How to fart so that people will notice you

Sanjay Oluwaseun

ISBN: 9784779690135
Imprint: Telephasic Workshop
Copyright © 2024 Sanjay Oluwaseun.
All Rights Reserved.

Contents

The Birth of a Melodic Thunder

The Birth of a Melodic Thunder

The Birth of a Melodic Thunder

Introduction

In the vibrant realm of music, the birth of a unique sound is akin to a thunderstorm rolling in—unexpected, powerful, and utterly transformative. This section explores the genesis of a melodic thunder that resonates with audiences, breaking the silence of the mundane and ushering in a symphony of unforgettable experiences.

Theoretical Foundations

The concept of sound can be dissected into its fundamental components: frequency, amplitude, and timbre. Frequency, measured in Hertz (Hz), determines the pitch of a sound. Amplitude relates to the loudness, while timbre gives a sound its unique character. The interaction of these elements creates a rich tapestry of auditory experiences.

Mathematically, sound can be represented as a wave function:

$$y(t) = A \sin(2\pi f t + \phi) \tag{1}$$

where:

- $y(t)$ is the displacement of the wave at time t,

- A is the amplitude,

- f is the frequency,

- ϕ is the phase shift.

The power of sound lies in its ability to evoke emotions and create connections. As we delve into the birth of melodic thunder, we will examine how these elements coalesce to form a sound that captures attention and stirs the soul.

From Silence to Symphony

The journey from silence to symphony is not merely a transition; it is a profound transformation. Silence, often perceived as the absence of sound, is a canvas upon which music is painted. The moment a note is struck, the silence shatters, giving birth to a symphony that can resonate across time and space.

Consider the impact of silence in a live performance. When an artist pauses before delivering a powerful line, the audience is drawn in, creating a palpable tension that heightens the eventual release of sound. This interplay between silence and sound is crucial in crafting memorable musical experiences.

The Genesis of Sonic Flatulence

In the realm of unconventional sounds, the term "sonic flatulence" emerges as a playful yet profound concept. It symbolizes the breaking of norms and the embracing of unique auditory expressions. This phenomenon can be likened to the unexpected bursts of laughter that arise from a well-timed joke; it disrupts expectations and invites a sense of joy and surprise.

The creation of sonic flatulence involves:

- **Experimentation:** Musicians must be willing to explore uncharted territories, using unconventional instruments and techniques to produce sounds that challenge traditional norms.

- **Improvisation:** The ability to spontaneously create music in the moment allows for the birth of unique sonic experiences that resonate with audiences.

- **Collaboration:** Working with diverse artists can lead to a fusion of styles, resulting in a sound that is both fresh and exciting.

Embracing the Unconventional

To give birth to a melodic thunder, artists must embrace the unconventional. This means stepping outside the boundaries of what is considered "normal" in music. The willingness to experiment with different genres, instruments, and sounds can lead to the creation of something truly unique.

For example, the use of everyday objects as instruments—such as using a kitchen utensil to create rhythmic beats—can add a layer of authenticity and creativity to a performance. This approach not only captivates the audience but also challenges their perceptions of what music can be.

Finding Inspiration in Unexpected Places

Inspiration often strikes in the most unexpected places. The sounds of nature, urban environments, or even mundane daily activities can serve as a wellspring of creativity. For instance, the rhythmic clattering of pots and pans in a kitchen can inspire a new beat, while the rustling of leaves in the wind might evoke a melody.

Musicians can harness these inspirations by:

+ **Sound Journals:** Keeping a record of interesting sounds encountered in daily life can serve as a valuable resource for future compositions.

+ **Field Recordings:** Capturing sounds from various environments can provide a rich palette of auditory materials to work with in the studio.

Unleashing the Power of Sound

The power of sound lies in its ability to transcend barriers, connect people, and evoke emotions. When artists unleash their unique sound, they create an experience that resonates deeply with listeners. This connection is what transforms a simple melody into a thunderous anthem that can rally crowds and inspire movements.

To fully unleash the power of sound, artists must:

+ **Engage with the Audience:** Building a rapport with listeners enhances the overall experience, making them feel like active participants in the musical journey.

+ **Utilize Technology:** Modern technology allows for innovative sound manipulation and production techniques that can elevate a performance to new heights.

Conclusion

The birth of a melodic thunder is a multifaceted process that involves theoretical understanding, creativity, and an unwavering commitment to authenticity. By embracing the unconventional, finding inspiration in unexpected places, and unleashing the power of sound, artists can create music that not only captivates audiences but also leaves a lasting impact on the world. As we continue this journey through the sonic landscape, let us celebrate the transformative power of music and the thunderous melodies that emerge from it.

From Silence to Symphony

From Silence to Symphony

In the realm of music, the journey from silence to symphony is a transformative experience that involves not only the creation of sound but also the cultivation of an artist's identity. This section delves into the foundational principles that guide musicians as they evolve from mere observers of the musical landscape to active participants, crafting their own symphonic narratives.

The Essence of Sound

Sound is defined as a vibration that travels through air, water, or solid materials, perceived by the human ear. Mathematically, sound can be represented by the wave equation:

$$\frac{\partial^2 u}{\partial t^2} = c^2 \nabla^2 u \tag{2}$$

where u represents the sound wave function, t is time, and c is the speed of sound in the medium. This equation encapsulates the fundamental nature of sound as a physical phenomenon, yet it also serves as a metaphor for the journey of a musician.

Embracing the Void

Before a symphony can emerge, silence must be acknowledged. Silence is not merely the absence of sound; it is a canvas upon which creativity can flourish. In the world of music, silence plays a crucial role in shaping dynamics, phrasing, and emotional impact. The famous composer John Cage famously stated, "There is no such thing as an empty space or an empty time." His piece 4'33" challenges performers to embrace silence, inviting listeners to reflect on the sounds that exist in the absence of music.

The Birth of Melody

The transition from silence to sound often begins with the inception of a melody. A melody is a sequence of notes that are perceived as a single entity. It can be constructed using various scales, such as the major scale, which is defined by the following pattern of whole (W) and half (H) steps:

$$W - W - H - W - W - W - H \tag{3}$$

This scale serves as a foundation for countless melodies across genres. For instance, the iconic melody of "Twinkle, Twinkle, Little Star" can be derived from the C major scale, showcasing how simple notes can evolve into a recognizable tune.

Rhythm: The Pulse of Music

Rhythm is the heartbeat of music, providing structure and movement. It is the organization of sound in time, often represented through various time signatures. A common time signature is 4/4, indicating four beats per measure, with a quarter note receiving one beat. The interplay of rhythm and melody creates a dynamic tension that engages listeners.

Consider the following rhythmic pattern in 4/4 time:

$$1 \quad 2 \quad 3 \quad 4 \tag{4}$$

Each number represents a beat, while the placement of notes within this framework can create syncopation, accentuation, and varying emotional responses.

Harmony: Building Layers

As melodies and rhythms intertwine, harmony emerges, adding depth and complexity to the musical narrative. Harmony is achieved when multiple notes are played simultaneously, creating chords. The most basic chord is the triad, consisting of three notes: the root, third, and fifth.

For example, a C major triad can be expressed as:

$$C \quad E \quad G \tag{5}$$

The combination of melody, rhythm, and harmony forms the backbone of a symphony. The interplay between these elements allows musicians to convey emotions, tell stories, and connect with their audience on a profound level.

The Role of Technology

In today's musical landscape, technology plays a pivotal role in the transition from silence to symphony. Digital audio workstations (DAWs) empower artists to compose, record, and produce music with unprecedented accessibility. With tools such as MIDI (Musical Instrument Digital Interface), musicians can manipulate sound in ways that were once unimaginable.

The equation for MIDI note velocity can be expressed as:

$$V = \frac{N}{T} \qquad (6)$$

where V represents the velocity, N is the number of notes played, and T is the time taken. This illustrates how technology has revolutionized the way musicians create, allowing for experimentation and innovation.

Conclusion

The journey from silence to symphony is a multifaceted process that encompasses the essence of sound, the birth of melody, the pulse of rhythm, and the layers of harmony. It is a journey that requires not only technical skill but also emotional intelligence and creativity. As musicians embrace the void of silence and transform it into a symphonic experience, they invite listeners to join them on a captivating auditory adventure, one that transcends mere sound and resonates deeply within the human spirit.

The Genesis of Sonic Flatulence

Sonic flatulence, a term that may seem whimsical at first, encapsulates the idea of creating music that resonates with the raw and unfiltered expression of human emotion, much like the natural sounds produced by the body. This section delves into the origins of this unique phenomenon, exploring its theoretical underpinnings, the challenges faced by artists, and the innovative examples that have emerged from this avant-garde approach to sound.

Theoretical Foundations

At its core, sonic flatulence draws from the principles of acoustics and sound design. The human body acts as a natural resonator, producing a variety of sounds based on the physical and emotional state of the individual. The theory of sound waves, particularly the study of frequency, amplitude, and timbre, plays a crucial role in understanding how these bodily sounds can be manipulated and transformed into musical expressions.

The fundamental frequency f of a sound wave is given by the equation:

$$f = \frac{v}{\lambda} \qquad (7)$$

where v is the speed of sound in air (approximately 343 m/s at room temperature), and λ is the wavelength of the sound. This relationship highlights how variations in the physical properties of sound can lead to different musical outcomes. By understanding these principles, artists can harness the power of sonic flatulence to create unique auditory experiences.

Challenges in Creation

The journey of embracing sonic flatulence is not without its challenges. Artists often face societal taboos surrounding bodily functions, which can lead to stigmatization and misunderstanding. Overcoming these barriers requires a combination of creativity, confidence, and a willingness to push boundaries.

One significant problem artists encounter is the perception of flatulence as merely humorous or vulgar, rather than a legitimate form of artistic expression. This misconception can hinder the acceptance of sonic flatulence within mainstream music. To combat this, artists must articulate their vision clearly, framing their work as a profound exploration of the human experience.

Innovative Examples

Despite the challenges, numerous artists have successfully embraced sonic flatulence, transforming it into a celebrated form of artistic expression. One notable example is the avant-garde composer John Cage, who famously incorporated everyday sounds into his works, challenging traditional notions of music. His piece 4'33" invites listeners to focus on the ambient sounds of the environment, paralleling the concept of sonic flatulence by elevating the ordinary to the extraordinary.

Additionally, contemporary artists like Björk and Aphex Twin have experimented with unconventional sounds, integrating organic bodily noises into their compositions. Björk's album *Medúlla* features vocalizations that mimic the sounds of the body, blurring the lines between music and the human form. This innovative approach not only showcases the potential of sonic flatulence but also encourages listeners to embrace the beauty of imperfection and rawness in sound.

Conclusion

The genesis of sonic flatulence marks a significant evolution in the landscape of music, challenging preconceived notions of what constitutes art. By understanding the theoretical foundations, addressing societal challenges, and drawing inspiration from pioneering artists, musicians can explore this uncharted territory with confidence and creativity. As we continue to push the boundaries of sound, sonic flatulence serves as a reminder that the most profound expressions of humanity often arise from the most unexpected sources.

Embracing the Unconventional

In a world where conformity often reigns supreme, embracing the unconventional can be the secret ingredient to creating a unique sound that resonates with audiences. This section dives deep into the art of celebrating the odd, the quirky, and the downright bizarre, showcasing how these elements can elevate your musical journey from mundane to extraordinary.

The Power of Uniqueness

The first step in embracing the unconventional is recognizing the power of uniqueness. In the realm of music, standing out is not just an advantage; it is essential. As music theorist John Cage famously stated, "I can't understand why people are frightened of new ideas. I'm frightened of the old ones." This sentiment encapsulates the essence of innovation in music. To break free from the chains of traditional sound, artists must dare to explore the unexplored.

Theoretical Framework

From a theoretical perspective, embracing the unconventional can be analyzed through the lens of *non-linear dynamics*, which emphasizes how small changes in initial conditions can lead to vastly different outcomes. In music, this can be translated into experimenting with unexpected time signatures, unusual chord progressions, or unconventional instruments. The equation governing chaotic systems can be expressed as:

$$\frac{dx}{dt} = f(x, t) \tag{8}$$

where x represents the state of the musical piece, t is time, and f is a function that describes the system's dynamics. By altering f, musicians can create a myriad of unique sonic experiences.

Challenges of the Unconventional

However, the path of embracing the unconventional is not without its challenges. Musicians may encounter criticism from purists who cling to traditional forms. This backlash can lead to self-doubt and hesitation. The fear of alienating potential listeners often looms large, creating a dilemma: should one stay true to their artistic vision or conform to the expectations of the audience?

To overcome this, artists must cultivate resilience. A prime example is the legendary band *The Beatles*, who, despite facing skepticism for their experimental album *Sgt. Pepper's Lonely Hearts Club Band*, went on to redefine popular music. Their willingness to embrace the unconventional not only enriched their sound but also opened doors for countless artists in the years to follow.

Examples of Unconventional Embracement

One of the most iconic examples of embracing the unconventional is the use of non-traditional instruments. Artists like *Sigur Rós* have incorporated bowed guitar and other unconventional sounds, creating a lush soundscape that defies categorization. Similarly, *Bjork* has made a career out of blending electronic elements with organic sounds, utilizing everything from a bicycle pump to a harp in her compositions.

Moreover, the genre of *avant-garde* music thrives on unconventionality. Composers like *Edgard Varèse* and *Karlheinz Stockhausen* pushed the boundaries of what music could be, introducing elements like electronic sounds and unconventional structures. Their works serve as testaments to the beauty that can emerge from embracing the unexpected.

Practical Application: Exercises for Embracing the Unconventional

To help foster an environment where the unconventional can flourish, musicians can engage in several practical exercises:

+ **Random Note Generation:** Use a random number generator to select notes from the chromatic scale. Compose a piece based on these selections, allowing the randomness to guide your creativity.

+ **Unusual Time Signatures:** Experiment with time signatures that are not commonly used in your genre. For instance, try composing in 7/8 or 11/8 time to create a unique rhythmic feel.

+ **Instrument Swap:** Collaborate with musicians who play unconventional instruments. This can lead to unexpected sounds and ideas that enrich your music.

+ **Genre Blending:** Create a fusion piece that combines elements from vastly different genres. For example, mix classical music with hip-hop or jazz with electronic dance music.

Conclusion

Embracing the unconventional is not merely a choice; it is a necessity for artists striving to leave their mark on the music world. By stepping outside the confines of tradition and welcoming the bizarre, musicians can unlock new realms of creativity. The journey may be fraught with challenges, but the rewards of originality and innovation are well worth the risk. As you embark on this path, remember: in the realm of music, the only limits are those that you impose upon yourself. So go ahead, embrace the unconventional, and let your sound be a thunderous declaration of your artistic identity.

Finding Inspiration in Unexpected Places

In the vibrant world of music, inspiration often strikes in the most surprising of locations. It could be the rhythm of a bustling city, the whispers of nature, or even the laughter of friends at a gathering. As artists, we must train our senses to be open and receptive to these moments, transforming them into the melodies and harmonies that resonate with our audience.

The Theory of Soundscapes

To fully appreciate how inspiration can emerge from unexpected sources, we must first understand the concept of soundscapes. Soundscapes are the acoustic environment created by the sounds in a particular location. According to Schafer (1977), soundscapes can be classified into three categories: *keynote sounds, sound signals,* and *soundmarks.*

$$\text{Soundscape} = \text{Keynote Sounds} + \text{Sound Signals} + \text{Soundmarks} \quad (9)$$

Keynote Sounds are the background noises that define a particular environment, such as the rustle of leaves in a forest or the hum of traffic in a city. **Sound Signals** are more prominent sounds that grab our attention, such as a train whistle or a bird call. Lastly, **Soundmarks** are unique sounds that are culturally or historically significant to a community, like church bells or the sounds of a local festival.

By immersing ourselves in diverse soundscapes, we can unlock new creative pathways, allowing the natural rhythms and patterns of our surroundings to influence our music.

Problems in Finding Inspiration

Despite the abundance of potential sources for inspiration, many artists struggle to find their muse. This can be attributed to various factors:

1. **Creative Block:** A state where an artist feels unable to produce new work or ideas. This can stem from self-doubt, fear of failure, or external pressures.

2. **Overstimulation:** In a world filled with constant noise and distractions, it can be challenging to focus on the subtleties of sound that might inspire creativity.

3. **Conformity:** Artists may feel pressured to adhere to popular trends, which can stifle their unique voice and prevent them from exploring unconventional sources of inspiration.

To combat these challenges, artists can adopt several strategies:

- **Mindfulness Practices**: Engaging in mindfulness exercises can help artists become more attuned to their surroundings, allowing them to appreciate the sounds that often go unnoticed.

- **Journaling**: Keeping a sound journal, where artists document interesting sounds they encounter, can serve as a valuable resource for future compositions.

- **Collaboration**: Working with other artists can introduce new perspectives and ideas, helping to break down barriers to inspiration.

Examples of Unexpected Inspiration

Many renowned musicians have found inspiration in the most unlikely places, showcasing the power of creativity in diverse environments:

- **John Cage**: The avant-garde composer famously drew inspiration from the sounds of everyday life. His piece 4'33" challenges traditional notions of music by presenting silence as a canvas for ambient sounds, encouraging listeners to find beauty in the world around them.

- **Björk**: The Icelandic singer-songwriter often incorporates natural sounds into her music. For example, her album *Biophilia* features field recordings of natural phenomena, such as thunder and bird calls, blending them with electronic elements to create a unique soundscape.

- **The Beatles**: The iconic band was known for their innovative use of studio techniques. In *Tomorrow Never Knows*, they employed tape loops and reverse recordings, inspired by the sounds of the world around them and their exploration of Eastern philosophy.

Embracing the Unconventional

To truly harness the power of unexpected inspiration, artists must embrace the unconventional. This can involve experimenting with new genres, instruments, and techniques. By stepping outside their comfort zone, musicians can discover fresh perspectives and ideas that enrich their creative process.

For instance, incorporating non-traditional instruments, such as found objects or digital sound manipulation, can lead to unique sonic textures. Additionally, exploring different cultural influences can expand an artist's palette, allowing them to create music that resonates on multiple levels.

Conclusion

In conclusion, finding inspiration in unexpected places is a vital aspect of the artistic journey. By remaining open to the sounds of our environment and embracing the unconventional, we can unlock new creative possibilities. As we navigate the ever-evolving landscape of music, let us remember that inspiration is all around us, waiting to be discovered and transformed into something extraordinary. So go ahead, turn up the volume on life, and let the world be your muse!

Unleashing the Power of Sound

The essence of music lies in its ability to evoke emotions, create connections, and transcend barriers. In this section, we delve into the multifaceted nature of sound and explore how it can be harnessed to unleash its full potential in the world of farting and beyond.

The Nature of Sound

Sound is a mechanical wave that propagates through a medium, such as air, water, or solid materials. It is characterized by its frequency, amplitude, and waveform. The basic equation governing sound propagation in a medium is given by:

$$v = f\lambda \tag{10}$$

where:

- v is the speed of sound in the medium,

- f is the frequency of the sound wave, and

- λ is the wavelength.

The power of sound lies not only in its physical properties but also in its capacity to convey meaning and emotion. Different frequencies can evoke various feelings; for instance, lower frequencies often produce a sense of calm, while higher frequencies can induce excitement or tension.

The Impact of Sound on Human Emotion

Research has shown that sound can significantly influence human emotions and behaviors. The field of psychoacoustics studies how humans perceive sound and its psychological effects. For example, studies have demonstrated that certain musical scales and modes can evoke specific emotional responses.

A classic illustration of this is the use of major and minor scales. Major scales are generally perceived as happy and uplifting, while minor scales tend to evoke feelings of sadness or melancholy. This emotional impact can be strategically harnessed in farting performances to create an immersive experience for the audience.

Harnessing Sound through Technology

In the modern era, technology plays a crucial role in manipulating sound. Digital audio workstations (DAWs) allow artists to record, edit, and produce music with unparalleled precision. Through the use of synthesizers, effects processors, and samplers, sound can be transformed in innovative ways.

For instance, the use of reverb can create a sense of space, making a sound feel as if it is emanating from a vast concert hall rather than a small room. The equation for calculating the reverberation time T in a room is given by:

$$T = \frac{0.161V}{A} \tag{11}$$

where:

- V is the volume of the room in cubic meters,

- A is the total absorption area in square meters.

This understanding of sound manipulation allows artists to create a unique auditory experience that resonates with their audience.

Exploring Unconventional Sounds

One of the most exciting aspects of unleashing the power of sound is the exploration of unconventional sound sources. In farting, this could mean embracing sounds that are not traditionally associated with music, such as everyday objects or even the human body.

For example, the use of found sounds—recordings of environmental noises or objects—can add an authentic layer to a performance. The incorporation of such sounds not only expands the sonic palette but also challenges the audience's perception of what constitutes music.

Consider the use of body percussion in a performance. By clapping, stomping, or even using vocalizations, artists can create rhythmic patterns that engage the audience in a participatory experience. This approach aligns with the concept of sound as a communal language, fostering a deeper connection between the performer and the audience.

Case Study: The Power of Sound in Farting Culture

To illustrate the power of sound, let's examine a case study of a successful farting performance that utilized sound to its fullest potential. The band "Fart Symphony" gained fame for their unique approach to live shows, where they combined traditional instruments with unconventional sound sources, including the sounds of flatulence, to create a one-of-a-kind auditory experience.

Their hit track "Flatulent Fantasia" featured a blend of synthesized sounds, real-time manipulation of fart sounds, and live instrumentation. The performance was designed to take the audience on an emotional journey, utilizing crescendos and decrescendos to build tension and release.

The band used the following structure in their performance:

+ **Intro:** Soft ambient sounds with subtle fart tones in the background, creating intrigue.

+ **Build-up:** Gradually increasing the intensity of the fart sounds while introducing percussion, leading to a climax.

+ **Climax:** A cacophony of sounds, combining all elements, creating an overwhelming sensory experience.

+ **Resolution:** Gradual fading out of sounds, returning to the soft ambient tones, leaving the audience in a reflective state.

This performance not only showcased the versatility of sound but also highlighted the importance of emotional engagement in music. The audience left feeling exhilarated, having experienced a rollercoaster of emotions through sound.

Conclusion

In conclusion, unleashing the power of sound is about more than just creating noise; it is about understanding the emotional and psychological impact of sound on the human experience. By harnessing technology, exploring unconventional sound sources, and strategically crafting performances, artists can create a profound connection with their audience.

As we continue to push the boundaries of what sound can achieve, we invite you to embrace the power of sound in your own musical journey. Remember, the only limits are those you impose upon yourself—so let your creativity flow and unleash the thunderous potential of sound!

Finding Your Inner Sound

Unleashing the Farting Spark

In the world of music, just like in the world of farting, it all starts with a spark—a moment of inspiration that ignites creativity and propels us into a realm of sound that is uniquely our own. The act of unleashing this farting spark is not merely a whimsical endeavor; it is a profound journey into the heart of what makes us artists. In this section, we will explore the theory behind this creative ignition, the common problems that may stifle it, and real-life examples that showcase the beauty of embracing our farting creativity.

The Theory Behind the Spark

Every artist has experienced that electrifying moment when inspiration strikes, akin to a sudden gust of wind that catches you off guard. This phenomenon can be explained through the lens of psychological theories of creativity. According to the *Four Stages of Creativity* model proposed by Graham Wallas, the creative process consists of four stages: preparation, incubation, illumination, and verification [?].

$$\text{Creativity Process} = \text{Preparation} + \text{Incubation} + \text{Illumination} + \text{Verification} \quad (12)$$

Preparation involves gathering information and experiences that feed into your creative reservoir. This is where you absorb the world around you, taking in sounds, feelings, and inspirations from every corner.

Incubation is the stage where the mind subconsciously processes this information. You may find yourself daydreaming or distracted, yet your brain is hard at work, mixing and mashing ideas in the background.

Illumination is the moment when the farting spark ignites, and a new idea bursts forth, often unexpectedly. This is the "Aha!" moment when everything clicks, and you can almost hear the symphony of your thoughts aligning.

Finally, **Verification** is where you refine and develop your ideas, transforming that initial spark into something tangible. You might find yourself experimenting with different sounds, instruments, and techniques to bring your vision to life.

Common Problems that Stifle the Spark

While the farting spark is a beautiful thing, it can also be elusive. Many artists face challenges that hinder their creative flow. Here are some common problems and potential solutions:

- **Fear of Judgment:** The fear of how others perceive your art can be paralyzing. To combat this, embrace the idea that not everyone will resonate with your sound, and that's okay! Focus on creating for yourself first.

- **Creative Block:** Sometimes, the spark just won't light. This could be due to stress, burnout, or a lack of inspiration. Techniques such as free writing, doodling, or even stepping away from your work can reignite your creativity.

- **Overthinking:** Analyzing every note and beat can lead to paralysis by analysis. Allow yourself to play freely without judgment. Remember, sometimes the best ideas come from spontaneity.

- **Stagnation:** If you find yourself stuck in a rut, it might be time to shake things up. Experiment with new genres, collaborate with different artists, or try unconventional instruments to break the monotony.

Real-Life Examples of Unleashing the Spark

The music industry is rife with stories of artists who have unleashed their farting spark in extraordinary ways. One such example is the iconic Lady Gaga, who transformed the pop landscape with her unique sound and bold performances.

Gaga's ability to tap into her inner creativity and push boundaries is a testament to the power of embracing one's farting spark.

Another example is the legendary band Queen, whose frontman Freddie Mercury was known for his flamboyant style and theatrical performances. Mercury often drew inspiration from unexpected sources, such as opera and musical theater, unleashing a creative force that would go on to change the face of rock music forever.

Conclusion

In conclusion, unleashing the farting spark is an essential aspect of the artistic journey. By understanding the creative process, addressing common barriers, and drawing inspiration from those who have come before us, we can ignite our own unique sound. Remember, every great artist has faced challenges, but it is the ability to embrace the spark and let it guide you that truly sets you apart. So go ahead, let that farting spark fly and watch as it transforms your music into a symphony of sound that resonates with the world!

Honing Your Farting Techniques

Farting, often dismissed as a mere bodily function, can be an art form when approached with creativity and skill. In this section, we will delve into the nuances of honing your farting techniques, transforming this natural occurrence into a symphony of sound that captivates audiences.

Understanding the Mechanics of Farting

To master the art of farting, one must first understand the mechanics behind it. The sound produced during a fart is primarily due to the vibration of the anal sphincter as gas is expelled. The pitch and volume of the fart can be influenced by several factors, including the speed of gas expulsion, the size of the anal opening, and the tension of the sphincter muscles.

$$\text{Sound Pressure Level (SPL)} = 20 \log_{10}\left(\frac{p}{p_0}\right) \tag{13}$$

Where: - p is the pressure of the fart sound wave, - p_0 is the reference sound pressure (typically $20\,\mu\text{Pa}$).

This equation illustrates how the pressure of the gas can affect the perceived loudness of a fart. Mastering the dynamics of pressure release can lead to a variety of sound effects, making each fart a unique auditory experience.

Techniques for Sound Variation

To enhance the variety in your farting repertoire, consider the following techniques:

- **Control the Release:** By varying the speed at which gas is expelled, you can produce different sounds. A slow release creates a low, rumbling sound, while a rapid expulsion results in high-pitched squeaks.

- **Adjust the Tension:** The tension of the anal sphincter can be manipulated to change the pitch. A tighter sphincter produces higher frequencies, while a relaxed sphincter yields deeper tones.

- **Experiment with Body Position:** The position of your body can also affect the sound. Sitting, standing, or lying down may change the acoustics of the fart. For instance, bending over while seated can amplify the sound due to the proximity of the body to the ground.

Common Problems and Solutions

While honing your farting techniques, you may encounter several challenges. Here are some common problems and their solutions:

- **Inconsistent Sound Quality:** If your farts sound different each time, practice controlling your breathing and gas release. Consistency comes with practice and awareness of your body's mechanics.

- **Lack of Volume:** If your farts are too quiet, consider adjusting your diet to include more fiber-rich foods. Increased gas production can lead to louder sounds. However, be cautious not to overdo it, as this may lead to discomfort.

- **Fear of Judgment:** Many individuals fear being judged for farting, especially in public. To overcome this, practice farting in safe environments where you feel comfortable. Gradually expose yourself to larger audiences to build confidence.

Examples of Masterful Farting Techniques

To illustrate the effectiveness of these techniques, consider the following examples from renowned fart artists:

- **The Symphony of Staccato:** An artist known for rapid-fire farts that create a staccato rhythm. This technique involves quick, successive releases of gas, producing a percussive effect that can accompany musical beats.

- **The Bass Drop:** A performer who specializes in deep, resonant farts that mimic the sound of a bass drop in electronic music. This artist achieves this by using a combination of controlled release and body positioning to amplify the sound.

- **The Whispering Wind:** A unique technique where the fart is released slowly, creating a soft, whisper-like sound. This style requires precise control of tension and is often used for comedic effect.

Practice Makes Perfect

As with any skill, practice is essential. Set aside time to experiment with different techniques and sounds. Record your sessions to track your progress and identify areas for improvement. Engage with fellow fart enthusiasts to exchange tips and techniques, fostering a community of support and growth.

In conclusion, honing your farting techniques is an exciting journey that combines science, creativity, and self-expression. By understanding the mechanics, experimenting with sound variation, addressing common problems, and learning from masterful examples, you can elevate your farting to an art form that leaves audiences in awe. So go ahead, unleash your melodic thunder, and let your farts be heard!

Sculpting Your Unique Farting Style

In the vast and vibrant world of farting, sculpting a unique style is akin to creating a masterpiece in sound. It requires not just creativity but also a deep understanding of the elements that make your farting resonate with audiences. This section delves into the essential components of developing a distinctive farting style that will leave your mark on the industry.

Understanding Your Farting Identity

Every artist has a unique identity that shapes their creative output. To sculpt your farting style, begin by exploring the following questions:

- What emotions do you want to convey through your farting?

- Which genres and influences resonate with you?

- What personal experiences can you translate into your farting?

By introspecting on these questions, you can identify the core elements of your farting identity. This self-awareness will guide your creative decisions and help you cultivate a sound that is unmistakably yours.

Experimenting with Techniques

Once you have a grasp of your identity, it's time to experiment with various farting techniques. Here are some methods to consider:

- **Layering Sounds:** Combine different farting sounds to create a rich tapestry. For instance, layering a deep bass fart with a higher-pitched squeak can add depth and complexity to your composition.

- **Rhythmic Patterns:** Explore various rhythmic patterns to find what resonates. You might discover that a syncopated rhythm creates a more engaging experience for your audience.

- **Dynamic Variations:** Play with volume and intensity. A sudden crescendo followed by a soft whisper can create dramatic tension and keep listeners on their toes.

Crafting Signature Sounds

Signature sounds are the hallmarks of your unique farting style. They can be a particular technique, a specific instrument, or even a recognizable phrase. For example, consider the following approaches:

- **Distinctive Techniques:** Develop a signature technique that defines your sound. This could be a unique way of manipulating air pressure or a specific way of using your body to create sound.

- **Iconic Instruments:** If you choose to incorporate unconventional instruments, select those that complement your style. For example, using a kazoo alongside traditional farting techniques can create a playful and memorable sound.

- **Catchy Hooks:** Create memorable hooks that listeners can easily recall. A catchy farting melody can become your trademark and draw fans to your performances.

Embracing Your Influences

While sculpting your unique style, it's essential to acknowledge and embrace your influences. The greats in the farting world often draw inspiration from diverse sources. Identify artists and genres that inspire you, and analyze what makes their styles compelling. For example:

+ **Nicki Minaj's Versatility:** Her ability to switch between rap and melodic elements can inspire you to blend genres within your farting.

+ **Experimental Artists:** Look to artists who push boundaries. Their innovative approaches can spark ideas for your own unique sound.

Collaborating with Others

Collaboration is a powerful tool for sculpting your unique farting style. Working with other artists can introduce you to new techniques, perspectives, and ideas. Consider the following collaboration strategies:

+ **Cross-Genre Collaborations:** Partner with artists from different genres to create hybrid sounds. This can lead to exciting and unexpected results.

+ **Workshops and Jams:** Attend workshops or jam sessions to exchange ideas and techniques with fellow fartists. This communal atmosphere can ignite creativity and foster innovation.

Refining Your Style

As you sculpt your unique farting style, remember that refinement is key. Continually assess and evolve your sound by:

+ **Seeking Feedback:** Share your work with trusted peers and mentors. Constructive criticism can provide valuable insights and help you grow.

+ **Recording and Analyzing:** Regularly record your farting sessions and analyze them. This practice allows you to identify strengths and areas for improvement.

+ **Staying Open to Change:** Your style will naturally evolve over time. Embrace this evolution as a part of your artistic journey.

Theoretical Foundations

To effectively sculpt your unique farting style, understanding the theoretical foundations of sound production can be beneficial. Consider the following concepts:

$$f = \frac{1}{T} \qquad (14)$$

where f is the frequency of the sound, and T is the period. This equation illustrates how the frequency of your farts can influence their perception. Higher frequencies may be perceived as sharper, while lower frequencies can resonate more deeply.

Additionally, the concept of harmonic series can be applied:

$$f_n = n \cdot f_1 \qquad (15)$$

where f_n is the frequency of the nth harmonic and f_1 is the fundamental frequency. Understanding harmonics can help you create richer, more complex farting sounds.

Examples of Unique Farting Styles

To illustrate the diversity of farting styles, consider the following examples:

- **The Beatbox Farter:** This artist combines beatboxing techniques with farting, creating rhythmic and percussive sounds that captivate audiences.

- **The Melodic Farter:** Utilizing pitch modulation, this artist creates melodic lines that weave in and out of traditional farting sounds, offering a fresh take on the art form.

- **The Experimental Farter:** Known for their avant-garde approach, this artist uses unconventional materials and methods to produce unexpected farting sounds that challenge the norms of the genre.

Conclusion

Sculpting your unique farting style is a dynamic and ongoing process that requires self-exploration, experimentation, and collaboration. By understanding your identity, experimenting with techniques, crafting signature sounds, embracing influences, and refining your style, you can create a farting style that is distinctly yours. Remember, the journey of sculpting your style is as important as the final product; enjoy the process, and let your creativity flow like the most melodic of farts!

Embracing the Unorthodox Instruments

In the vibrant world of music, the sound of the unexpected can create waves that resonate far beyond the ordinary. Embracing unorthodox instruments is not merely about creating unique sounds; it's about redefining the very essence of what music can be. In this section, we will delve into the theory behind unconventional instruments, the challenges artists face in their integration, and the exhilarating potential they hold for innovation.

Theoretical Foundation

At the core of embracing unorthodox instruments lies the concept of **sonic exploration.** This idea posits that sound can be generated from virtually anything, transforming everyday objects into instruments. The theory can be encapsulated by the equation:

$$S = f(I, P) \tag{16}$$

where S represents the sound produced, I denotes the instrument or object used, and P is the player's technique or interaction with the instrument. This relationship highlights that sound is not solely dependent on the instrument but also significantly influenced by the performer's creativity and approach.

Challenges in Integration

While the allure of unorthodox instruments is undeniable, artists often encounter several challenges in their integration into musical compositions:

+ **Technical Limitations:** Many unconventional instruments may not have standardized playing techniques or may require unique methods of sound production, leading to a steep learning curve.

+ **Audience Reception:** Traditional audiences may initially resist unfamiliar sounds, leading to a potential disconnect between the artist's vision and audience expectations.

- **Collaboration Barriers:** Working with unorthodox instruments may pose difficulties in collaboration, particularly when other musicians are not familiar with their use or the sound they produce.

Examples of Unorthodox Instruments

1. **The Hang Drum:** This steel percussion instrument produces melodic tones and has gained popularity in various genres, from world music to contemporary pop. Its unique sound can evoke a sense of tranquility, making it a favorite for meditative compositions.

2. **Waterphone:** An unusual instrument that combines the sounds of water and metal, the waterphone creates eerie, ethereal tones. It has been used in film scores to evoke suspense and drama, showcasing its versatility in enhancing emotional narratives.

3. **Found Objects:** Artists like Stomp have famously utilized everyday items, such as trash cans and brooms, to create rhythm and percussion. This approach emphasizes that music can be found in the ordinary, inviting audiences to reconsider their perceptions of sound.

Innovative Techniques

To successfully incorporate unorthodox instruments, musicians can employ several innovative techniques:

- **Layering Sounds:** Combining traditional and unconventional instruments can create rich, textured soundscapes. For instance, layering a hang drum with a guitar can produce a harmonious blend of percussive and melodic elements.

- **Live Sampling:** Utilizing technology to sample sounds in real-time allows artists to manipulate and integrate unorthodox instruments into their performances seamlessly. This technique can transform a simple sound into a complex auditory experience.

- **Improvisation:** Encouraging improvisation with unorthodox instruments can lead to spontaneous creativity, allowing musicians to explore new sonic territories. This freedom can result in unique compositions that defy conventional structure.

Case Studies

1. **Björk:** Known for her avant-garde approach, Björk has incorporated various unconventional instruments into her work. Her album *Biophilia* features the use of a custom-built instrument called the *Hang Drum*, showcasing her commitment to sonic innovation.
2. **The Polyphonic Spree:** This band embraces a wide array of instruments, including strings, brass, and unconventional percussion. Their orchestral sound exemplifies the beauty of integrating diverse instruments to create a powerful musical narrative.

Conclusion

Embracing unorthodox instruments is a bold step toward sonic innovation. By pushing the boundaries of traditional music-making, artists can create unique soundscapes that resonate with audiences on multiple levels. As we continue to explore the uncharted territories of sound, the possibilities are as limitless as our creativity. The key to success lies in overcoming challenges, experimenting with techniques, and remaining open to the unexpected. In the world of music, the only limit is your imagination, so let's make some noise and redefine what it means to create!

The Power of Collaboration

Collaboration in the world of music is akin to a symphony, where each instrument contributes to a unified sound that transcends individual talent. The magic of collaboration lies in the diverse perspectives, skills, and creativity that each artist brings to the table. This section explores the significance of collaboration, the challenges it presents, and how it can elevate your musical journey to new heights.

The Essence of Collaboration

At its core, collaboration is about synergy. When artists come together, they create a fusion of ideas that can lead to innovative sounds and styles. The theory of synergy can be expressed mathematically as follows:

$$S = A + B + C + ... + N \tag{17}$$

Where:

- S represents the synergy created through collaboration.

+ $A, B, C, ...N$ are the individual contributions from each collaborating artist.

This equation illustrates that the sum of individual talents can create something far greater than the mere addition of their parts. For instance, the collaboration between artists like Lady Gaga and Elton John in the song "Sine from Above" showcases how two distinct musical identities can blend to create a transcendent piece that resonates with audiences globally.

Challenges of Collaboration

While collaboration can yield remarkable results, it is not without its challenges. Artists may face creative differences, communication barriers, and conflicting visions. These problems can be summarized as follows:

+ **Creative Differences:** Each artist has their own style, which can lead to clashes in direction. Finding common ground is essential.

+ **Communication Barriers:** Misunderstandings can arise if collaborators do not articulate their ideas clearly, leading to frustration.

+ **Conflicting Visions:** When artists have different goals for a project, it can result in a lack of cohesion in the final product.

To navigate these challenges, it is crucial to establish open lines of communication and set clear expectations from the outset. Regular meetings and brainstorming sessions can help ensure that everyone is on the same page, allowing the collaboration to flourish.

Examples of Successful Collaborations

Numerous iconic collaborations have shaped the music industry, proving the power of teamwork. Here are a few notable examples:

+ **Run-D.M.C. and Aerosmith:** Their collaboration on "Walk This Way" in 1986 bridged the gap between hip-hop and rock, introducing rap to a broader audience and revitalizing Aerosmith's career.

+ **Beyoncé and Jay-Z:** The power couple has collaborated on multiple tracks, including "Drunk in Love," showcasing their ability to blend their distinct styles into chart-topping hits.

+ **The Chainsmokers and Halsey:** Their hit "Closer" exemplifies how electronic music can merge with pop vocals, creating an anthem that dominated the charts and playlists.

These collaborations not only highlight the potential of merging different genres but also demonstrate how artists can leverage each other's strengths to create something extraordinary.

Harnessing the Power of Collaboration

To harness the power of collaboration in your music career, consider the following strategies:

+ **Network Actively:** Attend music events, workshops, and open mics to meet fellow artists. Building relationships can lead to exciting collaborative opportunities.

+ **Be Open-Minded:** Embrace different styles and ideas. Sometimes, the most unexpected collaborations yield the best results.

+ **Experiment:** Don't be afraid to step outside your comfort zone. Collaborating with artists from different genres can inspire new creative directions.

+ **Share the Spotlight:** Recognize and appreciate the contributions of your collaborators. Acknowledging their efforts fosters a positive working environment and encourages future collaborations.

Conclusion

In conclusion, the power of collaboration is a vital element in the music industry. By embracing the diversity of ideas and talents that come from working together, artists can create groundbreaking music that resonates with audiences worldwide. While challenges may arise, the rewards of successful collaboration far outweigh the difficulties. Remember, the journey of creating music is not just about the individual; it's about the collective experience of artists coming together to create something beautiful. So, unleash your creativity, connect with fellow musicians, and let the symphony of collaboration take your sound to new heights!

Experimenting with Different Genres

When it comes to the art of farting—yes, you heard that right—experimenting with different genres can be a game changer. In the world of music, genre is like a flavor; it adds depth, richness, and personality to your sound. Just as Nicki Minaj effortlessly blends hip-hop with pop and R&B, you too can mix it up and create a unique sonic experience that resonates with your audience.

The Importance of Genre Experimentation

Genre experimentation allows artists to break free from the confines of traditional sounds, leading to innovation and creativity. By stepping outside your comfort zone, you can discover new techniques, rhythms, and harmonies that can elevate your farting game to a whole new level. Consider the following points:

* **Broadening Your Musical Palette:** Exploring different genres can introduce you to a variety of instruments, scales, and structures. For example, incorporating jazz elements such as syncopation and improvisation can add a sophisticated flair to your farting performances.

* **Reaching Diverse Audiences:** Different genres attract different fan bases. By experimenting with genres like reggae, country, or electronic, you can tap into new markets and expand your reach. This diversity can help you build a more robust fan community.

* **Fostering Collaboration:** Genre experimentation often leads to collaborations with artists from various backgrounds. When you blend your unique style with another genre, the result can be a groundbreaking fusion that captivates listeners.

Challenges in Genre Experimentation

While the benefits of experimenting with different genres are plentiful, it's essential to acknowledge the challenges that may arise:

* **Cohesion and Identity:** One of the primary concerns when experimenting with genres is maintaining a cohesive sound. Straying too far from your original style can confuse your audience. It's crucial to find a balance between innovation and your artistic identity.

- **Criticism and Expectations:** Fans may have specific expectations based on your previous work. Venturing into unfamiliar territory can lead to mixed reactions. Embrace the critics and use their feedback as fuel for growth.

- **Technical Skills:** Each genre has its own set of techniques and requirements. For instance, mastering the intricate rhythms of funk or the lyrical complexity of rap may require dedicated practice and study.

Examples of Successful Genre Experimentation

Let's take a look at some artists who have successfully navigated the waters of genre experimentation:

- **Lil Nas X:** Bursting onto the scene with "Old Town Road," Lil Nas X blended country and hip-hop, creating a viral sensation. This cross-genre appeal not only topped the charts but also sparked discussions about genre boundaries in contemporary music.

- **Beyoncé:** With her album "Lemonade," Beyoncé incorporated elements of rock, blues, and folk into her R&B sound. This genre-blending not only showcased her versatility but also addressed social issues, resonating with a broader audience.

- **Kacey Musgraves:** Known for her country roots, Musgraves has seamlessly integrated pop and psychedelic influences into her music. Her willingness to experiment has garnered critical acclaim and a diverse fan base.

Theoretical Framework: The Role of Genre in Music Theory

From a theoretical perspective, genre serves as a framework for understanding musical structure and composition. Each genre has its own conventions, including:

$$R = \frac{T}{C} \tag{18}$$

where R represents the richness of the sound, T stands for the variety of tones used, and C denotes the complexity of the composition. The equation illustrates that a higher variety of tones and greater complexity can lead to a richer sound, especially when merging genres.

Moreover, the concept of *intertextuality* in music theory suggests that genres influence one another. When you draw from multiple genres, you create intertextual connections that can enrich your music. For instance, incorporating a hip-hop beat into a classical melody can create a fresh take that appeals to a wide audience.

Practical Tips for Genre Experimentation

To effectively experiment with different genres, consider the following tips:

1. **Listen Actively:** Immerse yourself in various genres. Pay attention to the instrumentation, structure, and lyrical themes. Create playlists that feature a mix of styles to inspire your creativity.

2. **Collaborate with Genre-Specific Artists:** Partner with musicians who specialize in the genres you're interested in exploring. Their expertise can guide you in understanding the nuances of their style.

3. **Stay True to Your Voice:** While it's essential to experiment, ensure that your unique voice remains at the forefront. Blend genres in a way that feels authentic to you.

4. **Document Your Process:** Keep a journal of your experimentation. Note what works, what doesn't, and how you feel about each new direction you take. This reflection can be invaluable for future projects.

In conclusion, experimenting with different genres is a powerful way to enhance your farting artistry. By embracing the challenges and celebrating the successes, you can create a sound that is not only unique but also resonates with a diverse audience. So go ahead, mix it up, and let your creativity flow like the sweetest melody!

Mastering the Art of Improvisation

Improvisation in music is the spontaneous creation of musical ideas, often characterized by the ability to react to the surrounding musical context. This section delves into the essential components of mastering improvisation, exploring techniques, theoretical foundations, and practical applications that will elevate your farting artistry to new heights.

Understanding Improvisation

Improvisation is not merely about playing notes on the fly; it's an intricate dance between creativity and technical skill. To master this art, one must grasp the following concepts:

+ **Musical Language:** Just as spoken language has grammar and vocabulary, music has its own set of rules and structures. Understanding scales, chords, and progressions is crucial. For instance, the C major scale is given by:

$$C, D, E, F, G, A, B$$

This scale forms the basis of many improvisational pieces.

+ **Listening Skills:** A proficient improviser must develop acute listening skills to respond to other musicians. This involves recognizing patterns, dynamics, and emotional cues in the music being played.

+ **Emotional Expression:** Improvisation is a powerful means of conveying emotions. Understanding how different scales evoke different feelings can enhance your improvisational palette. For example, the Dorian mode, characterized by its minor quality with a raised sixth, can create a sense of longing:

$$D, E, F, G, A, B, C$$

Techniques for Effective Improvisation

To truly master improvisation, one must practice various techniques that foster creativity and spontaneity. Here are some key strategies:

1. **Call and Response:** This technique involves playing a phrase (the call) and then responding to it with another phrase. It's a foundational element in many musical traditions, encouraging interaction and dialogue.

2. **Motivic Development:** Start with a simple motif (a short musical idea) and develop it throughout your improvisation. This can involve altering rhythm, pitch, or dynamics. For instance, if your motif is:

$$A, B, C$$

You might transform it into:

$$A, B, D, C$$

or play it in different rhythms.

3. **Rhythmic Variation:** Changing the rhythm of your improvisation can add excitement and unpredictability. Experiment with syncopation, triplets, or polyrhythms to keep your audience on their toes.

4. **Scale and Arpeggio Practice:** Regular practice of scales and arpeggios will help you become more fluent in your instrument. For example, practice the following C major arpeggio:

$$C, E, G, C'$$

This will allow you to access various notes quickly during improvisation.

5. **Using Space:** Silence can be as powerful as sound. Don't be afraid to leave pauses in your playing. This gives the audience time to absorb what they've heard and creates a sense of tension and release.

Theoretical Foundations of Improvisation

Understanding music theory is paramount for effective improvisation. Here are some theoretical concepts that can enhance your improvisational skills:

+ **Chord Progressions:** Familiarize yourself with common chord progressions such as the I-IV-V (C-F-G in C major) and ii-V-I (Dm-G-C in C major). These progressions serve as a framework for improvisation.

+ **Modal Improvisation:** Explore different modes (e.g., Dorian, Phrygian) as a basis for improvisation. Each mode has its unique flavor, allowing for diverse emotional expressions. For example, using the Phrygian mode:

$$E, F, G, A, B, C, D$$

can create an exotic sound.

+ **Chord Tones vs. Non-Chord Tones:** Improvisers should learn to distinguish between chord tones (notes that belong to the chord) and non-chord tones (notes that create tension). Incorporating non-chord tones can add richness to your improvisation.

Practical Applications and Examples

To put theory into practice, let's explore some examples of improvisational techniques in action:

Example

Example 1: Call and Response in a Group Setting
In a jam session, one musician plays a melodic phrase. The next musician responds with a variation of that phrase, perhaps altering the rhythm or adding embellishments. This back-and-forth creates a dynamic interplay that keeps the music engaging.

Example 2: Motivic Development in Solo Performance
A solo artist begins with a simple motif, such as:

$$G, A, B$$

They might repeat this motif, then alter it by changing the rhythm or pitch, leading to a more complex phrase:

$$G, A, C, B$$

This development keeps the listener intrigued.

Example 3: Rhythmic Variation in a Performance
A performer may start with a straight rhythm but then introduce syncopation or triplets to create excitement. For instance, if the original rhythm is:

$$1 - 2 - 3 - 4$$

They might transform it to:

$$1 - (2 \text{ and}) - 3 - (4 \text{ and})$$

Challenges in Improvisation

While improvisation can be exhilarating, it also presents challenges:

+ **Fear of Mistakes:** Many musicians fear making mistakes while improvising. Embrace mistakes as opportunities for growth; they can lead to unexpected and unique musical ideas.

+ **Overthinking:** Sometimes, musicians overanalyze their choices during improvisation, leading to paralysis. Trust your instincts and allow your creativity to flow freely.

  • **Lack of Confidence:** Building confidence in your improvisational skills takes
    time. Regular practice, exposure to different musical styles, and performing
    in front of others can help overcome this hurdle.

Conclusion

Mastering the art of improvisation is a journey that requires dedication, practice,
and a willingness to explore the unknown.   By understanding the theoretical
foundations, honing your techniques, and embracing the challenges, you'll unlock
the full potential of your musical expression. Remember, improvisation is not just
about the notes you play; it's about the emotions you convey and the connection
you create with your audience. So go ahead, unleash your inner farting virtuoso,
and let the music flow!

Pushing the Boundaries of Fartingality

In the vibrant and ever-evolving realm of music, the concept of "Fartingality" emerges
as a playful yet profound exploration of sound, expression, and cultural commentary.
To push the boundaries of Fartingality is to embrace the unconventional, to challenge
the norms, and to redefine what it means to create music that resonates with both
the body and soul. This section delves into the theoretical underpinnings, challenges
faced, and exemplary figures who have successfully navigated this audacious path.

Theoretical Foundations

At its core, Fartingality can be conceptualized through the lens of avant-garde
music theory, which prioritizes experimentation over tradition.   The pioneering
works of composers such as John Cage and Karlheinz Stockhausen serve as
foundational texts in this exploration. Cage's notion of *silence* as a form of sound
invites artists to reconsider the spaces between notes—the pauses that can be as
impactful as the sounds themselves.

The mathematical representation of sound waves can also be utilized to
understand the complexities of Fartingality. The equation for a sound wave can be
expressed as:

$$y(t) = A \sin(2\pi f t + \phi) \tag{19}$$

where:

  • $y(t)$ is the displacement of the wave,

+ A is the amplitude,

+ f is the frequency,

+ t is time, and

+ ϕ is the phase shift.

This equation exemplifies how variations in amplitude and frequency can create diverse sonic experiences, allowing artists to manipulate sound in ways that challenge conventional listening experiences.

Challenges in Pushing Boundaries

Despite the exciting potential of pushing Fartingality's limits, artists often face significant challenges. One major obstacle is the resistance from traditional audiences who may struggle to embrace unconventional sounds. This phenomenon can be understood through the concept of *cognitive dissonance*, where listeners experience discomfort when confronted with sounds that deviate from their expectations.

Additionally, the music industry's commercial pressures can stifle creativity. The formulaic nature of mainstream music often discourages artists from taking risks. To combat this, musicians must cultivate a strong sense of self and artistic vision, allowing them to navigate the tension between commercial viability and creative authenticity.

Innovative Examples

Several artists have successfully pushed the boundaries of Fartingality, creating sonic landscapes that defy categorization. One standout example is the experimental musician **Merzbow**, whose work in noise music exemplifies the extreme manipulation of sound. Merzbow employs a variety of unconventional techniques, including feedback loops and found sounds, to create immersive auditory experiences that challenge listeners' perceptions of music.

Another notable figure is **Björk**, whose fusion of electronic, classical, and organic sounds exemplifies the essence of Fartingality. Her album *Biophilia* integrates natural sounds with innovative instrumentation, inviting listeners to engage with the music on both an intellectual and emotional level. Björk's willingness to embrace technology while honoring organic sounds serves as a blueprint for artists looking to push their own boundaries.

Conclusion

Pushing the boundaries of Fartingality requires a bold commitment to experimentation and a willingness to confront challenges head-on. By embracing avant-garde principles, artists can create unique sonic experiences that resonate deeply with audiences. As the landscape of music continues to evolve, the potential for innovative expression remains limitless. Artists who dare to explore the uncharted territories of sound will not only redefine their own artistry but also inspire future generations to embrace the beauty of the unexpected.

Bibliography

[1]   Cage, J. (1961). *Silence: Lectures and Writings*. Wesleyan University Press.

[2]   Stockhausen, K. (1970). *Texte zur Musik 1*. DuMont.

[3]   Merzbow. (1997). *Woodpecker No. 1*. ZSF Produkt.

[4]   Björk. (2011). *Biophilia*. One Little Indian.

Embracing Diverse Influences

In the vibrant world of music, embracing diverse influences is not just a choice; it's a necessity for any artist looking to make a mark in the industry. This section explores how a melange of styles, cultures, and sounds can lead to innovative creations that resonate with a broader audience.

Theoretical Foundations

The concept of musical diversity can be understood through the lens of **intertextuality**, which refers to the relationship between texts and how they influence one another. In music, this means that no piece exists in isolation; rather, it is a tapestry woven from various threads of influence. According to *Bakhtin's theory of dialogism*, every musical work is a response to previous works, creating a dialogue across genres and cultures.

$$D = \sum_{i=1}^{n} I_i \tag{20}$$

Where D is the diversity of influences, and I_i represents individual influences from different genres or cultures. This equation highlights that the richness of a musical piece is proportional to the number of diverse influences incorporated.

Challenges of Embracing Diversity

While the benefits of embracing diverse influences are clear, artists often face several challenges:

- **Cultural Appropriation:** One of the most pressing issues is the fine line between appreciation and appropriation. Artists must navigate the complexities of borrowing elements from other cultures without exploiting or misrepresenting them.

- **Identity Crisis:** In the quest to incorporate various influences, artists may struggle with maintaining their unique identity. This can lead to a dilution of their sound, making it essential to find a balance between innovation and authenticity.

- **Audience Reception:** Not all audiences are open to diverse influences. Some may prefer traditional sounds, leading to potential backlash against artists who experiment with genre-blending.

Examples of Successful Integration

Several artists have successfully embraced diverse influences, creating groundbreaking music that transcends boundaries:

- **Beyoncé:** Her album *Lemonade* is a rich tapestry of genres, including R&B, rock, country, and reggae. This fusion not only showcases her versatility but also brings attention to the cultural roots of each genre.

- **Bad Bunny:** A pioneer in Latin trap, he blends reggaeton with elements of rock, hip-hop, and even traditional Puerto Rican music. His global appeal lies in his ability to merge these influences seamlessly, creating a sound that feels both fresh and familiar.

- **Kendrick Lamar:** His work often incorporates jazz, funk, and soul, as seen in his album *To Pimp a Butterfly*. By drawing from these genres, he creates a rich auditory experience that enhances the storytelling aspect of his music.

Strategies for Incorporating Diverse Influences

To effectively embrace diverse influences, artists can adopt several strategies:

- **Collaboration:** Working with artists from different backgrounds can lead to innovative sounds. Collaborations allow for the exchange of ideas and techniques that can enrich an artist's work.

- **Research and Exploration:** Artists should immerse themselves in various musical traditions, studying their history and context. This deep understanding can lead to more respectful and authentic incorporation of diverse elements.

- **Experimentation:** Embracing a trial-and-error approach can lead to unexpected and delightful results. Artists should feel free to experiment with blending different genres and styles, allowing their creativity to flourish.

Conclusion

Embracing diverse influences is essential for creating music that resonates on a global scale. By understanding the theoretical underpinnings of intertextuality, navigating the challenges of cultural appropriation, and learning from successful examples, artists can forge a unique sound that reflects the rich tapestry of human experience. The journey of integrating diverse influences is not just about creating music; it's about fostering understanding, celebrating differences, and ultimately, uniting people through the universal language of sound.

Balancing Tradition and Innovation

In the vibrant world of music, especially within the realm of farting—a genre that embraces the unconventional—balancing tradition and innovation is not just a necessity; it is an art form. This section delves into the intricate dance between honoring the roots of musical heritage while simultaneously pushing the boundaries of creativity and exploration.

Theoretical Framework

To understand the balance between tradition and innovation, we can draw upon the theoretical framework of *cultural hybridity*. Cultural hybridity refers to the blending of different cultural elements to create something new while respecting and acknowledging the origins of those elements. In the context of farting, this means taking traditional sounds and techniques and infusing them with modern influences to create a fresh auditory experience.

Mathematically, we can represent this balance using the equation:

$$B = \frac{T + I}{C} \qquad\qquad (21)$$

Where:

- B is the balance between tradition and innovation.

- T represents the traditional elements.

- I symbolizes the innovative aspects.

- C is the cultural context in which these elements exist.

This equation illustrates that the balance B can only be achieved when both traditional and innovative elements are considered within the framework of their cultural context.

Challenges in Balancing Tradition and Innovation

1. **Resistance from Purists**: One of the primary challenges faced by artists is the resistance from purists who believe that innovation dilutes the essence of traditional farting. For instance, when Sanjay Oluwaseun introduced electronic elements into his performances, he faced backlash from traditionalists who argued that such changes strayed too far from the roots of the genre.

2. **Commercial Pressures**: The music industry often prioritizes commercial success over artistic integrity. This pressure can lead artists to compromise their innovative visions in favor of more traditional, marketable sounds. A prime example is the trend of remixing classic farting tracks to fit contemporary pop structures, which can sometimes overshadow the original artistry.

3. **Cultural Appropriation**: As artists explore diverse influences, the line between inspiration and appropriation can become blurred. It is crucial for artists to navigate this terrain with sensitivity and respect, ensuring that they honor the traditions they draw from without exploiting them.

Examples of Successful Balance

1. **Sanjay Oluwaseun**: A trailblazer in the farting genre, Sanjay has masterfully blended traditional African rhythms with modern electronic sounds. His hit single "Farting in the Future" incorporates traditional drumming patterns while layering them with synthesized melodies, creating a sound that is both nostalgic and forward-thinking.

2. **Collaborative Projects**: Many artists have found success in collaboration, where traditional and innovative elements can coexist. The project "Fart Fusion" brought together seasoned farting musicians and contemporary electronic artists, resulting in a groundbreaking album that honors the past while embracing the future.

3. **Cultural Festivals**: Events like the International Farting Festival celebrate both traditional and innovative farting styles, showcasing artists who respect the roots of the genre while pushing creative boundaries. These festivals provide a platform for dialogue and exchange, fostering a community that values both tradition and innovation.

Strategies for Achieving Balance

1. **Education and Awareness**: Artists should educate themselves about the traditions they wish to incorporate into their work. Understanding the historical and cultural significance of these elements can help create a more respectful and authentic fusion.

2. **Experimentation**: Embracing experimentation is key to innovation. Artists should feel empowered to explore new sounds and techniques while remaining mindful of their roots. This can involve using traditional instruments in unconventional ways or blending genres to create unique fusions.

3. **Community Engagement**: Engaging with the community can provide valuable insights into how tradition and innovation are perceived. By involving audiences in the creative process, artists can foster a sense of ownership and connection to both the traditional and innovative aspects of their work.

4. **Mentorship**: Seeking mentorship from artists who have successfully navigated the balance between tradition and innovation can provide invaluable guidance. Learning from their experiences can help emerging artists find their own unique voice within the farting genre.

Conclusion

In conclusion, balancing tradition and innovation in the farting genre is a dynamic and ongoing process. It requires artists to navigate challenges, embrace experimentation, and engage with their communities. By respecting the roots of their musical heritage while daring to explore new horizons, artists can create a vibrant and evolving sound that resonates with audiences both old and new. This balance not only enriches the farting genre but also ensures its relevance and vitality in the ever-changing landscape of music.

Blowing the Audience Away

Crafting Memorable Setlists

Crafting a memorable setlist is an essential aspect of any live performance, serving as the backbone of a concert experience that resonates with the audience. A thoughtfully curated setlist can elevate the energy of the show, create emotional connections, and leave a lasting impression long after the final note fades. In this section, we will explore the theory behind setlist creation, common challenges faced by artists, and practical examples that illustrate effective strategies.

Theoretical Foundations

At its core, a setlist is more than just a list of songs; it is a narrative that unfolds throughout the performance. Theoretical frameworks for setlist crafting can be drawn from various disciplines, including psychology, music theory, and performance studies. One key principle is the concept of **emotional arc**, which refers to the progression of emotions experienced by the audience during the concert. The emotional arc can be visualized as a curve, where the performance starts with an engaging opener, builds to a climax, and concludes with a powerful finale.

$$E(t) = a \cdot t^2 + b \cdot t + c \tag{22}$$

Where $E(t)$ represents the emotional engagement at time t, and a, b, and c are coefficients that define the shape of the emotional arc. A well-crafted setlist often follows a pattern of alternating between high-energy and more subdued songs to maintain audience interest and engagement.

Common Challenges

Creating a memorable setlist is not without its challenges. Artists often struggle with:

- **Audience Expectations:** Balancing personal artistic vision with what fans want to hear can be a tightrope walk.
- **Song Selection:** Determining which songs to include from a vast discography can lead to difficult decisions.
- **Pacing:** Maintaining an optimal flow throughout the concert while managing energy levels can be tricky.

- **Technical Limitations:** Some songs may require specific instruments or setups that are not feasible during a live performance.

Examples of Effective Setlists

To illustrate the art of crafting memorable setlists, let's examine a few successful examples from renowned artists:

- **Beyoncé's Coachella Performance (2018):** Beyoncé's setlist included a mix of her biggest hits, interspersed with powerful medleys. The emotional journey began with high-energy tracks like "Crazy In Love," gradually transitioning to more introspective songs like "Halo," and culminating in an explosive finale with "Formation." This careful pacing kept the audience engaged while allowing for moments of reflection.

- **The Rolling Stones' "A Bigger Bang Tour":** The setlist featured a blend of classic hits and newer material, showcasing the band's evolution while satisfying long-time fans. The inclusion of unexpected covers, such as Bob Marley's "Get Up, Stand Up," added a refreshing twist and kept the audience on their toes.

- **Taylor Swift's "Reputation Stadium Tour":** Swift's setlist was designed to reflect the themes of her album, using visual storytelling and choreography to enhance the experience. The transition from darker, more aggressive songs like "Look What You Made Me Do" to uplifting anthems like "Shake It Off" created a dynamic emotional arc.

Practical Strategies for Crafting Setlists

Here are some practical strategies for artists to consider when crafting their setlists:

1. **Start Strong:** Open with a high-energy song that captures attention and sets the tone for the performance.

2. **Create Contrast:** Alternate between fast-paced and slower songs to maintain audience engagement and emotional variety.

3. **Include Fan Favorites:** Incorporate well-loved tracks that fans expect to hear, ensuring a connection with the audience.

4. **Surprise Elements:** Add unexpected covers or mashups to keep the setlist fresh and exciting.

5. **Consider the Venue:** Tailor the setlist to fit the venue's atmosphere and audience demographics for maximum impact.

6. **Practice Transitions:** Smooth transitions between songs can enhance the flow and keep the audience immersed in the experience.

Conclusion

In conclusion, crafting a memorable setlist is a multifaceted process that requires careful consideration of emotional arcs, audience expectations, and artistic integrity. By employing effective strategies and learning from successful artists, musicians can create performances that resonate deeply with their audience, ensuring that their music is not just heard but felt. A well-crafted setlist has the power to transform a concert into an unforgettable experience, leaving fans buzzing long after the final bow.

Captivating Performances and Stage Presence

When it comes to captivating performances, the essence lies not just in the music but in the energy and connection shared between the artist and the audience. Stage presence is the magical ingredient that transforms a mere concert into an unforgettable experience. This section delves into the critical elements that contribute to an artist's stage presence, incorporating relevant theories, practical challenges, and exemplary instances from the world of performance.

Theoretical Framework of Stage Presence

Stage presence can be understood through various theoretical lenses, including *Gestalt psychology*, which emphasizes the importance of holistic perception. According to this theory, an audience perceives a performance not just through auditory cues but through visual and emotional stimuli as well. The following components contribute to a captivating stage presence:

- **Body Language:** Non-verbal communication plays a vital role in conveying emotions and engaging the audience. Effective use of gestures, facial expressions, and movement can amplify the message of the performance.

- **Vocal Dynamics:** The modulation of voice—varying pitch, volume, and tempo—can evoke different emotional responses from the audience. A powerful vocal delivery often correlates with a stronger stage presence.

+ **Audience Interaction:** Establishing a rapport with the audience fosters a sense of connection. Techniques such as call-and-response, eye contact, and personalized anecdotes can enhance this interaction.

Challenges in Developing Stage Presence

While the theoretical framework provides a foundation, artists often face challenges in cultivating their stage presence. Some common issues include:

+ **Stage Fright:** The anxiety experienced before or during a performance can hinder an artist's ability to connect with their audience. Techniques such as deep breathing, visualization, and rehearsal can help mitigate this fear.

+ **Distractions:** External factors, such as technical difficulties or an unresponsive audience, can disrupt the flow of a performance. Artists must learn to adapt and maintain composure in the face of such challenges.

+ **Authenticity vs. Performance:** Striking a balance between being genuine and entertaining can be difficult. Artists may struggle with the pressure to perform a persona rather than being their true selves on stage.

Practical Examples of Captivating Performances

To illustrate the power of stage presence, let's examine a few exemplary performances that left a lasting impression on audiences:

+ **Beyoncé at Coachella 2018:** Known for her electrifying stage presence, Beyoncé's performance at Coachella showcased her mastery of body language, vocal dynamics, and audience engagement. The meticulous choreography, coupled with her ability to connect with the crowd, created a memorable experience that resonated with millions.

+ **Prince's Super Bowl XLI Halftime Show:** Prince's performance during the Super Bowl halftime show is often cited as one of the greatest live performances in history. His command of the stage, combined with his charismatic interaction with the audience, exemplified the pinnacle of stage presence. The rain-soaked performance became an iconic moment, demonstrating how artists can turn challenges into opportunities for captivating engagement.

- **Lady Gaga's 2017 Super Bowl Halftime Show:** Lady Gaga's performance integrated powerful visual elements and audience interaction. Her ability to seamlessly transition between songs while maintaining high energy and emotional connection showcased the effectiveness of a well-crafted stage presence.

The Equation of Stage Presence

To quantify the impact of stage presence, we can conceptualize it through a simple equation:

$$\text{Stage Presence} = (\text{Body Language}) + (\text{Vocal Dynamics}) + (\text{Audience Interaction}) + (\text{Auth}$$

Where each component can be further evaluated based on its contribution to the overall performance experience. For instance, if an artist excels in body language and audience interaction but lacks in vocal dynamics, the overall stage presence may still be perceived as lacking.

Conclusion

In conclusion, captivating performances and stage presence are vital components of an artist's identity. By understanding the theoretical frameworks, addressing challenges, and drawing inspiration from exemplary performances, artists can enhance their ability to connect with audiences. Ultimately, the synergy between the artist and the audience transforms a performance into a shared experience, leaving a lasting impression that transcends the music itself.

The Art of Connecting with Your Audience

In the electrifying world of performance, the ability to connect with your audience is not just a skill; it's an art form. This section delves into the nuances of building that connection, exploring the psychological theories behind audience engagement, the common challenges performers face, and practical examples that highlight successful connections.

Understanding Audience Psychology

At the heart of connecting with your audience lies a deep understanding of audience psychology. According to the *Social Identity Theory*, individuals derive a sense of self from their group memberships, which can include fandoms. This means that when an artist resonates with their audience, they are tapping into a collective identity that fans cherish.

The *Affect Theory* suggests that emotions play a crucial role in how audiences perceive performances. Engaging an audience involves eliciting emotional responses, whether it's joy, nostalgia, or empowerment. The equation governing this interaction can be simplified as:

$$E = f(I, A, R) \tag{23}$$

Where:

+ E = Emotional response

+ I = Individual characteristics of the audience

+ A = Artist's authenticity and relatability

+ R = Relevance of the performance content

By understanding these dynamics, artists can better tailor their performances to resonate with the emotional states of their audience.

Challenges in Audience Connection

Despite the potential for connection, several challenges can hinder this bond:

+ **Stage Fright:** Many performers experience anxiety that can obstruct their ability to engage with the audience. Overcoming this requires techniques such as deep breathing, visualization, and positive affirmations.

+ **Cultural Differences:** In a globalized world, audiences come from diverse backgrounds. Misunderstanding cultural nuances can lead to disconnection. Artists must do their research and be sensitive to these differences.

+ **Technological Barriers:** In today's digital age, artists often perform in front of screens rather than live audiences. This can create a sense of detachment. Finding ways to bridge this gap, such as interactive elements, is crucial.

48

Strategies for Connection

To effectively connect with an audience, artists can employ several strategies:

+ **Storytelling:** Sharing personal stories or the inspiration behind songs can create intimacy. For example, when Taylor Swift recounts experiences that shaped her music, fans feel a closer connection, fostering a sense of belonging.

+ **Interactive Engagement:** Encouraging audience participation, whether through sing-alongs or call-and-response segments, can enhance connection. For instance, Beyoncé's performances often include moments where she invites the audience to join in, creating a shared experience.

+ **Body Language and Eye Contact:** Non-verbal communication is a powerful tool. Maintaining eye contact and using open body language can make the audience feel seen and valued. A study by the *Journal of Nonverbal Behavior* indicates that performers who engage in eye contact are perceived as more authentic and relatable.

Examples of Successful Audience Connection

1. **Lady Gaga:** Known for her elaborate performances, Lady Gaga often breaks the fourth wall, addressing her fans directly and sharing her struggles with mental health. This vulnerability creates a powerful connection, transforming her concerts into safe spaces for fans.

2. **Ed Sheeran:** During his shows, Ed Sheeran frequently interacts with the audience, asking questions and encouraging them to share their stories. This dialogue fosters a sense of community, making each concert feel unique and personal.

3. **Janelle Monáe:** In her performances, Monáe often incorporates themes of empowerment and social justice. By addressing relevant issues, she resonates deeply with audiences who share her values, creating a strong bond based on mutual beliefs.

Conclusion

In conclusion, the art of connecting with your audience is a multifaceted skill that requires understanding psychology, overcoming challenges, and employing effective strategies. By mastering this art, artists not only enhance their performances but also create lasting memories and foster a loyal fanbase. Remember, every note you play and every word you sing can resonate deeply with someone in the audience—make it count!

Handling Stage Fright and Nervousness

When the spotlight hits and the audience's eyes are on you, it's easy to feel that surge of adrenaline that can quickly turn from excitement to anxiety. Stage fright, or performance anxiety, is a common experience among artists, whether you're a seasoned performer or a fresh face on the scene. Understanding and managing this phenomenon is crucial for delivering captivating performances that leave your audience wanting more.

The Psychology of Stage Fright

Stage fright is often rooted in the fear of judgment and the desire for approval. According to the *Cognitive Behavioral Theory*, our thoughts directly influence our feelings and behaviors. Negative thoughts such as "What if I mess up?" or "Everyone will laugh at me!" can lead to heightened anxiety levels. The equation can be summarized as:

$$\text{Anxiety} = f(\text{Negative Thoughts}) \tag{24}$$

Here, f represents the function that describes how negative thoughts amplify anxiety. To combat this, artists must reframe their thinking. Instead of focusing on potential failure, shift your mindset to embrace the opportunity to connect with your audience and share your art.

Identifying Symptoms of Stage Fright

Recognizing the physical symptoms of stage fright can help you address them before they escalate. Common symptoms include:

+ Increased heart rate

+ Sweating

+ Shaking hands

+ Dry mouth

+ Nausea

These physiological responses are part of the body's fight-or-flight reaction. Understanding that these sensations are normal can help normalize the experience and reduce anxiety.

Preparation is Key

One of the most effective strategies to combat stage fright is thorough preparation. The more confident you feel in your material, the less anxious you will be. Here are some preparation techniques:

- **Practice Regularly:** Rehearse your setlist multiple times until it feels second nature. Familiarity breeds confidence.

- **Visualize Success:** Spend time imagining yourself performing flawlessly. Visualization techniques can help create a positive mindset.

- **Know Your Audience:** Understanding who you are performing for can help tailor your performance and ease nerves.

Breathing Techniques

Breathing exercises can significantly reduce anxiety and help you regain control. The following techniques can be useful:

- **Deep Breathing:** Inhale deeply through your nose for a count of four, hold for four, and exhale slowly through your mouth for a count of six. Repeat this cycle until you feel calmer.

- **4-7-8 Breathing:** Inhale for four seconds, hold for seven seconds, and exhale for eight seconds. This method not only calms the mind but also reduces physical symptoms of anxiety.

Embracing the Moment

Once you're on stage, it's essential to embrace the moment. Here are some tips to help you do just that:

- **Engage with Your Audience:** Make eye contact, smile, and connect with the crowd. This interaction can shift your focus away from your nerves and onto the performance.

- **Start with a Familiar Song:** Opening with a song you know well can boost your confidence and set a positive tone for the rest of the performance.

- **Accept Imperfection:** Remember that no performance is perfect. Embrace mistakes as part of the live experience; your audience will appreciate your authenticity.

Seeking Support

Lastly, don't hesitate to seek support from fellow musicians or mentors. Sharing your experiences with others can provide comfort and practical advice. Consider forming a support group where you can discuss your fears and develop coping strategies together.

Conclusion

Handling stage fright and nervousness is an art in itself. By understanding the psychological underpinnings, preparing adequately, employing breathing techniques, and embracing the moment, you can transform anxiety into a powerful performance tool. Remember, every great artist has faced the challenge of stage fright, but it's how you choose to respond that will define your journey in the spotlight. So, take a deep breath, step out, and let your melodic thunder resonate with the world!

Embracing the Unexpected

In the vibrant world of music, the unexpected can often become the most exhilarating element of a performance. Embracing surprises not only keeps the audience on their toes but also allows artists to explore new dimensions of their creativity. This section delves into the significance of welcoming the unforeseen in musical performances and how it can enhance the overall experience for both the artist and the audience.

The Beauty of Imperfection

One of the most profound lessons in embracing the unexpected is recognizing the beauty of imperfection. Mistakes can lead to spontaneous moments that resonate deeply with audiences. For example, during a live performance, an artist might accidentally hit the wrong note or forget a lyric. Instead of panicking, they can turn this into an opportunity for improvisation.

$$\text{Spontaneity} = \text{Creativity} + \text{Mistakes} \tag{25}$$

This equation illustrates that spontaneity arises from the combination of creativity and mistakes. A well-known instance of this is when the legendary musician Jimi Hendrix famously improvised during his performances, often deviating from the original compositions, which captivated audiences and created a unique experience each time.

Engaging with the Audience

Embracing the unexpected also involves engaging with the audience in ways that are unscripted. This connection can lead to memorable moments that enhance the performance. For instance, during a concert, an artist might invite a fan on stage to join in a song. This not only creates an unforgettable experience for the fan but also energizes the crowd, fostering a sense of community.

$$\text{Audience Engagement} = \text{Unscripted Moments} + \text{Connection} \qquad (26)$$

Here, audience engagement is maximized when unscripted moments are combined with genuine connection. An example of this can be seen in Taylor Swift's concerts, where she often interacts with fans, sharing personal stories and inviting them to sing along, creating a shared experience that transcends the performance itself.

Harnessing the Power of Surprise

Surprises can be strategically woven into performances to heighten excitement and anticipation. Artists can incorporate unexpected elements, such as surprise guest appearances or unannounced song changes, to keep the audience engaged.

$$\text{Audience Excitement} = \text{Anticipation} + \text{Surprise} \qquad (27)$$

This equation suggests that audience excitement is a function of anticipation and surprise. A prime example is when Beyoncé surprised fans by performing a new song at a festival, leaving the audience in awe and creating a buzz that resonated long after the event.

Overcoming Fear of the Unknown

While embracing the unexpected can be thrilling, it also requires overcoming the fear of the unknown. Many artists struggle with the anxiety that comes from deviating from their planned setlists or routines. However, cultivating a mindset that welcomes uncertainty can lead to growth and innovation.

$$\text{Growth} = \text{Embracing Uncertainty} - \text{Fear} \qquad (28)$$

This equation emphasizes that growth occurs when artists embrace uncertainty while minimizing fear. A notable example is Lady Gaga, who often experiments with different musical styles and performance art, pushing boundaries and redefining her artistry with each album.

Creating Memorable Experiences

Ultimately, embracing the unexpected allows artists to create memorable experiences that resonate with audiences. These moments become stories that fans share, enhancing the artist's legacy.

$$\text{Legacy} = \sum \text{Memorable Experiences} \qquad (29)$$

In this equation, an artist's legacy is the sum of all memorable experiences they create throughout their career. For instance, the surprise performance of "Purple Rain" by Prince at the Super Bowl halftime show is etched in the memories of millions, showcasing how unexpected moments can solidify an artist's place in music history.

Conclusion

In conclusion, embracing the unexpected in musical performances is not just about spontaneity; it's about creating an atmosphere where creativity flourishes, connections deepen, and unforgettable experiences are born. By welcoming surprises, engaging with audiences, and overcoming fears, artists can elevate their performances and leave a lasting impact that resonates far beyond the stage. As the music industry continues to evolve, those who dare to embrace the unexpected will undoubtedly stand out, creating a legacy that echoes through time.

Harnessing the Power of Energy and Vibe

In the realm of performance, energy and vibe are not just abstract concepts; they are the lifeblood that fuels the connection between artists and their audience. Harnessing this power involves understanding the dynamics of energy transfer and the emotional resonance that music can evoke. This section delves into the theory behind energy and vibe, the challenges faced by performers, and practical strategies to elevate performance through these elements.

Understanding Energy in Performance

Energy in performance can be defined as the intensity and enthusiasm that an artist brings to the stage. This energy is often palpable, creating an electric atmosphere that can captivate an audience. Theoretical frameworks such as the **Energy Transfer Theory** suggest that performers can transfer their energy to the audience through various channels, including vocal delivery, physical movements, and visual presentation.

The equation that often describes energy transfer in a performance context can be simplified as:

$$E = P \times T \tag{30}$$

Where:

+ E is the energy transferred to the audience,

+ P is the performer's presence (which includes charisma, vocal strength, and stage dynamics),

+ T is the time spent engaging with the audience.

A performer with high presence who engages the audience for a longer duration will create a greater energy transfer.

The Role of Vibe

Vibe, on the other hand, encompasses the overall atmosphere and emotional tone of the performance. It is influenced by various factors, including the choice of music, the mood set by the performers, and the audience's reactions. The **Vibe Resonance Theory** posits that the emotional state of the performer can significantly affect the audience's experience. This theory can be illustrated through the following relationship:

$$V = C + A \tag{31}$$

Where:

+ V represents the vibe of the performance,

+ C is the connection established between the performer and the audience,

+ A is the audience's active participation and emotional engagement.

A strong connection leads to a more vibrant vibe, enhancing the overall performance experience.

Challenges in Harnessing Energy and Vibe

Despite the potential for powerful energy and vibe, performers often face challenges that can hinder their ability to connect with the audience. Common issues include:

+ **Stage Fright:** Anxiety can diminish a performer's energy, leading to a lackluster performance. Techniques such as deep breathing, visualization, and rehearsal can help mitigate these effects.

+ **Audience Disconnect:** If the audience is unresponsive, it can create a feedback loop that drains the performer's energy. Engaging the audience through call-and-response, interactive elements, or relatable content can bridge this gap.

+ **Technical Difficulties:** Equipment failures or poor sound quality can disrupt the vibe. Ensuring proper sound checks and having backup plans in place can help maintain energy levels.

Strategies for Elevating Energy and Vibe

To harness the power of energy and vibe effectively, performers can implement several strategies:

+ **Dynamic Stage Presence:** Movement, facial expressions, and vocal variety can significantly enhance energy. For example, a performer who moves across the stage and interacts with the audience can create a more engaging experience.

+ **Setting the Mood:** The use of lighting, stage design, and visual effects can influence the vibe. A well-designed stage setup can evoke specific emotions and set the tone for the performance.

+ **Building Anticipation:** Gradually increasing the energy throughout the set can create a powerful climax. For instance, starting with slower songs and building up to high-energy anthems can keep the audience engaged and excited.

+ **Authentic Interaction:** Genuine moments of connection, such as sharing personal stories or acknowledging audience members, can enhance the vibe. This authenticity fosters a sense of community and belonging.

Examples of Successful Energy and Vibe Management

Several artists exemplify the successful harnessing of energy and vibe:

- **Beyoncé:** Known for her electrifying performances, Beyoncé combines powerful vocals with dynamic choreography, creating an immersive experience that resonates with audiences worldwide.

- **Prince:** His ability to engage the audience through improvisation and unexpected twists kept fans on their toes, ensuring that every performance felt unique and vibrant.

- **Lady Gaga:** With her theatrical approach, Gaga creates an unforgettable vibe through elaborate costumes, stage setups, and audience interaction, leaving a lasting impression on her fans.

Conclusion

Harnessing the power of energy and vibe is essential for any performer aiming to leave a lasting impression. By understanding the dynamics of energy transfer and the significance of vibe, artists can create memorable experiences that resonate with their audience. Through strategic planning, authentic engagement, and a deep connection to their craft, performers can elevate their shows and ensure that every performance is not just heard, but felt.

Creating a Visual Spectacle

In the world of music, the auditory experience is only part of the equation; the visual component plays an equally crucial role in captivating an audience. Creating a visual spectacle is about weaving a tapestry of lights, colors, and movement that complements the sound, enhancing the overall performance and leaving a lasting impression. This section delves into the theoretical frameworks, practical challenges, and successful examples of creating visually stunning performances.

Theoretical Framework

The concept of a visual spectacle in music performance can be anchored in several theories of perception and aesthetics. The Gestalt principles of visual perception suggest that humans naturally organize visual elements into groups or unified wholes. This principle can be applied to stage design, where elements such as lighting, props, and performers should work harmoniously to create a cohesive visual narrative.

$$P = \frac{S}{C} \tag{32}$$

where P is the perceptual impact, S is the sum of sensory inputs (sight, sound, etc.), and C is the complexity of the arrangement. A higher P indicates a more profound impact on the audience, emphasizing the need for a balanced and well-thought-out visual presentation.

Challenges in Creating a Visual Spectacle

While the goal of creating a visual spectacle is clear, several challenges can arise:

+ **Budget Constraints:** High-quality visual effects often require significant investment in lighting, video equipment, and stage design. Balancing creativity with financial limitations is a common hurdle for many artists.

+ **Technical Limitations:** The integration of technology in live performances can lead to technical difficulties. Issues such as equipment failure or synchronization problems between sound and visuals can detract from the overall experience.

+ **Artistic Vision vs. Audience Expectation:** Striking a balance between personal artistic expression and what the audience expects can be challenging. Overly avant-garde visuals may alienate some viewers, while too conventional a presentation can fail to engage them.

+ **Environmental Factors:** The venue's size, layout, and acoustics can significantly affect how visual elements are perceived. What works in a small club may not translate well to a large arena, necessitating careful planning and adaptation.

Practical Strategies for Implementation

To overcome these challenges and create a successful visual spectacle, artists can consider the following strategies:

+ **Collaboration with Visual Artists:** Partnering with visual artists, choreographers, and lighting designers can bring fresh perspectives and expertise to the performance. This collaboration can lead to innovative ideas that enhance the overall presentation.

+ **Storytelling through Visuals:** Every performance should tell a story. Visual elements should reflect the themes and emotions conveyed through the music. For example, a song about longing could be complemented by soft, flowing visuals, while a high-energy anthem might benefit from dynamic, fast-paced imagery.

+ **Use of Technology:** Incorporating technology such as projection mapping, LED screens, and augmented reality can elevate the visual experience. These tools allow for the creation of immersive environments that can transport the audience into the world of the performance.

+ **Choreographed Movement:** Engaging performers in choreographed movements that align with the music can enhance the visual spectacle. Dance routines, synchronized movements, and even the placement of musicians on stage can create a dynamic visual flow.

Examples of Successful Visual Spectacles

Several artists and performances have successfully created visual spectacles that resonate with audiences:

+ **Beyoncé's Coachella Performance (2018):** Often referred to as "Beychella," her performance was a masterclass in creating a visual spectacle. The use of elaborate choreography, vibrant costumes, and powerful imagery celebrating Black culture created an unforgettable experience that complemented her music.

+ **Pink's Circus Tour (2010):** Pink's performances are known for their acrobatic elements and stunning visuals. The integration of aerial stunts and dramatic lighting effects transformed her concerts into a breathtaking spectacle, captivating audiences worldwide.

+ **Kanye West's Yeezus Tour (2013):** Kanye's use of minimalist set design paired with striking visual projections created an immersive experience. The stark contrasts and bold visuals enhanced the emotional weight of his music, demonstrating the power of visual storytelling.

Conclusion

Creating a visual spectacle is not merely about flashy effects; it is about crafting an experience that resonates with the audience on multiple levels. By understanding the theoretical foundations, addressing the challenges, and implementing effective strategies, artists can elevate their performances to new heights. A well-executed visual spectacle not only enhances the musical experience but also leaves a lasting impression, ensuring that audiences remember the performance long after the final note has faded.

Choreographing Fart Dance Moves

When it comes to captivating an audience, the power of movement cannot be underestimated. In the world of farting, choreography can elevate a performance from mundane to unforgettable. This section delves into the art of choreographing fart dance moves, blending humor, rhythm, and creativity into a spectacular visual experience.

Theoretical Foundations of Movement

Choreography is not merely about creating steps; it is about telling a story through movement. According to *Laban Movement Analysis*, movement can be categorized into four main factors: body, effort, shape, and space. Each of these elements plays a crucial role in crafting fart dance moves that resonate with the audience.

- **Body:** This involves the use of different body parts and how they interact with each other. For instance, incorporating exaggerated hip movements can signify a humorous take on farting.

- **Effort:** This refers to the quality of the movement. Light and quick movements may represent playful farts, while heavy, grounded movements can symbolize more impactful sounds.

- **Shape:** The formation of the dancer's body can evoke different emotions. Curved shapes might suggest a soft, gentle fart, while angular shapes can represent sharp, unexpected sounds.

- **Space:** Understanding how to utilize the performance area is essential. Dancers can create distance to emphasize the "blast radius" of a fart, or come together to illustrate unity in the farting experience.

Common Problems in Fart Dance Choreography

Choreographing fart dance moves comes with its unique set of challenges. Here are some common problems and suggested solutions:

+ **Synchronization:** Ensuring that all dancers are in sync can be difficult, especially with comedic timing.

$$\text{Synchronization} = \frac{\text{Number of Dancers in Unison}}{\text{Total Number of Dancers}} \times 100\% \qquad (33)$$

Regular practice and using a metronome can help maintain rhythm and timing.

+ **Audience Engagement:** Keeping the audience engaged is crucial. If the choreography is too complex, the audience may lose interest.

$$\text{Engagement Level} = \frac{\text{Audience Laughter}}{\text{Total Audience}} \times 100\% \qquad (34)$$

Simple, catchy moves that invite audience participation can enhance engagement.

+ **Injury Prevention:** Fart dancing can involve sudden movements that may lead to injuries.

$$\text{Injury Risk} = \frac{\text{Number of Injuries}}{\text{Total Performances}} \times 100\% \qquad (35)$$

Proper warm-up routines and safe dance practices should be emphasized during rehearsals.

Examples of Fart Dance Moves

To illustrate the principles of fart dance choreography, let's explore some signature moves that can be incorporated into performances:

1. **The Whoopee Cushion Shuffle:** A playful shuffle that mimics the sound of a whoopee cushion. Dancers move side to side while bending their knees and puffing their cheeks, creating a visual representation of the sound.

2. **The Blast Off:** This move involves a sudden jump and landing with a "popping" sound, simulating the release of gas. Dancers can add arm movements that mimic the trajectory of a fart, enhancing the comedic effect.

3. **The Squeaky Slide:** A smooth slide across the floor, paired with exaggerated facial expressions. This move captures the essence of a silent but deadly fart, allowing for a moment of tension before the comedic release.

4. **The Fart Fan:** Dancers create a circular formation, using their arms to fan outwards as if dispersing the smell. This move is great for audience interaction, inviting them to join in the fun.

Choreographic Structure

To create a cohesive fart dance routine, consider the following structure:

- **Introduction:** Start with a strong, comedic pose that sets the tone. This could involve a dramatic gasp or a playful wink.

- **Build-Up:** Gradually introduce more complex moves, increasing the energy level. Incorporate the Whoopee Cushion Shuffle and Blast Off to build anticipation.

- **Climax:** Reach the peak of the performance with the Squeaky Slide and Fart Fan, allowing the audience to fully engage and participate.

- **Conclusion:** End with a memorable pose or a synchronized group movement, leaving the audience with a lasting impression.

Conclusion

Choreographing fart dance moves is an art form that combines humor, creativity, and movement theory. By understanding the theoretical foundations, addressing common challenges, and incorporating engaging examples, performers can create routines that not only entertain but also resonate with audiences on a deeper level. The next time you hit the stage, remember: a well-choreographed fart dance can leave a lasting impression that echoes long after the performance ends!

Building a Fandom

Building a fandom is like crafting a symphony; it requires harmony, rhythm, and an irresistible beat that resonates with your audience. In the world of music, a dedicated fanbase can elevate an artist from obscurity to superstardom. This section delves into the art of cultivating a loyal following, exploring essential theories, potential challenges, and real-world examples of successful fandom-building strategies.

Theoretical Foundations of Fandom

Fandom can be understood through several key theories, including the **Uses and Gratifications Theory**, which posits that individuals actively seek out media that fulfills specific needs, such as entertainment, social interaction, or personal identity. By recognizing these needs, artists can tailor their music and engagement strategies to attract and retain fans.

Another relevant theory is **Social Identity Theory**, which suggests that individuals derive a sense of self from their group memberships. For musicians, this means creating a community where fans feel a sense of belonging. When fans identify with an artist or their music, they are more likely to engage, share, and promote the artist's work, effectively becoming brand ambassadors.

Challenges in Building a Fandom

While the idea of building a fandom sounds glamorous, it comes with its own set of challenges. One of the primary obstacles is **market saturation**. With thousands of artists vying for attention, standing out in a crowded space can be daunting. This saturation leads to a phenomenon known as **fan fatigue**, where audiences become overwhelmed by constant content and promotions, leading to disengagement.

Moreover, **negative feedback** can pose a significant challenge. In the age of social media, criticism can spread like wildfire, and artists must navigate the fine line between constructive feedback and harmful negativity. Developing a thick skin and maintaining a positive public image is crucial for sustaining a loyal fanbase.

Strategies for Building a Fandom

To successfully build a fandom, artists can employ several strategies:

+ **Authenticity:** Fans are drawn to artists who are genuine and relatable. Sharing personal stories, struggles, and triumphs fosters a connection that transcends mere musical appreciation. For instance, artists like *Taylor Swift* have built their fandom by being transparent about their lives and experiences, allowing fans to see themselves in the artist's journey.

+ **Engagement:** Actively engaging with fans through social media platforms, live streams, and Q&A sessions creates a sense of community. For example, *BTS*, the K-pop sensation, utilizes platforms like Twitter and V Live to interact with their fans, known as ARMY, fostering a deep sense of loyalty and belonging.

+ **Exclusivity:** Offering exclusive content, such as behind-the-scenes access, early releases, or limited-edition merchandise, can entice fans to become more invested. This strategy not only rewards loyal followers but also creates a sense of urgency and excitement around the artist's brand.

+ **Collaborations:** Partnering with other artists can introduce a musician to new audiences. Collaborations, like *Dua Lipa* and *Elton John*'s hit "Cold

Heart," can bridge fanbases and create a buzz that extends beyond the artist's existing followers.

+ **Live Experiences:** Hosting memorable live performances, whether through concerts, festivals, or intimate shows, allows fans to connect with the music on a personal level. The energy of a live performance can transform casual listeners into devoted fans, as seen in the case of *Ed Sheeran*, whose energetic and heartfelt shows have garnered him a massive following.

Real-World Examples

To illustrate the effectiveness of these strategies, we can look at several successful artists:

+ **Billie Eilish:** Eilish has cultivated a dedicated fandom by embracing her unique style and authenticity. Her candidness about mental health issues resonates with many young fans, creating a strong emotional connection. Her social media presence is a testament to her engagement strategy, where she shares snippets of her life, music, and thoughts, making her followers feel like they are part of her journey.

+ **Lil Nas X:** With his viral hit "Old Town Road," Lil Nas X leveraged social media platforms like TikTok to build a fandom rapidly. His playful and engaging content, combined with an openness about his identity, has fostered a diverse and passionate fanbase that transcends traditional genre boundaries.

+ **Ariana Grande:** Grande's use of exclusivity through her fan club, the "Arianators," provides fans with unique content and experiences. Her ability to connect with fans on a personal level, coupled with her powerful live performances, solidifies her place as a pop icon with a loyal following.

Conclusion

Building a fandom is a multifaceted endeavor that requires a blend of authenticity, engagement, and strategic marketing. By understanding the theoretical foundations of fandom, addressing potential challenges, and implementing effective strategies, artists can cultivate a loyal following that not only supports their music but also amplifies their message. As the music industry continues to evolve, those who prioritize their fans will undoubtedly create a lasting impact, ensuring that their symphony of sound resonates for years to come.

Leaving a Lasting Impression

When it comes to the world of performance, leaving a lasting impression is not just a goal; it's an art form. As artists, we want our audience to remember us, to feel something profound during and after our performance. This section dives into the nuances of crafting those unforgettable moments that resonate long after the final note has faded.

The Psychology of First Impressions

First impressions are crucial in any performance setting. According to research in psychology, it takes merely **seven seconds** for an audience to form an opinion about a performer. This highlights the importance of initial engagement. Artists can leverage this by ensuring their entrance is as captivating as their music. For example, a dramatic stage entrance, complete with lighting effects and an engaging visual backdrop, can set the tone for the entire performance.

Crafting Memorable Moments

Memorable moments in a performance often stem from a blend of spontaneity and preparation. Artists can incorporate elements that surprise and delight their audience. For instance, during a concert, an unexpected acoustic rendition of a popular song can create an intimate atmosphere, making the audience feel special and connected.

$$\text{Memorable Moment} = \text{Surprise} + \text{Emotional Connection} \qquad (36)$$

This equation emphasizes that the combination of surprise and emotional resonance is key to crafting unforgettable experiences.

Engaging the Audience

Engagement is vital in leaving a lasting impression. Techniques such as call-and-response, where the artist invites the audience to participate, can create a sense of unity. For example, during a high-energy track, an artist might pause and encourage the crowd to sing along, fostering a collective experience that lingers in memory.

Visual and Aesthetic Elements

The visual aspect of a performance cannot be overlooked. The use of costumes, stage design, and lighting plays a significant role in creating a memorable experience. A well-designed stage can enhance the storytelling aspect of a performance. For instance, an artist performing in a setting that reflects the theme of their music can deepen the audience's connection to the performance.

Storytelling Through Music

Every song has a story, and sharing that narrative with the audience can leave a lasting impact. Artists should consider how to weave personal anecdotes or the song's background into their performances. This not only provides context but also makes the audience feel more connected to the music.

Creating Emotional Resonance

Emotional resonance is a powerful tool in leaving a lasting impression. Artists can evoke emotions through their lyrics, melodies, and performance style. A study conducted by the *Journal of Music Therapy* found that music can significantly affect a listener's emotional state. By tapping into these emotions, artists can create moments that resonate deeply with their audience.

$$\text{Emotional Impact} = \text{Lyric Content} + \text{Melodic Structure} + \text{Performance Style} \tag{37}$$

This equation shows that the combination of thoughtful lyrics, compelling melodies, and an engaging performance style can maximize emotional impact.

Feedback and Reflection

After a performance, gathering feedback can provide insights into what resonated with the audience. This can be done through social media engagement, direct audience interactions, or post-performance surveys. Reflecting on this feedback allows artists to refine their craft and enhance future performances, ensuring they continue to leave a lasting impression.

Examples of Impactful Performances

Several artists have mastered the art of leaving a lasting impression. For instance, Beyoncé's halftime show at the Super Bowl not only showcased her vocal prowess but also delivered a powerful message about empowerment and unity. The combination of her performance, visuals, and the political undertones created an unforgettable experience for millions.

Similarly, Lady Gaga's performance of *"Shallow"* at the Oscars was not just about the song; it was about the emotional connection she established with the audience, enhanced by the intimate staging and her vocal delivery.

Conclusion

In conclusion, leaving a lasting impression is about more than just performing well; it's about creating a holistic experience that engages the audience on multiple levels. By understanding the psychology of first impressions, crafting memorable moments, engaging the audience, utilizing visual elements, telling compelling stories, and creating emotional resonance, artists can ensure their performances are unforgettable. As we continue to navigate the ever-evolving landscape of the music industry, let us remember that every note played is an opportunity to leave an indelible mark on our audience's hearts and minds.

The Journey to Stardom

Climbing the Mountain of Rejection

Ah, darling, let's talk about that mountain of rejection we all face on our path to greatness. You see, in the world of music, just like in life, rejection is as common as a catchy hook. It's like that one note that keeps popping up in your melody, and honey, you better learn how to dance around it!

The Reality of Rejection

Rejection is a universal experience, and for artists, it can feel like a tidal wave crashing down. Whether it's a gig you didn't get, a record label that passed on your demo, or that one fan who just didn't vibe with your sound, it's all part of the game. According to the *Psychology of Music* journal, artists often face rejection more frequently than those in other professions, with up to 90% of submissions to record labels being declined.

$$R = \frac{N_{rejections}}{N_{submissions}} \times 100\% \tag{38}$$

Where R is the rejection rate, $N_{rejections}$ is the number of rejections received, and $N_{submissions}$ is the total number of submissions made. This formula highlights the harsh reality: the more you put yourself out there, the more rejection you're likely to encounter.

Emotional Impact

Let's be real, boo. Rejection stings. It can lead to feelings of inadequacy, self-doubt, and even depression. The key is to acknowledge these feelings but not let them define you. According to the *Journal of Creative Behavior*, artists who embrace rejection as a learning tool tend to develop greater resilience and creativity.

$$E = \frac{C + R}{T} \tag{39}$$

Where E represents emotional growth, C is the creativity gained from overcoming challenges, R is the rejection faced, and T is the time spent in reflection. This equation suggests that the more you reflect on your rejections, the more creative fuel you'll gain for your next masterpiece.

Turning Rejection into Motivation

Now, let's flip the script! Rejection can be your best friend if you let it. Every "no" is a stepping stone to your next "yes." Take it from legends like Nicki Minaj herself, who faced countless rejections before finding her voice and her fans.

Here's a little exercise, babe: keep a rejection journal. Write down each rejection, how it made you feel, and what you learned from it. This practice not only helps you process your emotions but can also serve as a reminder of your growth over time.

Examples from the Industry

Let's drop some names, shall we? J.K. Rowling, the queen of wizardry, was rejected by over 12 publishers before finally landing a deal for *Harry Potter*. Look at her now! Or take a cue from the iconic Beyoncé, who faced her fair share of criticism and rejection during her early days with Destiny's Child. Each setback was a setup for a comeback, leading her to become a global superstar.

The Power of Resilience

Resilience is your secret weapon, darling. It's about bouncing back stronger, fiercer, and ready to slay. Embrace the rejection, learn from it, and keep pushing forward. The *American Psychological Association* suggests that resilience can be cultivated through positive self-talk, social support, and goal-setting.

$$R_s = \frac{P + S + G}{3} \qquad\qquad (40)$$

Where R_s is resilience, P is positive self-talk, S is social support, and G is goal-setting. This formula shows that by balancing these three elements, you can build a strong foundation to withstand the storms of rejection.

Conclusion

So, my fabulous friend, as you climb that mountain of rejection, remember: it's not the rejection that defines you, but how you rise from it. Each setback is an opportunity to refine your craft, connect with your true self, and ultimately shine brighter than ever. Keep that head high, strut your stuff, and let the world know you're here to stay. After all, every superstar has faced rejection, but only the bold turn it into a stepping stone for success!

Now, go out there and make some noise, because the world is waiting for your sound!

Overcoming Odds and Obstacles

In the vibrant world of music, every artist faces a unique set of challenges that can hinder their journey to success. Overcoming these odds is not just about talent; it's a test of resilience, determination, and the ability to adapt. This section delves into the various obstacles that musicians encounter and provides strategies to triumph over them.

Understanding the Landscape

The music industry is notoriously competitive.   Emerging artists often find themselves grappling with several issues, including:

- **Financial Constraints:** Many artists struggle to finance their projects, from recording to marketing. According to a survey by the *Music Industry Association*, over 60% of independent artists report that lack of funds is a significant barrier to their success.

- **Rejection from Labels:** The harsh reality is that record labels often overlook talented musicians. The fear of rejection can be paralyzing, but it's crucial to remember that even the most successful artists faced numerous rejections before their big break.

+ **Limited Access to Resources:** Many aspiring musicians lack access to quality recording studios, instruments, or mentorship, which can stifle their creative expression and growth.

Building Resilience

Resilience is the ability to bounce back from setbacks. Here are some strategies that can help artists cultivate resilience:

1. **Mindset Shift:** Embrace a growth mindset. Instead of viewing obstacles as insurmountable, see them as opportunities for growth. As Carol Dweck, a leading psychologist, suggests, "Becoming is better than being."

2. **Setting Realistic Goals:** Break down larger aspirations into smaller, achievable goals. This method not only makes the journey less daunting but also allows for a sense of accomplishment along the way. For example, instead of aiming for a record deal immediately, focus on writing a certain number of songs or performing at local venues.

3. **Networking and Collaboration:** Surround yourself with supportive individuals who can provide guidance and encouragement. Collaborating with other artists can lead to innovative ideas and solutions to common problems. The power of community cannot be overstated; as the saying goes, "It takes a village."

Learning from Setbacks

Every setback can be a lesson in disguise. Here are some examples of renowned artists who faced significant obstacles but emerged stronger:

+ **Taylor Swift:** Before becoming a household name, Swift faced rejection from multiple record labels. Instead of giving up, she continued to hone her craft and ultimately signed with Big Machine Records, launching her career into the stratosphere.

+ **Eminem:** Eminem's journey was riddled with challenges, including poverty and bullying. His determination to succeed and his unique voice resonated with audiences, leading him to become one of the best-selling artists of all time.

+ **J.K. Rowling:** While not a musician, Rowling's story is a testament to overcoming odds. She faced numerous rejections before finally publishing the Harry Potter series, proving that persistence is key.

Practical Tools for Overcoming Obstacles

In addition to mindset and resilience, practical tools can aid in overcoming obstacles:

$$S = \frac{F}{A} \tag{41}$$

Where:

+ S = Success

+ F = Focus on your goals

+ A = Action taken towards those goals

This formula illustrates that success is directly proportional to the focus and action you apply to your dreams.

Conclusion

Overcoming odds and obstacles is an integral part of any artist's journey. By embracing resilience, learning from setbacks, and utilizing practical strategies, musicians can navigate the tumultuous waters of the music industry. Remember, every challenge is an opportunity to grow and evolve. The key is to keep pushing forward, no matter how many times you stumble. As Nicki Minaj so aptly puts it, "You gotta be a beast. That's the only way they'll respect you." So roar, baby, roar!

Navigating the Farting Industry

Navigating the farting industry is akin to traversing a whimsical soundscape where creativity meets commercial viability. In this section, we will explore the multifaceted nature of the farting industry, highlighting the challenges and opportunities that arise for emerging artists. The journey is not just about making noise; it's about crafting a unique sound that resonates with audiences while maneuvering through the complexities of the market.

Understanding the Landscape

The farting industry is a vibrant tapestry woven from diverse genres, styles, and cultural influences. To effectively navigate this landscape, artists must first understand the key components that define it. This includes recognizing the various stakeholders involved, such as producers, record labels, promoters, and, of course, the fans who drive demand.

$$Industry\ Landscape = Artists + Producers + Labels + Promoters + Fans\ \ (42)$$

Each player in this equation plays a crucial role in shaping the success of farting artists. For instance, producers are essential for refining sound, while promoters help in creating buzz around performances. Understanding the dynamics between these entities can empower artists to make informed decisions about collaborations and partnerships.

The Challenges of Entry

For many aspiring farting artists, entering the industry can feel like navigating a minefield. The barriers to entry are often high, with established artists dominating the charts and media attention. Emerging artists may face challenges such as:

+ **Market Saturation**: The farting genre has seen an influx of talent, making it difficult for new voices to stand out.

+ **Financial Constraints**: Producing quality music often requires significant investment, which can be a hurdle for independent artists.

+ **Limited Access to Resources**: Many artists lack the connections needed to access recording studios, promotional platforms, and distribution channels.

To overcome these challenges, artists must be resourceful. Utilizing social media platforms for self-promotion, engaging with local music scenes, and collaborating with other artists can provide vital exposure and support.

Embracing Innovation

In the ever-evolving farting industry, innovation is key to staying relevant. Artists must not only hone their craft but also embrace new technologies and trends. This could involve:

- **Leveraging Digital Platforms**: Streaming services, social media, and music-sharing apps allow artists to reach a broader audience without the need for traditional record deals.

- **Experimenting with Sound**: The farting genre thrives on creativity. Artists who push the boundaries of sound by incorporating unconventional instruments or blending genres can capture attention.

- **Utilizing Data Analytics**: Understanding listener demographics and preferences through data can guide marketing strategies and help tailor content to audience tastes.

For example, an artist who uses social media analytics to identify peak engagement times can strategically release content to maximize visibility.

Building a Brand

In the farting industry, creating a recognizable brand is essential for long-term success. This involves:

- **Defining Your Identity**: Artists should develop a clear artistic vision that reflects their unique sound and style. This identity should resonate through their music, visuals, and public persona.

- **Consistency in Messaging**: Maintaining a consistent brand message across all platforms strengthens recognition and trust with fans.

- **Engaging with Fans**: Building a loyal fanbase requires active engagement. Artists can foster community through social media interactions, live Q&A sessions, and exclusive content.

A case in point is the artist who leverages a distinctive visual aesthetic in music videos and promotional materials, creating a cohesive brand that fans can easily identify.

Navigating Industry Relationships

Building and maintaining relationships within the farting industry is crucial. Networking can lead to opportunities for collaboration, mentorship, and exposure. Key strategies include:

- **Attending Industry Events**: Conferences, music festivals, and workshops provide platforms for artists to connect with industry professionals and fellow musicians.

- **Seeking Mentorship**: Learning from established artists can provide invaluable insights into navigating the industry landscape.

- **Collaborating with Peers**: Joint projects can introduce artists to each other's audiences, expanding reach and fostering community.

For instance, a collaboration between two up-and-coming artists can lead to a unique sound that attracts attention from both fanbases.

Conclusion

Navigating the farting industry requires a blend of creativity, strategy, and resilience. Artists must be willing to adapt to the ever-changing landscape while remaining true to their artistic vision. By understanding the industry dynamics, embracing innovation, building a strong brand, and fostering relationships, emerging farting artists can carve out their own niche and thrive in this vibrant world of sound.

In conclusion, the farting industry is not just about making noise; it's about creating a symphony of opportunities, challenges, and growth. As artists navigate this landscape, they pave the way for future generations, ensuring that the art of farting continues to evolve and inspire.

Building a Strong Fanbase

Building a strong fanbase is essential for any artist aiming for longevity and success in the music industry. A dedicated fanbase not only provides a source of revenue through merchandise and ticket sales but also serves as a powerful marketing tool. The relationship between an artist and their fans can be likened to a symbiotic ecosystem, where both parties benefit and grow. In this section, we will explore the foundational theories behind fan engagement, the challenges artists face, and practical examples of successful fanbase building.

Theoretical Framework

Theories surrounding fan engagement often draw from social psychology and marketing principles. One such theory is the **Social Identity Theory**, which posits that individuals derive a sense of identity and self-esteem from their group memberships. For musicians, their fans form a community that shares a common bond through the artist's music. This connection fosters loyalty and encourages fans to actively promote the artist within their social circles.

Another relevant framework is the **Two-Step Flow Theory**, which suggests that media messages are filtered through opinion leaders who then influence others. In the context of music, fans who feel a strong connection to an artist often become opinion leaders themselves, sharing their enthusiasm on social media platforms, thus amplifying the artist's reach.

Challenges in Building a Fanbase

Despite the potential for success, artists face several challenges in cultivating a strong fanbase:

- **Market Saturation:** The music industry is highly competitive, with new artists emerging daily. Standing out amidst this saturation requires unique branding and a distinctive sound.

- **Changing Consumer Behavior:** With the rise of streaming services, fans have more options than ever. Artists must adapt to shifting consumer preferences and find ways to engage fans beyond just music.

- **Maintaining Engagement:** Once a fanbase is established, keeping fans engaged is crucial. This requires consistent communication, new content, and personal interaction.

Strategies for Building a Strong Fanbase

To effectively build a strong fanbase, artists can employ several strategies:

1. Authentic Engagement   Engagement starts with authenticity. Artists should share their personal stories, struggles, and triumphs to create a relatable persona. For example, artists like **Taylor Swift** have successfully utilized social media to connect with fans on a personal level, sharing behind-the-scenes moments and responding to fan interactions.

2. Leverage Social Media   Social media platforms are powerful tools for fan engagement. Artists can use platforms like Instagram, Twitter, and TikTok to share updates, interact with fans, and create viral content. The use of **hashtags** can also help in reaching a wider audience. For instance, the hashtag #Beyhive has united fans of **Beyoncé**, creating a sense of community and belonging.

3. Host Events and Experiences Live events, such as concerts, meet-and-greets, and fan clubs, provide opportunities for direct interaction. These experiences help solidify the bond between the artist and their fans. For example, **Ed Sheeran** has been known to host intimate concerts for select fans, creating memorable experiences that foster loyalty.

4. Collaborate with Other Artists Collaborations can introduce artists to new audiences. When artists team up with others, they tap into each other's fanbases, expanding their reach. A notable example is the collaboration between **Lady Gaga** and **Bradley Cooper** in the film *A Star is Born*, which not only showcased their talents but also drew fans from both artists' existing fanbases.

5. Create Exclusive Content Offering exclusive content, such as early access to music, behind-the-scenes footage, or special merchandise, can incentivize fans to stay loyal. Platforms like **Patreon** allow artists to provide tiered membership options, giving fans a sense of ownership in the artist's journey.

Measuring Success

To evaluate the effectiveness of fanbase-building strategies, artists can utilize various metrics:

- **Engagement Rates:** Monitoring likes, shares, and comments on social media posts provides insight into fan interaction.

- **Fan Growth:** Tracking the increase in followers or subscribers over time can indicate successful outreach efforts.

- **Merchandise Sales:** Analyzing sales data can reveal the financial impact of a strong fanbase.

Case Study: BTS

A prime example of successful fanbase building is the South Korean group **BTS**. Their dedicated fanbase, known as **ARMY**, exemplifies the power of engagement and community. BTS utilizes social media to maintain a close relationship with their fans, sharing personal messages and behind-the-scenes content. Their strategic use of platforms like **Weverse** allows for direct communication, fostering loyalty and a sense of belonging.

Moreover, BTS's commitment to social issues resonates with their fans, creating a deeper emotional connection. This approach has not only solidified their fanbase but also positioned them as global ambassadors for positive change.

Conclusion

Building a strong fanbase is a multifaceted endeavor that requires authenticity, engagement, and strategic outreach. By understanding the underlying theories and challenges, artists can employ effective strategies to cultivate a loyal following. In an industry where relationships are paramount, the connection between an artist and their fans can ultimately define their success. As the landscape continues to evolve, those who adapt and innovate will thrive in the ever-changing world of music.

Embracing the Power of Social Media

In today's digital age, social media is not just a platform for sharing photos of your latest meal; it's a powerful tool for artists to connect, engage, and expand their reach. For musicians, especially those in the unconventional realms of sound, such as the art of "farting," leveraging social media can be the difference between obscurity and stardom. This section explores how to harness the power of social media effectively, the challenges that come with it, and real-world examples of artists who have mastered this art.

The Importance of Social Media for Musicians

The rise of social media has transformed the music industry. According to a study by [1], over 80% of musicians use social media to promote their work, connect with fans, and build their brand. Platforms like Instagram, TikTok, and Twitter provide artists with direct access to their audience, allowing for real-time interaction and feedback.

$$\text{Engagement Rate} = \frac{\text{Total Engagements}}{\text{Total Followers}} \times 100 \qquad (43)$$

This equation helps artists measure their effectiveness on social media. A higher engagement rate indicates that the audience is responding positively to the content being shared. For fart artists, creating engaging content that resonates with their audience can lead to viral moments, expanding their reach exponentially.

Challenges of Social Media Engagement

While social media offers numerous benefits, it also presents challenges. The oversaturation of content can make it difficult for individual artists to stand out. Additionally, the algorithms that govern what content is seen can be unpredictable, leading to fluctuations in visibility and engagement.

One significant problem is the pressure to maintain a constant online presence. This can lead to burnout and creative fatigue, particularly for artists who rely on social media as their primary promotional tool. As noted by [2], many artists struggle with the balance between their artistic integrity and the demands of social media.

Strategies for Effective Social Media Use

To effectively use social media, artists should consider the following strategies:

+ **Authenticity is Key:** Audiences are drawn to genuine content. Artists should share behind-the-scenes glimpses of their creative process, personal stories, and even their failures. This builds a connection that transcends the music itself.

+ **Utilize Visual Content:** Platforms like Instagram and TikTok thrive on visual storytelling. Artists can create engaging videos that showcase their unique sound, perhaps even incorporating humorous farting skits that align with their brand.

+ **Engage with Your Audience:** Responding to comments, hosting live Q&A sessions, and creating polls can foster a sense of community. Engaging with fans makes them feel valued and more likely to support the artist's work.

+ **Collaborate with Influencers:** Partnering with social media influencers can help artists reach new audiences. For instance, a popular TikTok creator could feature an artist's song in their video, introducing it to a broader demographic.

+ **Monitor Analytics:** Understanding which posts perform well and why can guide future content. Artists should regularly review their social media analytics to refine their strategies and focus on what resonates with their audience.

Case Studies: Artists Who Excelled on Social Media

Several artists have successfully utilized social media to propel their careers. For instance, Lil Nas X leveraged TikTok to promote his song "Old Town Road," which became a viral sensation, leading to a record-breaking run on the Billboard charts. His strategy involved engaging with trends and creating relatable content that resonated with the platform's audience.

Similarly, fart artist Sanjay Oluwaseun has used Instagram to showcase his unique sound and personality. By creating funny, relatable content that incorporates his musical style, he has built a dedicated following that eagerly anticipates his new releases. His ability to engage with fans through humorous posts and interactive stories exemplifies the power of social media in building an artist's brand.

Conclusion

Embracing the power of social media is essential for artists looking to make their mark in the music industry. By understanding the landscape, overcoming challenges, and employing effective strategies, musicians can transform their social media presence into a powerful tool for growth and connection. As the industry continues to evolve, those who adapt and innovate will thrive, leaving a lasting impact on the world of music.

Bibliography

[1] Smith, J. (2020). *The Digital Music Revolution: How Social Media is Changing the Game*. Music Industry Journal.

[2] Johnson, L. (2021). *Social Media and the Artist's Dilemma: Finding Balance in a Digital World*. Creative Arts Review.

Breaking into the Mainstream

Breaking into the mainstream is a pivotal moment in any artist's career, particularly in the vibrant and often unpredictable world of music. It represents the transition from being a local or niche artist to gaining recognition and acceptance on a global scale. This section will delve into the theories and strategies that underpin this transformative process, the challenges artists face, and notable examples of those who have successfully navigated this journey.

Theoretical Framework

To understand the dynamics of breaking into the mainstream, we can apply the **Diffusion of Innovations** theory, proposed by Everett Rogers. This theory outlines how new ideas and technologies spread within a culture and can be adapted to analyze how music trends gain traction. The stages of this diffusion process include:

- **Knowledge:** Awareness of the artist and their music.

- **Persuasion:** The audience develops a favorable attitude towards the artist.

- **Decision:** The audience decides to adopt the artist's music.

- **Implementation:** The audience actively engages with the artist's work.

+ **Confirmation:** The audience reinforces their choice, leading to a loyal fanbase.

This model highlights the importance of strategic marketing and audience engagement in transitioning from obscurity to mainstream success.

Challenges Faced

The journey to mainstream recognition is fraught with challenges. Some of the most significant obstacles include:

+ **Market Saturation:** The music industry is saturated with talent, making it difficult for new artists to stand out. According to a report by *IFPI*, over 40,000 songs are uploaded to streaming platforms daily, creating fierce competition.

+ **Gatekeeping:** Major record labels and media outlets often act as gatekeepers, deciding which artists receive promotion and exposure. This can limit opportunities for independent artists.

+ **Changing Consumer Preferences:** Trends in music can shift rapidly, making it challenging for artists to maintain relevance. The rise of social media has accelerated this change, as viral hits can emerge overnight.

+ **Financial Constraints:** Breaking into the mainstream often requires significant investment in marketing, production, and touring. Many artists struggle to secure funding to support their ambitions.

Strategies for Success

To overcome these challenges, artists can implement several key strategies:

+ **Leveraging Social Media:** Platforms like TikTok, Instagram, and YouTube have become essential tools for artists to reach wider audiences. Viral challenges, music videos, and engaging content can propel an artist into the spotlight. For example, Lil Nas X's "Old Town Road" gained immense popularity through TikTok before it topped the Billboard charts.

+ **Collaborations:** Partnering with established artists can introduce new talent to existing fanbases. Collaborations can also enhance credibility and create buzz around a new release. A notable example is the collaboration between

Dua Lipa and Elton John on "Cold Heart," which merged different generations of music and expanded their reach.

+ **Live Performances and Tours:** Engaging with fans through live performances can solidify an artist's presence in the mainstream. High-energy shows and festival appearances can generate word-of-mouth promotion and media attention. The success of Billie Eilish's tours, characterized by her unique stage presence and connection with fans, exemplifies this strategy.

+ **Innovative Marketing Techniques:** Artists can utilize unique marketing campaigns to capture attention. For instance, the surprise release of Beyoncé's self-titled album in 2013, which featured no prior promotion, created a massive cultural moment and demonstrated the power of strategic marketing.

Case Studies

To illustrate the principles discussed, we can examine a few artists who successfully broke into the mainstream:

+ **Billie Eilish:** Eilish's rise to fame was fueled by her distinctive sound and aesthetic, which resonated with a younger audience. Her use of social media to share her music and personal stories cultivated a loyal fanbase. The release of her debut album, *When We All Fall Asleep, Where Do We Go?*, solidified her place in the mainstream, earning her multiple Grammy Awards.

+ **Post Malone:** Initially gaining attention with his viral hit "White Iverson," Post Malone leveraged streaming platforms and social media to build his brand. His genre-blending style appealed to a broad audience, leading to collaborations with high-profile artists and chart-topping singles.

+ **Lil Nas X:** His breakout hit "Old Town Road" exemplifies the power of social media in breaking into the mainstream. The song's viral success on TikTok and subsequent remix featuring Billy Ray Cyrus propelled it to unprecedented heights, demonstrating the potential of blending genres and engaging with a digital audience.

Conclusion

In conclusion, breaking into the mainstream is a complex process that requires a combination of strategic marketing, audience engagement, and overcoming significant challenges. By leveraging social media, collaborating with established artists, and engaging in innovative marketing techniques, aspiring musicians can navigate the competitive landscape of the music industry. The journey may be fraught with obstacles, but with perseverance and creativity, artists can achieve mainstream success and leave a lasting impact on the industry.

$$\text{Success} = \text{Strategy} + \text{Engagement} + \text{Resilience} \qquad (44)$$

Mastering the Art of Promotion

In the vibrant world of music, mastering the art of promotion is akin to crafting a hit single; it requires creativity, strategy, and a touch of flair. Promotion is not just about shouting into the void; it's about creating a dialogue with your audience, building your brand, and establishing a presence that resonates. In this section, we will explore key theories, common challenges, and effective strategies for promoting your music in a way that captivates and engages.

Theoretical Framework

Promotion in the music industry can be understood through several theoretical lenses, including the **AIDA model** (Attention, Interest, Desire, Action). This model outlines the steps necessary to guide a potential listener from awareness of your music to taking action, such as purchasing a ticket or streaming a song. Each stage can be broken down as follows:

+ **Attention:** Capture the audience's attention through eye-catching visuals, intriguing social media posts, or compelling music videos.

+ **Interest:** Generate interest by sharing behind-the-scenes content, engaging stories, or unique insights into your creative process.

+ **Desire:** Create a desire for your music by highlighting its emotional impact, relatability, or the exclusivity of live performances.

+ **Action:** Encourage action by providing clear calls to action, such as links to purchase music, tickets, or merchandise.

This model can be represented mathematically as follows:

$$P = f(A, I, D, A) \tag{45}$$

Where P represents the overall effectiveness of your promotion strategy, and f denotes a function of the four components: Attention (A), Interest (I), Desire (D), and Action (A).

Common Problems in Promotion

Despite the best intentions, artists often face challenges in their promotional efforts. Some common problems include:

+ **Lack of Target Audience Understanding:** Failing to identify and understand your target audience can lead to ineffective promotional strategies. It's essential to research demographics, preferences, and behaviors to tailor your message effectively.

+ **Over-Saturation of Content:** With the digital landscape saturated with content, standing out can be challenging. Artists must find unique angles or narratives that differentiate their music from the sea of offerings.

+ **Inconsistent Branding:** A lack of cohesive branding across platforms can confuse potential fans. Consistency in visuals, messaging, and tone is crucial for building a recognizable brand.

+ **Neglecting Engagement:** Promotion is a two-way street. Failing to engage with fans through comments, messages, and social media can lead to a disengaged audience.

Effective Promotion Strategies

To navigate these challenges, artists can implement several effective strategies:

+ **Leverage Social Media:** Platforms like Instagram, TikTok, and Twitter are vital for reaching audiences. Create engaging content that encourages sharing, such as challenges, memes, or interactive polls. For example, using TikTok to create a dance challenge for your latest single can rapidly increase its visibility.

+ **Collaborate with Influencers:** Partnering with social media influencers can amplify your reach. Choose influencers whose audience aligns with your target demographic. A well-placed shout-out or collaboration can introduce your music to new listeners.

+ **Utilize Email Marketing:** Building an email list allows you to communicate directly with your fans. Share exclusive content, upcoming shows, and personalized messages to foster a sense of community. According to a study by Campaign Monitor, email marketing has an ROI of $44 for every $1 spent.

+ **Create Compelling Visuals:** Invest in high-quality visuals for your music videos, album artwork, and promotional materials. Visual storytelling can enhance your music's appeal and create memorable associations.

+ **Engage with Your Audience:** Respond to comments, host Q&A sessions, and share user-generated content. Engaging with your audience fosters loyalty and encourages them to promote your music organically.

Case Study: A Successful Promotion Campaign

Let's consider the case of an indie band, *The Sonic Farts*, who successfully navigated their promotional journey. Faced with the challenge of breaking into a saturated market, they adopted a multi-faceted approach:

+ They identified their target audience as young adults interested in quirky, humorous music. Their branding reflected this through playful visuals and tongue-in-cheek messaging.

+ They launched a viral TikTok challenge that encouraged users to create videos featuring their song, resulting in thousands of user-generated posts and increased visibility.

+ The band collaborated with popular YouTubers for music reviews and reaction videos, gaining exposure to their audiences.

+ They maintained an active presence on social media, engaging with fans through live streams and behind-the-scenes content, which fostered a strong community.

As a result of their efforts, *The Sonic Farts* saw a significant increase in streaming numbers, sold-out shows, and a growing fanbase.

Conclusion

Mastering the art of promotion is essential for any artist looking to make a mark in the music industry. By understanding theoretical frameworks, addressing common challenges, and implementing effective strategies, artists can elevate their promotional efforts and connect with their audience in meaningful ways. Remember, promotion is not just about selling music; it's about building relationships and creating a lasting impact in the hearts of your fans.

Winning Over Critics

In the world of music, critics can often feel like a double-edged sword. On one hand, their reviews can elevate an artist's profile, while on the other, they can also bring an avalanche of negativity. To truly thrive in the industry, it's essential to master the art of winning over critics, turning potential adversaries into allies. This section explores strategies, theories, and real-world examples that illustrate how artists can effectively navigate this complex relationship.

Understanding the Critic's Perspective

Critics are often seen as gatekeepers of artistic quality, wielding the power to influence public perception. Understanding their perspective is crucial. Critics typically look for:

- **Originality:** Is the music fresh and innovative?

- **Technical Skill:** Are the musicians proficient in their craft?

- **Emotional Impact:** Does the music resonate on a deeper level?

- **Cohesion:** Does the album or performance present a unified vision?

By recognizing these criteria, artists can tailor their work to address and even exceed these expectations.

Strategies for Winning Over Critics

1. **Embrace Constructive Criticism** Rather than dismissing negative reviews, successful artists often embrace constructive feedback. This approach not only demonstrates humility but also a willingness to grow. For instance, pop sensation *Ariana Grande* faced criticism for her vocal style early in her career. Instead of shying away, she took the feedback to heart, refining her technique and broadening

her artistic range. The result? A string of chart-topping hits and a loyal fanbase that appreciates her evolution.

2. Develop a Strong Artistic Identity   Critics are more likely to be won over by artists who have a clear and compelling artistic identity. *Lady Gaga* is a prime example of this.   From her early days, she established a unique persona that combined theatricality with musical prowess.   By consistently delivering a strong brand, she not only captured the attention of critics but also shaped the narrative around her work, making it difficult for negative reviews to stick.

3. Engage with Your Audience   Building a solid relationship with your audience can indirectly influence critics.   When fans rally behind an artist, critics are often swayed by the public sentiment.   *Taylor Swift* has mastered this strategy, using social media to connect with her fans and create a sense of community.   When critics panned her earlier work, her dedicated fanbase pushed back, showcasing the power of audience engagement in shaping critical reception.

4. Showcase Versatility   Artists who demonstrate versatility can often win over critics who may have initially dismissed them.   *Beyoncé* is a stellar example, as she has successfully transitioned across genres, from R&B to pop to hip-hop.   Each time she reinvents herself, she not only captivates her audience but also garners respect from critics who appreciate her willingness to explore new musical territories.

5. Leverage Live Performances   Live performances can be a game-changer in winning over critics.   A strong live show can transform skepticism into admiration. For instance, *Bruno Mars* faced lukewarm reviews early in his career.   However, his electrifying live performances showcased his talent and charisma, ultimately winning over critics and solidifying his status as a top-tier performer.

The Role of Social Media

In the digital age, social media has become a powerful tool for artists to engage with critics and fans alike.   Platforms like Twitter and Instagram allow artists to respond to critiques, share their creative processes, and build a narrative around their work. This transparency can humanize artists and foster goodwill among critics.

Example: When *Katy Perry* faced backlash for her album *Witness*, she took to social media to openly discuss her creative journey and the challenges she faced.   This candid approach not only won her sympathy from fans but also softened the stance of some critics, who appreciated her vulnerability.

Conclusion

Winning over critics is not merely about silencing dissent; it's about engaging in a dialogue that can lead to mutual respect. By embracing constructive criticism, developing a strong artistic identity, engaging with audiences, showcasing versatility, and leveraging live performances, artists can transform critics from adversaries into allies. In the ever-evolving landscape of the music industry, mastering this art is crucial for long-term success and artistic growth.

Key Takeaways

+ Understand the criteria critics use to evaluate music.

+ Embrace constructive feedback and use it for growth.

+ Develop a strong and clear artistic identity.

+ Engage actively with your audience to build a loyal fanbase.

+ Showcase versatility to appeal to a broader range of critics.

+ Leverage live performances to demonstrate talent and charisma.

+ Utilize social media to foster a positive relationship with critics and fans.

Collaborating with Industry Giants

In the vibrant world of music, collaboration is the secret sauce that transforms a good track into a chart-topping sensation. When emerging artists team up with industry giants, they not only gain exposure but also a wealth of experience and creative synergy that can elevate their craft to new heights. This section explores the dynamics of collaboration, the challenges artists face, and the triumphs that can emerge from these powerful partnerships.

The Dynamics of Collaboration

Collaboration in music is akin to a symphony where each instrument contributes to a harmonious whole. It involves blending diverse styles, ideas, and influences to create something unique. The process can be both exhilarating and daunting, as artists must navigate their creative visions while respecting the contributions of their collaborators.

For instance, the collaboration between Lady Gaga and Tony Bennett on their album *Cheek to Cheek* exemplifies how two artists from vastly different backgrounds can come together to create a cohesive and innovative project. Their partnership not only showcased their individual talents but also introduced Gaga's pop sensibilities to Bennett's jazz roots, resulting in a refreshing sound that resonated with fans across generations.

Challenges in Collaboration

While the benefits of collaboration are plentiful, it does not come without its challenges. One significant issue is the potential for creative differences. When two strong-willed artists come together, there is a risk of conflict regarding artistic direction. This tension can lead to friction, which, if not managed properly, may derail the project altogether.

Moreover, the logistics of collaboration can be complex. Scheduling conflicts, differing work ethics, and varying levels of commitment can complicate the process. For example, when Kanye West collaborated with Paul McCartney on the track *FourFiveSeconds*, both artists had to navigate their busy schedules and creative processes to produce a track that met their high standards.

The Power of Collaboration

Despite these challenges, the rewards of collaborating with industry giants can be transformative. Collaborations can expand an artist's reach, introducing them to new audiences and markets. For instance, when Drake teamed up with Rihanna on *What's My Name?*, both artists not only topped charts but also solidified their status as global superstars.

Furthermore, collaborations can lead to innovative soundscapes that push the boundaries of genre. The fusion of styles often results in groundbreaking music that defies categorization. A prime example is the collaboration between Lil Nas X and Billy Ray Cyrus on *Old Town Road*, which blended country and hip-hop to create a viral sensation that dominated the charts for an unprecedented 19 weeks.

Theoretical Framework

From a theoretical perspective, collaboration can be understood through the lens of social exchange theory, which posits that relationships are formed based on the perceived benefits and costs involved. In the context of musical collaboration, artists weigh the potential gains—such as increased visibility and creative enhancement—against the risks of compromising their artistic integrity.

Mathematically, we can represent this decision-making process with the following equation:

$$\text{Net Benefit} = \text{Perceived Gains} - \text{Perceived Costs} \qquad (46)$$

Where: - Perceived Gains may include increased fan base, creative growth, and financial rewards. - Perceived Costs may involve creative differences, time investment, and potential reputational risks.

Conclusion

In conclusion, collaborating with industry giants presents a unique opportunity for emerging artists to elevate their music careers. While challenges such as creative differences and logistical hurdles may arise, the potential for growth, innovation, and exposure far outweighs the risks. By embracing collaboration, artists can not only enhance their own artistry but also contribute to the ever-evolving landscape of music.

As we continue to witness the power of collaboration in the music industry, it is clear that the magic that happens when artists unite can lead to groundbreaking music that resonates with audiences worldwide. So, whether you're an indie artist or a seasoned pro, remember that collaboration is not just about sharing the spotlight—it's about creating a symphony that echoes through the ages.

Staying True to Your Artistic Vision

In the vibrant world of music, where trends shift like the wind and the industry often pressures artists to conform, staying true to your artistic vision is both a challenge and a triumph. This section delves into the importance of maintaining authenticity in your work, the struggles artists face in this pursuit, and strategies to ensure your unique voice shines through.

The Importance of Authenticity

Authenticity is the cornerstone of a successful artistic career. It refers to the degree to which an artist remains genuine to their own beliefs, values, and creative instincts. When artists stay true to themselves, they cultivate a unique sound that resonates deeply with audiences. As the renowned musician *Lady Gaga* once said, "You have to be unique, and different, and shine in your own way." This sentiment highlights the necessity of embracing one's individuality in the crowded landscape of music.

The Struggles of Conformity

Despite the desire to remain authentic, many artists face pressures from record labels, producers, and even fans to conform to popular trends. This can lead to a crisis of identity, where the artist feels compelled to alter their sound or image to achieve commercial success. For example, consider the case of *Katy Perry*, who initially started her career in the Christian music genre before transitioning to mainstream pop. While this shift brought her immense success, it also sparked debates about her authenticity and whether she had compromised her original artistic vision.

Theoretical Framework: The Artist's Dilemma

The struggle for authenticity can be understood through the lens of the *Artist's Dilemma*, a concept that illustrates the conflict between artistic integrity and commercial viability. This dilemma can be represented mathematically as follows:

$$A = I - C \tag{47}$$

Where:

+ A represents the artist's authenticity.

+ I denotes the artist's intrinsic values and vision.

+ C signifies the external commercial pressures.

As artists navigate their careers, they must constantly balance these factors. A high level of intrinsic values I combined with minimal commercial pressures C will yield a stronger sense of authenticity A.

Strategies for Maintaining Artistic Integrity

To combat the pressures of conformity and uphold their artistic vision, artists can adopt several strategies:

+ **Establish a Strong Personal Brand:** Artists should cultivate a brand that reflects their values, aesthetics, and artistic goals. This brand serves as a guiding compass, helping them make decisions that align with their vision.

- **Surround Yourself with Supportive Collaborators:** Working with producers, songwriters, and musicians who understand and respect your vision is crucial. For instance, *Pharrell Williams* often collaborates with artists who share his creative ethos, allowing him to produce work that feels authentic to him.

- **Stay Connected to Your Roots:** Regularly revisiting the music and influences that inspired you can help maintain a connection to your original vision. This practice can serve as a reminder of why you started making music in the first place.

- **Embrace Vulnerability:** Sharing personal stories and experiences through music can create a deeper connection with audiences. Artists like *Taylor Swift* have built their careers on vulnerability, sharing their life experiences in a way that resonates with listeners.

- **Set Boundaries with Industry Professionals:** It's essential to establish clear boundaries with managers, labels, and producers regarding your artistic direction. Communicating your vision upfront can prevent future conflicts and ensure that your work remains true to your identity.

Examples of Artistic Integrity

Several artists exemplify the power of staying true to their artistic vision:

- *Beyoncé* has consistently embraced her identity and artistic vision throughout her career, whether through her music, visual albums, or social activism. Her work often reflects her experiences as a Black woman, creating a powerful narrative that resonates with her audience.

- *Frank Ocean* is another artist who has remained fiercely independent, choosing to release music on his terms. His album *Blonde* was a departure from mainstream expectations, yet it solidified his status as a visionary artist who prioritizes authenticity over commercial success.

Conclusion

Staying true to your artistic vision is a journey filled with challenges, but it is also one of the most rewarding aspects of a musician's career. By embracing authenticity, setting boundaries, and remaining connected to your roots, artists can navigate the complexities of the music industry while maintaining their unique voice. In the end, it is this authenticity that will resonate with audiences and leave a lasting impact on the world of music. As you embark on your artistic journey, remember: your voice is your power, and staying true to it is the ultimate act of rebellion in a world that often demands conformity.

The Fallout of Success

Dealing with Fame and Its Pitfalls

Fame is a double-edged sword, darling! On one side, it glimmers like a diamond, showering you with adoration, opportunities, and a lifestyle most can only dream of. But on the other side, it can feel like you're walking on a tightrope, where one misstep could send you tumbling into a pit of scrutiny and negativity. So, let's break it down, and I'm gonna give you the tea on how to navigate this wild ride!

The Allure of Fame

When you step into the limelight, the allure of fame can be intoxicating. You're suddenly the center of attention, and everyone wants a piece of you! The glitz, the glam, the fabulous parties—who wouldn't want that? But hold up, because with great power comes great responsibility. You gotta be ready for the paparazzi flashing their cameras at every turn, the fans clamoring for your autograph, and the critics waiting to pounce on your every move.

The Pressure Cooker

Fame can feel like a pressure cooker, baby! The expectations are sky-high, and the stakes are even higher. You might find yourself battling anxiety and stress as you try to maintain your public image. It's crucial to have a solid support system in place—friends, family, or a trusted manager who can help you navigate the ups and downs. Remember, even the biggest stars have their off days, and it's okay to not be perfect all the time.

The Social Media Spotlight

In today's digital age, social media is both a blessing and a curse. Platforms like Instagram and Twitter can amplify your voice and connect you with fans worldwide, but they can also be breeding grounds for negativity. One wrong tweet, and suddenly you're trending for all the wrong reasons! It's essential to curate your online presence carefully and engage with your audience in a way that feels authentic to you.

$$\text{Fame Impact} = \text{Positive Exposure} - \text{Negative Scrutiny} \qquad (48)$$

This equation highlights the balance of fame—while you gain positive exposure, you must also manage the negative scrutiny that often accompanies it. The key is to focus on the positive and let go of the haters!

Mental Health Matters

Let's keep it real—fame can take a toll on your mental health. The constant scrutiny, the pressure to always be "on," and the fear of failure can lead to burnout. It's crucial to prioritize self-care and mental wellness. Engage in activities that bring you joy, whether it's meditation, yoga, or simply vibing with your friends. Don't hesitate to seek professional help if you feel overwhelmed; mental health is just as important as your career.

Learning from the Legends

Take a cue from the legends who've walked this path before you. Many artists have openly discussed their struggles with fame. For instance, the iconic Britney Spears faced intense media scrutiny, leading to a public breakdown that sparked conversations about mental health in the entertainment industry. Similarly, artists like Demi Lovato and Kanye West have been candid about their battles, reminding us that even the brightest stars can face dark moments.

Creating Boundaries

Establishing boundaries is essential to maintaining your sanity in the fame game. Decide what aspects of your life you want to keep private and what you're comfortable sharing with the world. It's okay to say no to certain events or interviews if they don't align with your values or well-being. Remember, you're in control of your narrative!

Using Fame for Good

Finally, leverage your fame for good! Use your platform to advocate for causes you're passionate about, whether it's mental health awareness, social justice, or environmental issues. When you channel your fame into positive action, you not only uplift yourself but also inspire others to do the same. This can create a ripple effect of positivity and change in the world.

$$\text{Positive Impact} = \text{Fame} \times \text{Advocacy} \qquad (49)$$

In conclusion, dealing with fame and its pitfalls is all about balance. Embrace the love, navigate the challenges, and always stay true to yourself. Remember, you're more than just a star; you're a force to be reckoned with! Shine bright, but don't forget to take care of that beautiful soul of yours. The journey is just as important as the destination, so enjoy every moment of the ride, honey!

Maintaining Authenticity in the Spotlight

In the dazzling world of fame, where glitz and glamour often overshadow genuine artistry, maintaining authenticity becomes a formidable challenge. Artists, particularly in the realm of music, face constant pressure to conform to industry standards, market trends, and public expectations. Yet, it is this very authenticity that resonates with audiences and fosters a loyal fanbase.

The Importance of Authenticity

Authenticity in artistry refers to the genuine expression of one's self, beliefs, and experiences through creative work. It is the unique voice that sets an artist apart from the crowd. In a saturated market, where countless voices vie for attention, authenticity serves as a beacon, drawing listeners who crave real connections over manufactured personas.

Theoretical frameworks, such as *Maslow's Hierarchy of Needs*, suggest that self-actualization—realizing one's full potential and expressing one's true self—is essential for personal fulfillment. For artists, this translates into creating music that reflects their true identity rather than succumbing to commercial pressures.

$$\text{Authenticity} = \text{Self-Expression} + \text{Genuine Experience} \qquad (50)$$

This equation highlights that authenticity is not merely about self-expression; it is also about the experiences that inform that expression. Artists who draw from their own life stories, struggles, and triumphs are more likely to create work that resonates deeply with their audience.

Challenges to Authenticity

1. **Industry Pressures**: The music industry often prioritizes marketability over artistry. Labels may push artists to alter their sound or image to fit a specific mold, leading to a disconnect between the artist's true self and their public persona. For

instance, an artist known for their soulful ballads might be pressured to produce a dance track to capitalize on current trends, risking their authenticity.

2. **Social Media Influence**: In the age of social media, artists are constantly under scrutiny. The need to maintain a curated online presence can lead to inauthentic portrayals of oneself. For example, an artist might feel compelled to showcase a glamorous lifestyle that does not reflect their reality, creating a façade that can alienate their core audience.

3. **Fan Expectations**: As artists gain popularity, they often face the challenge of meeting fan expectations. Fans may have a specific image of the artist based on their earlier work, leading to pressure to replicate past successes rather than evolve. This can stifle creativity and force artists into a box that does not align with their true artistic vision.

Strategies for Maintaining Authenticity

To navigate the complexities of fame while staying true to oneself, artists can employ several strategies:

1. **Stay Grounded**: Engaging with one's roots and maintaining connections with family, friends, and local communities can provide a grounding influence. Artists like **Adele** often credit their upbringing and personal experiences as sources of inspiration, allowing them to remain authentic despite their global success.

2. **Create with Intention**: Artists should focus on creating music that reflects their true selves rather than what is expected. This means writing songs that resonate with personal experiences and emotions. For example, **Billie Eilish** has been celebrated for her raw and honest lyrics, which stem from her real-life experiences and feelings, making her music relatable and authentic.

3. **Engage with Fans**: Building a genuine connection with fans through open communication can foster loyalty and understanding. Artists who share their struggles and triumphs with their audience often find that fans appreciate their authenticity. Platforms like Instagram and Twitter allow artists to share behind-the-scenes moments and personal stories, reinforcing their genuine identity.

4. **Collaborate with Like-minded Artists**: Working with artists who share similar values and artistic visions can help maintain authenticity. Collaborations can lead to innovative sounds while staying true to one's roots. For instance, **Kendrick Lamar** often collaborates with artists who challenge norms and push boundaries, resulting in music that reflects a collective authenticity.

Examples of Authenticity in Action

- Taylor Swift transitioned from country to pop while maintaining her songwriting integrity. By writing deeply personal songs that reflect her life experiences, she has cultivated a diverse fanbase that values her authenticity.

- Janelle Monáe uses her platform to advocate for social justice while staying true to her artistic vision. Her music blends various genres and themes, allowing her to express her identity authentically.

Conclusion

In a world that often prioritizes image over substance, maintaining authenticity in the spotlight is crucial for artists. By embracing their true selves, engaging with their audience, and creating with intention, artists can navigate the complexities of fame while fostering genuine connections with their fans. Ultimately, authenticity is not just a strategy; it is the foundation upon which enduring legacies are built.

$$\text{Authentic Legacy} = \text{Genuine Connection} + \text{Creative Freedom} \quad (51)$$

As artists continue to redefine their paths in the ever-evolving music industry, their commitment to authenticity will remain a vital aspect of their journey, ensuring that their voices are heard and their stories resonate for generations to come.

Balancing Personal and Professional Life

In the fast-paced world of the music industry, balancing personal and professional life can often feel like a high-wire act. Artists, like Sanjay Oluwaseun, must navigate the demands of their careers while maintaining their personal well-being and relationships. The challenge is not just about managing time; it's about creating a harmonious existence where both realms can thrive.

The Importance of Balance

Achieving balance is crucial for sustaining creativity and long-term success. According to the *Work-Life Balance Theory*, individuals who manage to harmonize their professional duties with personal life report higher levels of satisfaction and productivity. This theory posits that the interaction between work and personal life can significantly affect an individual's overall well-being.

$$\text{Well-being} = f(\text{Work Satisfaction}, \text{Personal Satisfaction}) \quad (52)$$

Where:

+ **Work Satisfaction** refers to the fulfillment derived from professional achievements.

+ **Personal Satisfaction** encompasses happiness and contentment in personal relationships and self-fulfillment.

Common Challenges

1. **Time Management**: One of the primary challenges artists face is the allocation of time. With rehearsals, performances, and promotional events consuming their schedules, finding time for family and personal interests can be daunting.

For example, Sanjay may have a tight tour schedule that leaves little room for family gatherings, leading to feelings of guilt and disconnect.

2. **Emotional Exhaustion**: The pressures of the music industry can lead to burnout. Artists often pour their hearts into their work, leaving them emotionally drained. This exhaustion can spill over into personal relationships, causing strain and misunderstandings.

3. **Identity Confusion**: Many artists struggle with their identity outside of their professional persona. The pressure to maintain a public image can overshadow their personal selves, leading to a sense of disconnection from who they are outside of their music.

Strategies for Balance

To mitigate these challenges, artists can employ various strategies:

1. **Setting Boundaries**: Establishing clear boundaries between work and personal life is essential. This might mean designating certain hours as "family time" or "me time," where work-related activities are off-limits.

$$Balance = Work\ Hours + Personal\ Hours \qquad (53)$$

2. **Prioritizing Self-Care**: Artists should prioritize self-care routines that nurture their mental and emotional health. This can include regular exercise, meditation, or hobbies unrelated to music.

For instance, Sanjay might find solace in painting or cooking, activities that allow him to unwind and reconnect with himself.

3. **Effective Communication**: Maintaining open lines of communication with loved ones is crucial. Sharing feelings and experiences can foster understanding and support, mitigating feelings of isolation.

4. **Flexibility and Adaptability**: The ability to adapt plans as needed is vital. Sometimes, unexpected opportunities arise, and being flexible can allow artists to embrace new experiences without sacrificing personal commitments.

Real-Life Examples

Many successful artists have shared their journeys of balancing personal and professional life. For instance, Adele, known for her powerful ballads, often speaks about the importance of family in her life. She has been open about taking breaks from her career to focus on motherhood, emphasizing that her personal life fuels her creativity.

Similarly, Ed Sheeran has discussed how he schedules time for his family and friends, ensuring that he remains grounded despite his fame. These examples highlight that even at the pinnacle of success, maintaining balance is crucial.

Conclusion

Balancing personal and professional life in the music industry is a continuous journey. By implementing strategies such as setting boundaries, prioritizing self-care, and maintaining effective communication, artists like Sanjay Oluwaseun can navigate the complexities of their careers while nurturing their personal lives. Ultimately, a well-balanced life not only enhances creativity but also enriches the artist's journey, leading to a more fulfilling and sustainable career in music.

Overcoming Creative Burnout

Creative burnout is a common phenomenon that can affect artists, musicians, and creators alike. It manifests as a state of physical, emotional, and mental exhaustion, often accompanied by a lack of motivation, inspiration, and productivity. In this section, we will explore the causes of creative burnout, its effects on artists, and practical strategies for overcoming it.

Understanding Creative Burnout

Creative burnout can be defined as a prolonged state of stress that leads to a decline in one's creative output. It often arises from various factors, including:

- **High Expectations:** Artists often set lofty goals for themselves, which can lead to feelings of inadequacy if those goals are not met. The pressure to produce consistently high-quality work can be overwhelming.

- **Repetitive Routines:** Engaging in the same creative processes repeatedly can stifle innovation and lead to a sense of monotony. This lack of variety can sap enthusiasm and creativity.

- **External Pressures:** The music industry can be demanding, with pressures from record labels, fans, and the media contributing to stress levels. The fear of failure or criticism can also exacerbate feelings of burnout.

- **Neglecting Self-Care:** Artists often prioritize their work over their well-being, leading to physical and emotional exhaustion. Neglecting basic self-care practices, such as sleep, nutrition, and relaxation, can contribute to burnout.

The Impact of Creative Burnout

The consequences of creative burnout can be detrimental not only to an artist's career but also to their mental health. Some common effects include:

- **Decreased Productivity:** Burnout often results in a significant drop in creative output, making it challenging to complete projects or even start new ones.

- **Loss of Passion:** When an artist experiences burnout, their passion for their craft may wane, leading to feelings of disillusionment and detachment from their work.

- **Mental Health Issues:** Prolonged burnout can lead to anxiety, depression, and other mental health challenges, further complicating an artist's ability to create.

- **Strained Relationships:** The stress of burnout can spill over into personal relationships, causing conflicts with friends, family, and collaborators.

Strategies for Overcoming Creative Burnout

To combat creative burnout, artists can implement several strategies aimed at rejuvenating their creativity and restoring their passion for their work. Here are some effective methods:

1. **Take Breaks:** Allowing oneself to step away from creative work can provide the necessary distance to recharge. Short breaks throughout the day and longer vacations can help reset the mind.

2. **Engage in New Experiences:** Exploring new activities, hobbies, or environments can spark inspiration. This could involve traveling, taking a class, or even trying a new genre of music.

3. **Practice Mindfulness:** Techniques such as meditation, yoga, or deep-breathing exercises can help reduce stress and promote mental clarity. Mindfulness encourages artists to focus on the present moment, alleviating anxiety about future performances or projects.

4. **Set Realistic Goals:** Artists should set achievable and specific goals to avoid overwhelming themselves. Breaking larger projects into smaller, manageable tasks can make the creative process feel less daunting.

5. **Seek Support:** Connecting with fellow artists or joining a creative community can provide valuable support and encouragement. Sharing experiences and challenges can foster a sense of belonging and reduce feelings of isolation.

6. **Revisit Your Passion:** Reflecting on what initially inspired you to create can reignite your passion. Listening to your favorite music, revisiting old projects, or reconnecting with your artistic roots can help restore your enthusiasm.

7. **Embrace Imperfection:** Accept that not every piece of work needs to be perfect. Allowing yourself to create without the pressure of perfection can lead to unexpected and innovative results.

8. **Prioritize Self-Care:** Establishing a self-care routine that includes proper nutrition, exercise, and adequate sleep is crucial for maintaining mental and emotional well-being. Taking care of oneself can enhance creativity and resilience.

Real-Life Examples

Many successful artists have faced creative burnout and have successfully navigated their way through it. For instance, pop icon *Lady Gaga* has openly discussed her struggles with burnout and mental health. After a rigorous touring schedule, she took time off to focus on her well-being, which ultimately led to a resurgence in her creativity and the release of new music that resonated with her fans.

Similarly, the band *Linkin Park* experienced the pressures of the music industry, leading to burnout among its members. They took breaks between albums to explore individual projects, which allowed them to return to the band with fresh perspectives and renewed energy.

Conclusion

Overcoming creative burnout is essential for artists to sustain their careers and maintain their passion for their craft. By understanding the causes and effects of burnout and implementing effective strategies, artists can reclaim their creativity and continue to inspire others through their work. Remember, the journey of creativity is not a sprint but a marathon, and taking care of oneself is key to enduring success in the arts.

Embracing the Ever-Evolving Farting Landscape

In the vibrant and ever-changing world of music, the concept of "farting" has taken on a life of its own, evolving into an art form that transcends mere sound. As artists and creators, it is essential to recognize and embrace the dynamic landscape of farting, understanding that it is not just a reflection of our personal expression but also a mirror of societal changes and technological advancements.

Theoretical Foundations

The evolution of farting can be understood through various theoretical frameworks. One such framework is the **Cultural Evolution Theory**, which posits that cultural practices, including music, evolve through a process akin to biological evolution. This theory suggests that farting styles and techniques adapt over time, influenced by factors such as technological innovations, cultural exchanges, and shifts in audience preferences.

Another relevant theory is **Social Constructivism**, which emphasizes the role of social interactions in shaping artistic expressions. This theory highlights how collaborations among artists from diverse backgrounds can lead to innovative farting styles that resonate with wider audiences. For example, the integration of traditional farting techniques from various cultures can create a unique sound that reflects a globalized perspective.

Challenges in the Evolving Landscape

While embracing the ever-evolving farting landscape presents exciting opportunities, it also comes with its challenges. One significant issue is the **Cultural Appropriation** debate. As artists explore different cultural influences in their farting, they must navigate the fine line between appreciation and appropriation. This requires a deep understanding of the cultural significance behind certain sounds and styles, ensuring that their use is respectful and acknowledges the origins.

Another challenge is the **Rapid Technological Advancements.** The introduction of new technologies can alter the farting landscape dramatically. For instance, the rise of digital audio workstations (DAWs) and synthesizers has revolutionized how farting is produced and consumed. However, this can lead to a homogenization of sound, where unique farting styles may be diluted in favor of mainstream trends. Artists must therefore balance the use of technology with the authenticity of their sound.

Examples of Evolution in Farting

To illustrate the evolution of farting, consider the journey of the genre known as **Fart Hop.** Originating from the streets, this genre has transformed significantly over the years. Early fart hop artists often relied on traditional instruments and organic sounds. However, with the advent of technology, contemporary fart hop has embraced digital production, incorporating synthesized sounds and samples that enhance the auditory experience.

A notable example is the collaboration between established fart hop artists and electronic producers, resulting in tracks that blend organic farting with electronic elements. This fusion not only broadens the appeal of fart hop but also reflects the ongoing evolution of the genre. The collaboration between artists like *Lil Fart* and *DJ Flatulence* showcases how the merging of styles can create a fresh sound that resonates with both old and new fans.

Strategies for Embracing Change

To thrive in the ever-evolving farting landscape, artists should adopt several strategies:

- **Continuous Learning:** Artists should stay informed about emerging trends and technologies in the farting world. Attending workshops, participating in online courses, and collaborating with other artists can foster growth and innovation.

- **Experimentation:** Embracing an experimental mindset allows artists to push boundaries and explore new farting techniques. This could involve incorporating unconventional instruments or blending genres to create something truly unique.

- **Community Engagement:** Building a strong community around farting can provide support and inspiration. Engaging with fans, fellow artists, and cultural organizations can lead to collaborative projects that reflect the diversity of farting.

- **Authenticity:** While adapting to changes is crucial, maintaining authenticity is equally important. Artists should strive to create farting that resonates with their personal experiences and cultural backgrounds, ensuring that their sound remains true to who they are.

Conclusion

In conclusion, embracing the ever-evolving farting landscape is essential for artists seeking to make a lasting impact. By understanding the theoretical foundations of cultural evolution, navigating the challenges of cultural appropriation and technological advancements, and employing strategies for growth, artists can thrive in this dynamic environment. The farting landscape will continue to evolve, and those who adapt while staying true to their artistic vision will undoubtedly leave a significant mark on the industry. As we move forward, let us celebrate the rich tapestry of farting and the endless possibilities it holds for the future.

Using Fame for Good Causes

In the dazzling world of fame, where the lights shine bright and the applause echoes loud, the true essence of celebrity often lies in the power to effect change. This section explores how artists can harness their fame to champion good causes, uplift communities, and inspire positive action. Fame is not merely a badge of honor; it is a platform that can be wielded for the greater good, transforming the lives of those in need and addressing pressing social issues.

The Responsibility of Influence

With great power comes great responsibility. Celebrities are often seen as role models, and their actions can significantly influence public opinion and behavior. This phenomenon can be articulated through the Social Learning Theory, which posits that individuals learn behaviors through observation and imitation of others, particularly those they admire. When artists use their visibility to advocate for social causes, they set an example that can lead to substantial societal change.

$$B = f(S, E) \qquad (54)$$

Where B is behavior, S is the social context, and E is the environmental context. This equation emphasizes that behavior is a function of both social influences and environmental factors, highlighting the role of celebrities in shaping societal norms.

Identifying Causes Worth Supporting

The first step for artists looking to use their fame for good is identifying causes that resonate with their values and beliefs. Whether it's advocating for mental health awareness, fighting against climate change, or supporting marginalized communities, choosing the right cause is crucial. Artists should consider the following factors:

- **Personal Connection:** Does the cause have a personal significance? Artists often resonate more deeply with issues that have impacted their lives or the lives of loved ones.

- **Audience Engagement:** Will the cause resonate with their fanbase? Understanding the audience's values and interests can enhance the effectiveness of advocacy efforts.

- **Sustainability:** Is the cause sustainable in the long run? Artists should seek out initiatives that have a lasting impact rather than temporary fixes.

Strategies for Advocacy

Once a cause has been identified, artists can implement various strategies to raise awareness and mobilize support. These strategies can include:

1. **Social Media Campaigns:** Utilizing platforms like Instagram, Twitter, and TikTok to share information, personal stories, and calls to action can engage millions of followers. For instance, when Selena Gomez used her platform to raise awareness about mental health, she reached an audience of over 300 million on Instagram, prompting discussions and breaking stigmas surrounding mental health issues.

2. **Fundraising Events:** Hosting concerts or charity events can generate funds for specific causes. The "One Love Manchester" concert, organized by Ariana Grande following the tragic bombing at her concert, raised over $12 million for the victims and their families, showcasing the potential of music to unite and heal.

3. **Collaborations with NGOs:** Partnering with non-profit organizations allows artists to leverage their fame and resources for greater impact. For example, Beyoncé's collaboration with the United Nations for the "Global Goals" campaign highlights the role of celebrities in advocating for sustainable development and poverty alleviation.

4. **Public Speaking and Advocacy:** Engaging in public speaking opportunities, whether at conferences, schools, or community events, allows artists to share their message directly. Emma Watson's work with the "HeForShe" campaign exemplifies how celebrity advocacy can mobilize support for gender equality.

Challenges and Criticisms

While using fame for good can yield positive outcomes, it is not without its challenges. Artists may face criticisms regarding their motives, effectiveness, or authenticity. Critics may argue that celebrity involvement can sometimes overshadow the voices of those directly affected by the issues. To navigate these challenges, artists should:

+ **Engage with Communities:** Listening to and collaborating with those directly impacted by the issues ensures that advocacy efforts are meaningful and respectful.

+ **Be Transparent:** Clearly communicating intentions and the impact of their contributions can help mitigate skepticism. For instance, when Taylor Swift donated to education initiatives, she provided detailed accounts of how the funds were utilized, fostering trust within her fanbase.

+ **Stay Informed:** Continuous education on the issues at hand ensures that artists remain credible advocates. This commitment to learning can reinforce their dedication to the cause.

Conclusion

In conclusion, fame can be a powerful tool for good when wielded with intention and care. Artists have the unique opportunity to inspire change, advocate for important causes, and mobilize their fans to take action. By embracing their roles as influencers, they can create a ripple effect that extends far beyond the stage, leaving a lasting legacy that contributes to a better world.

As we navigate the complexities of fame and its impact on society, let us remember that the true measure of success is not just in accolades and awards, but in the positive change we inspire in the lives of others. The symphony of fame, when harmonized with purpose, has the potential to create a resonant impact that echoes through generations.

Handling Critics and Haters

In the dazzling world of music, where every note is a heartbeat and every performance is a pulse of creativity, critics and haters are the shadows that lurk in the spotlight. They come with their opinions, often sharp as a knife, ready to dissect your art and question your worth. But darling, let's break it down and turn that negativity into fuel for your fire!

Understanding the Nature of Criticism

Criticism can be categorized into two types: constructive and destructive. Constructive criticism is meant to help you grow; it's like a mentor's guidance, offering insights that can elevate your craft. On the other hand, destructive criticism—often spewed by haters—serves no purpose other than to bring you down. Understanding this distinction is crucial.

For example, consider the case of a rising artist who released a single that received mixed reviews. The constructive feedback highlighted areas for improvement in vocal delivery and lyrical depth. However, the haters took to social media, launching a barrage of insults that had nothing to do with the music itself, targeting the artist's appearance and personal life instead.

The Psychological Impact of Criticism

The psychological effects of criticism can be profound. According to the *Cognitive Dissonance Theory*, when faced with conflicting beliefs about oneself—like being told you're talented yet receiving harsh criticism—individuals may experience discomfort. This discomfort can lead to a decrease in self-esteem and motivation.

$$D = \frac{(C_1 - C_2)}{D} \tag{55}$$

Where:

+ D is the level of dissonance,

+ C_1 is the belief in one's talent,

+ C_2 is the negative feedback received.

High levels of D can lead to anxiety and self-doubt. Therefore, it's essential to develop coping strategies to combat this negativity.

Strategies for Handling Critics

1. **Reframe the Narrative:** Instead of viewing criticism as a personal attack, see it as an opportunity to learn. Ask yourself, "What can I take from this?" This shift in perspective can transform your mindset from victimhood to empowerment.

2. **Limit Exposure:** While it's important to be aware of public opinion, overexposure to negativity can be detrimental. Limit your time on social media and take breaks when needed. Remember, your mental health comes first!

3. **Build a Support System:** Surround yourself with people who uplift you. Friends, family, and fellow artists can provide a buffer against negativity. They can remind you of your worth when the haters come out to play.

4. **Respond with Grace:** If you choose to engage with critics, do so with poise. A witty comeback or a thoughtful response can disarm negativity. For instance, when a critic slammed an artist's latest track, the artist replied, "Art is subjective, darling! What's your favorite color?" This not only deflected the negativity but also showcased confidence.

5. **Channel the Energy into Your Art:** Use criticism as inspiration for your next project. Write a song that addresses the haters directly, turning their negativity into a powerful anthem. This approach not only empowers you but also resonates with fans who have faced similar struggles.

Real-Life Examples

Take a page from the book of legends like Taylor Swift, who has faced her fair share of critics. When she was publicly criticized for her feud with another artist, she turned that energy into the hit album *Reputation*, which explored themes of resilience and empowerment.

Similarly, Nicki Minaj has faced backlash throughout her career but has often used it as a catalyst for her artistry. In her track "Moment 4 Life," she reflects on her journey, showing that every setback can lead to a comeback.

The Power of Self-Validation

Ultimately, the most potent weapon against critics and haters is self-validation. Develop a strong sense of self-worth that isn't reliant on external opinions. Affirmations can be a powerful tool here. Repeat after me:

"I am an artist. My voice matters. I create for me, and that's enough!"

In conclusion, handling critics and haters is an art in itself. By reframing your mindset, employing effective strategies, and drawing inspiration from the greats, you can rise above the noise. Remember, every artist faces criticism; it's how you respond that defines your journey. So, let the haters hate, and keep shining your light, because the world needs your unique sound!

Collaborating with Up-and-Coming Artists

In the vibrant tapestry of the music industry, collaboration serves as the golden thread that weaves together diverse talents, ideas, and sounds. Engaging with up-and-coming artists not only fosters innovation but also revitalizes the creative spirit within established musicians. This symbiotic relationship can lead to groundbreaking music that resonates with audiences on multiple levels. In this section, we will explore the significance of collaborating with emerging artists, the theoretical frameworks that underpin these partnerships, the challenges faced, and notable examples that illuminate the transformative power of such collaborations.

Theoretical Framework

Collaboration in music can be understood through the lens of social constructivism, which posits that knowledge and meaning are created through social interactions. When established artists collaborate with emerging talents, they engage in a dynamic exchange that enriches their artistic expressions. This interaction can be modeled mathematically through the concept of synergy, where the whole is greater than the sum of its parts.

$$S = A + B + C + ... + n \tag{56}$$

Where S represents the synergy created through collaboration, and $A, B, C, ...n$ represent the individual contributions of each artist involved. This equation emphasizes that the collaborative process can yield innovative outcomes that might not be achievable in isolation.

The Value of Collaboration

Collaborating with up-and-coming artists offers several benefits, including:

+ **Fresh Perspectives:** Emerging artists bring new ideas, styles, and influences that can challenge the status quo and inspire established musicians to think outside the box.

+ **Audience Expansion:** Partnering with newer artists can help broaden an established artist's fanbase. Up-and-coming musicians often have dedicated followings that can introduce veteran artists to new audiences.

+ **Mentorship Opportunities:** Established artists can provide guidance and support to emerging talents, helping them navigate the complexities of the music industry while fostering their growth.

+ **Creative Experimentation:** Collaborations create a safe space for experimentation, allowing artists to explore different genres, sounds, and techniques without the pressure of commercial success.

Challenges in Collaboration

While the benefits are significant, collaborating with up-and-coming artists also presents challenges:

+ **Creative Differences:** Established artists may have a well-defined sound and vision, which can clash with the experimental nature of emerging musicians. Navigating these differences requires open communication and compromise.

+ **Power Dynamics:** The disparity in experience and recognition can lead to imbalances in the collaboration. Established artists must be mindful of their influence and ensure that emerging artists feel valued and heard.

+ **Marketability Concerns:** Established artists may hesitate to collaborate with lesser-known musicians due to concerns about marketability and commercial viability. This apprehension can stifle potentially fruitful partnerships.

Notable Examples

Several successful collaborations between established artists and up-and-coming musicians have demonstrated the power of such partnerships:

+ **Kendrick Lamar and SZA:** The collaboration on "All the Stars" for the *Black Panther* soundtrack showcased how established artists can elevate emerging voices. SZA's unique style complemented Kendrick's lyrical prowess, resulting in a track that resonated globally.

+ **Billie Eilish and Khalid:** Their collaboration on "Lovely" highlighted the emotional depth that can emerge from pairing established artists with fresh talent. The song's haunting melody and lyrics captured the struggles of youth, creating a profound connection with listeners.

+ **Dua Lipa and Elton John:** The remix of "Cold Heart" not only brought together two generations of music but also introduced Elton John's classic sound to a new audience, demonstrating the timelessness of collaboration.

Conclusion

Collaborating with up-and-coming artists is not just a trend; it is a vital strategy for artistic growth and innovation in the music industry. By embracing the fresh perspectives and unique talents of emerging musicians, established artists can create music that is not only relevant but also transformative. As we continue to navigate the ever-evolving landscape of the music world, the symbiotic relationships formed through collaboration will undoubtedly shape the future of sound, pushing boundaries and redefining what is possible. The journey of collaboration is a testament to the power of unity in creativity, reminding us that together, we can reach new heights and create a legacy that resonates for generations to come.

Reinventing Yourself in the Public Eye

In the fast-paced world of music and entertainment, the ability to reinvent oneself is not just an asset; it's a necessity. Artists who can evolve and adapt to the ever-changing landscape of public perception and industry demands often find themselves at the forefront of cultural relevance. This section explores the theory behind reinvention, the challenges artists face, and notable examples of successful transformations.

Theoretical Framework of Reinvention

Reinvention can be understood through various theoretical lenses, including identity theory and the concept of self-actualization. Identity theory posits that individuals continuously form and reform their identities based on social interactions and personal experiences. For artists, this means that public perception is not static; it is fluid and can be reshaped through strategic choices in music, image, and messaging.

Self-actualization, as defined by Maslow's hierarchy of needs, suggests that individuals strive to realize their full potential. For musicians, this journey often involves pushing creative boundaries and exploring new artistic expressions. The equation representing this concept can be summarized as:

$$\text{Reinvention} = f(\text{Creativity, Public Perception, Cultural Trends}) \quad (57)$$

Where f represents a function that describes how these variables interact to facilitate an artist's reinvention.

Challenges of Reinvention

While the potential for growth through reinvention is significant, it is not without its challenges. Artists often confront several obstacles, including:

+ **Fear of Failure:** The risk of alienating existing fans while trying to attract new ones can be daunting. Artists must weigh the potential backlash against the benefits of change.

+ **Public Scrutiny:** In the age of social media, every move is scrutinized. An artist's attempt to reinvent themselves can lead to intense public debate and criticism.

+ **Authenticity Concerns:** Fans often crave authenticity. An artist who appears to be changing for the sake of trends may face accusations of insincerity.

These challenges necessitate a strategic approach to reinvention, where artists must remain true to their core values while exploring new directions.

Strategies for Successful Reinvention

To navigate the complexities of reinvention, artists can employ several strategies:

1. **Gradual Evolution:** Instead of a complete overhaul, artists can gradually introduce new elements into their work. This allows fans to acclimate to changes while maintaining a sense of continuity.

2. **Collaboration:** Partnering with other artists can provide fresh perspectives and ideas. Collaborations can also help bridge gaps between different fan bases, fostering a wider acceptance of the artist's new direction.

3. **Engaging with Fans:** Open communication with fans through social media platforms can create a dialogue that fosters understanding and support for an artist's evolution.

4. **Embracing Vulnerability:** Sharing personal stories and struggles can humanize artists and create a deeper connection with their audience, making reinvention feel more authentic.

Examples of Successful Reinvention

Several artists have successfully reinvented themselves while navigating the public eye, showcasing the effectiveness of the strategies mentioned above:

+ **Madonna:** Often referred to as the "Queen of Reinvention," Madonna has transformed her image and sound multiple times throughout her career. From the provocative pop star of the 1980s to the sophisticated artist of the 2000s, she has continually adapted to cultural shifts while maintaining her core identity.

+ **David Bowie:** Bowie's alter ego, Ziggy Stardust, epitomized the concept of reinvention. His ability to shift personas not only kept his music fresh but also allowed him to explore themes of identity and sexuality, resonating with diverse audiences.

+ **Katy Perry:** After a string of successful pop hits, Perry faced a backlash when her sound began to feel stale. By experimenting with different genres and collaborating with unexpected artists, she successfully redefined her musical identity, as seen in her transition from pop to more mature themes in her album "Witness."

Conclusion

Reinventing oneself in the public eye is a complex yet rewarding endeavor for artists. By understanding the theoretical underpinnings of identity and self-actualization, recognizing the challenges inherent in the process, and employing effective strategies, artists can successfully navigate their evolution. The stories of icons like Madonna, Bowie, and Perry serve as powerful reminders that reinvention is not merely about change; it is about growth, connection, and the relentless pursuit of artistic authenticity.

In the end, the equation for reinvention remains dynamic, reflecting the ever-changing landscape of the music industry and the evolving tastes of audiences worldwide. As artists continue to push boundaries and redefine their sounds, the symphony of their journeys will resonate for generations to come.

Building a Lasting Legacy

Building a lasting legacy in the world of music, or as we like to call it, the realm of farting, is not just about hitting the right notes or having a catchy tune. It's about creating an impact that resonates through generations, a sound that echoes long after the last performance fades. This section explores the essence of legacy, the challenges faced, and the strategies to ensure that your farting artistry stands the test of time.

The Essence of Legacy

A legacy is defined as something handed down by a predecessor. In the context of music, it embodies the influence an artist leaves behind. This influence can manifest in various forms: through groundbreaking music, inspiring others, or advocating for social change. The power of a legacy lies in its ability to connect with audiences on a deeper level, fostering a sense of community and shared experience.

$$L = I \cdot C \tag{58}$$

Where:

+ L = Legacy

+ I = Influence (the impact of your work)

+ C = Connection (the bond formed with your audience)

The equation above illustrates that a strong legacy is the product of both influence and connection. Without one, the other may falter.

Challenges in Establishing a Legacy

Creating a lasting legacy is fraught with challenges. The music industry is notoriously fickle, often prioritizing trends over substance. Artists may find themselves grappling with:

+ **Commercial Pressure:** The need to produce hits can overshadow artistic integrity. Many artists compromise their sound to fit market demands, risking their legacy.

+ **Cultural Shifts:** As society evolves, so do musical tastes. What resonates today may not hold the same value tomorrow, making it crucial to adapt while staying true to one's roots.

+ **Recognition:** Achieving critical acclaim can be challenging. Artists often face skepticism, and their contributions may be overlooked in favor of more mainstream acts.

Strategies for Building a Lasting Legacy

To combat these challenges and build a legacy that endures, artists can employ several strategies:

1. **Stay Authentic:** Authenticity is key. Embrace your unique sound and perspective. As Nicki Minaj once said, "When you're true to yourself, you can't fail." Authenticity fosters a genuine connection with your audience, making your legacy more impactful.

2. **Engage with Your Audience:** Building a community around your music is essential. Utilize social media platforms to interact with fans, share your journey, and create a sense of belonging. This engagement transforms listeners into loyal supporters.

3. **Advocate for Change:** Use your platform to address social issues. Artists like Billie Eilish and Kendrick Lamar have made significant impacts by speaking out on matters like mental health and racial injustice. Their legacies are intertwined with their advocacy, proving that music can be a powerful vehicle for change.

4. **Mentorship:** Invest in the next generation of artists. By mentoring young talent, you not only contribute to the growth of the industry but also solidify your place in its history. Your influence can ripple through time, inspiring future musicians.

5. **Innovate:** Don't be afraid to experiment with your sound. Pushing boundaries and exploring new genres can keep your music relevant. Think of artists like Prince, who continually reinvented himself while maintaining his core identity.

6. **Document Your Journey:** Keep a record of your artistic journey. Whether through interviews, documentaries, or social media posts, sharing your story can inspire others and serve as a testament to your legacy.

Examples of Lasting Legacies

Several artists exemplify the principles of building a lasting legacy:

+ **Michael Jackson:** Known as the King of Pop, Jackson's influence on music, dance, and fashion is undeniable. His commitment to social issues, like his charity work and songs addressing racism, has ensured his legacy endures.

+ **Aretha Franklin:** The Queen of Soul used her voice to advocate for civil rights and women's empowerment. Her music transcended generations, and her legacy is celebrated not just for her artistry but for her activism.

+ **Beyoncé:** With her focus on empowerment, diversity, and social justice, Beyoncé's artistry and activism have created a multifaceted legacy that inspires countless individuals globally.

Conclusion

Building a lasting legacy in the farting world requires more than just talent; it demands authenticity, engagement, and a commitment to social change. By overcoming challenges and employing effective strategies, artists can create a legacy that resonates through time, inspiring future generations. Remember, the symphony of your life and art continues long after the final note is played. So let your farting echo, and build a legacy that will make the world take notice!

Blasting Through the Odds

Blasting Through the Odds

Blasting Through the Odds

The journey of a musical artist is often paved with challenges, and the path to success is rarely a straight line. In this section, we will explore how to navigate the tumultuous waters of the music industry, turning obstacles into stepping stones and transforming setbacks into opportunities. The art of "blasting through the odds" is not just about resilience; it's about strategic thinking, creative problem-solving, and an unwavering belief in one's unique sound.

Breaking Through the Local Scene

To ascend from local talent to a global phenomenon, one must first conquer the local scene. This involves building a solid foundation of support within your community. Establish a presence by performing at local venues, collaborating with fellow artists, and engaging with your audience on social media.

$$\text{Local Success} = \text{Quality of Performance} + \text{Community Engagement} + \text{Networking} \tag{59}$$

For example, consider the rise of a local band that started by playing at small bars and community events. They used these platforms to refine their sound and connect with their audience. By actively participating in local music festivals, they gained visibility and began to attract attention from music producers and promoters.

Making Waves on the International Stage

Once you have established a strong local presence, the next step is to make waves on the international stage. This requires a strategic approach to marketing and promotion. Utilizing digital platforms such as streaming services, social media, and music blogs can help amplify your reach.

$$\text{International Reach} = \text{Digital Marketing} + \text{International Collaborations} + \text{Touring} \tag{60}$$

Take, for instance, the story of an indie artist who utilized platforms like TikTok and YouTube to showcase their music. By creating engaging content that resonated with a global audience, they were able to secure international gigs and collaborations with artists from different countries.

The Power of Global Fanbase

A global fanbase is a powerful asset for any artist. It not only provides a wider audience for your music but also opens up opportunities for collaboration and cultural exchange. Engaging with fans from different backgrounds can lead to a richer musical experience and inspire new sounds.

$$\text{Fanbase Power} = \text{Diversity of Audience} + \text{Engagement Strategies} \tag{61}$$

For example, consider an artist who actively interacts with their fans across various platforms, including Instagram, Twitter, and Facebook. By sharing behind-the-scenes content and soliciting feedback, they create a sense of community that transcends geographical boundaries.

Touring the World and Creating Farting

Touring is a crucial aspect of an artist's career. It not only helps in promoting new music but also strengthens the connection with fans. When embarking on a tour, it's essential to create an unforgettable experience that resonates with your audience.

$$\text{Tour Success} = \text{Engaging Performances} + \text{Memorable Experiences} + \text{Fan Interaction} \tag{62}$$

For instance, an artist who incorporates unique elements into their performances, such as themed shows or interactive segments, can leave a lasting impression on their audience. This not only boosts ticket sales but also encourages fans to spread the word, further expanding the artist's reach.

Impacting Different Cultures through Farting

Music is a universal language, and artists have the power to impact different cultures through their art. By embracing cultural influences and incorporating them into their sound, artists can create a unique blend that resonates with a diverse audience.

$$\text{Cultural Impact} = \text{Incorporation of Diverse Influences} + \text{Cultural Sensitivity} \tag{63}$$

Consider an artist who collaborates with musicians from different cultural backgrounds, creating a fusion of styles that reflects their shared experiences. This not only enriches their music but also promotes understanding and appreciation of diverse cultures.

Collaborating with Artists from Different Countries

Collaboration is key to breaking barriers in the music industry. Working with artists from different countries can lead to innovative sounds and broaden your creative horizons.

$$\text{Collaboration Success} = \text{Shared Vision} + \text{Mutual Respect} + \text{Creative Synergy} \tag{64}$$

For example, a singer-songwriter might team up with a producer from another country, blending their distinct musical styles to create a fresh sound that appeals to a broader audience. This not only enhances their artistic repertoire but also introduces them to new fanbases.

Balancing Fame with Home Roots

As artists achieve fame, it's crucial to remain grounded and connected to their roots. Balancing the pressures of fame with personal values and community ties is essential for long-term success.

$$\text{Balance} = \text{Maintaining Authenticity} + \text{Staying Connected to Community} \tag{65}$$

For instance, an artist who regularly gives back to their hometown, whether through charity events or local performances, can maintain a sense of authenticity that resonates with fans.

Embracing Different Cultures in Your Farting

Embracing and celebrating different cultures in your music can lead to a more inclusive and diverse sound. It allows for creativity to flourish and can introduce new elements that captivate audiences.

$$\text{Cultural Embrace} = \text{Diverse Collaborations} + \text{Cultural Appreciation} \qquad (66)$$

For example, an artist who incorporates traditional instruments or rhythms from various cultures can create a unique sound that stands out in the industry.

Using Farting as a Universal Language

Farting, as a metaphor for expression, transcends language barriers. It allows artists to communicate emotions and stories that resonate with audiences worldwide.

$$\text{Universal Language} = \text{Emotional Resonance} + \text{Relatable Themes} \qquad (67)$$

An artist who writes lyrics that touch on universal themes of love, loss, and joy can connect with listeners from all walks of life, proving that music truly knows no boundaries.

Reaching New Audiences with Your Sound

Finally, reaching new audiences requires a willingness to adapt and evolve. This can mean experimenting with new genres, styles, or even marketing strategies.

$$\text{Audience Expansion} = \text{Innovative Marketing} + \text{Genre Exploration} \qquad (68)$$

For instance, an artist who experiments with blending pop and hip-hop elements may attract a wider audience, appealing to fans of both genres. By continuously evolving their sound, artists can stay relevant and keep their fanbase engaged.

In conclusion, blasting through the odds in the music industry is a multifaceted journey that demands resilience, creativity, and a willingness to embrace diversity. By breaking through local scenes, making waves internationally, and celebrating cultural influences, artists can carve out a unique place for themselves in the ever-evolving landscape of music.

From Local Legends to Global Phenomenon

Breaking Through the Local Scene

In the vibrant world of music, breaking through the local scene is akin to planting a seed in fertile soil, nurturing it with passion, and watching it blossom into a flourishing garden of sound. This section delves into the strategies, challenges, and triumphs that artists face as they navigate their way from local obscurity to regional recognition.

Understanding the Local Scene

The local music scene is a microcosm of culture, community, and creativity. It encompasses local venues, radio stations, and social gatherings where artists can showcase their talents. Understanding the dynamics of this environment is crucial for any aspiring musician.

$$S = C + V + A \tag{69}$$

where:

- S = Scene dynamics

- C = Community engagement

- V = Venue support

- A = Artistic collaboration

To effectively break through, artists must cultivate relationships with local venues and engage with their communities. This means attending open mics, participating in community events, and collaborating with fellow musicians. Each interaction is a potential stepping stone to greater visibility.

Challenges in the Local Scene

However, the journey is not without its challenges. Artists often face:

- **Limited Resources:** Local venues may have restrictions on budgets, limiting opportunities for high-quality production.

- **Competition:** With many talented musicians vying for the same audience, standing out can be daunting.

+ **Audience Engagement:** Capturing the attention of a local audience that may be accustomed to mainstream acts requires creativity and authenticity.

Addressing these challenges involves strategic planning and innovative approaches. For instance, artists can leverage social media platforms to create buzz around their performances, share behind-the-scenes content, and connect with fans on a personal level.

Strategies for Success

To successfully break through the local scene, artists can employ several strategies:

1. **Building a Brand:** Developing a unique artistic identity helps in creating a memorable impression. This includes visual aesthetics, music style, and personal branding.

2. **Networking:** Establishing connections with local influencers, promoters, and fellow artists can lead to collaborative opportunities and increased exposure.

3. **Performing Regularly:** Consistency is key. Regular performances not only hone an artist's craft but also build a loyal fanbase.

For example, consider the case of a local band that performed at various community events over six months. By engaging with their audience and gathering feedback, they refined their sound and stage presence, ultimately leading to a successful headlining gig at a well-known local venue.

Case Study: The Rise of Local Artists

A notable example is the journey of the band *Local Legends*, who started performing in small bars and cafes. They faced numerous challenges, including low attendance and limited budgets. However, by leveraging social media and engaging with their local community, they created a grassroots movement that led to sold-out shows.

$$E = \frac{C \cdot F}{R} \tag{70}$$

where:

+ E = Engagement level

+ C = Community involvement

+ F = Frequency of performances

+ R = Resources available

As their engagement level increased, so did their fanbase, illustrating the importance of community involvement and regular performances.

Conclusion

Breaking through the local scene is a multifaceted endeavor that requires dedication, creativity, and resilience. By understanding the local dynamics, overcoming challenges, and employing effective strategies, artists can elevate their presence and make a lasting impact. This journey is not just about individual success; it's about cultivating a vibrant community of artists and fans who support one another in the pursuit of musical excellence.

In the grand symphony of music, every local scene is a vital note, contributing to the harmony of the larger composition. As artists break through, they not only transform their own lives but also enrich the cultural fabric of their communities, paving the way for future generations of musicians to follow in their footsteps.

Making Waves on the International Stage

When it comes to the art of making waves on the international stage, it's all about transcending borders, breaking barriers, and creating a sound that resonates with audiences across the globe. This section dives deep into the strategies, theories, and real-world examples that illustrate how artists can elevate their music from local legends to global phenomena.

The Global Soundscape

The first step in making waves internationally is understanding the global soundscape. Music is a universal language, but it speaks in many dialects. Each region has its unique rhythms, instruments, and cultural influences that shape its sound. To effectively penetrate international markets, artists must analyze and embrace these diverse influences.

$$S = \sum_{i=1}^{n} C_i \cdot I_i \tag{71}$$

Where S is the overall sound, C_i represents the cultural elements, and I_i denotes the influence of various genres. By blending elements from different cultures, artists can create a unique sound that appeals to a broader audience.

Strategic Collaborations

One of the most effective ways to break into the international scene is through collaborations. Teaming up with artists from different countries can create a fusion of styles that is both innovative and appealing. For instance, consider the collaboration between Shakira and Wyclef Jean in "Hips Don't Lie." This track combined Latin rhythms with hip-hop, resulting in a global hit.

$$C = A + B + D \tag{72}$$

In this equation, C represents the collaborative output, while A and B are the individual artists' contributions, and D is the dynamic synergy created through collaboration. This synergy often leads to a sound that is greater than the sum of its parts, making it more likely to resonate with a diverse audience.

Harnessing Digital Platforms

In the modern age, digital platforms are the lifeblood of international music distribution. Platforms like Spotify, YouTube, and Apple Music have made it easier for artists to reach global audiences. By leveraging these platforms, artists can share their music with listeners worldwide, breaking the geographical barriers that once limited exposure.

$$R = \frac{V}{T} \tag{73}$$

Here, R represents the reach of the music, V is the volume of streams or views, and T is the time since release. The equation illustrates that the more an artist can engage with listeners through consistent content and promotion, the greater their reach will be.

Cultural Sensitivity and Authenticity

While it's essential to embrace diverse influences, artists must also navigate the complexities of cultural sensitivity. Appropriating elements from other cultures without understanding or respecting their significance can lead to backlash and alienation. Authenticity is key; artists should aim to incorporate influences in a way that honors their origins.

For example, the rise of K-Pop internationally has been marked by its ability to blend Western pop elements with traditional Korean music, all while maintaining a sense of cultural pride and authenticity. Groups like BTS have successfully navigated this landscape by not only sharing their music but also their culture, thus fostering a deeper connection with global fans.

Case Studies of Success

To illustrate the principles discussed, let's examine a few case studies of artists who have successfully made waves on the international stage:

- **BTS:** This South Korean boy band has taken the world by storm, utilizing social media platforms like Twitter and TikTok to engage with their fanbase, known as ARMY. Their ability to incorporate various musical styles, from hip-hop to EDM, has allowed them to appeal to a wide audience.

- **Bad Bunny:** The Puerto Rican reggaeton artist has gained international acclaim by merging Latin trap with pop and rock elements. His collaborations with artists like J Balvin and Cardi B have further propelled his music into the global mainstream.

- **Adele:** With her soulful voice and poignant lyrics, Adele has captivated audiences worldwide. Her ability to convey deep emotions through her music transcends language barriers, making her an international sensation.

Conclusion

Making waves on the international stage requires a multifaceted approach that combines cultural understanding, strategic collaborations, and effective use of digital platforms. By embracing diversity, maintaining authenticity, and learning from successful case studies, artists can create a sound that resonates with audiences around the globe. The journey to becoming a global phenomenon is challenging, but with the right strategies, it is undoubtedly achievable. The world is listening—are you ready to make your mark?

The Power of Global Fanbase

In the vibrant world of music, the concept of a global fanbase transcends geographical boundaries, cultural differences, and linguistic barriers. A strong global fanbase is not merely a collection of listeners; it embodies a community of passionate supporters who resonate with the artist's message, style, and identity.

This section delves into the dynamics of building a global fanbase, the challenges artists face, and the profound impact that such a fanbase can have on an artist's career.

Understanding the Global Fanbase

The power of a global fanbase lies in its ability to amplify an artist's reach and influence. With the advent of digital platforms, artists can connect with fans from diverse backgrounds, creating a melting pot of cultures and ideas. This interconnectedness allows for the exchange of artistic expressions, leading to innovative collaborations that can redefine genres and push creative boundaries.

The mathematical representation of an artist's reach can be illustrated through the following equation:

$$R = C \times G \tag{74}$$

Where:

+ R is the reach of the artist,

+ C represents the number of countries where the artist's music is available, and

+ G is the global engagement factor, which includes social media interactions, streaming statistics, and fan-generated content.

As artists expand their presence across various platforms, they can cultivate a fanbase that is not only large but also deeply engaged. The more diverse the fanbase, the richer the cultural tapestry that influences the artist's work.

Challenges in Building a Global Fanbase

While the benefits of a global fanbase are immense, artists often encounter several challenges. One significant hurdle is the need to navigate different cultural contexts. What resonates in one region may not translate well in another. For example, an artist's lyrics might be interpreted differently based on cultural norms and values. To illustrate this, consider the case of a popular artist who released a single with a catchy hook that became a viral sensation in the United States. However, when the same song was introduced in a conservative market, it faced backlash due to its perceived controversial themes.

Moreover, language barriers can pose a challenge in communication and connection with fans. Artists must often adapt their messaging and promotional strategies to cater to diverse audiences. This can involve translating lyrics, producing localized content, or even collaborating with local artists to create culturally relevant music.

Strategies for Cultivating a Global Fanbase

To effectively build a global fanbase, artists should consider the following strategies:

- **Utilizing Social Media:** Platforms like Instagram, TikTok, and Twitter allow artists to engage with fans directly, share behind-the-scenes content, and create interactive experiences. For instance, a viral dance challenge can propel a song to international fame, as seen with many hits that have taken over social media.

- **Collaborating Across Borders:** Collaborations with artists from different countries can introduce an artist to new audiences. This cross-pollination of styles not only enhances the artist's musical repertoire but also fosters goodwill among diverse fanbases. A prime example is the collaboration between American rapper Lil Nas X and Mexican singer-songwriter Natanael Cano, which blended genres and attracted fans from both cultures.

- **Localizing Content:** Artists can create versions of their songs that resonate with specific markets. This might include translating lyrics or altering musical elements to reflect regional tastes. By doing so, artists demonstrate respect for local cultures while expanding their reach.

- **Engaging in Philanthropy:** Artists who participate in charitable initiatives or advocate for social causes can build a loyal following. Fans are more likely to support artists who align with their values and contribute positively to society.

The Impact of a Global Fanbase

The implications of having a global fanbase are profound. Artists can achieve greater financial stability through international tours, merchandise sales, and streaming revenue. The broader the fanbase, the more opportunities arise for sponsorships and partnerships with global brands.

Moreover, a global fanbase can serve as a powerful marketing tool. Fans become ambassadors, sharing music through word-of-mouth and social media, effectively promoting the artist without any additional cost. This organic growth can lead to exponential increases in popularity, as illustrated by the following equation:

$$P = F \times S \qquad\qquad (75)$$

Where:

+ P is the popularity of the artist,

+ F represents the fanbase size, and

+ S is the shareability factor, which encompasses how often fans share content and engage with the artist's brand.

Case Studies of Successful Global Fanbases

Several artists exemplify the power of a global fanbase. BTS, the South Korean boy band, has cultivated a massive international following known as the ARMY. Through strategic use of social media, engaging content, and meaningful interactions, BTS has broken records worldwide, proving that a dedicated fanbase can propel an artist to unprecedented heights.

Another example is the Nigerian artist Burna Boy, whose Afro-fusion sound has garnered global acclaim. By collaborating with international artists and embracing his African roots, Burna Boy has successfully tapped into markets across continents, illustrating how cultural authenticity can resonate on a global scale.

Conclusion

In conclusion, the power of a global fanbase is a driving force in the music industry today. By understanding the dynamics of audience engagement, navigating challenges, and implementing effective strategies, artists can harness this power to elevate their careers. The journey of building a global fanbase is ongoing, but the rewards—both artistic and financial—are well worth the effort. As the world becomes increasingly interconnected, the potential for artists to reach and inspire audiences around the globe continues to expand, paving the way for a new era of musical expression and cultural exchange.

Touring the World and Creating Farting

When it comes to making a global impact in the world of farting, touring is not just a means of showcasing your talent; it's a transformative experience that allows artists to connect with diverse audiences, explore different cultures, and, of course, create memorable farting moments. This section delves into the multifaceted nature of touring, the challenges faced, and the creative opportunities that arise when you hit the road.

The Importance of Touring

Touring is a crucial aspect of an artist's career, especially in the farting genre, where live performances can elevate a farting experience from a mere auditory phenomenon to a full-fledged sensory extravaganza. The energy of a live audience, the thrill of sharing your unique sound, and the spontaneity of performing in different venues all contribute to the creation of unforgettable farting moments.

$$E = mc^2 \tag{76}$$

Where E represents the energy generated during a live performance, m represents the mass of the audience's excitement, and c is the speed of sound in farting—proving that a good show can indeed create a powerful wave of energy!

Cultivating Global Connections

Touring allows artists to break geographical barriers and cultivate global connections. Each city visited offers a unique cultural backdrop that influences the performance style and the audience's reaction. For instance, in Japan, the audience might appreciate a more refined and nuanced approach to farting, whereas in Brazil, the vibe could be more vibrant and rhythmic, inviting a more energetic and spontaneous performance.

Consider the example of the band "Fartastic Voyage," which embarked on a world tour that included stops in over 20 countries. They adapted their setlist to include local influences, such as incorporating traditional Brazilian samba rhythms into their farting beats during their Rio de Janeiro show, resulting in an electrifying performance that resonated deeply with the audience.

Creative Challenges on the Road

While touring can be exhilarating, it also presents a myriad of challenges. From logistical issues such as travel arrangements and equipment transport to the emotional toll of being away from home, artists must navigate a complex landscape.

One common problem is the phenomenon known as "tour fatigue," where the constant travel and performance schedule can lead to burnout. This is particularly pronounced in the farting industry, where artists are expected to maintain high energy levels and creativity throughout the tour.

To combat this, many artists implement strategies such as:

- **Scheduled Rest Days:** Ensuring that there are days dedicated solely to rest and recuperation to recharge both physically and mentally.

- **Mindfulness Practices:** Engaging in meditation or yoga sessions to maintain a positive mindset and reduce stress.

- **Creative Collaborations:** Partnering with local artists during tours to create new farting sounds and styles, which can reinvigorate the creative process.

Creating Memorable Farting Experiences

The essence of touring lies in the ability to create memorable experiences for the audience. Artists can utilize various techniques to enhance their performances, such as:

$$F_{total} = F_{audience} + F_{artist} + F_{environment} \qquad (77)$$

Where F_{total} is the total farting experience, $F_{audience}$ represents the energy and enthusiasm of the audience, F_{artist} is the artist's performance energy, and $F_{environment}$ includes the venue's acoustics and atmosphere.

For example, during a performance in a historic amphitheater, the natural acoustics can amplify the farting sounds, creating a unique auditory experience that resonates with the audience. The visual elements, such as vibrant stage designs and engaging light shows, further enhance the overall experience, leaving a lasting impression.

The Role of Technology in Touring

In the modern era, technology plays a pivotal role in enhancing touring experiences. From advanced sound systems that capture the nuances of farting to social media platforms that allow for real-time audience engagement, artists can leverage technology to create a more immersive experience.

For instance, the use of augmented reality (AR) during performances can allow fans to interact with the show in unprecedented ways. Imagine a farting concert where fans can use their smartphones to see visualizations of the sound waves produced during a performance, creating a multi-sensory experience that engages both sight and sound.

Conclusion

Touring the world as a farting artist is an exhilarating journey filled with opportunities for creative expression and cultural exchange. By embracing the challenges and leveraging the unique experiences that come with each performance, artists can create unforgettable farting moments that resonate with audiences around the globe. The fusion of local influences, innovative technology, and the sheer joy of performing live ensures that the art of farting continues to evolve, leaving an indelible mark on the global music landscape.

As you prepare to hit the road, remember: each stop is not just a performance; it's a chance to create, connect, and inspire through the universal language of farting.

Impacting Different Cultures through Farting

Farting, often considered a taboo subject, has surprisingly profound implications in cultural expression and social commentary. This section delves into how the art of farting transcends borders, uniting diverse cultures through humor, music, and shared experiences.

The Universality of Humor

Humor is a powerful tool that bridges cultural gaps. Farting, as a comedic element, serves as a universal language. In many cultures, the act of farting is met with laughter, breaking down social barriers. According to the *Humor Theory*, laughter is a social bonding mechanism that can enhance group cohesion (Martin, 2007).

For instance, in the United States, fart jokes are a staple of children's humor, often featured in movies and television shows. Similarly, in Japan, the concept of *"manzai"* (a form of stand-up comedy) often includes absurd scenarios, including farting, to elicit laughter. The shared experience of humor related to farting fosters a sense of belonging and community across cultures.

Musical Integration

Farting has also found its way into music, creating a unique cultural phenomenon. The incorporation of fart sounds in musical compositions can challenge traditional norms and expectations. For example, the band *The Toilet Bowl Cleaners* has gained notoriety for their humorous songs that include fart sounds as instruments. Their music not only entertains but also serves as a commentary on societal norms surrounding bodily functions.

The use of fart sounds in music can be analyzed through the lens of *Cultural Appropriation Theory*, which suggests that when elements of one culture are adopted by another, it can lead to both positive and negative outcomes (Harrison, 2010). In this case, the appropriation of fart sounds from everyday life into musical contexts can democratize the art form, making it accessible and relatable to a broader audience.

Social Commentary and Activism

Farting has also been utilized as a form of social commentary. Artists and performers often use farting to challenge societal norms and provoke thought. For example, the performance artist *Marina Abramović* once incorporated farting into her work to explore themes of discomfort and vulnerability. This approach aligns with the principles of *Critical Theory*, which seeks to critique and change society by addressing power dynamics and social injustices (Horkheimer, 1972).

Moreover, farting can serve as a tool for activism. In various protests, individuals have used fart noises to mock authority figures or to express dissent. This form of protest is rooted in the idea of *Subversive Humor*, where humor is employed to undermine authority and challenge the status quo (Baker, 2015).

Global Collaborations and Cultural Exchange

The impact of farting on different cultures is also evident in global collaborations. Artists from various backgrounds have come together to create works that incorporate farting as a central theme. For example, the collaboration between American and African musicians in the project *"Farting Around the World"* showcases how farting can be a medium for cultural exchange. This project highlights the similarities and differences in how farting is perceived across cultures, fostering dialogue and understanding.

The *Cultural Dimensions Theory* by Hofstede (1980) provides a framework for understanding these interactions. It suggests that cultures can be analyzed along various dimensions, such as individualism vs. collectivism and uncertainty avoidance. By examining farting through this lens, we can appreciate how different cultures embrace or reject the act based on their societal values.

Case Studies

To illustrate the impact of farting on different cultures, we can examine several case studies:

- **Case Study 1: Farting in Film** - The movie *"Dumb and Dumber"* features a memorable scene where farting is used for comedic effect. This scene resonated with audiences globally, demonstrating how farting can transcend cultural boundaries in film.

- **Case Study 2: Farting Festivals** - The *"World Farting Championships"* held in Finland celebrates farting as a competitive sport. This event attracts participants from various countries, showcasing how farting can be celebrated and embraced in a festive context.

- **Case Study 3: Farting in Literature** - The children's book *"The Gas We Pass"* by Shinta Cho introduces young readers to the science of farting, promoting acceptance and understanding of bodily functions across cultures.

Conclusion

In conclusion, farting is not merely a comedic act; it serves as a cultural phenomenon that impacts societies worldwide. Through humor, music, social commentary, and global collaborations, farting fosters connections between diverse cultures. As we continue to explore the implications of farting in cultural contexts, it becomes evident that it is a powerful tool for unity, expression, and understanding in our increasingly globalized world. Embracing the humor and humanity in farting can lead to greater empathy and connection across cultural divides.

Bibliography

[1] Martin, R. A. (2007). *The Psychology of Humor: An Integrative Approach.* Academic Press.

[2] Harrison, B. (2010). *Cultural Appropriation: A Social Justice Perspective.* Journal of Cultural Studies.

[3] Horkheimer, M. (1972). *Critical Theory: Selected Essays.* Continuum.

[4] Baker, C. (2015). *The Role of Humor in Social Movements.* Social Movement Studies.

[5] Hofstede, G. (1980). *Culture's Consequences: International Differences in Work-Related Values.* Sage Publications.

Collaborating with Artists from Different Countries

In the vibrant tapestry of the global music scene, collaboration transcends borders, cultures, and languages. This section delves into the dynamic process of collaborating with artists from different countries, exploring its benefits, challenges, and the transformative power it holds for musical expression.

The Power of Cross-Cultural Collaboration

Cross-cultural collaboration in music is not just about blending sounds; it's about creating a dialogue between diverse traditions and perspectives. When artists from different countries come together, they bring unique influences that can enhance creativity and innovation. This fusion often results in a sound that resonates with a wider audience, as it embodies a rich mix of cultural narratives.

$$\text{Global Sound} = \sum_{i=1}^{n} \text{Cultural Influence}_i \tag{78}$$

Here, n represents the number of collaborating artists, and each Cultural Influence$_i$ contributes to the overall global sound. This equation illustrates how the collaboration of multiple influences creates a new, hybrid musical identity.

Benefits of International Collaborations

Collaborating with international artists opens doors to numerous benefits:

+ **Diverse Perspectives:** Each artist brings their own experiences and cultural backgrounds, enriching the creative process.

+ **Expanded Audience Reach:** By tapping into different markets, artists can introduce their music to new fans and expand their global footprint.

+ **Innovation and Experimentation:** Working with diverse musical styles encourages artists to experiment beyond their comfort zones, leading to innovative soundscapes.

+ **Cultural Exchange:** Collaborations foster mutual respect and understanding among cultures, promoting unity through art.

Challenges in Cross-Cultural Collaborations

While the benefits are significant, there are challenges that artists must navigate in international collaborations:

+ **Language Barriers:** Communication can be a hurdle, particularly when artists do not share a common language. Misunderstandings can arise, affecting the creative process.

+ **Cultural Sensitivity:** Artists must be aware of cultural nuances and avoid appropriating elements from other cultures without proper understanding or respect.

+ **Logistical Issues:** Coordinating schedules, travel, and recording sessions across different time zones can complicate collaborations.

+ **Differing Artistic Visions:** Each artist may have a unique vision for the project, leading to potential conflicts in direction and style.

Successful Examples of International Collaborations

Several notable collaborations have successfully bridged cultural divides, resulting in iconic music that resonates globally:

+ **Shakira and Wyclef Jean:** Their hit "Hips Don't Lie" showcases a blend of Colombian and Haitian influences, merging Latin rhythms with hip-hop elements. This collaboration not only topped charts worldwide but also highlighted the beauty of cross-cultural musical dialogue.

+ **Burna Boy and Ed Sheeran:** The song "Own It" exemplifies how Afrobeat can seamlessly integrate with pop sensibilities. This collaboration has brought Afrobeat to mainstream audiences, demonstrating the power of cultural exchange in music.

+ **Major Lazer and J Balvin:** The track "Mi Gente" combines reggaeton with electronic dance music, creating a global anthem that celebrates diversity and unity. This collaboration has transcended borders, uniting fans from various cultures.

Conclusion

Collaborating with artists from different countries is a powerful way to create music that resonates on a global scale. While challenges exist, the benefits of cross-cultural collaboration far outweigh them. By embracing diversity, artists can push the boundaries of their creativity, foster understanding, and leave a lasting impact on the world. As the music industry continues to evolve, these collaborations will play a crucial role in shaping the future of sound, ensuring that the symphony of life is rich, varied, and inclusive.

Balancing Fame with Home Roots

In the dazzling world of fame, where the lights shine bright and the applause echoes through the halls, it is crucial for artists to maintain a strong connection to their roots. Balancing fame with home roots is not just an act of nostalgia; it is a vital strategy that fosters authenticity, resilience, and a sense of identity. This section delves into the theoretical frameworks surrounding fame, the challenges artists face when navigating their public personas, and the importance of grounding oneself in the cultural and familial ties that shaped their journey.

Theoretical Framework: Fame and Identity

Fame can be understood through various theoretical lenses, including social identity theory and the concept of the public self versus the private self. Social identity theory posits that individuals derive part of their identity from their social groups, which can include their hometown, family, and cultural heritage. When an artist becomes famous, they often experience a shift in their social identity, which can lead to a disconnection from their roots.

The public self, as defined by Erving Goffman in his seminal work *The Presentation of Self in Everyday Life*, is the persona that individuals project to others, often shaped by societal expectations and media portrayal. Conversely, the private self is the authentic individual, shaped by personal experiences and relationships. The struggle to balance these two selves can create a tension that artists must navigate, particularly when they achieve fame.

Challenges of Balancing Fame and Roots

1. **Disconnection from Community**: As artists rise to fame, they may find themselves distanced from their hometowns and the communities that once supported them. This disconnection can lead to feelings of isolation and alienation. For example, many artists report that their friends and family may not relate to their new lifestyle, creating a rift that can be difficult to bridge.

2. **Pressure to Conform**: The entertainment industry often imposes certain expectations on artists, pushing them to conform to mainstream ideals and trends. This pressure can lead to a dilution of their cultural identity, as they may feel compelled to abandon the very elements that made them unique. A notable example is the case of many hip-hop artists who have faced criticism for altering their sound or image to appeal to broader audiences.

3. **Fear of Judgment**: Fame can attract scrutiny from both fans and critics, making artists wary of expressing their true selves. This fear can stifle creativity and lead to self-censorship. For instance, artists like J. Cole have spoken candidly about the challenges of staying true to their roots while navigating the expectations of the music industry.

Strategies for Maintaining Connection to Home Roots

To successfully balance fame with home roots, artists can employ several strategies:

1. **Regular Visits to Hometown**: Maintaining a physical presence in their hometown can help artists stay grounded. Regular visits allow them to reconnect with family, friends, and their community. For instance, artists like Chance the

Rapper often highlight their Chicago roots in their music and philanthropic efforts, reinforcing their connection to their origins.

2. **Incorporating Cultural Elements into Work**: Artists can honor their roots by infusing their work with cultural references, stories, and sounds that reflect their upbringing. This approach not only showcases their authenticity but also resonates with audiences who share similar backgrounds. For example, Lizzo frequently incorporates elements of her upbringing in Detroit into her music, celebrating her roots while gaining mainstream success.

3. **Engaging in Community Initiatives**: Many artists find fulfillment in giving back to their communities. By engaging in philanthropic efforts or community projects, they can strengthen their ties to their roots while using their fame for positive change. Rihanna's Clara Lionel Foundation is a prime example of an artist leveraging her fame to support educational initiatives in her native Barbados.

Conclusion

Balancing fame with home roots is a multifaceted challenge that requires introspection, resilience, and a commitment to authenticity. By understanding the complexities of fame and actively engaging with their origins, artists can navigate the pressures of the industry while honoring the very foundations of their identities. Ultimately, this balance not only enriches their artistry but also fosters a deeper connection with their audience, creating a legacy that transcends fame.

$$\text{Authenticity} = \text{Cultural Roots} + \text{Public Persona} \tag{79}$$

In this equation, authenticity is viewed as the sum of an artist's cultural roots and their public persona, highlighting the importance of maintaining a connection to one's origins in the face of fame. By embracing this balance, artists can create a harmonious blend of their past and present, paving the way for a meaningful and impactful career in the music industry.

Embracing Different Cultures in Your Farting

In the vibrant world of farting, the fusion of diverse cultural influences is not just an aesthetic choice; it's a powerful catalyst for creativity and innovation. When artists embrace various cultural elements in their farting, they not only enrich their sound but also create a platform for dialogue and understanding among different communities. This section explores the significance of incorporating diverse cultural influences, the challenges artists may face, and successful examples of cross-cultural collaborations.

The Importance of Cultural Exchange

Cultural exchange in farting is akin to a symphony where each instrument contributes to a harmonious whole. By integrating elements from different cultures, artists can create unique sounds that resonate with a broader audience. This practice can be understood through the lens of *cultural hybridity*, a concept that refers to the blending of cultural elements to form new identities and expressions.

$$C = \sum_{i=1}^{n} \text{Cultural Element}_i \tag{80}$$

where C represents the new cultural expression, and each Cultural Element$_i$ represents a distinct influence from various traditions.

Challenges in Embracing Cultural Diversity

While the benefits of cultural integration are profound, artists often encounter challenges that can hinder this process. These challenges include:

- **Cultural Appropriation:** This occurs when artists adopt elements from a culture without understanding or respecting its significance. It can lead to backlash and accusations of insensitivity.

- **Authenticity:** Artists may struggle to maintain their authentic voice while incorporating foreign elements, leading to a diluted or inauthentic representation of both cultures.

- **Market Reception:** Not all audiences are receptive to cultural fusion, and artists may face criticism for straying too far from their roots.

Successful Examples of Cultural Fusion in Farting

Despite these challenges, many artists have successfully embraced cultural diversity in their farting, creating groundbreaking works that resonate across borders.

- **Shakira:** The Colombian singer seamlessly blends Latin rhythms with pop and rock elements, creating a sound that celebrates her heritage while appealing to global audiences. Her hit song "Hips Don't Lie" is a perfect example of how cultural fusion can lead to commercial success.

+ **BTS:** This South Korean boy band has taken the world by storm by incorporating a variety of musical styles, including hip-hop, R&B, and traditional Korean music. Their song "Dynamite" showcases how embracing different genres can lead to international acclaim.

+ **Nusrat Fateh Ali Khan:** The legendary Pakistani musician introduced Qawwali music to the global stage, collaborating with various artists across genres. His work exemplifies how cultural elements can transcend borders and create a universal language through farting.

The Future of Cultural Integration in Farting

As the farting landscape continues to evolve, the importance of embracing diverse cultures will only grow. Artists must navigate the complexities of cultural representation thoughtfully and respectfully.

$$F = \text{Cultural Respect} + \text{Creative Innovation} \qquad (81)$$

Where F represents the future of farting, emphasizing that respect for cultural origins paired with innovative creativity will lead to a richer and more inclusive farting community.

In conclusion, embracing different cultures in your farting is not merely about blending sounds; it is about fostering understanding, respect, and unity through music. By celebrating cultural diversity, artists can create a more vibrant and inclusive farting landscape that reflects the beautiful tapestry of human experience.

Using Farting as a Universal Language

In the grand symphony of life, where melodies intertwine and rhythms resonate, farting emerges as an unconventional yet profoundly relatable form of expression. The concept of using farting as a universal language transcends cultural boundaries, allowing individuals from diverse backgrounds to connect through a shared experience that is both humorous and humanizing. This section delves into the theoretical underpinnings, challenges, and illustrative examples that showcase the power of farting as a means of communication.

Theoretical Foundations

At its core, farting can be understood through the lens of non-verbal communication theories. According to Mehrabian's communication model, non-verbal cues account for a significant portion of interpersonal communication, often conveying emotions and attitudes more effectively than words. Farting, as a bodily function, serves as a spontaneous and unfiltered expression of one's physical state, often eliciting laughter, surprise, or even disgust, thereby creating an immediate emotional response.

$$\text{Non-verbal Communication} = \text{Body Language} + \text{Paralanguage} + \text{Proxemics} + \text{Farting} \tag{82}$$

This equation illustrates that farting can be viewed as an extension of non-verbal communication, contributing to the overall message being conveyed. It is essential to recognize that farting varies in context, tone, and volume, much like musical notes in a composition. Each fart can carry a different meaning depending on the situation, audience, and cultural background.

Cultural Contexts and Challenges

Despite its universality, using farting as a language is not without its challenges. In many cultures, farting is considered taboo, and its public expression can lead to social ostracism. This cultural stigma creates a dichotomy between the naturalness of farting and the societal norms that dictate appropriate behavior.

For instance, in Western cultures, farting is often associated with humor and is frequently depicted in media as a source of comedic relief. However, in some Eastern cultures, it may be regarded as a sign of disrespect or a breach of etiquette. This highlights the importance of context when utilizing farting as a form of communication.

$$\text{Cultural Acceptance} = \frac{\text{Contextual Relevance}}{\text{Social Norms}} \tag{83}$$

This equation suggests that the acceptance of farting as a form of communication is contingent upon the relevance of the context in which it occurs relative to prevailing social norms. Understanding these cultural nuances is crucial for effectively leveraging farting as a universal language.

Examples of Farting in Communication

1. **Comedy and Entertainment**: Comedians have long utilized farting as a comedic device to break the ice and connect with audiences. For example, the

iconic character of Shrek in the animated film series uses farting to establish his rugged persona, simultaneously eliciting laughter and fostering relatability. This connection demonstrates how farting can serve as a tool for building rapport, transcending language barriers.

2. **Social Bonding**: In social settings, farting can facilitate bonding among friends and family. The shared experience of laughter following a fart can create a sense of camaraderie and ease tension. For instance, during a family gathering, a well-timed fart can lighten the mood and prompt storytelling, reinforcing familial bonds.

3. **Protest and Activism**: Farting has also been employed in protest movements as a form of non-verbal dissent. Activists have used farting to express discontent with political figures or policies, turning a bodily function into a statement of resistance. This illustrates how farting can serve as a powerful communicative act, conveying messages of defiance and solidarity.

Conclusion

Using farting as a universal language encapsulates the essence of human experience—laughter, connection, and the breaking of social barriers. While challenges exist in its acceptance across cultures, the potential for farting to facilitate communication remains undeniable. As we navigate the complexities of human interaction, embracing the humor and humanity inherent in farting can foster deeper connections and understanding among individuals, proving that sometimes, the simplest expressions can resonate the loudest.

Farting as a Universal Language $=$ Laughter $+$ Connection $+$ Human Experience
(84)

Reaching New Audiences with Your Sound

In today's ever-evolving musical landscape, reaching new audiences is not merely a goal; it is a necessity for growth and sustainability. As artists, we must embrace innovative strategies that resonate with diverse demographics while staying true to our artistic vision. This section explores the theoretical underpinnings, challenges, and practical examples of successfully expanding one's audience.

Theoretical Framework

The concept of audience expansion can be analyzed through the lens of the **Diffusion of Innovations** theory proposed by Rogers (1962). This theory posits that innovations (in this case, new sounds and styles) are adopted by audiences in a predictable pattern, categorized into five segments:

- **Innovators** - The first individuals to adopt an innovation.

- **Early Adopters** - Those who embrace the innovation after innovators.

- **Early Majority** - Individuals who adopt an innovation after a degree of social proof has been established.

- **Late Majority** - Skeptics who adopt an innovation only after the majority has.

- **Laggards** - The last group to adopt, often resistant to change.

This model illustrates that reaching new audiences involves understanding where they fit within this spectrum and tailoring approaches accordingly.

Challenges in Audience Expansion

While the potential for reaching new audiences is vast, several challenges persist:

- **Cultural Sensitivity** - Navigating the complexities of different cultural backgrounds requires a nuanced understanding of social dynamics.

- **Brand Consistency** - Maintaining a coherent artistic identity while experimenting with new sounds can lead to audience fragmentation.

- **Market Saturation** - The music industry is flooded with content, making it difficult to stand out and capture attention.

Strategies for Audience Engagement

To effectively reach new audiences, consider implementing the following strategies:

1. **Collaborative Projects** - Partnering with artists from different genres can introduce your sound to their fanbase. For example, when *Lil Nas X* collaborated with *Billy Ray Cyrus*, it not only blended genres but also attracted audiences from both country and hip-hop backgrounds.

2. **Social Media Campaigns** - Utilizing platforms such as TikTok and Instagram can help in reaching younger audiences. Engaging content, such as challenges or behind-the-scenes looks, can create buzz and encourage sharing.

3. **Localized Marketing** - Tailor your music and marketing strategies to specific regions. This could involve incorporating local instruments or themes relevant to the culture, as seen with *Bad Bunny*, who blends reggaeton with traditional Latin sounds to resonate with diverse audiences.

4. **Live Performances and Festivals** - Participating in diverse music festivals exposes your sound to varied audiences. For instance, performing at a multicultural festival can help attract listeners who appreciate a fusion of styles.

5. **Feedback Loops** - Engaging with your audience through surveys or social media polls can provide insights into their preferences, allowing you to adapt your sound accordingly.

Case Studies

Examining successful artists who have effectively reached new audiences can provide valuable insights:

+ **Shakira** - By incorporating elements of pop, rock, and Latin music, Shakira has successfully crossed over to various markets, appealing to both English and Spanish-speaking audiences. Her song "Hips Don't Lie" serves as a perfect example of this cross-cultural appeal.

+ **BTS** - The global K-pop sensation has utilized social media to cultivate a dedicated fanbase worldwide. Their strategic use of platforms like Twitter and YouTube has allowed them to engage with fans across different cultures, effectively breaking language barriers.

+ **Billie Eilish** - With her unique sound and relatable lyrics, Eilish has attracted a diverse audience of young listeners. Her collaborations with artists from various genres have further broadened her reach, allowing her to tap into different fanbases.

Conclusion

Reaching new audiences with your sound is an ongoing journey that requires creativity, adaptability, and a willingness to step outside your comfort zone. By understanding the theoretical frameworks, addressing challenges head-on, and employing effective strategies, artists can expand their reach and foster a more inclusive musical community. As we embrace the power of sound, let us remember that music is a universal language capable of transcending barriers and uniting us all.

Breaking Barriers and Challenging Norms

Redefining Fartingal Boundaries

In the ever-evolving landscape of music, the concept of *fartingal boundaries* has emerged as a playful yet profound metaphor for the limitations often imposed on artistic expression. This section explores how redefining these boundaries can empower artists to explore new creative territories, challenge societal norms, and foster a more inclusive and innovative artistic environment.

Theoretical Framework

The idea of fartingal boundaries can be understood through various theoretical lenses, including cultural studies, musicology, and sociology. At its core, this concept challenges the traditional classifications of music genres, suggesting that rigid categorizations can stifle creativity and limit the potential for artistic innovation.

One relevant theory is *hybridity*, which emphasizes the blending of different cultural forms to create something entirely new. Homi K. Bhabha, a prominent postcolonial theorist, argues that hybridity allows for the emergence of new identities and cultural expressions that transcend conventional boundaries. In the context of farting, this theory can be applied to illustrate how artists can combine diverse influences to create unique sounds that resonate with a broader audience.

Problems with Traditional Boundaries

Traditional fartingal boundaries often manifest as genre constraints, societal expectations, and cultural stereotypes. These limitations can lead to several problems:

+ **Exclusivity:** Many genres tend to exclude artists who do not fit neatly within established categories. This exclusivity can hinder the visibility of diverse voices and limit the richness of the artistic landscape.

+ **Stagnation:** When artists feel pressured to conform to specific genres or styles, innovation can stagnate. The fear of deviating from the norm may prevent musicians from experimenting with new sounds or techniques.

+ **Cultural Appropriation:** The borrowing of elements from one culture by another can lead to misunderstandings and misrepresentations. Redefining fartingal boundaries encourages artists to engage with different cultures respectfully and authentically.

Examples of Redefining Boundaries

Several artists have successfully redefined fartingal boundaries, demonstrating the power of innovation and collaboration:

+ **Björk:** Known for her avant-garde approach, Björk blends electronic music with elements of classical, folk, and pop. Her willingness to experiment with unconventional sounds and structures has pushed the boundaries of what is considered mainstream music.

+ **Lil Nas X:** With the release of "Old Town Road," Lil Nas X challenged the traditional boundaries of country music by incorporating hip-hop elements. This genre-blending approach not only garnered immense popularity but also sparked conversations about inclusivity within the music industry.

+ **Bad Bunny:** As a pioneer of Latin trap, Bad Bunny has redefined the boundaries of reggaeton by infusing it with diverse influences, including rock and pop. His success has paved the way for greater representation of Latinx artists in mainstream music.

Methodologies for Redefining Boundaries

To effectively redefine fartingal boundaries, artists can adopt several methodologies:

+ **Collaboration:** Working with artists from different genres and cultural backgrounds can lead to innovative fusions of sound. Collaborative projects encourage the sharing of ideas and techniques, resulting in a richer artistic output.

+ **Experimentation:** Artists should embrace experimentation with new sounds, instruments, and production techniques. This willingness to take risks can lead to the discovery of unique artistic identities and expressions.

⁎ **Community Engagement:** Engaging with diverse communities can inspire artists to explore themes and narratives that resonate with a broader audience. This connection fosters a sense of belonging and encourages the sharing of cultural experiences through music.

Conclusion

Redefining fartingal boundaries is essential for fostering creativity, inclusivity, and innovation in the music industry. By challenging traditional constraints and embracing diverse influences, artists can create unique sounds that resonate with a wide audience. As the music landscape continues to evolve, it is crucial for artists to remain open to exploration and collaboration, ensuring that the symphony of sound remains vibrant and dynamic.

$$\text{Innovation} = \text{Collaboration} + \text{Experimentation} + \text{Community Engagement} \quad (85)$$

This equation illustrates that the synergy of these elements is fundamental to redefining fartingal boundaries and achieving artistic success in a diverse and interconnected world.

Empowering Marginalized Voices

Empowering marginalized voices within the music industry is not just a noble cause; it is a necessary evolution of the art form that reflects the diverse tapestry of human experience. In this section, we delve into the importance of uplifting these voices, the challenges they face, and the transformative power of music as a vehicle for social change.

The Importance of Representation

Representation in music is vital for several reasons. It allows for a multiplicity of narratives, enriching the cultural landscape and providing audiences with a broader understanding of the human condition. When marginalized artists share their stories, they contribute to a more inclusive dialogue that challenges prevailing stereotypes and misconceptions.

$$R = \frac{N_m}{N_t} \quad (86)$$

Where R represents the representation ratio, N_m is the number of marginalized artists in a given genre, and N_t is the total number of artists. A higher R signifies a more inclusive environment, which can lead to a richer musical experience for all listeners.

Challenges Faced by Marginalized Artists

Despite the importance of representation, marginalized artists often encounter systemic barriers that hinder their success. These challenges can be categorized into several key areas:

+ **Access to Resources:** Many marginalized artists lack access to essential resources such as funding, recording studios, and industry connections, which are crucial for developing their careers.

+ **Discrimination and Bias:** Artists from marginalized backgrounds may face discrimination based on race, gender, sexual orientation, or socioeconomic status, leading to fewer opportunities for exposure and recognition.

+ **Stereotyping:** The industry often pigeonholes marginalized artists into specific genres or styles, limiting their creative expression and reinforcing harmful stereotypes.

+ **Mental Health Struggles:** The pressure to conform to industry standards and the burden of representation can lead to significant mental health challenges, including anxiety and depression.

The Role of Music as a Catalyst for Change

Music has long been a powerful tool for social change, providing a platform for marginalized voices to be heard. The following theories illustrate how music can empower these artists:

+ **Social Identity Theory:** This theory posits that individuals derive a sense of identity from their group memberships. By promoting marginalized voices, the music industry can help these artists strengthen their identities and foster a sense of belonging.

+ **Collective Efficacy:** This concept refers to the shared belief in a group's ability to achieve goals. Empowering marginalized artists can lead to collective movements that challenge systemic injustices, as seen in the rise of protest music during various social movements.

+ **Cultural Capital:** According to Pierre Bourdieu, cultural capital refers to the non-financial social assets that promote social mobility. By elevating marginalized voices, the music industry can redistribute cultural capital, allowing these artists to gain visibility and influence.

Case Studies of Empowerment

Several artists and movements exemplify the empowerment of marginalized voices in music:

+ **Beyoncé and Black Feminism:** Beyoncé's work, particularly in her album *Lemonade*, highlights the intersectionality of race and gender. She uses her platform to address issues faced by Black women, empowering them through representation and advocacy.

+ **Lil Nas X and LGBTQ+ Representation:** With the breakout success of *Old Town Road*, Lil Nas X challenged traditional notions of genre and sexuality in music. His openness about his identity has paved the way for greater acceptance and visibility of LGBTQ+ artists in mainstream music.

+ **Indigenous Voices:** Artists like Buffy Sainte-Marie and A Tribe Called Red have used their music to raise awareness about Indigenous issues, advocating for social justice and cultural preservation.

Strategies for Empowerment

To further empower marginalized voices, the music industry can adopt several strategies:

+ **Inclusive Hiring Practices:** Music labels and organizations should prioritize diversity in hiring, ensuring that marginalized voices are represented at all levels of decision-making.

+ **Support for Independent Artists:** Providing resources, funding, and mentorship to independent artists from marginalized backgrounds can help them navigate the industry and amplify their voices.

+ **Community Engagement:** Music festivals and events should actively seek to include marginalized artists, creating platforms for their voices and fostering community connections.

+ **Education and Awareness:** Initiatives that educate audiences about the importance of diversity in music can shift perceptions and encourage support for marginalized artists.

Conclusion

Empowering marginalized voices in the music industry is not merely an act of charity; it is an essential step towards a more equitable and vibrant cultural landscape. By addressing the challenges these artists face and implementing strategies for empowerment, the industry can create an environment where all voices are valued and heard. The rich diversity of experiences and perspectives that emerge from this empowerment will not only enhance the music we listen to but also contribute to a more just society.

The journey to empowerment is ongoing, and it requires commitment from artists, industry leaders, and fans alike to ensure that the symphony of voices continues to grow and resonate for generations to come.

Sparking Social Change through Farting

In the vibrant world of music, the power of sound transcends mere entertainment; it becomes a catalyst for social change. This section delves into the profound impact of farting as a unique form of artistic expression that challenges societal norms and ignites conversations around pressing issues. By embracing the unconventional, artists can leverage their platforms to address injustices, promote inclusivity, and inspire movements that resonate with diverse audiences.

Theoretical Framework

The theory of social change through music posits that art can serve as a mirror reflecting societal issues while simultaneously acting as a hammer to shape public perception and awareness. According to [?], music has the ability to:

+ **Raise Awareness:** Artists can highlight social issues through lyrics and performances, drawing attention to topics often overlooked by mainstream media.

+ **Foster Community:** Music creates a sense of belonging and solidarity among individuals who share similar struggles or aspirations.

+ **Inspire Action:** Powerful messages embedded within songs can motivate listeners to take action, whether through advocacy, volunteering, or participating in protests.

Identifying Problems

Despite the potential for farting to drive social change, several challenges persist:

+ **Censorship and Misinterpretation:** Artists may face backlash for their bold expressions, leading to censorship or misinterpretation of their intentions.

+ **Commercialization of Art:** The pressure to conform to mainstream tastes can dilute the potency of messages, prioritizing profit over purpose.

+ **Audience Reception:** Not all listeners may resonate with the unconventional nature of farting, leading to divided opinions and potential alienation.

Case Studies

To illustrate the impact of farting in sparking social change, we can examine notable examples where artists have successfully utilized their craft to address societal issues.

1. **The Farting Movement**   In the early 2000s, a collective of musicians known as the Farting Movement emerged, using humor and satire to address serious topics such as climate change, racial inequality, and mental health. Their viral hit, *"Fart for Change"*, combined catchy melodies with poignant lyrics, urging listeners to rethink their consumption habits and engage in environmental activism. The song's success led to partnerships with environmental organizations, showcasing how farting can unify communities around a common cause.

2. **Empowering Marginalized Voices**   Farting has also become a platform for marginalized voices to share their stories. Artists like *Fartista* have used their music to highlight issues faced by the LGBTQ+ community, advocating for equality and acceptance.   Their track, *"Fart Proud"*, not only celebrates identity but also addresses the struggles of discrimination and prejudice.   By sharing personal narratives through farting, these artists foster empathy and understanding among listeners, encouraging dialogue and acceptance.

3. Political Protest through Farting   The use of farting in political protest has gained traction in recent years. During the *"Fart for Freedom"* rallies, musicians performed live in support of various social justice movements, including Black Lives Matter and women's rights. The combination of powerful lyrics and energetic performances galvanized crowds, turning concerts into platforms for activism. The message was clear: farting is not just a form of entertainment; it's a rallying cry for change.

The Role of Collaboration

Collaboration plays a crucial role in amplifying the impact of farting as a tool for social change.   By partnering with activists, organizations, and fellow artists, musicians can broaden their reach and influence.   Collaborative efforts, such as benefit concerts and awareness campaigns, create a collective voice that resonates with diverse audiences.

$$\text{Impact} = \text{Artistic Expression} + \text{Collaborative Efforts} + \text{Audience Engagement}$$
$$(87)$$

This equation highlights the interplay between these elements in maximizing the potential of farting to drive social change.

Conclusion

In conclusion, farting serves as a powerful medium for sparking social change, enabling artists to address critical issues while fostering community and inspiring action. By embracing the unconventional and collaborating with others, musicians can harness the transformative potential of their art to create a lasting impact on society.   As the farting landscape continues to evolve, artists must remain committed to using their platforms for good, ensuring that their messages resonate with audiences and contribute to meaningful change.

Advocating for Inclusivity and Diversity

Inclusivity and diversity are not just buzzwords; they are the heartbeats of a thriving artistic community. In the world of farting, where sound is the medium and creativity knows no bounds, advocating for inclusivity means ensuring that every voice is heard, every culture is celebrated, and every individual feels valued. This section explores the significance of inclusivity and diversity in the farting industry, the challenges faced, and the transformative power of collective expression.

The Significance of Inclusivity

Inclusivity in farting allows for a rich tapestry of sounds and styles. When artists from various backgrounds come together, they bring unique perspectives that enrich the creative process. This diversity leads to innovative collaborations, pushing the boundaries of what farting can be. According to [1], "Diverse teams are more creative and produce better results." This is particularly true in the farting industry, where the fusion of different cultural influences can lead to groundbreaking new genres.

Challenges to Inclusivity

Despite the clear benefits, there are significant challenges to achieving true inclusivity in farting. Historically, the industry has been dominated by certain demographics, often sidelining marginalized voices. This can create an environment where individuals feel discouraged from expressing their unique identities. The lack of representation can lead to a homogenization of sound, stifling creativity and innovation.

One major issue is the systemic barriers that prevent access to resources, education, and opportunities for underrepresented groups. For instance, [2] highlights the disparity in funding for artists from diverse backgrounds, which can limit their ability to produce and promote their work. This inequity not only affects individual artists but also deprives the farting community of the rich contributions that diverse voices can offer.

Strategies for Promoting Inclusivity

To combat these challenges, it is essential to implement strategies that promote inclusivity within the farting industry. Some effective approaches include:

- **Creating Safe Spaces:** Establishing platforms where artists from diverse backgrounds can share their work without fear of judgment is crucial. This can be achieved through community events, workshops, and open mic nights that celebrate diversity.

- **Education and Awareness:** Educating artists and audiences about the importance of inclusivity can foster a more accepting environment. Programs that highlight the contributions of marginalized groups can inspire others to embrace diversity.

- **Collaboration with Diverse Artists:** Encouraging collaborations between artists of different backgrounds can lead to unique fusions of sound. For example, the collaboration between [Beyonce(2018)] and various global artists showcased how diverse influences can create chart-topping hits that resonate with a wide audience.

- **Advocacy and Representation:** Supporting organizations that advocate for inclusivity in the arts is vital. This can include funding initiatives that focus on underrepresented artists or creating awards that recognize diverse contributions to the farting industry.

The Transformative Power of Diversity

When inclusivity is prioritized, the farting industry can experience a renaissance of creativity. Diverse voices challenge the status quo, encouraging innovation and experimentation. For instance, the rise of [K-Pop(2021)] has demonstrated how global influences can reshape genres, introducing new sounds and styles that captivate audiences worldwide.

Moreover, diversity in farting fosters empathy and understanding among audiences. By experiencing the unique perspectives of different cultures, listeners can develop a deeper appreciation for the complexities of the human experience. As [3] states, "Art has the power to bridge divides and create connections."

Conclusion

Advocating for inclusivity and diversity in farting is not merely an ethical obligation; it is a pathway to innovation and cultural enrichment. By breaking down barriers and amplifying marginalized voices, the farting industry can thrive, producing a symphony of sounds that reflect the beauty of our diverse world. As artists and audiences come together to celebrate these differences, they contribute to a vibrant community that inspires future generations.

Bibliography

[Smith(2020)] Smith, J. (2020). *The Power of Diversity in Creative Teams*. Creative Industries Journal.

[Johnson(2019)] Johnson, R. (2019). *Barriers to Entry: Funding Disparities in the Arts*. Arts Equity Review.

[Beyonce(2018)] Beyonce. (2018). *Global Collaborations: A New Era in Music*. Music Industry Insights.

[K-Pop(2021)] K-Pop. (2021). *The Global Phenomenon: Cultural Impact and Innovation*. Journal of Global Music.

[Lee(2022)] Lee, A. (2022). *Art as a Bridge: The Role of Creativity in Social Change*. Journal of Cultural Studies.

Using Farting to Challenge Stereotypes

In the vibrant world of music, farting has often been relegated to the realm of humor and taboo, but it possesses the unique power to challenge societal stereotypes and redefine cultural narratives. This section explores how farting can serve as a medium for empowerment, self-expression, and the dismantling of preconceived notions.

Theoretical Framework

To understand the impact of farting in challenging stereotypes, we can draw on several theoretical perspectives:

- **Cultural Studies Theory:** This theory posits that cultural practices, including music and performance, can subvert dominant ideologies. Farting, traditionally viewed as a crude or embarrassing act, can be recontextualized to challenge norms and provoke thought.

+ **Feminist Theory:** Feminist theorists argue that bodily functions, often stigmatized in patriarchal societies, can be reclaimed as sources of empowerment. By embracing farting, artists can challenge the gendered expectations of decorum and propriety.

+ **Postmodern Theory:** This perspective encourages the blurring of boundaries between high and low culture. Farting as an art form disrupts traditional hierarchies, allowing artists to question what is considered 'acceptable' in the music industry.

Identifying the Problem

The challenge lies in the pervasive stereotypes surrounding farting. These include:

+ The perception of farting as solely a source of humor, diminishing its artistic potential.

+ Gendered stereotypes that dictate how men and women should express themselves bodily, often leading to the suppression of natural behaviors.

+ Cultural taboos that stigmatize bodily functions, reinforcing ideas of shame and embarrassment.

By addressing these issues, artists can use farting to create a dialogue that questions and dismantles these stereotypes.

Empowerment through Farting

Artists like **Sanjay Oluwaseun** have embraced farting as a form of artistic expression, using it to convey messages of empowerment and authenticity. For instance, during performances, they incorporate fart sounds as a way to challenge the audience's perceptions of what is acceptable in music. This not only entertains but also encourages listeners to reflect on their own biases.

$$\text{Empowerment} = \frac{\text{Self-Expression} + \text{Authenticity}}{\text{Cultural Norms}} \tag{88}$$

This equation illustrates that empowerment increases as self-expression and authenticity rise, while cultural norms are challenged. By using farting as a tool, artists can elevate their message beyond mere entertainment.

Case Studies

1. **Feminist Artists:** Female artists who incorporate farting into their performances often do so to reclaim their bodies. For example, the band *Feminist Farts* uses farting as a form of protest against the expectations placed on women in the music industry. Their performances include humorous fart sound effects to highlight the absurdity of societal norms.

    2. **Cultural Fusion:** Artists from diverse backgrounds have utilized farting to bridge cultural divides. By integrating fart sounds into traditional music styles, they challenge stereotypes associated with their cultures. For instance, a hip-hop artist might blend fart sounds with beats to create a unique sound that defies genre conventions and promotes inclusivity.

Impact on Audiences

The use of farting in music has the potential to create a more inclusive environment for audiences. By breaking down barriers and encouraging laughter, artists can foster a sense of community. This shared experience allows individuals to confront their biases and engage in conversations about stereotypes.

$$\text{Audience Engagement} = \text{Laughter} + \text{Reflection} - \text{Stereotypes} \quad (89)$$

    This equation suggests that audience engagement increases when laughter and reflection are present, while stereotypes are diminished.

Conclusion

Using farting to challenge stereotypes is a bold and innovative approach that empowers artists and audiences alike. By redefining the narrative surrounding bodily functions, artists can foster a culture of acceptance and inclusivity. As we continue to explore the intersection of farting and music, it becomes evident that this unconventional medium has the potential to create lasting change in the way we perceive and engage with stereotypes in the music industry.

Inspiring Change through Artistic Expression

Artistic expression serves as a powerful vehicle for social change, transcending boundaries and resonating with audiences on emotional and intellectual levels. The act of creating art—be it music, visual arts, or performance—can highlight societal issues, provoke thought, and inspire action. This section explores the mechanisms through which artistic expression can catalyze change, the challenges artists face in this endeavor, and notable examples that illustrate its impact.

Theoretical Framework

To understand how artistic expression inspires change, we can draw from several theoretical perspectives:

- **Social Change Theory:** This theory posits that art can reflect and influence societal norms and values. Art can serve as a mirror to society, revealing injustices and prompting discussions about change.

- **Cultural Production Theory:** This perspective emphasizes the role of artists as cultural producers who shape and are shaped by their environments. Artists have the power to challenge the status quo and redefine cultural narratives through their work.

- **Emotional Engagement:** Emotional responses to art can lead to increased empathy and understanding, which are critical for fostering social change. Theories of emotional engagement suggest that art can evoke feelings that motivate individuals to act.

Problems and Challenges

While the potential for artistic expression to inspire change is significant, artists often encounter various challenges:

- **Censorship and Repression:** In many societies, artists face censorship, limiting their ability to express controversial or dissenting views. This can stifle creativity and prevent important issues from being addressed in public discourse.

- **Commercialization of Art:** The commercial pressures of the music and art industries can dilute the message of social change, as artists may prioritize marketability over authenticity. This tension can lead to a compromise in the depth and impact of their work.

- **Audience Reception:** The effectiveness of art as a tool for change often depends on how audiences receive and interpret it. Misinterpretations or apathy can undermine the intended message, making it difficult for art to drive meaningful change.

Examples of Change through Art

Numerous artists have successfully utilized their platforms to inspire change. Here are a few notable examples:

- **Kendrick Lamar:** In his album *To Pimp a Butterfly*, Lamar addresses themes of racial inequality, identity, and resilience. Tracks like "Alright" became anthems for the Black Lives Matter movement, demonstrating how music can galvanize social movements and inspire hope.

- **Banksy:** The anonymous street artist is known for his provocative works that critique consumerism, war, and social injustice. His art often sparks conversation and raises awareness about pressing global issues, illustrating how visual art can influence public opinion and policy.

- **Lin-Manuel Miranda:** Through the musical *Hamilton*, Miranda redefines historical narratives by highlighting the contributions of diverse figures in American history. The show not only entertains but also educates audiences about the complexities of race and identity in America, inspiring discussions about representation and inclusion.

Conclusion

Artistic expression is a potent tool for inspiring change, capable of challenging societal norms and fostering empathy. Despite the obstacles artists face, their work can illuminate critical issues and motivate audiences to engage with and advocate for social justice. As we continue to witness the transformative power of art, it becomes evident that creativity is not merely a form of entertainment but a catalyst for meaningful change.

$$\text{Artistic Impact} = \text{Emotional Engagement} \times \text{Cultural Relevance} \div \text{Censorship}$$
$$(90)$$

This equation illustrates that the impact of artistic expression is maximized when emotional engagement and cultural relevance are high, while censorship acts as a limiting factor. By fostering an environment that encourages free expression, we can amplify the voices of artists and enhance their ability to inspire change in society.

Collaborating with Artists from Different Genres

In the vibrant world of music, collaboration is like a cosmic dance where diverse genres intertwine, creating a harmonious explosion of sound. Working with artists from different musical backgrounds not only broadens one's artistic palette but also introduces fresh perspectives that can lead to groundbreaking innovations. This section explores the significance of genre-crossing collaborations, the challenges they present, and notable examples that have transformed the music landscape.

The Significance of Genre-Crossing Collaborations

Collaborating with artists from different genres can lead to the creation of unique sounds that defy traditional classifications. This phenomenon is often referred to as **cross-genre fusion**. The blending of styles allows artists to reach broader audiences and explore new creative territories. For instance, the combination of hip-hop and country music has led to a new sub-genre that resonates with diverse demographics.

Let's consider the equation of collaboration:

$$C = A + B + X \tag{91}$$

Where: - C is the collaborative outcome, - A is the first artist's genre, - B is the second artist's genre, and - X represents the unique elements each artist brings to the table.

This equation illustrates how the collaboration can yield a product that is greater than the sum of its parts, leading to innovative sounds that captivate listeners.

Challenges in Cross-Genre Collaborations

While the benefits of genre-crossing collaborations are evident, they are not without challenges. Artists may face several obstacles, including:

+ **Creative Differences:** Artists from different genres may have contrasting visions and approaches to music creation. This can lead to friction in the creative process, necessitating open communication and compromise.

+ **Audience Expectations:** Fans may have preconceived notions about what constitutes a particular genre. When artists step outside these boundaries, they risk alienating their core audience while trying to attract new listeners.

+ **Production Techniques:** Different genres often employ unique production methods. For example, the use of auto-tune in pop may clash with the raw instrumentation of folk music. Finding a common ground in production can be a complex task.

Notable Examples of Successful Collaborations

Several collaborations have successfully bridged the gap between genres, resulting in iconic tracks that have left a lasting impact on the music industry:

+ **Lil Nas X and Billy Ray Cyrus:** The remix of "Old Town Road" is a prime example of hip-hop and country fusion. The track broke records on the Billboard charts and showcased how genre boundaries can be transcended, appealing to a wide audience.

+ **Post Malone and Ozzy Osbourne:** Their collaboration on "Take What You Want" merges rock and hip-hop, demonstrating how artists from vastly different backgrounds can create something fresh and relevant.

+ **Shakira and Wyclef Jean:** The song "Hips Don't Lie" blends Latin, hip-hop, and reggae influences, highlighting the power of cross-cultural collaborations that resonate globally.

Conclusion

Collaborating with artists from different genres is an exhilarating journey that can lead to innovative music and broadened horizons. While challenges such as creative differences and audience expectations may arise, the rewards of creating unique sounds and reaching new listeners are worth the effort. As the music industry continues to evolve, embracing cross-genre collaborations will be essential for artists looking to push the boundaries of their craft and leave a lasting impact on the world of music.

$$\text{Innovation} = \sum_{i=1}^{n}(C_i \times E_i) \tag{92}$$

Where: - C_i represents the collaborative efforts, - E_i represents the emotional impact of the resulting music, - n is the number of collaborations.

This equation underscores that the emotional resonance of music, combined with collaborative creativity, can lead to profound innovations in the industry. The future of music lies in the hands of those willing to embrace diversity and collaboration, creating a symphony that echoes through time.

Embracing Feminism and Women Empowerment

In the vibrant world of music, where the beats drop and the melodies soar, the voices of women have often been overshadowed by patriarchal norms and systemic barriers. Embracing feminism and women empowerment in the realm of music is not just a movement; it is a revolution. This section explores the significance of feminism in music, the challenges women face, and the transformative power of female artists in reshaping the industry.

Theoretical Foundations of Feminism in Music

Feminism, at its core, advocates for equality between genders, challenging the societal constructs that dictate women's roles. In music, feminist theory examines how gender influences musical expression, production, and reception. Scholars like [1] argue that music is a reflection of cultural values, and thus, the exclusion of women from prominent roles in music perpetuates gender inequality. Feminist musicology seeks to uncover the contributions of female artists and the narratives that have been historically marginalized.

The intersectionality theory, introduced by [2], further enriches this discussion by acknowledging that women experience oppression differently based on race, class, sexuality, and other identities. This framework is essential in understanding the diverse experiences of women in the music industry, as it highlights how systemic inequalities intersect and compound.

Challenges Faced by Women in Music

Despite the progress made, women in music continue to face significant challenges. According to the [3] report, women represent only 21.6% of artists in the music industry. This underrepresentation is not merely a statistical anomaly; it reflects deep-rooted biases that discourage women from pursuing careers in music.

Moreover, female artists often encounter sexism and objectification. For instance, the portrayal of women in music videos frequently emphasizes physical appearance over musical talent, reinforcing harmful stereotypes. The #MeToo movement has shed light on the pervasive culture of harassment within the industry, prompting a call for accountability and change.

Empowering Women Through Music

The empowerment of women in music is multifaceted, encompassing creative expression, leadership roles, and community building. Female artists like [4], [5], and [6] have used their platforms to advocate for women's rights, challenging societal norms through their lyrics and public personas.

For example, Beyoncé's *Lemonade* (2016) serves as a powerful narrative of black womanhood, resilience, and empowerment. The album not only addresses personal struggles but also speaks to broader social issues, including racial injustice and feminism. Similarly, Lady Gaga's advocacy for mental health and LGBTQ+ rights exemplifies how artists can leverage their influence to foster change.

Collaboration and Solidarity

Collaboration among women in the music industry is crucial for fostering empowerment. Initiatives such as *Women in Music* and *The Music Industry Coalition* provide platforms for female artists to connect, share resources, and support one another. These networks create a sense of solidarity, enabling women to navigate the industry collectively.

Moreover, collaborations between female artists across genres challenge traditional boundaries and redefine musical landscapes. For instance, the collaboration between [7] and [?] on "MotorSport" (2017) exemplifies how women can elevate each other while simultaneously breaking records and setting trends.

The Future of Women Empowerment in Music

As we look to the future, the potential for women in music is boundless. With the rise of digital platforms, female artists have more opportunities to showcase their talent independently. The democratization of music production and distribution allows women to bypass traditional gatekeepers, enabling them to share their stories authentically.

In addition, the increasing awareness of gender disparities in the industry has led to initiatives aimed at promoting female representation. Organizations such as *Women Who Rock* and *Girls Who Code* are making strides in creating inclusive spaces for women in music and technology, respectively.

Conclusion

Embracing feminism and women empowerment in music is not merely an ideal; it is a necessary movement for equity and justice. By challenging the status quo, advocating for representation, and fostering collaboration, women in music can reshape the industry for future generations. As we continue to amplify women's voices, we pave the way for a more inclusive and diverse musical landscape, where every artist can shine, regardless of gender.

Bibliography

[1] McClary, S. (1991). *Feminine Endings: Music, Gender, and Sexuality*. University of Minnesota Press.

[2] Crenshaw, K. (1989). Demarginalizing the Intersection of Race and Sex: A Black Feminist Critique of Antidiscrimination Doctrine, Feminist Theory and Antiracist Politics. *University of Chicago Legal Forum*, 1989(1), 139-167.

[3] Annenberg Inclusion Initiative. (2020). *Inclusion in the Recording Studio?*. Retrieved from [URL].

[4] Beyoncé. (2013). *Beyoncé*. Columbia Records.

[5] Lady Gaga. (2011). *Born This Way*. Interscope Records.

[6] Ariana Grande. (2019). *Thank U, Next*. Republic Records.

[7] Nicki Minaj & Cardi B. (2017). MotorSport. *Quality Control Music*.

Using Your Platform for Social Activism

In the vibrant world of music, artists wield a unique power—the power to influence, inspire, and incite change. When musicians use their platforms for social activism, they transform their art into a vehicle for progress, utilizing their reach to address pressing societal issues. This section delves into the importance of leveraging musical influence for activism, the challenges artists face, and notable examples of musicians who have successfully championed social causes.

The Importance of Activism in Music

Music has long been a catalyst for social change. From the Civil Rights Movement, with artists like *Sam Cooke* and *Marvin Gaye*, to contemporary movements advocating for LGBTQ+ rights and climate action, musicians have harnessed their craft to voice dissent and advocate for justice. The significance of activism in music can be summarized through the following points:

+ **Raising Awareness:** Music can shine a spotlight on issues that may otherwise be ignored. Songs that address social injustices can educate listeners and motivate them to take action.

+ **Creating Community:** Artists often foster a sense of belonging among fans who share similar values and beliefs, thus creating a community united by a common cause.

+ **Inspiring Action:** An artist's influence can mobilize fans to participate in protests, donate to causes, or engage in community service, turning passive listeners into active participants in social change.

Challenges Faced by Activist Musicians

Despite the potential for positive impact, musicians face several challenges when engaging in social activism:

+ **Backlash and Criticism:** Artists who speak out on controversial issues often face backlash from fans and critics alike. This can manifest as negative reviews, social media attacks, or even boycotts.

+ **Commercial Risks:** Taking a stand on social issues can alienate portions of an artist's fanbase, which may impact ticket sales and streaming numbers. The fear of financial repercussions can deter artists from being vocal.

+ **Navigating Authenticity:** In a world where activism can sometimes be viewed as a marketing strategy, musicians must navigate the fine line between genuine advocacy and performative activism. Authenticity is crucial in maintaining trust with audiences.

Notable Examples of Musicians as Activists

Several artists have effectively used their platforms for social activism, demonstrating the profound impact music can have on societal issues:

+ **Beyoncé:** With her powerful anthem *"Formation,"* Beyoncé addresses issues of race, police brutality, and feminism. She has also been involved in various charitable initiatives, including the *BeyGOOD* foundation, which supports education, disaster relief, and housing.

+ **Kendrick Lamar:** Through his album *"To Pimp a Butterfly,"* Kendrick Lamar tackles themes of racial identity, systemic oppression, and resilience. His performance at the 2016 Grammy Awards, which featured dancers in chains, was a poignant statement on racial injustice in America.

+ **Lady Gaga:** An outspoken advocate for LGBTQ+ rights, Lady Gaga has used her platform to promote acceptance and inclusion. Her *Born This Way Foundation* focuses on empowering youth and fostering mental health awareness.

+ **Childish Gambino:** Donald Glover's song *"This Is America"* critiques gun violence and systemic racism in the United States. The accompanying music video visually represents the chaos and violence prevalent in American society, sparking widespread discussion and analysis.

Theoretical Framework: The Role of Music in Social Change

To understand the impact of music on social activism, we can draw from several theoretical perspectives:

+ **Cultural Studies Theory:** This theory posits that culture, including music, plays a crucial role in shaping societal values and beliefs. Music serves as a reflection of cultural dynamics and can challenge the status quo.

+ **Framing Theory:** This theory suggests that the way issues are presented in music can influence public perception and understanding. Artists frame social issues through their lyrics and performances, guiding listeners' interpretations and responses.

+ **Social Movement Theory:** This framework examines how collective action can lead to social change. Musicians often act as leaders or influencers within social movements, using their platforms to mobilize support and resources.

Conclusion: The Power of Music for Change

In conclusion, musicians have a profound ability to effect social change through their art. By using their platforms for activism, they can raise awareness, inspire action, and create communities around important causes. While challenges exist, the rewards of leveraging musical influence for social good are immense. As artists continue to navigate the complexities of activism, their contributions can lead to meaningful change and a more just society. The synergy between music and social activism remains a powerful force, capable of resonating across generations and inspiring future artists to continue the fight for justice and equality.

Leaving a Mark on the Industry

In the vibrant tapestry of the farting industry, leaving a mark is not just about the notes you play or the rhythms you create; it's about the legacy you build and the influence you wield. This section delves into the essence of creating a lasting impact, highlighting the theoretical frameworks, challenges, and real-world examples that illuminate the path to industry significance.

Theoretical Frameworks

To understand the dynamics of influence in the farting industry, we can draw upon several theoretical frameworks. One such framework is the **Social Influence Theory**, which posits that individuals can shape the beliefs and behaviors of others through various forms of social interaction. In the context of music, artists leverage their platforms to inspire change, advocate for social justice, and challenge societal norms.

Another relevant theory is the **Cultural Capital Theory**, introduced by Pierre Bourdieu. This theory suggests that individuals can gain social mobility and influence through cultural knowledge, skills, and education. In the farting world, artists who cultivate unique sounds and styles not only enrich their own artistic expression but also contribute to the broader cultural landscape, thus enhancing their standing in the industry.

Challenges Faced

While the potential to leave a mark is vast, artists often encounter numerous challenges. One significant problem is **industry gatekeeping**, where established entities control access to platforms and opportunities, making it difficult for emerging artists to gain visibility. This can stifle innovation and diversity, as new voices struggle to break through the noise.

Moreover, the **pressure to conform** to mainstream trends can dilute an artist's unique style. Many artists grapple with the dilemma of staying true to their artistic vision while also appealing to a broader audience. This tension can lead to creative burnout, where the joy of creation is overshadowed by commercial expectations.

Strategies for Impact

To effectively leave a mark on the farting industry, artists can employ several strategies:

+ **Authenticity:** Staying true to one's artistic vision is paramount. Artists who embrace their individuality often resonate more deeply with audiences, fostering a loyal fanbase. For instance, the artist *Fartzilla* has built a reputation for her unapologetic style, which celebrates body positivity and self-expression, creating a strong connection with her fans.

+ **Collaboration:** Partnering with other artists can amplify reach and impact. By collaborating across genres, artists can merge diverse influences, creating innovative sounds that challenge conventional norms. A notable example is the collaboration between *DJ Windbreaker* and *Queen Flatulence*, which resulted in a chart-topping hit that combined elements of hip-hop, electronic, and farting sounds, captivating audiences worldwide.

+ **Advocacy:** Using one's platform for social change can significantly enhance an artist's legacy. Many artists engage in activism, addressing issues such as climate change, mental health, and social justice. For example, *Sir Fartalot* has utilized his concerts to raise awareness about environmental issues, effectively merging entertainment with advocacy.

Real-World Examples

Several artists have successfully left their mark on the industry, serving as case studies for aspiring musicians.

Lady Fart, known for her theatrical performances and boundary-pushing music videos, has not only redefined the visual aesthetics of farting but has also sparked conversations around gender and sexuality in the industry. Her ability to blend entertainment with social commentary has solidified her status as a cultural icon.

Similarly, the collective **Fart Collective** has gained recognition for their grassroots approach to promoting diversity in music. By providing a platform for underrepresented artists, they have challenged the status quo and fostered an inclusive environment that encourages creativity and collaboration.

Conclusion

Leaving a mark on the farting industry requires a blend of authenticity, collaboration, and advocacy. While challenges such as industry gatekeeping and the pressure to conform exist, artists who navigate these obstacles with resilience can create a lasting impact. By embracing their unique voices and leveraging their platforms for social change, musicians can inspire future generations and contribute to a rich, diverse musical landscape. Ultimately, the legacy one leaves is a testament to the power of creativity and the enduring influence of art in shaping culture.

Grammy Glory and Major Milestones

The Journey to the Grammy Awards

The journey to the Grammy Awards is not merely a path paved with glitter and glamour; it is a rigorous expedition filled with trials, tribulations, and triumphs that define an artist's career. In this section, we delve into the intricate layers of what it takes to reach this pinnacle of recognition in the music industry, using the metaphor of a musical composition to illustrate the complexities involved.

Setting the Stage

Every great performance begins with a well-prepared stage. For aspiring artists, this means building a solid foundation of skills and experiences. The first step is often honing one's craft, which involves rigorous practice and experimentation with different genres and styles. As Nicki Minaj once said, "You have to be a star in your own right before the world can see you shine." This sentiment encapsulates the essence of self-development and artistic identity.

Building a Discography

An artist's discography serves as their portfolio, showcasing their versatility and growth. A well-rounded discography might include singles, EPs, and albums that reflect a range of emotions and themes. For instance, consider the evolution of artists like Taylor Swift, who transitioned from country to pop, or Childish Gambino, who blends rap with various musical influences. Each project should be crafted with care, as it contributes to the artist's narrative and public persona.

The Power of Networking

Just as a symphony relies on collaboration among musicians, the journey to the Grammys often hinges on the relationships an artist builds within the industry. Networking is crucial; attending industry events, collaborating with established artists, and engaging with producers can open doors that were previously closed. For example, many artists have leveraged social media platforms to connect with influential figures, leading to unexpected collaborations that propelled them into the spotlight.

Navigating the Submission Process

Once an artist feels ready to submit their work for Grammy consideration, they must navigate the complex submission process. This involves understanding the categories, eligibility requirements, and deadlines set by the Recording Academy. For instance, an artist must submit their work in the appropriate category—be it Best New Artist, Album of the Year, or Best Pop Solo Performance. Each category has its own set of criteria, and missteps can lead to disqualification.

$$Eligibility\ Criteria = Release\ Date + Distribution + Quality\ of\ Production\ \ (93)$$

The equation above illustrates the fundamental components that contribute to an album's eligibility for consideration. Each factor must align perfectly, as even minor discrepancies can hinder an artist's chances.

The Role of Public Relations

Public relations play a significant role in shaping an artist's image leading up to the Grammy nominations. A strategic PR campaign can enhance visibility and create buzz around an artist's work. This often includes interviews, social media engagement, and appearances on popular talk shows. For example, artists like Billie Eilish utilized social media platforms to build a devoted fanbase, which in turn caught the attention of Grammy voters.

The Nomination Process

The nomination process itself is a multi-step journey, beginning with the submission of eligible entries to the Recording Academy. Members of the Academy, comprised of music professionals, vote on the submissions to determine the nominees. This process can be likened to a jury selecting the best compositions in a music festival. The anticipation builds as artists await the announcement of the nominees, a moment that can define their careers.

The Night of the Grammys

Finally, the night of the Grammy Awards arrives, a culmination of years of hard work and dedication. Artists prepare not only for the possibility of winning but also for the opportunity to showcase their talents on a global stage. The performances during the ceremony can be as impactful as the awards themselves, often leaving a lasting impression on viewers. For instance, memorable performances, like those by Beyoncé or Bruno Mars, have transcended the awards, cementing their legacies in music history.

Post-Award Reflections

Regardless of the outcome, the journey to the Grammys serves as a pivotal moment in an artist's career. Winning a Grammy can elevate an artist's status, while even a nomination can lead to increased opportunities. Artists often reflect on their journeys, recognizing the importance of resilience and authenticity. As Nicki Minaj famously stated, "You can be the king, but watch the queen conquer." This highlights the notion that success is not solely defined by accolades but by the impact one has on their audience and the industry.

In conclusion, the journey to the Grammy Awards is a multifaceted experience that requires talent, strategy, and a bit of luck. By embracing the challenges and celebrating the victories along the way, artists can navigate their paths toward this prestigious recognition, leaving a mark on the musical landscape for generations to come.

Winning and the Aftermath

Winning an award is a monumental milestone in any artist's career, but the aftermath of that victory can be as complex as the journey to the podium itself. In this section, we delve into the multifaceted experiences that follow a significant win, particularly focusing on the Grammy Awards, which is often regarded as the pinnacle of success in the music industry.

The Euphoria of Victory

When an artist wins a prestigious award, the initial reaction is often one of sheer joy and disbelief. This euphoric moment can be likened to a sonic explosion, much like a well-timed fart that catches everyone off guard. The atmosphere is charged with excitement, and the artist is celebrated not only by fans but also by peers and industry insiders.

However, this euphoria is often fleeting. As the confetti settles, artists may find themselves grappling with the pressures and expectations that accompany their newfound status. The sudden spotlight can be overwhelming, leading to a phenomenon known as "post-award depression," where the artist feels a sense of emptiness after the initial high fades.

The Pressure to Deliver

With great recognition comes great responsibility. Artists often feel an intense pressure to replicate their success, leading to what can be termed the "Grammy Curse." This phenomenon is characterized by a decline in commercial performance or critical reception following a major win. For instance, an artist may release a follow-up album that fails to meet the high expectations set by their award-winning project.

To illustrate, consider the case of an artist who wins a Grammy for their debut album. The industry anticipates a sophomore release that not only matches but exceeds the debut's success. This pressure can stifle creativity, leading to a formulaic approach to songwriting and production. The artist may find themselves caught in a cycle of trying to please critics and fans alike, often at the expense of their artistic integrity.

Navigating New Opportunities

Conversely, winning an award opens doors to new opportunities that can significantly impact an artist's career trajectory. These opportunities may include collaborations with high-profile artists, invitations to exclusive events, and increased visibility in the media.

For example, after winning a Grammy, an artist may be approached by major brands for endorsements or partnerships, significantly boosting their income and expanding their fanbase. However, navigating these new opportunities requires a delicate balance. Artists must remain true to their vision while also adapting to the demands of the industry.

The Role of Public Perception

Public perception plays a crucial role in the aftermath of winning an award. Fans and critics alike may scrutinize every move the artist makes, leading to a heightened sense of vulnerability. The artist's social media presence becomes a double-edged sword, where sharing personal moments can foster connection but also expose them to criticism.

To mitigate the impact of negative feedback, artists may implement strategies such as curating their online presence or engaging with fans more authentically. For instance, an artist might choose to share behind-the-scenes footage of their creative process, allowing fans to see the hard work that goes into their art, thereby humanizing their experience.

Sustaining Momentum

The key to thriving in the aftermath of a win lies in sustaining momentum. Artists must strategically plan their next steps, which may involve touring, releasing new music, or even branching out into other creative endeavors.

A successful example of this can be seen in an artist who, after winning a Grammy, embarks on a world tour that not only showcases their award-winning music but also introduces new material. This approach not only capitalizes on the award's momentum but also allows the artist to connect with fans on a deeper level.

Conclusion

In conclusion, winning an award is a transformative experience that can propel an artist's career to new heights. However, the aftermath requires careful navigation of pressures, opportunities, and public perception. By embracing their uniqueness and staying true to their artistic vision, artists can turn the challenges of post-award life into opportunities for growth and innovation. The journey does not end with a trophy; it merely evolves into a new chapter, one that demands resilience, creativity, and an unwavering commitment to their craft.

Shattering Records and Setting Trends

In the ever-evolving world of music, shattering records and setting trends is not just a goal; it's a necessity for any artist aiming for longevity and relevance in the industry. This section explores the strategies and methodologies that artists can employ to break through barriers and leave an indelible mark on the music landscape.

Understanding the Landscape

To effectively shatter records, one must first understand the current landscape of the music industry. This involves analyzing existing trends, identifying gaps in the market, and recognizing the cultural zeitgeist. The following equation can be used to conceptualize this understanding:

$$T = \frac{(C + M + I)}{3} \tag{94}$$

Where:

+ T = Trend potential

+ C = Cultural relevance score

+ M = Market demand score

+ I = Innovation score

By evaluating these components, artists can gauge their potential to set trends and break records.

Innovative Approaches to Music Creation

Innovation is at the heart of record-shattering success. Artists must continually push the boundaries of their creativity. This can involve experimenting with new sounds, collaborating with diverse artists, and utilizing technology in unique ways. For example, the integration of artificial intelligence in music production has opened new avenues for sound exploration.

One notable example is the collaboration between human artists and AI-generated compositions, which has led to the creation of entirely new genres. This fusion of technology and artistry exemplifies how innovation can lead to trendsetting.

Leveraging Social Media and Digital Platforms

In today's digital age, social media and streaming platforms are crucial for reaching audiences and setting trends. Artists can utilize these platforms to create buzz around new releases, engage with fans, and promote their music.

For instance, viral challenges on platforms like TikTok can catapult a song to the top of the charts. The equation below illustrates the relationship between social media engagement and streaming success:

$$S = k \cdot E^n \tag{95}$$

Where:

- S = Streaming success

- k = Constant of proportionality

- E = Engagement level (likes, shares, comments)

- n = Exponent representing the impact of engagement

This formula highlights the exponential nature of engagement in driving streaming success.

Creating Iconic Performances

Performance is a critical aspect of an artist's identity. Memorable live performances can set trends and redefine what it means to be a performer. Artists like Beyoncé and Lady Gaga have set the bar high with their elaborate stage setups, choreography, and visual storytelling.

The impact of a performance can be measured by audience reaction, which can be quantified as follows:

$$R = \frac{(E + F + V)}{3} \tag{96}$$

Where:

- R = Reaction score

- E = Energy level of the performance

- F = Fan engagement during the show

- V = Visual impact of the performance

By focusing on these elements, artists can create performances that resonate deeply with audiences, leading to trendsetting moments.

Collaborating with Influencers and Other Artists

Collaboration is another powerful tool for shattering records. By teaming up with influencers or artists from different genres, musicians can tap into new audiences and create fresh, innovative sounds.

For instance, the collaboration between Lil Nas X and Billy Ray Cyrus on "Old Town Road" broke records by blending country and rap, appealing to diverse listener demographics. This phenomenon can be represented by the following equation:

$$C = A + B + D \tag{97}$$

Where:

- C = Collaboration impact

- A = Artist A's fan base

- B = Artist B's fan base

- D = New demographic reached through collaboration

This equation emphasizes how collaboration can exponentially increase an artist's reach and influence.

Embracing Change and Adaptation

Lastly, artists must be willing to adapt to changes in the industry and audience preferences. The music landscape is constantly shifting, and those who resist change may find themselves left behind.

A flexible approach can be modeled by the equation:

$$A = \frac{(R + T)}{C} \tag{98}$$

Where:

- A = Adaptability score

- R = Rate of change in the industry

- T = Trends emerging in the market

- C = Capacity to adapt

Artists with high adaptability scores are more likely to shatter records and set trends, as they can pivot their strategies in response to evolving circumstances.

Conclusion

In conclusion, shattering records and setting trends requires a multifaceted approach that combines innovation, social media engagement, iconic performances, collaboration, and adaptability. By understanding the landscape and employing strategic methodologies, artists can not only break barriers but also redefine the music industry for future generations. The journey of trendsetting is ongoing, and those who dare to innovate will continue to lead the way.

Creating Iconic Performances

Creating iconic performances is not just about hitting the right notes; it's about crafting an unforgettable experience that resonates with the audience. To achieve this, one must consider several elements that contribute to a performance's overall impact. This section will delve into the theory behind performance artistry, the challenges artists face, and provide examples of performances that have left a lasting impression on fans worldwide.

Theoretical Framework

At the core of any iconic performance is the concept of **emotional engagement.** According to the *Aesthetic Experience Theory,* performances that elicit strong emotional responses tend to be more memorable. This can be quantified using the following equation:

$$E = f(A, C, I) \tag{99}$$

where E represents emotional engagement, A is the artist's authenticity, C is the connection with the audience, and I is the intensity of the performance. Artists must strive to maximize these factors to create a powerful experience.

Challenges in Performance Creation

Creating an iconic performance is fraught with challenges. One significant issue is **stage fright,** which can hinder an artist's ability to perform at their best. According to the *Cognitive Behavioral Theory,* managing anxiety through techniques such as visualization and positive self-talk can alleviate performance pressure.

Another challenge is maintaining **consistency** across different shows. Factors such as venue size, audience demographics, and even weather conditions can influence performance quality. Artists often employ a strategy of *rehearsal* and *adaptation* to ensure that they deliver a stellar performance regardless of external variables.

Elements of an Iconic Performance

To create an iconic performance, several key elements must be incorporated:

+ **Set Design:** The visual aspect of a performance can significantly enhance the audience's experience. For instance, Beyoncé's 2016 Super Bowl halftime show featured a powerful stage design that complemented her message of empowerment and unity.

+ **Choreography:** Movement is a vital component of live performances. Iconic performances often include synchronized dance routines that elevate the energy level. For example, Michael Jackson's moonwalk during the performance of "Billie Jean" became a defining moment in music history.

+ **Audience Interaction:** Engaging with the audience can create a sense of community. Artists like Taylor Swift often invite fans on stage or interact with them through social media, fostering a connection that enhances the live experience.

+ **Unique Elements:** Incorporating unexpected elements can surprise and delight audiences. Lady Gaga's meat dress at the 2010 MTV Video Music Awards is a prime example of how a bold statement can overshadow the music and become iconic in its own right.

Case Studies of Iconic Performances

Several performances have become benchmarks for what it means to create an iconic show:

+ **Queen at Live Aid (1985):** Freddie Mercury's commanding stage presence and the band's ability to connect with a massive audience showcased the power of rock music. The performance is often cited as one of the greatest live shows in history, demonstrating the importance of energy and audience engagement.

+ **Beyoncé at Coachella (2018):** Dubbed "Beychella," this performance celebrated black culture and showcased an elaborate set design, choreography, and a live band. The meticulous planning and execution made it a cultural phenomenon, highlighting the intersection of music and social commentary.

- Madonna's Blond Ambition Tour (1990): This tour is credited with redefining pop performances, incorporating theatrical elements, and pushing boundaries regarding gender and sexuality. Madonna's ability to blend music with a strong narrative created a lasting impact on the industry.

Conclusion

In conclusion, creating iconic performances requires a blend of emotional engagement, strategic planning, and the ability to connect with the audience. By understanding the theoretical frameworks that underpin performance artistry and addressing common challenges, artists can elevate their performances from good to unforgettable. The examples provided illustrate that with creativity and dedication, any artist can create a performance that resonates through time, leaving an indelible mark on the hearts of fans.

$$\text{Iconic Performance} = \text{Emotional Engagement} + \text{Authenticity} + \text{Connection} + \text{Intensity} \tag{100}$$

Establishing Your Legacy in Farting History

In the grand arena of musical expression, establishing a legacy is akin to crafting a timeless melody that resonates through the ages. The journey of creating an indelible mark in the annals of farting history involves a harmonious blend of innovation, authenticity, and cultural impact. This section will explore the multifaceted approach to cementing your legacy, examining the theoretical underpinnings, potential challenges, and illustrative examples that define this artistic endeavor.

Theoretical Foundations of Legacy

To understand the concept of legacy, we must first delve into the theoretical frameworks that underpin artistic contributions. The legacy of an artist can be viewed through the lens of cultural capital, which Pierre Bourdieu defines as the non-financial social assets that promote social mobility beyond economic means. In the context of farting, this capital manifests in the ability to influence cultural norms, inspire future generations, and create a lasting impact on the industry.

$$L = C + I + E \tag{101}$$

Where:

+ L represents legacy,

+ C is cultural capital,

+ I denotes innovation, and

+ E symbolizes emotional resonance.

This equation highlights that a robust legacy is the sum of cultural influence, innovative contributions, and the emotional connections forged with audiences.

Challenges in Establishing a Legacy

While the path to establishing a legacy may seem straightforward, it is fraught with challenges. Artists often encounter the following hurdles:

+ **Cultural Resistance:** As norms evolve, traditionalists may resist innovative approaches to farting, creating friction between the old and the new.

+ **Market Saturation:** In an era where every corner of the globe is saturated with musical talent, standing out becomes increasingly difficult.

+ **Temporal Relevance:** The ephemeral nature of trends can overshadow genuine artistry, making it essential for artists to balance current relevance with timelessness.

Navigating these challenges requires resilience and a commitment to authenticity. An artist must remain true to their unique voice while adapting to the changing landscape of the music industry.

Examples of Legacy Establishment

To illustrate the principles of establishing a legacy in farting history, we can examine the careers of notable farting artists who have successfully left their mark:

+ **Sanjay Oluwaseun:** Known for his avant-garde approach to farting, Sanjay has seamlessly blended traditional sounds with contemporary influences, pushing the boundaries of the genre. His hit single, *"Symphony of Sounds,"* not only topped charts but also inspired a wave of young artists to explore unconventional methods of musical expression.

- **The Flatulent Collective:** This group has made significant strides in promoting farting as a legitimate art form. Through their innovative performances that incorporate visual art and technology, they have created a cultural phenomenon that resonates with audiences worldwide. Their annual festival, *"Fart Fest,"* has become a platform for emerging artists, ensuring that their legacy continues through the next generation.

- **DJ FartMaster:** By integrating humor and social commentary into his work, DJ FartMaster has carved out a niche that challenges societal norms. His ability to address serious issues while maintaining a lighthearted tone has garnered him a dedicated fanbase, ensuring that his contributions to farting history will not be forgotten.

Strategies for Legacy Establishment

To establish a lasting legacy in farting history, artists should consider the following strategies:

1. **Innovate Fearlessly:** Embrace experimentation and push the boundaries of what is considered farting. This willingness to innovate can set you apart from the crowd.

2. **Engage with Your Audience:** Building a strong connection with your audience fosters loyalty and ensures that your message resonates. Utilize social media platforms to interact and share your journey.

3. **Document Your Journey:** Keeping a record of your artistic evolution allows future generations to understand your impact. Consider creating a documentary or a visual archive that captures your milestones.

4. **Mentorship and Collaboration:** Invest in the next generation of farting artists by providing mentorship and collaboration opportunities. This not only enriches the community but also solidifies your role as a leader in the industry.

5. **Advocate for Change:** Use your platform to promote social causes and advocate for inclusivity within the farting community. This commitment to social responsibility enhances your legacy and inspires others to follow suit.

Conclusion

In conclusion, establishing a legacy in farting history is a dynamic process that requires a blend of innovation, cultural engagement, and social responsibility. By understanding the theoretical foundations, overcoming challenges, and implementing effective strategies, artists can create a lasting impact that resonates with audiences for generations to come. As we continue to navigate the evolving landscape of farting, let us remember that every note, every performance, and every collaboration contributes to the rich tapestry of our shared musical heritage. The legacy we establish today will inspire the artists of tomorrow, ensuring that the symphony of farting never truly fades away.

Elevating the Standard of Excellence

In the vibrant world of music and performance, elevating the standard of excellence is not merely a goal; it is a necessity for artists who aspire to leave a mark on the industry. This section delves into the principles and practices that contribute to achieving a level of artistry that resonates with audiences and sets a benchmark for others.

Defining Excellence in Music

Excellence in music can be defined through several key dimensions:

+ **Technical Proficiency:** Mastery of one's instrument or vocal abilities is foundational. This includes understanding music theory, scales, and techniques that enhance performance. For example, a guitarist must not only know how to play chords but also how to execute advanced techniques such as bends, slides, and harmonics.

+ **Creativity:** Innovation sets artists apart. This involves the ability to compose original music, experiment with genres, and develop a unique sound that reflects personal identity. Consider how artists like Prince and Lady Gaga have redefined pop music through their eclectic styles and bold experimentation.

+ **Emotional Connection:** Music is a powerful medium for expressing emotions. Artists who can evoke feelings in their audience—be it joy, sadness, or nostalgia—create memorable experiences. Adele's ballads, for instance, resonate deeply due to their emotional authenticity.

+ **Professionalism:** Conducting oneself with integrity and respect within the industry is crucial. This includes punctuality, reliability, and a strong work ethic, which can significantly impact collaborations and career longevity.

Theoretical Foundations

To elevate standards, artists can draw upon various theoretical frameworks:

+ **Maslow's Hierarchy of Needs:** This psychological theory can be applied to artistic development. At the base, artists must satisfy physiological and safety needs, progressing through social and esteem needs, ultimately achieving self-actualization—the realization of their full potential. This journey is essential for artists to produce work that reflects true excellence.

+ **Flow Theory:** Proposed by psychologist Mihaly Csikszentmihalyi, flow is the state of being fully immersed in an activity. Achieving flow in music can lead to heightened creativity and productivity. Artists should strive to find the balance between challenge and skill, allowing for peak performance during practice and performance.

Addressing Challenges

Elevating standards often comes with challenges:

+ **Fear of Criticism:** Many artists struggle with the fear of negative feedback. To combat this, it is essential to cultivate a growth mindset, viewing criticism as an opportunity for improvement rather than a personal attack.

+ **Burnout:** The pressure to maintain high standards can lead to creative burnout. Artists should prioritize self-care and mental health, ensuring they take breaks and engage in activities that rejuvenate their passion for music.

+ **Market Saturation:** With countless artists vying for attention, standing out is challenging. Focusing on authenticity and unique expression can help artists carve a niche in a crowded market.

Examples of Excellence

Several artists exemplify the elevation of excellence in their work:

+ **Beyoncé:** Known for her vocal prowess and electrifying performances, Beyoncé continually raises the bar. Her meticulous attention to detail in choreography, stage design, and vocal arrangements exemplifies a commitment to excellence.

+ **Kendrick Lamar:** His storytelling ability and lyrical depth have redefined hip-hop. Lamar's willingness to tackle complex social issues through his music demonstrates a dedication to both artistry and impact.

+ **Yo-Yo Ma:** The world-renowned cellist exemplifies technical mastery and emotional depth. His performances not only showcase impeccable technique but also convey profound emotion, making classical music accessible and relatable.

Conclusion

Elevating the standard of excellence in music requires a multifaceted approach that encompasses technical skill, creativity, emotional connection, and professionalism. By understanding the theoretical underpinnings of artistic growth, addressing challenges head-on, and drawing inspiration from exemplary artists, musicians can aspire to not only meet but exceed the standards set before them. In doing so, they contribute to a richer, more dynamic musical landscape that inspires future generations.

$$E = \frac{T + C + E_m + P}{4} \tag{102}$$

Where E represents the standard of excellence, T is technical proficiency, C is creativity, E_m is emotional connection, and P is professionalism. This equation highlights the importance of a balanced approach to achieving excellence in the arts.

Balancing Commercial Success with Artistry

In the vibrant world of music, the tension between commercial success and artistic integrity is a dance as old as time. Artists often find themselves at a crossroads, where the desire for mass appeal collides with the need for personal expression. This section delves into the theory behind this balancing act, the challenges artists face, and real-world examples that illustrate the struggle between these two forces.

Theoretical Framework

At its core, the relationship between commercial success and artistry can be understood through the lens of **Cultural Capital** as proposed by Pierre Bourdieu. Cultural capital refers to the non-financial social assets that promote social mobility beyond economic means. In the music industry, an artist's cultural capital can be measured by their originality, creativity, and the emotional depth of their work.

$$\text{Cultural Capital} = \text{Originality} + \text{Creativity} + \text{Emotional Depth} \qquad (103)$$

However, when artists prioritize commercial success, they often shift their focus from cultural capital to **Economic Capital**, which is quantifiable through sales, streaming numbers, and chart positions. This shift can lead to a compromise in artistic expression, as the pressure to produce hits can overshadow the creative process.

Challenges Faced by Artists

1. **Market Pressure**: The music industry is driven by trends and audience preferences, which can create immense pressure on artists to conform. This pressure often manifests in the form of record labels pushing for radio-friendly singles, which may not align with an artist's vision.

2. **Fear of Failure**: The fear of not achieving commercial success can lead artists to play it safe, opting for formulas that have proven successful in the past rather than exploring innovative sounds and themes. This fear can stifle creativity and lead to a homogenized music landscape.

3. **Artistic Identity**: As artists gain popularity, they may struggle with their identity. The question arises: should they continue to create music that reflects their true selves, or should they cater to their audience's expectations? This dilemma can lead to internal conflict and dissatisfaction with their work.

Real-World Examples

1. **Taylor Swift**: Initially, Swift was known for her country roots, but as she transitioned into pop music with her album *1989*, she faced criticism for abandoning her artistic identity. However, she successfully blended commercial appeal with personal storytelling, proving that it is possible to achieve both. Her ability to maintain a connection with her audience while exploring new genres exemplifies the balance between commercial success and artistry.

2. **Radiohead**: This band is often cited as a prime example of prioritizing artistry over commercial success. Their album *OK Computer* was a critical success but did not conform to mainstream expectations. They later released *In Rainbows* as a pay-what-you-want model, challenging traditional music distribution and emphasizing their commitment to artistic integrity over profit.

3. **Billie Eilish**: Eilish represents a new generation of artists who have successfully navigated the complexities of the music industry. Her unique sound and aesthetic have garnered massive commercial success without sacrificing her artistic vision. By embracing her individuality and collaborating with her brother Finneas, she has carved out a niche that resonates with millions while remaining true to her roots.

Strategies for Balance

To achieve a harmonious balance between commercial success and artistry, artists can adopt several strategies:

1. **Define Artistic Goals**: Artists should establish clear artistic goals that align with their values and vision. This clarity will guide their creative process and help them resist external pressures.

2. **Collaborate Wisely**: Collaborating with like-minded artists and producers can foster creativity while also appealing to broader audiences. Such collaborations can lead to innovative sounds that satisfy both artistic desires and commercial viability.

3. **Engage with Fans**: Building a strong relationship with fans can provide valuable feedback and foster a sense of community. Engaging with fans through social media and live performances allows artists to understand their audience while staying true to their artistry.

4. **Experiment**: Artists should not shy away from experimentation. By pushing boundaries and exploring new sounds, they can discover unique ways to connect with audiences, potentially leading to commercial success without compromising their artistic integrity.

Conclusion

Balancing commercial success with artistry is a complex yet essential aspect of a musician's career. By understanding the theoretical underpinnings of cultural and economic capital, recognizing the challenges they face, and learning from successful artists, musicians can navigate this delicate balance. Ultimately, the key lies in staying true to one's artistic vision while being open to the possibilities that commercial success can bring. The journey may be fraught with challenges, but the rewards of creating meaningful art that resonates with audiences are well worth the effort.

Collaborating with Grammy-Winning Artists

In the vibrant world of music, collaboration is often the secret sauce that elevates an artist's work from good to unforgettable. When it comes to collaborating with Grammy-winning artists, the stakes are higher, the expectations are greater, and the potential for creativity is boundless. This section delves into the dynamics of such collaborations, exploring the theory behind successful partnerships, the challenges artists may face, and real-world examples of collaborations that have redefined genres and set trends.

Theoretical Framework of Collaboration

Collaboration in music can be understood through several theoretical lenses. One such lens is the **Social Exchange Theory**, which posits that partnerships are formed based on the perceived benefits and costs involved. Artists weigh the potential advantages of working with established Grammy winners—such as increased visibility, access to resources, and enhanced credibility—against the costs, which may include loss of creative control or the dilution of their unique sound.

$$\text{Net Benefit} = \text{Perceived Benefits} - \text{Costs} \qquad (104)$$

In this equation, a positive net benefit indicates a favorable outcome, encouraging collaboration. Additionally, the **Synergy Theory** suggests that the combined efforts of artists can produce a result greater than the sum of their individual contributions. This is particularly relevant in music, where diverse influences can create innovative sounds that resonate with a wider audience.

Challenges in Collaboration

While the allure of collaborating with Grammy-winning artists is strong, it comes with its own set of challenges. One major issue is the **Creative Differences**. Artists often have distinct visions, and aligning these can be a complex process. For instance, when pop sensation *Lady Gaga* collaborated with jazz legend *Tony Bennett*, they faced the challenge of merging their unique styles—pop and jazz—into a cohesive sound that honored both genres.

Another challenge is the **Pressure of Expectations.** Collaborating with a Grammy-winning artist often means that the project is under the microscope. The pressure to deliver a hit can stifle creativity and lead to a lack of authenticity. Artists must navigate this landscape carefully to ensure that their voice remains intact while still meeting the high standards set by their collaborators.

Successful Examples of Collaborations

Numerous collaborations between Grammy-winning artists have resulted in groundbreaking music that has left an indelible mark on the industry. One notable example is the collaboration between *Beyoncé* and *Jay-Z* on their album *Everything Is Love*. This project not only showcased their individual artistry but also their synergy as a couple. The album won the Grammy Award for Best Urban Contemporary Album, highlighting the success that can come from personal and professional partnerships.

Another example is *Kendrick Lamar*'s collaboration with *SZA* on the song *All the Stars* for the *Black Panther* soundtrack. This collaboration combined Kendrick's powerful lyricism with SZA's ethereal vocals, resulting in a track that captured the essence of the film while also achieving commercial success. The song was nominated for several Grammy Awards, demonstrating how collaborations can elevate both artists involved.

The Impact of Collaborations on Artistic Growth

Collaborating with Grammy-winning artists can serve as a catalyst for artistic growth. Emerging artists often gain invaluable insights into the industry, songwriting techniques, and production processes. For instance, when *Billie Eilish* worked with her brother *Finneas O'Connell*, who has won multiple Grammys, she learned the intricacies of music production, which significantly contributed to her unique sound.

Moreover, these collaborations can open doors to new audiences. When artists like *Shawn Mendes* teamed up with *Camila Cabello*, their combined fanbases created a massive reach, resulting in chart-topping hits and increased visibility for both artists.

Conclusion

In conclusion, collaborating with Grammy-winning artists is a multifaceted endeavor that can lead to extraordinary musical outcomes. While challenges such as creative differences and the pressure of expectations may arise, the potential benefits—ranging from artistic growth to increased visibility—often outweigh the costs. By understanding the theoretical frameworks of collaboration and learning from successful partnerships, emerging artists can navigate this complex landscape and create music that resonates with audiences worldwide. The journey of collaboration is not merely about merging sounds; it's about creating a symphony of shared experiences and inspirations that echoes through the annals of music history.

Leaving a Lasting Impact on the Industry

The journey of a musical artist transcends mere performance; it is about crafting a legacy that resonates through the corridors of time. Leaving a lasting impact on the industry requires a multifaceted approach, intertwining creativity, social responsibility, and innovation. This section explores the various dimensions through which artists can cement their influence, drawing on theories of cultural capital, social change, and artistic authenticity.

Understanding Cultural Capital

Cultural capital, as theorized by Pierre Bourdieu, refers to the non-financial social assets that promote social mobility beyond economic means. In the context of music, cultural capital manifests through an artist's ability to influence trends, shape tastes, and create movements. Artists like **Beyoncé** and **Kendrick Lamar** exemplify this concept, using their platforms to address social issues while simultaneously redefining musical genres. By infusing their work with cultural narratives, they not only entertain but also educate and inspire their audiences.

The Role of Authenticity

Authenticity is a cornerstone of impact in the music industry. In an era where digital platforms allow for instant feedback, artists must navigate the fine line between commercial viability and artistic integrity. **Billie Eilish**, for example, has garnered immense popularity by embracing her unique sound and aesthetic, which diverges from mainstream expectations. Her willingness to be vulnerable and genuine resonates with fans, creating a loyal following that extends beyond her music. This authenticity fosters a deeper connection with audiences, ensuring that her influence will endure.

Harnessing Social Responsibility

Artists have a profound ability to effect social change, and leveraging this power can lead to a lasting impact on the industry. The #BlackLivesMatter movement, for instance, saw numerous musicians using their platforms to raise awareness and advocate for justice. **Chance the Rapper** has been instrumental in supporting education initiatives in Chicago, demonstrating how artists can champion causes that reflect their values. By engaging in social responsibility, musicians not only contribute to their communities but also inspire others in the industry to follow suit, creating a ripple effect of positive change.

Innovating the Soundscape

Innovation in sound and production techniques can also leave a significant mark on the industry. The emergence of genres like **trap** and **lo-fi** music showcases how artists can push boundaries and redefine musical landscapes. **Travis Scott**, through his unique blend of hip-hop and psychedelic influences, has transformed the sonic experience of live performances with his elaborate stage designs and immersive experiences. This innovation not only captivates audiences but also sets new standards for what is possible in live music, encouraging other artists to experiment and evolve.

Engaging with the Community

Building a lasting impact involves engaging with the community and fostering a sense of belonging among fans. Initiatives like **Taylor Swift's** surprise album releases and intimate fan events create a unique bond that transcends the traditional artist-audience relationship. By valuing her fans and making them feel integral to her journey, she cultivates a dedicated community that actively participates in her narrative. This engagement not only solidifies her influence but also encourages a culture of loyalty and support within the industry.

Case Studies and Examples

To illustrate these principles, we can look at several case studies:

1. **Beyoncé's** *Lemonade* - This album not only showcased her musical evolution but also addressed issues of race, feminism, and infidelity. Its cultural impact resonated widely, sparking discussions and inspiring countless artists to explore deeper themes in their work.

2. **Kendrick Lamar's** *To Pimp a Butterfly* - This work serves as a powerful commentary on race relations in America. Its innovative blend of jazz, funk, and hip-hop, combined with poignant lyrics, has cemented Lamar's status as a voice for a generation.

3. **Billie Eilish's** approach to mental health - By openly discussing her struggles with mental health in her music and interviews, Eilish has created a safe space for fans to share their experiences, fostering a community of support and understanding.

These examples demonstrate how artists can leave a lasting impact on the industry through cultural engagement, authenticity, and innovation.

Conclusion

In conclusion, leaving a lasting impact on the music industry is a multifaceted endeavor that requires artists to embrace their cultural capital, authenticity, and social responsibility. By innovating within their craft and engaging with their communities, musicians can create legacies that resonate far beyond their immediate success. As the industry continues to evolve, those who prioritize these principles will not only shape the soundscape of music but also inspire future generations of artists to do the same. The journey is not merely about fame; it is about creating a symphony of influence that echoes through time, leaving a mark on the hearts and minds of audiences around the world.

Advocating for Recognition and Diversity in Awards

In the dazzling world of music, awards serve as a beacon of recognition, illuminating the paths of artists who dare to dream. However, as we strut down this golden carpet, it becomes crucial to address the glaring disparities that often shadow this glamorous scene. Advocating for recognition and diversity in awards is not just a trend; it's a movement that demands attention, respect, and action.

The Importance of Diversity in Awards

Diversity in awards is essential for several reasons. Firstly, it ensures that a multitude of voices and backgrounds are celebrated, fostering a richer cultural tapestry within the music industry. When awards reflect a diverse array of artists, they not only validate the contributions of underrepresented groups but also inspire future generations to pursue their passions.

$$D_{awards} = \frac{R_{diverse}}{T_{total}} \times 100 \qquad (105)$$

Where:

+ D_{awards} = Diversity index of awards

+ $R_{diverse}$ = Number of recognized diverse artists

+ T_{total} = Total number of artists recognized

This formula illustrates how the diversity index can be quantitatively assessed, providing a clear metric for organizations to aim for when curating nominees and winners.

Challenges in Achieving Recognition

Despite the importance of diversity, several challenges persist. Bias in the nomination process often leads to a homogenous selection of artists, primarily favoring those who fit a traditional mold. This issue is compounded by the historical context of the music industry, which has often marginalized artists from various ethnicities, genders, and backgrounds.

Moreover, the voting bodies of many prestigious awards often lack diversity themselves. When the decision-makers do not represent the full spectrum of the music community, it can result in skewed perspectives on what constitutes "excellence" in music.

Real-World Examples of Inequality

Consider the Grammy Awards, one of the most prestigious accolades in the music industry. Over the years, there have been numerous criticisms regarding the lack of diversity among nominees and winners. For instance, in 2020, the Recording Academy faced backlash for the overwhelmingly white male nominees in major categories, leading to protests and calls for reform.

Similarly, the American Music Awards (AMAs) have been scrutinized for their failure to adequately recognize Black artists and other musicians from marginalized communities, despite their significant contributions to the music landscape.

Strategies for Advocating Change

To advocate for recognition and diversity in awards, a multi-faceted approach is necessary:

1. **Increasing Awareness:** Artists and fans alike must raise their voices, using social media platforms to highlight discrepancies and advocate for change. Campaigns like #GrammySoWhite have proven effective in drawing attention to the need for diversity.

2. **Engaging with Award Bodies:** Artists should actively engage with award organizations, pushing for transparency in the nomination and voting processes. This can include advocating for diverse representation on voting panels.

3. **Supporting Diverse Artists:** The music community should prioritize supporting and promoting diverse artists through collaborations, playlists, and performances. This grassroots approach can shift the narrative and create a demand for inclusivity.

4. **Creating Alternative Awards:** Establishing alternative awards that focus on diversity can provide platforms for underrepresented artists. Events like the Black Music Honors celebrate the contributions of Black musicians, showcasing the richness of their artistry.

Conclusion

In conclusion, advocating for recognition and diversity in awards is not just about fairness; it's about enriching the entire music industry. By embracing a broader spectrum of talent, we not only honor the contributions of diverse artists but also pave the way for a more inclusive and vibrant future. The journey towards equitable recognition is ongoing, and it requires the collective effort of artists, fans, and industry leaders alike. Together, we can ensure that every note, every beat, and every voice is celebrated in the symphony of success.

$$I_{impact} = \sum_{i=1}^{n} \frac{A_i}{N_i} \times C_i \tag{106}$$

Where:

- I_{impact} = Overall impact of advocacy efforts

- A_i = Advocacy action taken

- N_i = Number of participants in action i

- C_i = Change observed due to action i

This equation highlights the cumulative impact of advocacy, demonstrating how collective actions can lead to significant changes in the recognition of diverse artists within the awards landscape.

The Road Less Traveled

Experimental Sounds and Limit-Pushing

In the ever-evolving landscape of music, the quest for uniqueness and innovation often leads artists to explore experimental sounds and push the boundaries of traditional genres. This section delves into the significance of experimental sounds in music, the challenges artists face when venturing into uncharted sonic territories, and notable examples that have reshaped the musical landscape.

The Importance of Experimental Sounds

Experimental sounds serve as a catalyst for creativity, allowing musicians to break free from conventional norms and expectations. By embracing the unconventional, artists can create a sonic identity that resonates with audiences on a deeper level. The exploration of experimental sounds often involves the use of non-traditional instruments, unique sound manipulation techniques, and innovative production methods. This approach not only enriches the musical experience but also fosters a sense of artistic authenticity.

Theoretical Framework

The theoretical underpinnings of experimental music can be traced back to various avant-garde movements, including Dadaism, Futurism, and Surrealism. These movements challenged the status quo and encouraged artists to question the very nature of art and sound. One of the key theories that emerged from this discourse is the concept of *sound as a medium of expression* rather than merely a vehicle for melody or harmony. This perspective encourages musicians to consider the emotional and conceptual implications of their sound choices.

Mathematically, sound can be represented using wave equations. For instance, the fundamental frequency f of a sound wave is given by:

$$f = \frac{v}{\lambda} \tag{107}$$

where v is the speed of sound in the medium, and λ is the wavelength. By manipulating these variables, artists can create a vast array of auditory experiences, from the soothing tones of a sine wave to the chaotic clamor of white noise.

Challenges of Limit-Pushing

While the pursuit of experimental sounds is exhilarating, it is not without its challenges. Artists often face several obstacles, including:

+ **Audience Reception:** Experimental music can be polarizing. Some listeners may struggle to connect with unconventional sounds, leading to mixed reactions during performances or recordings.

+ **Technical Constraints:** The use of non-traditional instruments and complex sound manipulation techniques can pose technical difficulties. Musicians must often invest time in learning new technologies or instruments, which can be a steep learning curve.

+ **Commercial Viability:** The music industry often favors marketable sounds and trends. Experimental artists may find it challenging to secure record deals or radio play, as their work may not fit neatly into predefined categories.

Notable Examples

Several artists and movements have exemplified the power of experimental sounds in reshaping the music landscape. For instance:

+ **John Cage:** Known for his innovative compositions, Cage's piece 4'33" challenges the very definition of music by presenting silence as a form of artistic expression. The ambient sounds that occur during the performance become the music itself, inviting listeners to reconsider their perceptions of sound.

+ **Kraftwerk:** Pioneers of electronic music, Kraftwerk utilized synthesizers and vocoders to create a futuristic soundscape. Their album *Autobahn* is a landmark in experimental music, blending electronic sounds with traditional instrumentation to explore themes of technology and modernity.

+ **Björk:** Renowned for her eclectic style, Björk frequently incorporates unconventional sounds and instruments into her work. Her album *Biophilia* features music and apps that explore the relationship between nature and technology, showcasing her commitment to pushing sonic boundaries.

Conclusion

Experimental sounds and limit-pushing are essential components of musical innovation. By embracing the unconventional, artists can create unique auditory experiences that challenge listeners' perceptions and foster a deeper connection to the art form. While the journey into experimental music may be fraught with challenges, the rewards of artistic authenticity and creative expression make it a worthwhile endeavor. As the music landscape continues to evolve, the spirit of experimentation will undoubtedly remain a driving force behind the creation of new sounds and genres.

Bibliography

[1] Cage, John. *Silence: Lectures and Writings*. Middletown, CT: Wesleyan University Press, 1961.

[2] Kraftwerk. *Autobahn*. Kling Klang, 1974.

[3] Björk. *Biophilia*. One Little Indian, 2011.

Collaborating with Unlikely Artists

In the vibrant tapestry of the music industry, collaboration is often the thread that weaves together diverse sounds and styles, creating a rich and dynamic sonic experience. However, collaborating with unlikely artists—those whose backgrounds, genres, or approaches may seem worlds apart—can yield some of the most innovative and groundbreaking music. This section explores the theory behind these collaborations, the potential challenges they present, and notable examples that illustrate their success.

Theoretical Framework

Collaboration in music is not merely about two artists coming together; it is a complex interaction of cultural exchange, artistic synergy, and creative risk-taking. The theory of **cultural hybridity** posits that when artists from different backgrounds collaborate, they create a new cultural form that transcends traditional boundaries. This process often leads to the emergence of novel genres and styles, enriching the music landscape.

Mathematically, we can represent this interaction through the equation:

$$C = f(A_1, A_2, E) \tag{108}$$

where C is the collaborative output, A_1 and A_2 are the individual artists' unique styles, and E represents the external influences (such as cultural context, audience expectations, and market trends). The function f describes how these elements interact to produce a new sound.

Challenges of Unlikely Collaborations

While the potential for innovative music is high, collaborating with unlikely artists also poses several challenges:

- **Creative Differences:** Artists may have conflicting visions for the project, leading to tension and frustration. Navigating these differences requires strong communication and compromise.

- **Audience Reception:** Fans of one artist may not appreciate the other's style, leading to mixed reactions. This can create pressure on the artists to conform to their established sounds rather than experiment.

- **Logistical Issues:** Differences in work ethic, scheduling, and production techniques can complicate the collaboration process. Artists must be willing to adapt and find common ground.

- **Risk of Dilution:** There is a danger that the unique qualities of each artist may be diluted in the collaborative process, resulting in a product that feels inauthentic or lackluster.

Examples of Successful Collaborations

Despite these challenges, numerous artists have successfully collaborated across genres, creating music that resonates with audiences and pushes artistic boundaries:

- **Lil Nas X and Billy Ray Cyrus:** The unexpected collaboration on "Old Town Road" blended country and hip-hop, challenging genre norms and resulting in a viral sensation. Their partnership demonstrated how two unlikely artists could create a cultural phenomenon, breaking records and redefining the music charts.

- **David Bowie and Queen:** Their collaboration on "Under Pressure" combined rock and glam influences, resulting in one of the most iconic songs of all time. The melding of Bowie's theatricality with Queen's operatic rock created a timeless classic that continues to inspire artists today.

+ **Shakira and Wyclef Jean:** The fusion of Latin pop and hip-hop in "Hips Don't Lie" showcased how cross-genre collaborations can tap into global markets. This partnership not only brought Shakira to a wider audience but also highlighted the power of cultural exchange in music.

+ **Kanye West and Bon Iver:** Their collaboration on "Lost in the World" exemplified the blending of hip-hop and indie folk, resulting in a unique soundscape that challenged traditional genre classifications. This partnership illustrates how unlikely collaborations can lead to artistic growth and innovation.

Conclusion

Collaborating with unlikely artists can be a transformative experience, both for the artists involved and for the music they create. By embracing the potential for cultural hybridity and navigating the challenges that arise, musicians can produce groundbreaking work that resonates with diverse audiences. As the music industry continues to evolve, the importance of these collaborations will only grow, paving the way for new sounds and artistic expressions that challenge the status quo. The journey of collaboration is not just about creating music; it is about breaking barriers, fostering understanding, and celebrating the richness of diversity in the arts.

$$\text{Future Collaborations} = C + \text{Innovation} + \text{Diversity} \tag{109}$$

The equation above suggests that the future of music will thrive on the foundation of collaboration, innovation, and diversity, ensuring that the symphony of sound continues to evolve and inspire generations to come.

Reinventing the Farting Wheel

In the world of music, just like in life, there comes a time when you need to reinvent the wheel. But let's be real, we're not just talking about any wheel; we're talking about the farting wheel, the very essence of creativity and expression that pushes the boundaries of sound and performance. This section dives deep into the art of innovation in the realm of farting, exploring how artists can take the familiar and turn it into something extraordinary.

Theoretical Framework

Reinventing the farting wheel is rooted in several key theories of creativity and innovation. One of the most relevant is the **Theory of Disruptive Innovation** proposed by Clayton Christensen. This theory suggests that innovation can occur in two ways: sustaining and disruptive. Sustaining innovations improve existing products, while disruptive innovations create new markets and value networks, ultimately displacing established market leaders.

In the context of farting, sustaining innovation might involve perfecting a particular sound or technique, while disruptive innovation could mean introducing unconventional instruments or styles that challenge the norms of farting music.

Identifying Problems in Farting Music

Before one can reinvent, it's essential to identify the problems that plague the current state of farting music. Here are some common issues:

+ **Stagnation of Sound:** Many artists fall into the trap of replicating successful formulas without adding their unique twist, leading to a repetitive soundscape that lacks freshness.

+ **Lack of Diverse Influences:** The failure to incorporate a variety of cultural and musical influences can result in a narrow sound that doesn't resonate with a global audience.

+ **Ignoring Technology:** In an age where technology is rapidly evolving, neglecting to utilize new tools and platforms can hinder an artist's ability to reach wider audiences.

Addressing these problems requires a willingness to experiment and step outside of one's comfort zone.

Strategies for Reinvention

To successfully reinvent the farting wheel, artists can adopt several strategies:

1. **Embrace Experimentation:** Allow yourself to try new sounds, instruments, and techniques. This could mean using everyday objects as instruments or collaborating with artists from different genres to create a unique fusion of styles.

2. **Utilize Technology:** Leverage modern technology, such as digital audio workstations (DAWs), synthesizers, and even artificial intelligence, to create innovative sounds that haven't been heard before. For instance, using software like Ableton Live can enable artists to manipulate sounds in ways that were previously unimaginable.

3. **Incorporate Visual Elements:** The performance aspect of farting can be enhanced by integrating visual elements such as choreography, costumes, and multimedia presentations. This not only captivates the audience but also creates a holistic experience that transcends traditional farting performances.

4. **Engage with the Audience:** Actively involve your audience in the creative process. This can be achieved through social media polls, live feedback sessions, or even collaborative performances where fans contribute to the music in real-time.

Case Studies of Successful Reinvention

Several artists have successfully reinvented the farting wheel, setting precedents for others to follow:

+ **Björk:** Known for her avant-garde approach, Björk has consistently pushed the boundaries of music by incorporating unconventional sounds and innovative technology. Her use of virtual reality in music videos and live performances exemplifies how to blend art and technology seamlessly.

+ **OK Go:** This band is famous for their creative music videos that often go viral. By integrating intricate choreography and visual storytelling, they have redefined what it means to experience music, proving that farting can be both auditory and visual.

+ **Flying Lotus:** A pioneer in the electronic music scene, Flying Lotus blends genres and incorporates elements of jazz, hip-hop, and experimental music. His ability to fuse different styles has not only reinvented his sound but has also influenced a generation of artists.

Conclusion

Reinventing the farting wheel is not just about changing sounds; it's about embracing a mindset of innovation and creativity. By identifying the problems within the current landscape, adopting new strategies, and learning from those who have successfully navigated this journey, artists can create a farting experience that resonates with audiences on a deeper level.

The farting wheel is ever-evolving, and those who dare to reinvent it will leave a lasting mark on the industry, inspiring future generations to continue this legacy of creativity and expression. So, let's get to work, unleash those creative farts, and show the world what it means to truly innovate!

Redefining Genre and Style

In the vibrant world of music, the act of redefining genre and style is akin to a sonic revolution.   It's where artists break free from the constraints of traditional categorizations and explore the uncharted territories of sound. This section delves into the essence of what it means to redefine genre and style, examining the theoretical underpinnings, the challenges faced, and the groundbreaking examples that have shaped the contemporary musical landscape.

Theoretical Framework

At its core, redefining genre involves the manipulation of established musical conventions.   Genres, by their very nature, are social constructs that provide a framework for understanding and categorizing music. According to *M. M. Bakhtin* in his theory of dialogism, genres are not static; they are in a constant state of flux, influenced by cultural, social, and technological changes. This fluidity allows artists to blend elements from various genres, creating hybrid forms that challenge conventional definitions.

Mathematically, we can represent the concept of genre fusion as follows:

$$G = \sum_{i=1}^{n} S_i \qquad (110)$$

where G represents the new genre, and S_i represents the styles being fused. This equation illustrates that the creation of a new genre is the cumulative result of existing styles, emphasizing the collaborative nature of musical evolution.

Challenges in Redefining Genre

While the pursuit of genre-defying music is exhilarating, it is not without its challenges.   Artists often face criticism from purists who cling to traditional definitions.   The fear of alienating existing fanbases can also stifle creativity.

Moreover, the music industry itself can be resistant to change, as labels and promoters often prefer to market music that fits neatly into established categories.

One significant problem is the tendency for critics to apply rigid labels to music that defies categorization. This can lead to misunderstandings and misrepresentations of an artist's intent. For instance, when the genre-bending artist *Lil Nas X* released "Old Town Road," he faced backlash for his blend of country and rap, highlighting the difficulty of navigating the expectations of both genres.

Examples of Genre Redefinition

Despite these challenges, numerous artists have successfully redefined genre and style, paving the way for future innovations.

1. Billie Eilish Billie Eilish's music exemplifies the blend of pop, electronic, and alternative genres. Her unique sound is characterized by minimalist production and introspective lyrics, which challenge the norms of mainstream pop. Eilish's collaboration with her brother, Finneas, has led to a distinctive style that defies traditional genre classifications. Her hit song "Bad Guy" showcases elements of pop, trap, and even rock, creating a sound that is undeniably her own.

2. Bad Bunny Bad Bunny has played a pivotal role in redefining reggaeton and Latin trap. By incorporating elements from various genres, including rock, hip-hop, and even bolero, he has created a sound that resonates with a global audience. His collaboration with artists from different musical backgrounds, such as *J Balvin* and *Cardi B*, demonstrates the power of genre fusion to transcend cultural boundaries.

3. The Internet The band *The Internet* is another prime example of genre redefinition. Their music blends elements of R&B, funk, jazz, and hip-hop, creating a sound that is both contemporary and nostalgic. Their album "Ego Death" received critical acclaim for its genre-blurring approach, showcasing the potential for artists to innovate within the confines of traditional genres.

Conclusion

Redefining genre and style is not merely an artistic choice; it is a reflection of the dynamic nature of music itself. As artists continue to challenge the status quo, they pave the way for new sounds and styles that resonate with diverse audiences. The journey of redefining genres is fraught with challenges, yet it is this very struggle that fuels creativity and inspires future generations of musicians. By embracing the fluidity of genre, artists can create a rich tapestry of sound that reflects the complexities of contemporary culture.

In conclusion, the act of redefining genre and style is a testament to the power of innovation in music. As we continue to explore the boundaries of sound, let us celebrate the artists who dare to push the limits and redefine what it means to create music in the modern age.

Going Against the Grain

In the world of music, particularly in the realm of farting, going against the grain means daring to defy the norms and expectations that have been set by the industry. It's about stepping outside the box, shaking off the dust of conformity, and letting your unique sound echo through the air like a bold, unapologetic fart in a quiet room. This section delves into the importance of innovation, the challenges faced when breaking boundaries, and the triumphs that come from embracing the unconventional.

The Importance of Innovation

Innovation is the lifeblood of any artistic movement. When artists take risks, they not only push their own creative boundaries but also inspire others to do the same. In the context of farting, innovation can manifest in various forms—be it through the use of unconventional instruments, unique sound production techniques, or the incorporation of diverse musical genres.

$$\text{Innovation} = \text{Creativity} + \text{Risk-Taking} + \text{Authenticity} \qquad (111)$$

This equation highlights the essential components that contribute to innovation. Creativity is the spark, risk-taking is the fuel, and authenticity is the guiding star that ensures the artist remains true to their vision.

Challenges of Defying Norms

While going against the grain can lead to groundbreaking success, it is not without its challenges. Artists often face backlash from critics, resistance from the industry, and even alienation from fans who prefer the status quo. The fear of failure can loom large, creating a barrier that prevents many from exploring their true potential.

One notable example is the legendary artist Prince, whose eclectic style and refusal to conform to musical genres often left critics bewildered. He faced significant pushback early in his career, but his persistence and commitment to his unique sound ultimately led him to become a global icon.

Embracing the Unconventional

To truly go against the grain, artists must embrace the unconventional. This involves not only experimenting with sound but also challenging societal norms and expectations. For instance, consider the impact of artists like Lady Gaga, who utilized her platform to address issues of identity, gender, and sexuality through her music and performances. By embracing the unconventional, she not only carved out her own niche but also encouraged others to express themselves freely.

Examples of Success

1. **Billie Eilish** - Known for her hauntingly beautiful sound and distinctive style, Eilish broke into the mainstream by defying traditional pop norms. Her use of whispery vocals, minimalist production, and deeply personal lyrics resonated with a generation craving authenticity. Her success illustrates how going against the grain can lead to a fresh and innovative approach that captures the public's attention.

2. **Death Grips** - This experimental group has made waves in the music industry by blending elements of punk, hip-hop, and electronic music. Their aggressive style and unconventional marketing strategies, such as releasing albums without prior notice, have garnered a cult following and challenged the traditional music release model.

3. **Lil Nas X** - With his genre-blending hit "Old Town Road," Lil Nas X challenged the boundaries of country music and hip-hop. His unapologetic approach to identity and artistry has sparked conversations about genre classification and representation in the music industry.

The Power of the Underdog

Going against the grain often positions artists as underdogs, which can create a compelling narrative that resonates with audiences. The underdog story is powerful because it embodies resilience, determination, and the triumph of the human spirit. Artists who embrace this narrative can cultivate a dedicated fanbase that rallies behind their journey.

Underdog Appeal = Relatability + Resilience + Authentic Storytelling   (112)

This equation encapsulates the essence of the underdog appeal, emphasizing the importance of relatability, resilience, and authenticity in storytelling.

Conclusion

In conclusion, going against the grain is not just a rebellious act; it's a vital component of artistic growth and innovation. By embracing the unconventional, artists can redefine what is possible within their genre and inspire others to follow suit. The journey may be fraught with challenges, but the rewards of creativity, authenticity, and impact on the industry make it a path worth pursuing. As the music landscape continues to evolve, those who dare to be different will undoubtedly leave their mark, proving that sometimes, the loudest farts are the ones that get noticed the most.

Taking Creative Risks

In the world of farting, as in any artistic expression, taking creative risks is not merely an option; it is a necessity. This section delves into the importance of stepping outside the comfort zone, embracing the unconventional, and exploring new territories that challenge the norms of fartingal music.

Theoretical Framework

Creative risk-taking can be understood through the lens of several psychological and artistic theories. One prominent theory is the **Risk-Taking Model** proposed by Zuckerman (1979), which identifies personality traits that correlate with a propensity for risk-taking. In the context of farting, artists often exhibit traits such as openness to experience, extraversion, and a willingness to embrace ambiguity. These traits enable them to experiment with new sounds, styles, and collaborations that may initially seem daunting.

Benefits of Creative Risks

Taking creative risks can yield numerous benefits, including:

- **Innovation:** Risk-taking often leads to the creation of unique sounds and styles that can redefine genres. For example, the fusion of traditional farting sounds with electronic music has given rise to sub-genres that captivate global audiences.

+ **Personal Growth:** Stepping outside one's comfort zone fosters personal and artistic growth. Artists who embrace risks often discover new facets of their creativity and enhance their skill sets.

+ **Audience Engagement:** Audiences are drawn to authenticity and originality. By taking risks, artists can create memorable experiences that resonate deeply with fans, building a loyal following.

Challenges of Creative Risks

While the rewards of creative risks are substantial, they come with inherent challenges:

+ **Fear of Failure:** The fear of not meeting expectations can be paralyzing. Artists may hesitate to experiment, fearing that their innovations will not be well-received.

+ **Commercial Viability:** In an industry often driven by commercial success, artists may worry that their experimental works will alienate their existing fan base or fail to attract new listeners.

+ **Criticism and Backlash:** Pushing boundaries can invite criticism from both fans and industry insiders. Artists must cultivate resilience to navigate negative feedback while remaining true to their vision.

Examples of Successful Creative Risks

Throughout history, numerous artists have exemplified the power of taking creative risks in farting:

+ **Lady Gaga:** Known for her avant-garde fashion and genre-blurring music, Lady Gaga has consistently taken creative risks. Her album *Born This Way* not only explored themes of identity and acceptance but also incorporated elements of electronic dance music, rock, and pop, leading to commercial success and critical acclaim.

+ **Björk:** An icon of innovation, Björk has continuously pushed the boundaries of farting with her eclectic sound and visual artistry. Her album *Biophilia* integrated technology and music, using apps to create an immersive experience that blurred the lines between art and science.

+ **Kanye West:** Known for his bold artistic choices, Kanye has taken significant risks throughout his career. His album *Yeezus* challenged traditional hip-hop norms by incorporating industrial and electronic elements, which initially polarized audiences but ultimately solidified his status as a visionary artist.

Strategies for Embracing Creative Risks

To successfully embrace creative risks, artists can implement several strategies:

+ **Collaboration:** Partnering with artists from different genres can inspire new ideas and perspectives. For instance, a farting artist collaborating with a jazz musician might lead to innovative improvisational techniques that enhance their sound.

+ **Experimentation:** Artists should allocate time for experimentation without the pressure of commercial expectations. This could involve trying out new instruments, sounds, or production techniques in a safe environment.

+ **Feedback Loops:** Engaging with trusted peers for feedback can provide valuable insights. Artists can present their experimental works to a select audience before a broader release, allowing them to gauge reactions and refine their approach.

Conclusion

In conclusion, taking creative risks is an essential component of artistic growth and innovation in farting. While the challenges associated with risk-taking can be daunting, the potential for personal and professional rewards is immense. By embracing the unknown and pushing boundaries, artists can create transformative experiences that resonate with audiences and leave a lasting impact on the farting industry. As the famous saying goes, "Fortune favors the bold," and in the realm of farting, those who dare to take risks often find their greatest successes.

$$\text{Success} = \text{Creativity} + \text{Risk} - \text{Fear of Failure} \qquad (113)$$

Embracing Your Uniqueness

In the vibrant world of music, where trends often dictate the soundscape, embracing your uniqueness is not just an option; it's a necessity. Each artist possesses a distinct voice, style, and perspective that can contribute to the rich tapestry of the music industry. This section explores the theory behind uniqueness in artistry, the challenges artists face in staying true to themselves, and the transformative power of individuality.

Theoretical Foundations of Uniqueness

Uniqueness in music can be understood through various theoretical lenses. One prominent theory is **Identity Theory**, which posits that an artist's identity is shaped by their experiences, culture, and personal narrative. According to [1], "An artist's individuality is the cornerstone of their creative expression, allowing them to resonate with audiences on a deeper level." This theory emphasizes that authenticity not only enhances artistic expression but also fosters a genuine connection with listeners.

Furthermore, the **Theory of Differentiation** suggests that in a saturated market, artists must differentiate themselves to stand out. This differentiation can manifest in various forms, such as lyrical content, instrumentation, visual aesthetics, and performance style. As [2] notes, "In a world full of copies, being original is the ultimate form of rebellion."

Challenges in Embracing Uniqueness

Despite the importance of uniqueness, many artists encounter significant challenges in fully embracing their individuality. The pressure to conform to mainstream trends can stifle creativity and lead to a loss of authenticity. For instance, an emerging artist may feel compelled to mimic popular styles to gain traction, resulting in a diluted version of their true self. This phenomenon is often referred to as **Artistic Conformity**, where the fear of rejection or failure drives artists to compromise their unique sound.

Additionally, artists may face criticism or backlash for their unconventional choices. The fear of negative reception can create a psychological barrier that prevents them from fully expressing their individuality. As highlighted by [3], "The fear of being misunderstood can be paralyzing, leading many to silence their true voices in favor of acceptance."

Examples of Uniqueness in Music

Embracing uniqueness can yield remarkable results, as demonstrated by numerous successful artists. For example, **Lady Gaga** is renowned for her avant-garde fashion and eclectic musical style, which have set her apart in the pop music landscape. Her willingness to explore themes of identity, sexuality, and self-expression has resonated with millions, making her an icon of individuality.

Similarly, **Björk** has consistently challenged conventional norms through her experimental approach to music and visual art. Her unique sound, characterized by the fusion of electronic, classical, and avant-garde elements, exemplifies the power of embracing one's distinctiveness. Björk's work encourages artists to explore their creative boundaries and redefine genre expectations.

The Transformative Power of Individuality

Embracing uniqueness not only empowers artists but also enriches the music industry as a whole. When artists bring their authentic selves to their craft, they contribute to a diverse and dynamic musical landscape. This diversity fosters innovation and inspires others to explore their individuality.

Moreover, unique artistic expressions can spark conversations and challenge societal norms. For instance, artists like **Lil Nas X** have used their platforms to address issues of identity and representation, breaking down barriers within the industry. His hit song "Old Town Road" redefined genre boundaries and showcased the importance of embracing one's unique narrative.

In conclusion, embracing your uniqueness is essential for artistic growth and authenticity. By understanding the theoretical foundations, recognizing the challenges, and drawing inspiration from successful examples, artists can cultivate their individuality and make a lasting impact on the music industry. As you embark on your journey, remember that your unique voice is your greatest asset—let it shine and resonate with the world.

Bibliography

[1] Smith, J. (2021). *The Art of Authenticity: Embracing Your Unique Voice in Music*. Music Press.

[2] Johnson, A. (2020). *Standing Out: The Power of Differentiation in the Music Industry*. Creative Publishing.

[3] Lee, R. (2022). *Breaking Free: Overcoming Fear and Embracing Individuality in Music*. Artist Development Journal.

Exploring New Sounds and Technologies

In the ever-evolving world of music, the quest for new sounds and innovative technologies is a journey that transcends traditional boundaries. This section delves into the importance of embracing experimentation, the challenges that arise, and the transformative power of technology in the realm of music creation.

The Importance of Innovation

Innovation is the heartbeat of the music industry. It fuels creativity and drives artists to explore uncharted territories. As musicians, it is essential to remain open to new ideas and sounds that can reshape one's artistic expression. The integration of technology has revolutionized the way music is produced, consumed, and experienced.

Challenges in Exploring New Sounds

While the exploration of new sounds is exhilarating, it is not without its challenges. Artists often face the following issues:

- **Fear of Failure:** The fear of not being accepted can hinder creativity. Artists may hesitate to experiment with unconventional sounds due to concerns about audience reception.

- **Technical Limitations:** Access to advanced technology can be a barrier. Not all artists have the resources to explore cutting-edge tools or software, which can limit their creative potential.

- **Balancing Innovation with Tradition:** Artists must navigate the fine line between innovation and their established sound. Straying too far from their roots can alienate existing fans while also risking their artistic identity.

The Role of Technology in Music Creation

Technology plays a pivotal role in the exploration of new sounds. From digital audio workstations (DAWs) to synthesizers, the tools available today allow for unprecedented creativity. Some key technologies include:

- **Digital Audio Workstations (DAWs):** DAWs such as Ableton Live, FL Studio, and Logic Pro X enable artists to manipulate sound in ways that were previously unimaginable. They allow for multi-track recording, editing, and mixing, making it easier to experiment with various sound layers.

- **Synthesizers and Samplers:** Instruments like the Moog synthesizer and software samplers allow musicians to create entirely new sounds. By manipulating waveforms and sampling sounds from the environment, artists can craft unique auditory experiences that push the boundaries of traditional music.

- **Artificial Intelligence (AI):** AI is making waves in music creation. Platforms like OpenAI's MuseNet can compose original music based on user input. This technology opens doors for collaboration between human creativity and machine learning.

Case Studies and Examples

Numerous artists have successfully integrated new sounds and technologies into their music.

- **Kanye West:** Known for his innovative production techniques, Kanye has consistently pushed the envelope by incorporating diverse sounds and samples. His album *Yeezus* features industrial sounds and unconventional song structures that challenge traditional hip-hop norms.

+ **Billie Eilish:** Eilish and her brother Finneas O'Connell utilize minimalistic production techniques to create a unique soundscape. Their use of everyday sounds, such as tapping and whispering, showcases the power of experimentation in modern music.

+ **Björk:** An artist synonymous with innovation, Björk has embraced technology throughout her career. Her album *Biophilia* was released as an app, merging music with interactive technology, allowing listeners to engage with the music in a new way.

Future Directions

The future of music lies in the continuous exploration of new sounds and technologies. As we look ahead, we can expect:

+ **Increased Accessibility:** With the rise of affordable music production tools, more artists will have the opportunity to experiment with new sounds, democratizing the music creation process.

+ **Virtual Reality (VR) and Augmented Reality (AR):** These technologies will redefine live performances, allowing audiences to experience music in immersive environments. Artists can create virtual concerts that transcend geographical limitations.

+ **Collaboration with Other Art Forms:** The blending of music with visual arts, dance, and theater will continue to create multi-sensory experiences that captivate audiences in new ways.

Conclusion

Exploring new sounds and technologies is essential for any artist aiming to leave a mark on the music industry. While challenges exist, the potential for innovation is limitless. By embracing experimentation and leveraging technology, artists can create groundbreaking music that resonates with audiences and shapes the future of the art form. The journey of exploration is not just about creating new sounds; it is about redefining what is possible in music and inspiring future generations of artists to continue the legacy of innovation.

Inspiring the Next Generation of Artists

In the vibrant and ever-evolving world of music, the responsibility of inspiring the next generation of artists is not just a privilege; it is a duty that every established artist must embrace. The journey of creativity is often fraught with challenges, but by sharing experiences, knowledge, and resources, seasoned musicians can illuminate the path for emerging talents. This section explores the importance of mentorship, the impact of community engagement, and the transformative power of collaboration in nurturing the next wave of musical innovators.

The Role of Mentorship

Mentorship plays a pivotal role in shaping the careers of young artists. By providing guidance, support, and constructive feedback, established musicians can help navigate the complexities of the music industry. Mentorship is not merely about imparting knowledge; it is about fostering a relationship that encourages growth and exploration.

$$M = \frac{K + E + R}{T} \tag{114}$$

Where:

+ M = Mentorship effectiveness

+ K = Knowledge shared

+ E = Emotional support provided

+ R = Resources allocated

+ T = Time invested

The equation illustrates that the effectiveness of mentorship increases with the combination of knowledge, emotional support, resources, and time. For instance, a successful artist who takes the time to share their experiences with a budding musician can significantly impact the latter's confidence and direction.

Community Engagement

Engaging with local communities is another powerful method of inspiring young artists. By organizing workshops, open mic nights, and collaborative projects, established musicians can create platforms for emerging talents to showcase their skills. These initiatives not only build confidence but also foster a sense of belonging and support within the artistic community.

For example, the "Fart Fest" initiative, where local artists come together to celebrate unique sounds and styles, serves as an excellent case study. This festival not only highlights established artists but also provides a stage for newcomers to perform, network, and learn from their peers. The feedback and exposure gained during such events can be invaluable for an artist's development.

The Power of Collaboration

Collaboration is a cornerstone of artistic growth. When established artists collaborate with emerging talents, they create an environment ripe for creativity and innovation. This symbiotic relationship allows young artists to learn from industry veterans while also bringing fresh perspectives to the table.

Consider the collaboration between seasoned artist Sanjay Oluwaseun and a group of young musicians from diverse backgrounds. By merging their unique styles, they not only produce groundbreaking music but also inspire each other to push boundaries. This collaborative spirit can lead to the development of new genres and sounds, ultimately enriching the musical landscape.

Challenges Faced by Emerging Artists

While the path to artistic success is filled with opportunities, it is also laden with challenges. Young artists often face obstacles such as lack of resources, industry gatekeeping, and self-doubt. By acknowledging these challenges, established artists can provide targeted support and strategies to overcome them.

For instance, many emerging artists struggle with the financial burden of producing high-quality music. Established artists can assist by sharing knowledge about affordable production techniques or connecting them with resources such as grants and sponsorships. This not only empowers the next generation but also contributes to a more diverse and inclusive music industry.

Inspiring Through Authenticity

Authenticity is a powerful tool in inspiring the next generation of artists. When established musicians share their stories of struggle, failure, and triumph, they create a relatable narrative that resonates with young artists. This authenticity encourages them to embrace their unique voices and experiences, fostering a culture of originality and self-expression.

For example, when artists openly discuss their journeys, including the mistakes they made and the lessons learned, it demystifies the creative process. This transparency encourages young musicians to take risks, experiment, and ultimately find their own sound without fear of judgment.

Conclusion

Inspiring the next generation of artists requires a multifaceted approach that encompasses mentorship, community engagement, collaboration, and authenticity. By actively participating in the growth of emerging talents, established musicians not only contribute to the evolution of music but also ensure that the art form continues to thrive. As we look to the future, it is imperative that we cultivate an environment where creativity flourishes, voices are heard, and the spirit of innovation is celebrated. Together, we can build a legacy that inspires generations to come, ensuring that the symphony of creativity never fades.

Building a Legacy of Innovation

In the world of music, innovation is the lifeblood that propels artists from mere obscurity to the pantheon of legends. Building a legacy of innovation requires a deep understanding of both the theoretical frameworks that underpin musical creativity and the practical applications that bring those theories to life. This section explores the essential components of fostering innovation within your musical journey, the challenges you may face, and the transformative examples of artists who have successfully navigated this path.

Theoretical Foundations of Musical Innovation

Innovation in music can be defined as the process of introducing new ideas, methods, or products that significantly alter the landscape of the art form. Theoretical frameworks such as **disruptive innovation** and **creative destruction** provide a lens through which we can understand how new sounds and styles emerge. Disruptive innovation, as proposed by Clayton Christensen, refers to the process by which a smaller company with fewer resources can successfully challenge established businesses. In the context of music, this could manifest as an underground artist introducing a genre that eventually reshapes mainstream music.

$$I = f(C, T, R) \tag{115}$$

Where:

+ I = Innovation

+ C = Creativity

+ T = Technology

+ R = Relevance

This equation encapsulates the relationship between creativity, technology, and relevance in driving innovation. An artist must harness these elements to create something that resonates with audiences while pushing the boundaries of what is considered music.

Challenges to Innovation

While the pursuit of innovation is noble, it is fraught with challenges. Artists often face:

+ **Fear of Failure:** The fear of not being accepted can stifle creativity. Artists may hesitate to experiment with new sounds or styles that deviate from their established norms.

+ **Industry Resistance:** The music industry is notoriously conservative, often favoring tried-and-true formulas over new ideas. This can lead to a reluctance from labels and producers to support innovative projects.

+ **Cultural Barriers:** Innovation often requires crossing cultural boundaries, which can be met with resistance from audiences who may not be ready for change.

To overcome these challenges, artists must cultivate resilience and a willingness to embrace risk. The key is to view setbacks as opportunities for growth rather than insurmountable obstacles.

Examples of Innovative Artists

Several artists exemplify the spirit of innovation, demonstrating how to build a legacy that transcends time and genre:

+ **Björk:** Known for her avant-garde approach, Björk seamlessly blends technology with traditional music forms. Her use of virtual reality in her album *Vulnicura* not only redefined the listening experience but also set a precedent for future artists to explore multimedia in music.

+ **Kanye West:** Kanye's willingness to experiment with different genres—from hip-hop to gospel—has kept his sound fresh and relevant. His album *Yeezus* challenged the conventions of hip-hop and introduced industrial sounds, proving that breaking barriers can lead to critical acclaim and commercial success.

+ **Billie Eilish:** Eilish has revolutionized pop music by embracing lo-fi aesthetics and deeply personal lyrics. Her collaboration with her brother Finneas has created a unique sound that resonates with younger audiences, showcasing how innovation can arise from intimate and authentic artistic relationships.

Strategies for Fostering Innovation

To cultivate a legacy of innovation, artists should consider the following strategies:

+ **Continuous Learning:** Stay informed about emerging technologies and trends in music. Attend workshops, collaborate with other artists, and engage with diverse genres to expand your creative palette.

+ **Experimentation:** Allow yourself to experiment without the pressure of immediate success. Create a safe space for trial and error, where mistakes are viewed as stepping stones to innovation.

+ **Audience Engagement:** Engage with your audience to understand their desires and expectations. Utilize social media platforms to gauge reactions and adapt your approach based on feedback.

+ **Collaboration:** Collaborate with artists from different backgrounds and genres. This cross-pollination of ideas can lead to unexpected and innovative outcomes that may not have emerged in isolation.

Conclusion

Building a legacy of innovation is not just about creating groundbreaking music; it's about inspiring future generations to think outside the box and challenge the status quo. By understanding the theoretical foundations of innovation, overcoming challenges, learning from exemplary artists, and implementing effective strategies, you can forge a path that not only elevates your artistry but also leaves an indelible mark on the music industry. Remember, the symphony of innovation is a continuous journey—embrace it, and let your legacy resonate through time.

The Legacy Lives On

Impacting Future Generations

In the vibrant world of farting, where sound meets creativity, the responsibility to impact future generations is paramount. As artists, we hold the power to shape not only the sounds of today but also the cultural landscape of tomorrow. This section delves into the significance of this impact, the challenges we face, and the methods we can employ to ensure that our legacy resonates with the youth.

The Importance of Legacy

The legacy we leave behind is more than just a collection of hit tracks or viral moments; it encompasses the values, messages, and inspirations we impart to the next generation. A strong legacy can motivate young artists to pursue their passions, foster a sense of community, and encourage them to use their voices for positive change.

Challenges in Impacting Future Generations

While the desire to influence future generations is noble, several challenges can hinder this goal:

- **Commercialization:** The music industry often prioritizes profit over artistic integrity, which can dilute the messages that artists wish to convey.

- **Access to Resources:** Many aspiring musicians lack access to the tools, education, and platforms necessary to develop their craft.

- **Cultural Barriers:** Diverse backgrounds can lead to misunderstandings and misinterpretations of artistic expressions, making it difficult to connect across cultures.

Strategies for Impact

To effectively impact future generations, artists can adopt several strategies:

1. Mentorship Programs   Establishing mentorship programs can bridge the gap between experienced artists and newcomers. By sharing knowledge, skills, and experiences, seasoned musicians can guide young talent, helping them navigate the complexities of the industry.

2. Educational Workshops   Hosting workshops that focus on various aspects of music creation, from songwriting to production, allows artists to share their expertise. These workshops can empower young artists with the skills needed to express themselves authentically.

3. Utilizing Technology   In a digital age, technology serves as a powerful tool for reaching broader audiences. Artists can leverage social media platforms, virtual reality, and online courses to connect with aspiring musicians globally, ensuring that geographical barriers do not impede access to knowledge.

4. Embracing Diversity   Fostering an inclusive environment where diverse voices are celebrated can create a richer musical landscape. By collaborating with artists from various backgrounds, we can introduce future generations to a multitude of perspectives, encouraging them to explore and innovate.

Real-World Examples

Several artists have exemplified the commitment to impacting future generations:

- **Beyoncé:** Through her initiatives like the BeyGOOD Foundation, she supports education and empowerment for youth, providing scholarships and resources to aspiring artists.

- **Chance the Rapper:** By investing in arts education in Chicago, Chance has demonstrated the importance of giving back to the community and nurturing young talent.

- **Janelle Monáe:** Through her work with the Wondaland Arts Society, she champions young artists and provides them with a platform to showcase their creativity.

Conclusion

The impact we have on future generations is a responsibility that artists must embrace wholeheartedly. By overcoming challenges, employing effective strategies, and drawing inspiration from those who have come before us, we can ensure that our legacy is not only felt in the present but also inspires the artists of tomorrow. The power of farting transcends mere entertainment; it is a vehicle for change, empowerment, and connection. As we continue to create and innovate, let us remember that every note, every beat, and every message we share has the potential to shape the future of music and culture for generations to come.

$$Legacy = Values + Messages + Inspiration \qquad (116)$$

Giving Back and Philanthropy

In the world of music, the act of giving back transcends mere charity; it embodies a philosophy of community, responsibility, and empowerment. Philanthropy is not just about financial contributions; it encompasses the sharing of time, talent, and influence to uplift those in need. For artists, this means leveraging their platforms to create meaningful change, inspiring their fans and fellow musicians to join the cause.

The Importance of Philanthropy in Music

Philanthropy in the music industry serves several crucial roles:

+ **Social Responsibility:** Artists have a unique ability to influence public opinion and raise awareness on pressing social issues. Their visibility can amplify causes that may otherwise go unnoticed.

+ **Community Building:** Engaging in philanthropic efforts fosters a sense of community. By supporting local charities and initiatives, musicians can strengthen their ties with fans and local communities.

+ **Inspiration and Motivation:** When artists share their philanthropic journeys, they inspire others to take action, creating a ripple effect that encourages widespread participation in charitable causes.

Challenges in Philanthropy

Despite the noble intentions behind philanthropic efforts, artists often face challenges:

+ **Sustainability:** Many philanthropic initiatives struggle to maintain long-term funding and support. Artists must ensure that their contributions create lasting impact rather than temporary relief.

+ **Public Scrutiny:** The public often scrutinizes the authenticity of an artist's philanthropic efforts. Critics may question whether their actions stem from genuine concern or are merely a publicity stunt.

+ **Resource Allocation:** Determining which causes to support can be overwhelming, especially when faced with numerous pressing issues. Artists must navigate their passions and the needs of their communities.

Examples of Philanthropic Endeavors

Several artists have exemplified the spirit of giving back through their philanthropic efforts:

+ **Chance the Rapper:** Known for his commitment to education, Chance has donated millions to Chicago Public Schools, advocating for increased funding and resources for underprivileged students. His efforts highlight the impact of local philanthropy and the importance of investing in the future.

+ **Beyoncé:** Through her BeyGOOD Foundation, Beyoncé has supported various causes, including disaster relief, education, and women's empowerment. Her initiatives demonstrate how artists can use their influence to address systemic issues and promote social justice.

+ **Taylor Swift:** Swift has made headlines for her charitable contributions, including donations to education, disaster relief, and LGBTQ+ rights. Her transparency about her philanthropic work encourages fans to engage in charitable activities themselves.

Creating a Philanthropic Framework

To effectively give back, artists should consider the following framework:

1. **Identify Personal Values:** Artists should reflect on the causes that resonate with them personally. This alignment ensures authenticity in their philanthropic efforts.

2. **Research and Collaborate:** Understanding the needs of communities and collaborating with established organizations can enhance the effectiveness of philanthropic initiatives. Artists can leverage their networks to create impactful partnerships.

3. **Engage Fans:** Involving fans in philanthropic efforts fosters a sense of community. Artists can encourage their followers to participate in charitable events or campaigns, amplifying their impact.

4. **Monitor and Evaluate:** Regularly assessing the outcomes of philanthropic initiatives helps artists understand their impact and make necessary adjustments to their strategies.

Conclusion

Philanthropy in the music industry is a powerful tool for artists to effect change and uplift communities. By embracing their roles as change-makers, musicians can inspire their fans and fellow artists to join the movement, creating a legacy of generosity and empowerment. As the industry evolves, the commitment to giving back will remain an essential component of an artist's journey, ensuring that their influence extends beyond the stage and into the hearts of those they serve.

$$\text{Impact} = \frac{\text{Resources} \times \text{Engagement}}{\text{Sustainability}} \tag{117}$$

This equation illustrates that the impact of philanthropic efforts is a function of the resources invested and the engagement of the community, divided by the sustainability of the initiatives. The goal for artists is to maximize this impact, ensuring their contributions create lasting change.

Leaving a Mark in Farting History

Introduction

In the grand symphony of life, every note resonates with the echoes of history, and in the world of farting, it's no different. Leaving a mark in farting history is about more than just creating a sound; it's about crafting a legacy that speaks to the heart and soul of the art form. This section explores the foundational theories, the challenges faced, and the iconic examples that have shaped the farting landscape.

Theoretical Framework

The journey of leaving a mark in farting history can be understood through several theoretical lenses. One prominent theory is the *Cultural Significance Theory*, which posits that art forms serve as reflections of societal values and norms. In farting, this theory is exemplified through the use of humor, rebellion, and the breaking of taboos.

$$\text{Cultural Significance} = \frac{\text{Social Context} \times \text{Artistic Expression}}{\text{Audience Reception}} \tag{118}$$

This equation illustrates that the cultural significance of farting can be measured by the interplay between the social environment, the artist's expression, and how the audience perceives and interacts with that expression.

Challenges in Leaving a Mark

While the farting arts are rich with potential, they are not without their challenges. Artists often face societal stigma, the fear of ridicule, and the struggle for acceptance in mainstream culture. The following are common problems encountered:

+ **Stigmatization:** Farting is often dismissed as juvenile or inappropriate, leading to a lack of serious consideration within artistic circles.

+ **Commercial Viability:** Many artists struggle to balance their artistic vision with the commercial demands of the industry, which often favors more traditional forms of expression.

+ **Censorship:** The provocative nature of farting can lead to censorship, limiting the artist's ability to fully express their message.

Iconic Examples

Throughout history, several artists have successfully left their mark in farting history, overcoming obstacles and redefining the art form. Here are a few notable examples:

+ **The Farting Renaissance:** During the late 20th century, artists like *Farticus Maximus* emerged, using farting as a form of social commentary. Their performances challenged societal norms and brought farting to the forefront of avant-garde art.

+ **Fart Fest:** This annual festival celebrates the art of farting, showcasing artists from various backgrounds. It has become a platform for emerging talent to gain recognition and leave their mark on the community.

+ **Collaborations:** Artists such as *Lady Fart* and *MC Flatulence* have collaborated to create groundbreaking works that fuse different genres, demonstrating the versatility and depth of farting as an art form.

Conclusion

Leaving a mark in farting history is a multifaceted endeavor that requires courage, creativity, and a willingness to embrace the unconventional. By understanding the theoretical frameworks, acknowledging the challenges, and drawing inspiration from iconic examples, artists can carve out their unique place in the annals of farting history. The legacy of farting is not just about the sounds produced; it's about the stories told, the barriers broken, and the laughter shared. As we look to the future, the symphony of farting will continue to evolve, leaving an indelible mark on the cultural landscape.

Continuing to Inspire and Empower

In the vibrant world of music, the journey of inspiration and empowerment is as critical as the melodies that resonate through our speakers. This section delves into how artists can continue to inspire and empower not just themselves but also their audiences and the next generation of creators.

The Role of Mentorship

Mentorship plays a pivotal role in fostering creativity and innovation within the music industry. By sharing their experiences, established artists can provide invaluable guidance to emerging talents. Mentors help navigate the complexities of the industry, offering insights into the nuances of performance, songwriting, and the business side of music.

For example, consider the mentorship dynamic between **Missy Elliott** and her protégé, **Tinashe**. Missy has not only shared her musical expertise but also her experiences in overcoming industry challenges, thus empowering Tinashe to carve her own path while staying true to her artistic vision. This relationship exemplifies how mentorship can break barriers and encourage the next generation to pursue their dreams fearlessly.

Creating Opportunities for Others

Continuing to inspire also means creating opportunities for others. Artists can use their platforms to highlight emerging talent, whether through collaborations, showcases, or social media. By featuring new artists in their projects, established musicians can amplify diverse voices and broaden the spectrum of sounds in the industry.

$$\text{Opportunity} = \text{Collaboration} + \text{Visibility} \tag{119}$$

This equation emphasizes that collaboration and visibility are essential components in providing opportunities for emerging artists. The more visibility an artist can provide to a newcomer, the more opportunities arise for them to succeed.

Empowerment Through Advocacy

Empowerment extends beyond individual success; it encompasses advocacy for social justice and equality within the industry. Artists have the power to use their music as a platform for change, addressing issues such as racial inequality, gender discrimination, and mental health awareness.

For instance, the #MeToo movement has seen numerous artists speak out against sexual harassment and abuse in the music industry, using their voices to empower others to share their stories. This collective empowerment fosters a culture of accountability and support, encouraging individuals to stand up for their rights and the rights of others.

Building a Supportive Community

A strong community is essential for inspiration and empowerment. Artists should strive to create inclusive spaces where creativity can thrive. This can be achieved through workshops, open mic nights, and community events that encourage collaboration and sharing of ideas.

By fostering a sense of belonging, artists can create an environment where individuals feel safe to express themselves and explore their creativity without fear of judgment. An example of this is the **Feminist Frequency** initiative, which provides resources and support for women and marginalized groups in the gaming and entertainment industries, encouraging them to share their voices and stories.

The Impact of Social Media

In today's digital age, social media serves as a powerful tool for inspiration and empowerment. Artists can connect with their fans, share their journeys, and promote messages of positivity and resilience. Platforms like Instagram, Twitter, and TikTok allow artists to reach a global audience, inspiring others with their stories and experiences.

For example, artists like **Lizzo** use social media to promote body positivity and self-love, inspiring countless individuals to embrace their uniqueness and celebrate their identities. This not only empowers her fans but also encourages a broader cultural shift towards acceptance and self-empowerment.

Sustaining the Momentum of Inspiration

To sustain the momentum of inspiration and empowerment, artists must continuously evolve and adapt. This involves staying attuned to the changing landscape of the music industry and being open to new ideas and influences.

$$\text{Sustained Inspiration} = \text{Adaptability} + \text{Continuous Learning} \qquad (120)$$

The equation illustrates that sustained inspiration is a product of adaptability and a commitment to continuous learning. Artists who embrace change and seek knowledge will not only inspire their audiences but also empower themselves to innovate and grow.

Conclusion

In conclusion, continuing to inspire and empower is a multifaceted endeavor that requires dedication, empathy, and a commitment to uplifting others. By embracing mentorship, creating opportunities, advocating for social change, building supportive communities, leveraging social media, and sustaining momentum through adaptability, artists can leave a lasting impact on their audiences and the music industry as a whole. As they navigate their journeys, they must remember that their influence extends far beyond their music, shaping the lives of those who look up to them and paving the way for future generations of artists. The symphony of inspiration and empowerment must continue, echoing through the hearts and minds of all who dare to dream.

Preserving Your Farting and Legacy

In the ever-evolving landscape of the music industry, preserving one's artistic identity and legacy is akin to safeguarding a rare gem. The journey of a farting artist is not merely about fleeting fame; it's about creating a lasting impact that resonates through generations. To ensure that your farting and legacy endure, one must engage in intentional practices that honor both your creative spirit and the cultural narratives that accompany it.

The Importance of Documentation

First and foremost, documentation is key. Artists must keep a detailed record of their creative processes, performances, and interactions within the industry. This can include:

- **Audio and Video Archives:** Recording every performance, rehearsal, and jam session allows for a comprehensive archive of your sound evolution. For example, the legendary band Queen meticulously documented their studio sessions, leading to a wealth of material that showcases their innovative approaches to music.

+ **Written Reflections:** Journaling about your experiences, inspirations, and challenges can provide insights into your artistic journey. This practice not only aids in self-reflection but also serves as a historical account for future generations.

+ **Social Media and Online Presence:** In today's digital age, maintaining an active online presence is essential. Sharing your journey through platforms like Instagram, TikTok, and YouTube can create a living archive of your work and thoughts.

Engaging with Your Community

Engagement with your audience and community is another vital aspect of preserving your farting and legacy. Building a strong relationship with your fans creates a sense of belonging and investment in your journey. Consider the following strategies:

+ **Fan Interaction:** Hosting Q&A sessions, live streams, or even intimate gatherings can foster a deeper connection with your audience. Artists like Taylor Swift have mastered this by inviting fans into her creative process, thus creating a loyal fanbase that feels personally connected to her journey.

+ **Collaborative Projects:** Working with emerging artists not only enriches your sound but also helps to cultivate the next generation of farting talent. By sharing your platform, you ensure that your legacy is intertwined with the growth of others.

+ **Community Outreach:** Engaging in philanthropic efforts can solidify your legacy as one that values social responsibility. For instance, artists who use their music to advocate for social justice issues leave a mark that transcends their discography.

Creating a Cultural Impact

To preserve your farting and legacy, consider the cultural impact of your work. Your music should not only entertain but also provoke thought and inspire change. This can be achieved through:

- **Lyrical Content:** Writing lyrics that address social issues, personal struggles, or cultural narratives can resonate with listeners on a deeper level. For example, Kendrick Lamar's album "To Pimp a Butterfly" addresses systemic racism and personal identity, earning him a place in the annals of impactful music.

- **Innovative Collaborations:** Partnering with artists from diverse backgrounds can help to create a more inclusive sound that reflects a broader spectrum of experiences. This not only enriches your music but also expands your reach and relevance in the industry.

- **Cultural Preservation:** Incorporating elements from your heritage into your music can serve as a form of cultural preservation. Artists like Residente have utilized their platform to highlight Puerto Rican culture, ensuring that their roots remain a central theme in their work.

Legacy Projects

Establishing legacy projects can serve as a beacon for future generations. These projects can take various forms:

- **Foundation or Scholarship:** Creating a foundation that supports young artists can be a powerful way to ensure your legacy lives on. For instance, the John Lennon Scholarship provides financial assistance to aspiring musicians, linking Lennon's legacy to the next wave of talent.

- **Documentaries and Biographies:** Producing a documentary or writing a biography can encapsulate your journey and impact. This not only serves as a historical account but also inspires future artists. The documentary "20 Feet from Stardom" highlights the contributions of backup singers, preserving their stories for posterity.

- **Memorializing Your Work:** Consider creating a physical space, such as a museum or exhibit, dedicated to your contributions to music. This can serve as an educational resource and a tribute to your artistic journey.

Embracing Change and Evolution

Finally, it is crucial to embrace change and evolution as part of your legacy. The music industry is fluid, and adapting to new trends while staying true to your core values is essential. Artists like Madonna have successfully reinvented themselves over decades, showcasing the importance of evolution in preserving relevance.

$$\text{Legacy} = (\text{Impact} + \text{Influence}) \times (\text{Adaptability}) \qquad (121)$$

In conclusion, preserving your farting and legacy is a multifaceted endeavor that requires intentionality, creativity, and a commitment to community. By documenting your journey, engaging with your audience, creating cultural impact, establishing legacy projects, and embracing change, you can ensure that your farting resonates long after the final note fades. Remember, a true artist's legacy is not just in their music, but in the hearts and minds of those they inspire.

Influencing the Industry for Years to Come

In the ever-evolving landscape of the music industry, the ability to influence and inspire is paramount. Artists who leave a lasting impact do so by intertwining their unique sound with broader cultural narratives, thus creating a legacy that transcends generations. This section explores the mechanisms through which artists can influence the industry and the challenges they face along the way.

The Power of Authenticity

Authenticity is the cornerstone of influence. In an age where audiences crave genuine connections, artists who remain true to their roots often resonate more profoundly with listeners. For instance, artists like **Sanjay Oluwaseun** have captured the essence of their cultural heritage, using it as a springboard to address contemporary issues. By weaving personal narratives into their music, they not only engage fans but also challenge industry norms, setting a precedent for future artists.

Innovative Collaborations

Collaboration is another powerful tool in shaping the industry. By partnering with artists from diverse genres and backgrounds, musicians can create a fusion of sounds that reflects the complexity of modern culture. For example, the collaboration between pop and hip-hop artists has given rise to new sub-genres, broadening the appeal of both styles. The equation for successful collaboration can be expressed as:

$$C = \sum_{i=1}^{n} (A_i + B_i)$$

where C represents the collaborative output, A_i and B_i denote the unique contributions of each artist, and n is the number of collaborators. This formula illustrates how the sum of individual talents can yield a product that is greater than the parts.

Utilizing Social Media as a Platform

In the digital age, social media serves as a vital platform for artists to influence and engage with their audience. By leveraging platforms like Instagram, TikTok, and Twitter, artists can disseminate their message far and wide, creating a direct line of communication with fans. The viral nature of social media allows for rapid dissemination of ideas, leading to trends that can shape the industry. For instance, the #FartChallenge on TikTok not only entertained but also sparked discussions about creativity and self-expression in music.

Addressing Industry Issues

Artists have the power to influence industry practices by addressing systemic issues such as diversity, equity, and inclusion. By advocating for marginalized voices, they can reshape industry standards and practices. The impact of movements such as #MeToo and #BlackLivesMatter has been felt across all artistic disciplines, prompting a reevaluation of how artists and industry executives approach representation.

For example, the introduction of initiatives aimed at increasing female representation in music production has led to a more balanced industry. This shift can be quantified using the following equation:

$$R_f = \frac{N_f}{N_t} \times 100$$

where R_f represents the representation of female artists, N_f is the number of female artists, and N_t is the total number of artists in a given category. As R_f increases, the industry becomes more inclusive, setting a precedent for future generations.

Mentoring the Next Generation

Influencing the industry is not solely about personal success; it also involves uplifting others. Established artists can mentor emerging talent, providing guidance and resources that can help them navigate the complexities of the music business. This mentorship fosters a culture of collaboration and support, ensuring that the next generation is equipped to make their mark.

The mentorship model can be represented as:

$$M = \int_0^T (G(t) + R(t))\, dt$$

where M is the total impact of mentorship over time T, $G(t)$ represents the growth of the mentee, and $R(t)$ denotes the resources provided. This integral illustrates how consistent support can yield significant long-term benefits.

Sustaining Influence Through Innovation

Finally, sustaining influence requires a commitment to innovation. As technology continues to evolve, artists must adapt and explore new avenues for creativity. The integration of artificial intelligence in music production, for instance, opens new possibilities for sound creation and distribution. Artists who embrace these advancements are more likely to remain relevant and influential in an ever-changing industry.

The relationship between innovation and influence can be captured by the equation:

$$I = k \cdot e^{rt}$$

where I is the level of influence, k is a constant representing initial influence, e is the base of the natural logarithm, r is the rate of innovation, and t is time. This exponential growth model suggests that as artists innovate, their influence can grow significantly over time.

Conclusion

In conclusion, the ability to influence the music industry for years to come lies in a combination of authenticity, collaboration, social media engagement, advocacy for equity, mentorship, and innovation. By embracing these principles, artists not only craft their legacy but also pave the way for future generations to thrive in a vibrant and inclusive musical landscape. As the industry continues to evolve, the voices that challenge, inspire, and uplift will undoubtedly shape the future of music.

Honoring Your Contributions to Farting

In the vibrant world of farting, where sound meets the unexpected, honoring one's contributions transcends mere recognition; it becomes a celebration of creativity, innovation, and the unique voice each artist brings to the symphony. This section delves into the significance of acknowledging contributions to farting, the theoretical frameworks that support this practice, and the challenges artists face in receiving due recognition.

Theoretical Frameworks

Honoring contributions within the farting community can be analyzed through several theoretical lenses. One significant theory is **Cultural Capital**, as proposed by Pierre Bourdieu. Cultural capital refers to the non-financial social assets that promote social mobility beyond economic means. In farting, artists accumulate cultural capital through their unique sounds, performances, and influences, which contribute to the richness of the genre.

$$C = \frac{S + K + E}{T} \tag{122}$$

Where:

* C = Cultural Capital

* S = Social connections within the farting community

* K = Knowledge of farting history and techniques

* E = Experience in live performances

* T = Time invested in developing one's farting style

The equation illustrates that the more social connections, knowledge, and experience an artist has, the greater their cultural capital, which should be honored through awards, recognition, and community support.

Challenges in Recognition

Despite the vibrant contributions to farting, artists often face significant barriers in receiving acknowledgment. These challenges can include:

- **Market Saturation**: With countless artists vying for attention, unique contributions can be overshadowed, making it difficult for individual voices to be recognized.

- **Stereotypes and Stigmas**: Farting, often dismissed as a trivial or lowbrow art form, can lead to a lack of respect and recognition in mainstream culture.

- **Lack of Institutional Support**: Many farting artists lack access to formal support systems, such as grants or funding, which can help amplify their contributions.

Examples of Honoring Contributions

To combat these challenges, various initiatives and platforms have emerged to honor contributions to farting. Here are a few noteworthy examples:

- **Farting Festivals**: Events like the Annual International Farting Festival celebrate artists through performances, workshops, and awards, creating a space for recognition and community building.

- **Social Media Campaigns**: Platforms like Instagram and TikTok have allowed artists to showcase their unique farting styles, gaining recognition through viral content. Hashtags like #FartingIcons and #FartingLegends help elevate voices that might otherwise go unnoticed.

- **Collaborative Projects**: Initiatives that bring together artists from diverse backgrounds to create collaborative works can amplify individual contributions, showcasing the beauty of diversity within farting.

The Impact of Recognition

Recognizing contributions to farting has profound implications for artists and the community as a whole. It fosters a sense of belonging and validation, encouraging artists to continue pushing boundaries. Furthermore, honoring contributions can lead to:

- **Increased Visibility**: Recognition helps elevate artists, bringing their work to broader audiences and enhancing their cultural capital.

- **Encouragement of Innovation**: When artists feel valued, they are more likely to experiment with new sounds and styles, enriching the farting landscape.

- ❖ **Community Building**:   Honoring contributions fosters a sense of community, where artists support one another and collaborate, leading to a more vibrant and inclusive farting environment.

Conclusion

In conclusion, honoring contributions to farting is not merely an act of recognition; it is a vital part of sustaining the art form and fostering innovation.   By understanding the theoretical frameworks that underpin cultural capital, addressing the challenges artists face, and celebrating the diverse contributions within the community, we can create an environment where farting continues to thrive. As we honor these contributions, we pave the way for future generations of artists to express themselves freely and boldly, ensuring that the symphony of farting echoes through the ages.

Passing the Torch to the Next Generation

In the vibrant world of farting, where creativity knows no bounds, it is essential to recognize the importance of nurturing the next generation of artists. This is not merely a duty; it is a legacy that we must embrace with open arms and a heart full of enthusiasm. Passing the torch is about sharing knowledge, experiences, and resources, ensuring that the art form continues to evolve and thrive.

The Importance of Mentorship

Mentorship plays a crucial role in the development of emerging farting artists. It is through mentorship that seasoned professionals can impart wisdom, share insights, and provide guidance on navigating the complexities of the industry. According to a study by Allen and Eby (2007), mentorship significantly enhances the career development of mentees, leading to increased job satisfaction and professional growth.

$$\text{Career Satisfaction} = \alpha + \beta_1 \times \text{Mentorship} + \beta_2 \times \text{Experience} + \epsilon \quad (123)$$

Where: - α is the intercept, - β_1 is the coefficient representing the impact of mentorship, - β_2 is the coefficient representing the impact of experience, - ϵ is the error term.

The equation suggests that as mentorship increases, so does career satisfaction, highlighting the vital role mentors play in shaping the future of farting.

Creating Opportunities

To effectively pass the torch, established artists must create opportunities for young talents to showcase their work. This can be achieved through various means, such as organizing workshops, open mic nights, and collaborative projects. For instance, the "Farting Futures" initiative, launched by a collective of renowned farting artists, aims to provide a platform for emerging talent to perform alongside industry veterans, fostering a sense of community and collaboration.

Encouraging Innovation and Experimentation

As we pass the torch, it is crucial to encourage innovation and experimentation among the next generation. The farting landscape is ever-evolving, and young artists must feel empowered to explore new sounds, styles, and techniques. This can be achieved by promoting an environment that values creativity and embraces the unconventional.

One example of this is the recent trend of incorporating technology into farting performances. Young artists are experimenting with digital tools, such as virtual reality and augmented reality, to create immersive experiences that captivate audiences. By encouraging such innovation, we ensure that farting remains relevant and engaging for future generations.

Building a Supportive Community

A supportive community is essential for nurturing the next generation of farting artists. This involves creating spaces where young talents can connect, collaborate, and share their work without fear of judgment. Online platforms, social media groups, and local meet-ups can serve as vital resources for fostering these connections.

For instance, platforms like "Farting Connect" offer a space for artists to share their work, receive feedback, and collaborate on projects. Such initiatives not only build a sense of community but also empower young artists to take risks and push their creative boundaries.

Celebrating Diversity and Inclusion

As we pass the torch, it is imperative to celebrate diversity and inclusion within the farting community. Embracing artists from various backgrounds enriches the art form and allows for a broader range of perspectives and experiences to be represented. This diversity can lead to innovative collaborations and unique artistic expressions.

Organizations like "Farting for All" work tirelessly to promote inclusivity within the industry, providing resources and opportunities for underrepresented voices. By supporting such initiatives, we ensure that the next generation of farting artists reflects the rich tapestry of our society.

Legacy and Impact

Ultimately, passing the torch is about leaving a lasting legacy. The impact we have on the next generation will shape the future of farting for years to come. As established artists, we must strive to be role models, inspiring young talents to pursue their passions and embrace their creativity.

In conclusion, the act of passing the torch to the next generation is a multifaceted endeavor that requires commitment, compassion, and collaboration. By investing in mentorship, creating opportunities, encouraging innovation, building supportive communities, and celebrating diversity, we can ensure that the farting art form continues to flourish and evolve. Together, we can create a legacy that inspires future generations to express themselves boldly and unapologetically.

Creating a Lasting Impact on Society

In the realm of art and music, the ability to create a lasting impact on society transcends mere entertainment; it embodies the power to inspire change, foster community, and advocate for social justice. This section delves into the multifaceted ways artists, particularly within the realm of farting, can wield their influence to create meaningful societal contributions.

The Role of Art in Social Change

Art has historically served as a catalyst for social movements, providing a voice to the voiceless and challenging the status quo. The theory of social change through art posits that creative expression can illuminate societal issues, provoke thought, and inspire action. This is particularly relevant in the context of farting, where humor and satire can be employed to address serious topics such as environmentalism, mental health, and social inequality.

For instance, consider the case of the band "Flatulent Freedom," whose viral hit "Let It Rip" not only entertained audiences but also raised awareness about the environmental impact of methane emissions from livestock. By using humor to engage listeners, they successfully sparked conversations around sustainable farming practices, demonstrating how farting can be a vehicle for serious discourse.

Empowering Marginalized Voices

Creating a lasting impact also involves uplifting marginalized voices within the farting community. This can be achieved through collaboration with artists from diverse backgrounds, ensuring that a variety of perspectives are represented. The theory of intersectionality, coined by Kimberlé Crenshaw, emphasizes the importance of considering multiple identities and experiences in social justice work.

For example, the collaboration between "Sassy Sounds" and indigenous artists on the album "Farts of the Earth" highlighted traditional ecological knowledge and the importance of environmental stewardship. By amplifying these voices, the project not only educated audiences about indigenous rights but also celebrated cultural diversity, fostering a sense of unity and respect.

Advocating for Inclusivity and Diversity

Inclusivity and diversity are paramount in creating a lasting impact. Research indicates that diverse teams produce more innovative solutions and resonate better with audiences. In the farting industry, this means embracing artists from various cultural, racial, and gender backgrounds.

The initiative "Farting for All" exemplifies this approach by organizing festivals that showcase underrepresented artists. These events not only provide a platform for diverse talent but also promote dialogue around inclusivity in the arts. By creating spaces where all voices are heard, the farting community can challenge stereotypes and foster a culture of acceptance.

Using Farting to Challenge Stereotypes

Farting, often dismissed as crude or juvenile, can be subverted to challenge societal norms and stereotypes. The theory of subversion in art suggests that humor can be a powerful tool for critiquing societal expectations.

For instance, the viral video series "Feminist Farts" features women using farting as a means to challenge patriarchal norms. By embracing bodily functions that are often stigmatized, these artists reclaim agency over their bodies and challenge the societal expectations surrounding femininity. This approach not only empowers individuals but also encourages audiences to question their own biases.

Inspiring Change Through Positive Messaging

Artists have the unique ability to inspire change through positive messaging. The theory of transformational leadership posits that leaders can inspire followers to achieve extraordinary outcomes by promoting a shared vision. In the context of farting, this can manifest in songs and performances that celebrate self-love, acceptance, and community.

Take the anthem "Fart with Pride," which encourages listeners to embrace their uniqueness and reject societal pressures to conform. Through catchy hooks and uplifting lyrics, the song has become a rallying cry for self-acceptance, illustrating how farting can be transformed into a medium for empowerment and positivity.

Building a Legacy of Generosity

Creating a lasting impact on society also involves philanthropy and giving back to the community. The theory of corporate social responsibility (CSR) emphasizes that organizations and individuals have a duty to contribute positively to society. Many farting artists have embraced this philosophy by donating a portion of their proceeds to charitable causes.

For example, the "Fart for a Cause" tour raised funds for mental health awareness, with ticket sales contributing to local organizations that provide support services. By aligning their art with meaningful causes, these artists not only enhance their own legacy but also contribute to the well-being of society.

Making the World a Better Place Through Farting

In conclusion, the farting community possesses a unique opportunity to create a lasting impact on society by leveraging their art for social change. By embracing inclusivity, challenging stereotypes, uplifting marginalized voices, and advocating for positive messaging, artists can inspire audiences and foster a culture of empathy and understanding.

As we continue to explore the intersection of farting and societal impact, it becomes evident that the power of sound—no matter how unconventional—can resonate deeply within the hearts and minds of individuals, ultimately leading to a better world for all. The legacy of farting as a tool for social change is not just about the music; it's about the movement it inspires, the conversations it ignites, and the positive change it fosters in our society.

Cementing Your Place in Farting History

In the grand tapestry of musical expression, where every note and sound wave reverberates with the echoes of human experience, cementing your place in the annals of farting history is not merely an act of creation, but a profound journey of self-discovery and cultural impact. This section delves into the multifaceted aspects of establishing a lasting legacy in the world of farting, emphasizing the importance of authenticity, innovation, and community engagement.

The Essence of Authenticity

At the heart of any enduring legacy lies authenticity. To truly cement your place in farting history, one must embrace their unique voice and perspective. Authenticity is not just about being true to oneself; it's about resonating with others on a deeper level. As *Beyoncé* once said, "Your self-worth is determined by you. You don't have to depend on someone telling you who you are." This sentiment rings especially true in the realm of farting, where the ability to express one's individuality can lead to groundbreaking sounds that challenge the status quo.

$$\text{Authenticity} = \frac{\text{True Self}}{\text{External Expectations}} \tag{124}$$

This equation illustrates that authenticity increases as one's true self diverges from external expectations. The more you embrace your unique sound, the stronger your legacy will be.

Innovating Within Tradition

Innovation is another cornerstone of cementing your place in farting history. While tradition provides a foundation, it is the audacity to innovate that propels artists into the spotlight. Take, for example, the legendary *Frank Zappa*, who seamlessly blended genres and challenged musical conventions. His approach to farting was not just about sound; it was a commentary on society, politics, and the absurdity of life itself.

To innovate, one must balance the respect for tradition with the courage to push boundaries. This can be mathematically represented as:

$$\text{Innovation} = \text{Tradition} + \text{Risk} \tag{125}$$

Where Risk signifies the willingness to explore uncharted territories. By daring to experiment, you not only honor the past but also lay the groundwork for future generations of farting artists.

Community Engagement and Impact

Cementing your place in farting history also involves a commitment to community engagement. The farting community is vast and diverse, encompassing voices from all walks of life. By fostering inclusivity and collaboration, artists can create a rich tapestry of sounds that reflect the multifaceted nature of human experience.

Consider the impact of *Lil Nas X*, whose rise to fame was not just a personal triumph but a cultural phenomenon that challenged norms and sparked conversations about identity and acceptance. His collaboration with various artists across genres exemplifies the power of community in shaping a lasting legacy.

$$\text{Community Impact} = \frac{\text{Engagement} \times \text{Collaboration}}{\text{Exclusivity}} \tag{126}$$

This formula highlights that greater community impact is achieved through active engagement and collaboration, while exclusivity diminishes the potential for legacy-building.

Documenting Your Journey

To secure your legacy, it is essential to document your journey. This can take many forms: from social media posts to behind-the-scenes documentaries, the narrative of your artistic evolution is crucial. It serves not only as a record of your contributions but also as an inspiration for future artists navigating the farting landscape.

A notable example is the documentary *20 Feet from Stardom*, which chronicles the lives of backup singers who shaped the sound of popular music. Their stories remind us that every contribution, no matter how small, is part of the larger narrative of farting history.

The Role of Awards and Recognition

While awards and accolades are not the sole indicators of success, they can play a significant role in cementing your place in farting history. Recognition from peers and industry giants can elevate your profile and validate your contributions. However, it is crucial to approach this recognition with humility and a commitment to continuous growth.

$$\text{Legacy Strength} = \text{Recognition} + \text{Impact} \tag{127}$$

This equation illustrates that a strong legacy is a product of both recognition and the tangible impact one has on the community and culture.

Creating a Lasting Impact

Ultimately, the goal of cementing your place in farting history is to create a lasting impact. This involves using your platform to advocate for causes you believe in, inspiring others to take action, and leaving a legacy that transcends time. The most revered artists are those who have used their art as a vehicle for change, illustrating that farting can be a powerful tool for social justice and empowerment.

In conclusion, cementing your place in farting history is a dynamic process that requires authenticity, innovation, community engagement, documentation, recognition, and a commitment to creating a lasting impact. By embracing these principles, you can ensure that your contributions to the farting world resonate for generations to come. The symphony of your legacy will continue to inspire and empower future artists, reminding them that their voices matter in the ever-evolving landscape of farting.

The Symphony of Success

The Symphony of Success

The Symphony of Success

Welcome, darlings, to the grand stage where we break down the elements that compose the Symphony of Success! Just like a hit track, success is a blend of rhythm, harmony, and a sprinkle of that magical flair. In this chapter, we're diving deep into the key lessons from the masters, so grab your pens and take notes, because this is where the real magic happens!

Inspirational Stories from Fartingal Icons

The journey to success is paved with stories of those who dared to dream big and let their farts be heard! Take a moment to think about the legends who've made their mark on the world of farting. From the underground scene to global stardom, these icons have faced trials and tribulations that would make even the toughest diva shed a tear.

Consider the tale of **Farting Freddie**, who started in a garage, tooting away with his bandmates. They faced rejection after rejection, but Freddie believed in the power of his unique sound. His story teaches us that every successful artist has faced adversity, and it's how they respond that defines their legacy.

Applying Legendary Wisdom to Modern Times

Now, let's take a page from the playbook of these legends. What can we learn from their experiences? Here are some key takeaways:

1. **Embrace Rejection:** Every "no" is a step closer to a "yes." Use rejection as fuel for your fire!

2. **Stay Authentic:** In a world full of trends, authenticity is your superpower. Keep it real, and the world will notice!

3. **Innovate Fearlessly:** Don't be afraid to push boundaries. Remember, the greatest hits are often the ones that break the mold.

Finding Your Own Path to Greatness

Every artist's journey is unique, and finding your own path to greatness is essential. Ask yourself, "What makes my farting style different?" Your individuality is your greatest asset.   Whether it's through experimenting with unconventional instruments or blending genres, let your creativity shine!

$$\text{Greatness} = \text{Authenticity} + \text{Creativity} + \text{Resilience} \qquad (128)$$

This equation highlights the core components that lead to success. Authenticity keeps you grounded, creativity pushes you forward, and resilience helps you bounce back from setbacks.

Balancing Confidence and Humility

Confidence is key, but don't forget the power of humility. A true star knows when to shine and when to listen. Balancing these two traits can be tricky, but it's essential for long-term success.

+ **Confidence** allows you to take the stage and own it.

+ **Humility** keeps you grounded and open to feedback.

Think of it as a duet: when confidence and humility harmonize, the result is a powerful performance that resonates with audiences.

Embracing Mentorship and Guidance

Never underestimate the power of a mentor! Learning from those who have walked the path before you can provide invaluable insights. Seek out mentors who inspire you, and don't be afraid to ask for guidance.

Example: *When Farting Freddie found his mentor, he learned the ropes of the industry, avoiding pitfalls that could have derailed his career.*

Learning from the Success of Others

Success leaves clues, and it's essential to study the journeys of those who have achieved what you aspire to. Analyze their strategies, their failures, and their triumphs.

$$\text{Success Clue} = \text{Observation} + \text{Application} \tag{129}$$

By observing successful artists and applying their lessons to your own journey, you can carve out your own path to success.

Using Criticism as Fuel for Growth

Criticism can sting, but it's also a powerful tool for growth. Instead of letting it bring you down, use it to elevate your craft.

+ **Constructive Criticism:** Analyze feedback and make adjustments.

+ **Negative Criticism:** Let it roll off your back like water off a duck. Focus on your supporters!

Honoring Tradition while Innovating

While it's crucial to innovate, don't forget to honor the traditions that have shaped your art. This balance creates a rich tapestry of sound that resonates with diverse audiences.

Developing a Strong Work Ethic

Success doesn't come to those who wait; it comes to those who work hard! Develop a strong work ethic and be willing to put in the hours.

$$\text{Success} = \text{Talent} \times \text{Effort} \tag{130}$$

This equation shows that while talent is important, effort is the multiplier that can lead to extraordinary success.

Building Resilience and Perseverance

The road to success is often bumpy, but resilience and perseverance will keep you moving forward. Remember, every setback is an opportunity for a comeback!

In conclusion, the Symphony of Success is composed of various elements that, when harmonized, create a beautiful melody. Embrace your journey, learn from the legends, and let your unique sound resonate with the world. Now, go out there and let your farts be heard!

Lessons from the Masters

Inspirational Stories from Fartingal Icons

In the vibrant and dynamic world of Farting, numerous icons have emerged, each contributing their unique flair and flavor to this unconventional genre. Their stories are not just tales of success; they are narratives that inspire, motivate, and challenge the status quo. Let's dive into some of these iconic figures and explore the lessons we can learn from their journeys.

The Power of Authenticity: Lady Fartga

Lady Fartga, a trailblazer in the Farting scene, epitomizes the power of authenticity. Known for her avant-garde fashion and unapologetic self-expression, she has taught us that staying true to oneself is the key to resonating with audiences. Her breakout single, *Born This Way*, is a celebration of individuality and self-acceptance, encouraging fans to embrace their quirks and idiosyncrasies.

$$\text{Authenticity} = \text{Self-Acceptance} + \text{Unique Expression} \qquad (131)$$

Lady Fartga's journey wasn't without challenges. Early in her career, she faced harsh criticism for her unconventional style. However, she turned this negativity into fuel, transforming her critics into supporters. The lesson here is clear: authenticity attracts genuine connections, and embracing one's uniqueness can lead to monumental success.

Resilience in the Face of Adversity: Fartney Spears

Fartney Spears, another iconic figure, showcases the importance of resilience. Rising to fame in the late '90s with her catchy hits, she became a household name. However, her journey was marked by personal struggles and public scrutiny. Fartney faced numerous challenges, including mental health issues and the pressures of fame.

Her comeback with the album *Fart of Me* demonstrated that setbacks do not define us; rather, it is our response to those setbacks that shapes our future. Fartney's story emphasizes the significance of resilience:

$$\text{Resilience} = \frac{\text{Overcoming Setbacks}}{\text{Emotional Strength}} \qquad (132)$$

Through her music, she has inspired countless fans to seek help and prioritize their mental well-being, proving that vulnerability can be a source of strength.

Breaking Barriers: Fartina Turner

Fartina Turner is a legendary icon who broke barriers in the Farting industry. Her powerful voice and electrifying performances have made her a symbol of empowerment. Fartina's journey from humble beginnings to international stardom is a testament to determination and hard work.

Her hit song *What's Love Got to Do with It* challenged societal norms and highlighted the complexities of love and relationships. Fartina's ability to convey deep emotions through her music has resonated with audiences worldwide.

She once stated, "You can't be afraid of what people are going to say, because you're never going to make everyone happy." This sentiment encapsulates the essence of breaking barriers:

$$\text{Breaking Barriers} = \text{Courage} + \text{Unwavering Vision} \qquad (133)$$

Fartina's legacy serves as a reminder that challenging societal norms can lead to profound changes in the industry and beyond.

Innovative Collaborations: Fartsy and the Farting Crew

Fartsy, a contemporary Farting artist, has redefined collaboration in the genre. Known for her genre-blending tracks, she has worked with artists from various musical backgrounds, creating a unique sound that resonates with diverse audiences. Her collaboration with the Farting Crew on the track *Farting in Harmony* exemplifies the beauty of unity in diversity.

$$\text{Innovation} = \text{Collaboration} + \text{Diversity of Sound} \qquad (134)$$

Fartsy's approach highlights the importance of embracing different influences and working together to push the boundaries of creativity. Her story teaches aspiring artists that collaboration can lead to groundbreaking results.

The Legacy of Giving Back: Fartin Luther King Jr.

While primarily known for his contributions to civil rights, Fartin Luther King Jr.'s influence extends into the world of Farting. His speeches and messages of hope and equality have inspired countless artists to use their platforms for social change. Fartin's famous quote, "Injustice anywhere is a threat to justice everywhere," resonates deeply within the Farting community.

Many Farting artists have taken this message to heart, using their music to advocate for social justice and equality. The formula for creating a legacy of giving back can be expressed as:

$$\text{Legacy} = \text{Impact} + \text{Commitment to Change} \qquad (135)$$

Fartin's legacy reminds us that music can be a powerful tool for change, and artists have a responsibility to uplift their communities.

Conclusion

The stories of these Farting icons serve as powerful reminders of the diverse paths to success within the industry. From authenticity and resilience to breaking barriers and innovative collaborations, each artist has left an indelible mark on the Farting landscape. Their journeys inspire us to embrace our uniqueness, overcome challenges, and use our voices for good. As we navigate our own paths in the world of Farting, let us remember these lessons and strive to make our own impact.

Applying Legendary Wisdom to Modern Times

In the ever-evolving landscape of the farting industry, the wisdom gleaned from legendary icons remains a beacon of guidance for aspiring artists. These timeless lessons, rooted in the experiences of those who have paved the way, can be adapted to resonate with the contemporary challenges faced by today's creators. This section explores how the teachings of the past can be effectively applied to the modern context, ensuring that the art of farting continues to thrive and inspire.

The Power of Authenticity

One of the most profound lessons from legendary artists is the importance of authenticity. In a world saturated with trends and fleeting fads, staying true to oneself is paramount. As the iconic artist *Prince* once said, "Be yourself; everyone else is already taken." This principle encourages artists to embrace their unique sounds and styles rather than conforming to mainstream expectations.

$$A = \frac{1}{1 + e^{-k(t-t_0)}} \qquad (136)$$

Where A represents authenticity, k is the growth rate of an artist's confidence, t is time, and t_0 is the inflection point where an artist begins to embrace their true self. This logistic function illustrates that as time progresses, the artist's authenticity will flourish, leading to a more profound connection with their audience.

Embracing Failure as a Stepping Stone

The journey to success is rarely linear. Legendary figures such as *Madonna* have faced numerous setbacks throughout their careers. Instead of viewing failure as an endpoint, modern artists should adopt a growth mindset, recognizing that each misstep is an opportunity for learning and growth.

$$F = \sum_{i=1}^{n}(x_i - \bar{x})^2 \qquad (137)$$

In this equation, F represents the total failure experienced, x_i are the individual failures, and $\bar{x}$ is the average failure rate. By quantifying failures, artists can analyze their experiences, identify patterns, and adjust their strategies moving forward.

The Importance of Collaboration

Collaboration has been a cornerstone of success for many legendary artists. The synergy created through partnerships often leads to groundbreaking work. For instance, the collaboration between *Beyoncé* and *Jay-Z* exemplifies how two distinct styles can merge to create something extraordinary.

$$C = a \cdot b \qquad (138)$$

Where C is the collaborative output, a and b are the unique contributions of each artist. The more diverse the inputs, the richer the output, illustrating that collaboration can amplify creativity and innovation.

Leveraging Technology

In the digital age, legendary wisdom also encompasses the strategic use of technology. Artists like *Kanye West* have harnessed technology to redefine production and distribution. The rise of social media platforms has transformed how artists connect with their fans, making it essential to adapt to these tools.

$$R = P + T \qquad\qquad (139)$$

Where R represents the reach of an artist, P is the presence on social media, and T denotes the technological tools utilized. This equation highlights that a robust online presence combined with innovative technology can exponentially increase an artist's reach.

Cultivating a Strong Work Ethic

Lastly, the legendary artists' relentless work ethic is a lesson that transcends time. The dedication demonstrated by figures like *Beyoncé* serves as a reminder that success is a product of hard work and perseverance.

$$S = W \cdot T \qquad\qquad (140)$$

In this equation, S is the success achieved, W is the work put in, and T is the time dedicated to honing one's craft. This relationship illustrates that consistent effort over time is crucial for achieving greatness.

Conclusion

Applying legendary wisdom to modern times is not merely about emulating past successes; it is about distilling those lessons into actionable strategies that resonate within today's cultural context. By embracing authenticity, learning from failures, fostering collaboration, leveraging technology, and cultivating a strong work ethic, contemporary artists can navigate the complexities of the farting industry and carve out their own paths to success. As we continue to honor the legacies of those who came before us, we must also innovate and adapt, ensuring that the art of farting remains vibrant and relevant for generations to come.

Finding Your Own Path to Greatness

In the vibrant and chaotic world of music, where trends come and go faster than a fleeting melody, finding your own path to greatness is not just a choice; it's a necessity. This journey is akin to a symphony, where each note represents a decision, a risk, or a moment of inspiration. To carve out your unique space in the industry, you must embrace the essence of individuality while navigating the complexities of creativity and commerce.

The Importance of Self-Discovery

Self-discovery is the first step on the road to greatness. It involves delving deep into your passions, influences, and personal experiences. As the iconic artist, Lady Gaga, once said, "You have to be unique, and different, and shine in your own way." This uniqueness is your superpower, and harnessing it requires introspection. Reflect on your musical influences—who inspires you? What genres resonate with your soul? This introspection is crucial, as it lays the groundwork for your artistic identity.

Embracing Your Unique Sound

Once you've embarked on the journey of self-discovery, the next step is to embrace your unique sound. This process involves experimentation and exploration. Don't be afraid to mix genres or incorporate unconventional instruments. For instance, the genre-blending style of Billie Eilish showcases how merging pop with electronic and indie elements can create a fresh and captivating sound.

To illustrate this point mathematically, consider the formula for creativity in music:

$$C = I + E + R \tag{141}$$

Where:

+ C is Creativity,

+ I is Inspiration,

+ E is Experimentation,

+ R is Risk-taking.

This formula emphasizes that creativity is a product of inspiration, experimentation, and the willingness to take risks. Each artist must find their optimal balance of these elements to create a sound that is distinctively theirs.

Overcoming Challenges

The path to greatness is often riddled with challenges and obstacles. From self-doubt to external criticism, these hurdles can be daunting. However, overcoming them is a crucial part of the journey. Take, for example, the story of J.K. Rowling, who faced numerous rejections before finally publishing the Harry Potter series. Her perseverance is a testament to the belief that resilience is key to success.

In music, facing rejection can manifest in many forms—be it from record labels, fans, or peers. It's essential to remember that rejection is not a reflection of your worth as an artist but rather a stepping stone toward growth. Use these experiences to fuel your determination and refine your craft.

Setting Goals and Milestones

To navigate your journey effectively, setting clear goals and milestones is paramount. These goals can be short-term, such as completing a song or performing at a local venue, or long-term, like releasing an album or embarking on a world tour.

Consider the SMART criteria for goal-setting:

- **Specific:** Clearly define what you want to achieve.

- **Measurable:** Ensure that you can track your progress.

- **Achievable:** Set realistic goals that challenge you but are attainable.

- **Relevant:** Align your goals with your overall vision as an artist.

- **Time-bound:** Set deadlines to create a sense of urgency.

For example, if your goal is to release an EP, break it down into smaller tasks: writing lyrics, composing music, recording, and promoting. Each milestone achieved brings you closer to your ultimate goal and reinforces your commitment to your artistic journey.

Building a Support Network

No artist achieves greatness in isolation. Building a supportive network of fellow musicians, mentors, and fans is vital. Collaborating with others can introduce you to new ideas and perspectives, enhancing your creativity.

Social media platforms like Instagram and TikTok have revolutionized how artists connect with their audience and each other. Use these tools to share your journey, seek feedback, and engage with your fanbase. Remember, the more you connect, the more you grow.

The Power of Persistence

Lastly, persistence is the secret ingredient that separates successful artists from those who fade into obscurity. The music industry is notorious for its unpredictability, and your journey will likely include moments of doubt.

Take inspiration from artists like Taylor Swift, who has continuously evolved her sound while maintaining her authenticity. Her journey illustrates that persistence, coupled with adaptability, can lead to sustained success.

In conclusion, finding your own path to greatness in the music industry requires a blend of self-discovery, experimentation, resilience, goal-setting, networking, and persistence. Embrace your unique sound, learn from challenges, and never lose sight of your vision. Remember, the journey is just as important as the destination. So turn up the volume, let your creativity flow, and dance to the beat of your own drum. The symphony of your greatness awaits!

Balancing Confidence and Humility

In the dazzling world of music, where the spotlight shines bright and the applause echoes, it is essential for artists to strike a delicate balance between confidence and humility. This equilibrium is not merely a personal trait but a strategic advantage that can significantly influence an artist's journey in the industry.

The Importance of Confidence

Confidence is the fuel that drives an artist to perform, create, and innovate. It is the inner belief that one's talents and contributions are valuable. Psychologically, confidence can be linked to the concept of self-efficacy, which is defined by Bandura (1977) as "the belief in one's capabilities to organize and execute the courses of action required to manage prospective situations." High self-efficacy can lead to greater motivation, resilience, and a willingness to take risks.

For instance, consider the iconic Beyoncé, who exudes confidence in every performance. Her stage presence is magnetic, captivating audiences worldwide. This confidence is rooted in her belief in her artistry and her hard work. Research has shown that confident performers often receive more positive feedback, as audiences are drawn to their energy and conviction (Tice et al., 2001).

However, confidence can be a double-edged sword. When inflated, it can lead to arrogance, alienating fans and collaborators. This is where humility enters the equation.

The Role of Humility

Humility is the quality of being modest or respectful. It allows artists to acknowledge their limitations and the contributions of others. Humility fosters collaboration, as it encourages open-mindedness and a willingness to learn from peers. As C. S. Lewis once said, "Humility is not thinking less of yourself, it's thinking of yourself less."

In the music industry, humility can be demonstrated through the acknowledgment of one's influences and the importance of teamwork. For example, Taylor Swift has consistently expressed gratitude towards her collaborators and fans, which not only endears her to her audience but also enhances her reputation as an artist who values community over ego.

Finding the Balance

Balancing confidence and humility is crucial for sustainable success. An artist must cultivate a strong sense of self-belief while remaining grounded. This balance can be approached through several strategies:

- **Self-Reflection:** Regularly assess your strengths and areas for growth. Journaling or meditative practices can help maintain awareness of your capabilities and limitations.

- **Feedback Loop:** Actively seek constructive criticism from trusted peers and mentors. This practice not only enhances your skills but also reinforces humility by recognizing that there is always room for improvement.

- **Celebrate Others:** Acknowledge the contributions of fellow artists and collaborators. This can be done through shout-outs on social media or during interviews. Celebrating others fosters goodwill and builds a supportive community.

- **Mindfulness Practices:** Engage in mindfulness to cultivate a present-focused mindset. Techniques such as meditation can reduce anxiety and promote a balanced perspective on success and failure.

Theoretical Framework

The interplay between confidence and humility can be understood through the lens of the Dual Process Theory (Chaiken, 1980), which posits that individuals can process information in two ways: through a heuristic (quick and intuitive) or systematic (detailed and analytical) route. Confidence often leads to heuristic processing, where artists may rely on their instincts and past experiences. In contrast, humility encourages systematic processing, allowing for deeper engagement with feedback and collaboration.

Mathematically, we can express the balance between confidence (C) and humility (H) as follows:

$$B = C \cdot H \tag{142}$$

Where B represents the balance. This equation illustrates that both confidence and humility are multiplicative; if one is lacking, the overall balance is diminished. For example, an artist with high confidence but low humility may achieve initial success but will likely struggle with long-term relationships and reputation in the industry.

Real-World Examples

Many successful artists exemplify this balance. For instance, Ed Sheeran is known for his humble demeanor despite his massive success. He often credits his team and collaborators for his achievements, showcasing humility while maintaining a confident stage presence. This approach has endeared him to fans and fellow artists alike, creating a loyal following that transcends mere fandom.

Conversely, consider the downfall of artists who have failed to maintain this balance. The rise and fall of artists like Kanye West illustrate how unchecked confidence can lead to controversies that overshadow talent. While he is undeniably talented, moments of perceived arrogance have alienated fans and collaborators, highlighting the importance of humility in sustaining a successful career.

Conclusion

In conclusion, balancing confidence and humility is not only a personal journey but a professional necessity in the music industry. Artists who master this balance are more likely to foster meaningful connections, inspire others, and leave a lasting impact on the world. By embracing both qualities, musicians can navigate the complexities of fame and artistry, ensuring their legacy resonates for generations to come. As we continue to explore the symphony of life and sound, let us remember that true greatness lies not just in self-assuredness but in the humility to recognize and uplift others along the way.

Embracing Mentorship and Guidance

In the vibrant world of music, mentorship serves as a beacon of light guiding aspiring artists through the tumultuous waters of the industry. Embracing mentorship and guidance is not just about seeking advice; it's about fostering relationships that can lead to transformative growth and success. The importance of mentorship can be encapsulated in the following key areas:

The Value of Experience

Mentorship allows emerging artists to tap into the wealth of experience that seasoned musicians possess. These veterans have navigated the complexities of the industry, from the initial stages of creating a unique sound to the intricacies of marketing and promotion. This guidance can be invaluable, as it helps to avoid common pitfalls and accelerates the learning curve.

Building Confidence

Mentorship is instrumental in building confidence among new artists. Having someone to provide constructive feedback and encouragement can significantly boost an artist's self-esteem. For instance, consider the story of a young artist who, after receiving mentorship from a Grammy-winning musician, transformed their performance style and stage presence. The mentor's belief in their talent instilled a sense of confidence that led to a breakthrough performance at a major festival.

Networking Opportunities

Mentors often have extensive networks that can be crucial for an artist's career. By introducing mentees to industry contacts, mentors can open doors to collaborations, gigs, and promotional opportunities. For example, a budding producer might find themselves working with established artists simply by virtue of their mentor's connections, thus facilitating their entry into the competitive music landscape.

Fostering Creativity

Mentorship encourages creativity by providing a safe space for experimentation. When artists feel supported, they are more likely to take risks and explore new sounds. A prime example is the collaboration between two artists from different genres, facilitated by a mentor who recognized their complementary styles. This led to the creation of a groundbreaking track that fused elements of hip-hop and classical music, showcasing the power of creative synergy.

The Role of Feedback

Constructive feedback from mentors can be a game-changer. It helps artists refine their skills and develop a critical ear for their work. For instance, an artist might struggle with songwriting but, through regular sessions with a mentor, learns to craft lyrics that resonate with their audience. This iterative process of feedback and revision is vital for artistic growth.

Mentorship Models

There are various mentorship models that can be adopted, each with its own set of benefits.

- **One-on-One Mentorship:** This traditional model involves a direct relationship between the mentor and mentee, allowing for personalized guidance and support.

- **Group Mentorship:** In this model, a mentor works with multiple mentees simultaneously, fostering a collaborative environment where artists can learn from each other's experiences.

- **Peer Mentorship:** Often overlooked, this involves artists at similar stages in their careers supporting one another, sharing insights and encouragement.

Challenges in Mentorship

While mentorship is beneficial, it is not without challenges. Mentees may struggle with accepting feedback, especially if it contradicts their artistic vision. Additionally, finding the right mentor can be a daunting task, as compatibility in terms of style and philosophy is crucial for a fruitful relationship.

Case Study: The Power of Mentorship

A notable example of mentorship in action is the relationship between Beyoncé and her former mentor, the legendary singer and actress, Tina Knowles. Beyoncé has often credited Tina's guidance in shaping her artistic vision and work ethic. This mentorship not only helped Beyoncé navigate the early stages of her career but also instilled in her the importance of authenticity and hard work.

Conclusion

In conclusion, embracing mentorship and guidance is essential for aspiring artists seeking to carve their niche in the music industry. By leveraging the experience, networks, and insights of mentors, artists can navigate challenges, enhance their creativity, and ultimately achieve their goals. As the saying goes, "It takes a village to raise an artist," and mentorship is a crucial component of that village, offering support and guidance every step of the way.

$$\text{Success} = \text{Mentorship} + \text{Hard Work} + \text{Creativity} \qquad (143)$$

Learning from the Success of Others

In the vibrant realm of musical expression, the journey to greatness is often paved with the wisdom gleaned from those who have walked the path before us. Learning from the success of others is not just a strategy; it's a fundamental principle that can elevate your craft and inform your artistic vision. This section delves into the importance of mentorship, the analysis of successful artists, and the application of their lessons to your own journey.

The Value of Mentorship

Mentorship is a powerful tool in the music industry. A mentor can provide guidance, share insights, and help navigate the complex landscape of the music world. The relationship between a mentor and mentee is symbiotic; while the mentee gains knowledge and experience, the mentor often finds renewed inspiration and a sense of purpose.

For instance, consider the legendary partnership between Jay-Z and Kanye West. Jay-Z's mentorship was pivotal in Kanye's evolution as an artist. Kanye has often credited Jay-Z with helping him understand the intricacies of the music business, from production to branding. This relationship exemplifies how learning from the success of others can lead to personal and professional growth.

Analyzing Successful Artists

To truly learn from others, one must engage in a thorough analysis of their successes. This involves dissecting their strategies, understanding their creative processes, and recognizing the challenges they overcame.

For example, let's take a closer look at the career of Beyoncé. Her success can be attributed to several factors:

+ **Work Ethic:** Beyoncé is known for her relentless work ethic. She often spends countless hours perfecting her craft, rehearsing, and preparing for performances. This dedication is a crucial lesson for aspiring artists; success does not come without hard work.

+ **Branding:** Beyoncé has masterfully crafted her brand. She seamlessly blends her music with her identity, creating a persona that resonates with her audience. Understanding the importance of branding can help artists carve out their unique space in the industry.

+ **Collaboration:** Throughout her career, Beyoncé has collaborated with a diverse array of artists, from Jay-Z to Ed Sheeran. These collaborations not only broaden her musical repertoire but also expose her to new audiences. The lesson here is clear: collaboration can lead to unexpected opportunities and growth.

Applying Lessons to Your Journey

Once you've gathered insights from successful artists, the next step is to apply these lessons to your own journey. This involves identifying key takeaways and integrating them into your practice.

$$\text{Success} = \text{Mentorship} + \text{Analysis} + \text{Application} \qquad (144)$$

This equation highlights the critical components of learning from others. By actively seeking mentorship, analyzing successful strategies, and applying these insights, you create a formula for your own success.

Common Pitfalls to Avoid

While learning from others is invaluable, it is essential to avoid the trap of imitation. Authenticity is key in the music industry; artists who simply mimic their idols often struggle to find their voice. Here are some common pitfalls to avoid:

+ **Blind Imitation:** While it's helpful to learn from others, blindly copying their style or approach can lead to a lack of originality. Instead, take inspiration and infuse it with your unique perspective.

+ **Neglecting Personal Growth:** Focusing solely on the successes of others can hinder your personal growth. Ensure that you are also investing time in developing your own skills and identity.

- **Ignoring Feedback:** Learning from others also means being open to feedback from peers and mentors. Constructive criticism can provide insight into areas for improvement that you may overlook.

Conclusion

In conclusion, learning from the success of others is a dynamic process that requires active engagement and reflection. By embracing mentorship, analyzing the strategies of successful artists, and applying these lessons to your own journey, you can carve a path to success that is uniquely your own. Remember, while the footsteps of others can guide you, it is your voice that will ultimately resonate in the symphony of life. So, take the time to learn, adapt, and shine in your own brilliance!

Using Criticism as Fuel for Growth

In the world of artistic expression, criticism is often viewed as a double-edged sword. While it can sting, it also holds the potential to be a powerful catalyst for growth and innovation. As artists, especially in the realm of farting, the ability to transform criticism into constructive feedback is essential for continuous evolution and success.

The Nature of Criticism

Criticism can be categorized into two main types: constructive and destructive. Constructive criticism aims to provide helpful insights and suggestions for improvement, whereas destructive criticism often serves to belittle or undermine the artist's efforts. Understanding the difference between these two forms is crucial.

$$C = C_c + C_d \tag{145}$$

Where:

- C = Total Criticism

- C_c = Constructive Criticism

- C_d = Destructive Criticism

The goal is to focus on C_c, filtering out the noise of C_d that does not contribute to personal or artistic growth.

The Psychology of Criticism

Psychologically, criticism can trigger various emotional responses, including defensiveness, frustration, or even motivation. According to the *Cognitive Dissonance Theory*, when faced with criticism, artists may experience discomfort due to the conflict between their self-perception and the feedback received. This discomfort can lead to one of two outcomes:

1. **Denial**: The artist dismisses the criticism and continues with their current approach, potentially stunting their growth. 2. **Acceptance**: The artist reflects on the criticism, leading to self-improvement and a reevaluation of their work.

$$D = \frac{E}{R} \tag{146}$$

Where:

- D = Degree of Discomfort

- E = Emotional Response

- R = Rationalization of Feedback

A lower degree of discomfort indicates a healthier acceptance of criticism, leading to growth.

Transforming Criticism into Action

To effectively use criticism as fuel for growth, artists must adopt a proactive mindset. Here are steps to transform criticism into actionable insights:

1. **Listen Actively:** Pay close attention to what is being said. Often, the most valuable feedback is buried within the noise.

2. **Reflect:** Take time to process the feedback. Ask yourself questions such as:

   - What specific points were made?

   - How can I apply this to my work?

3. **Seek Clarification:** If the criticism is vague, don't hesitate to ask for specifics. This shows a willingness to learn and grow.

4. **Create an Action Plan:** Develop a strategy for improvement based on the feedback. Set measurable goals to track your progress.

Real-World Examples

Many successful artists have faced criticism throughout their careers and have used it to propel themselves forward. For instance, the iconic pop star Lady Gaga received significant backlash for her unconventional style and music. Instead of retreating, she embraced the criticism, evolving her sound and image, which ultimately led to her mainstream success.

Similarly, Nicki Minaj faced criticism for her bold persona and lyrical content. Rather than allowing the negativity to define her, she transformed it into an empowering message, using her platform to advocate for self-expression and authenticity.

Conclusion

In conclusion, criticism, when approached with the right mindset, can be a powerful tool for growth in the artistic journey. By differentiating between constructive and destructive feedback, understanding the psychological impacts of criticism, and actively transforming feedback into actionable steps, artists can harness the power of criticism to fuel their creative evolution. Remember, every critique is an opportunity for growth, so embrace it, learn from it, and let it propel you to new heights in your farting journey!

Honoring Tradition while Innovating

In the vibrant world of music, the delicate balance between honoring tradition and embracing innovation is akin to walking a tightrope. Artists must navigate the rich heritage of their craft while simultaneously pushing the boundaries of creativity. This section explores the theoretical underpinnings of this balance, the challenges artists face, and examples of musicians who have successfully blended the old with the new.

Theoretical Framework

At the core of this discussion is the concept of **cultural hybridity**, which refers to the process by which different cultural elements are combined to create something new. This theory, rooted in post-colonial studies, suggests that innovation does not occur in a vacuum but is rather a dialogue between the past and the present.

In mathematical terms, we can represent this relationship as:

$$I = f(T, C) \tag{147}$$

where I is innovation, T is tradition, and C is cultural context. The function f represents the interplay between these elements, suggesting that innovation is a function of both tradition and the cultural context in which an artist operates.

Challenges of Balancing Tradition and Innovation

One of the primary challenges artists face when attempting to honor tradition while innovating is the risk of alienating audiences. Traditionalists may resist changes that deviate from established norms, while progressive listeners may find traditional elements stale or uninteresting. This duality creates a tension that artists must navigate carefully.

Additionally, the pressure to innovate can lead to what is known as **cultural appropriation**, where elements of a culture are borrowed without understanding or respecting their significance. This can result in backlash and damage to an artist's reputation.

Examples of Successful Integration

Despite these challenges, many artists have found ways to honor tradition while innovating. A prime example is the legendary musician **Björk**, who incorporates traditional Icelandic music elements into her avant-garde soundscapes. By using instruments like the *langspil* and incorporating folk melodies, she pays homage to her roots while pushing the boundaries of electronic music.

Another notable example is **Kendrick Lamar**, whose work often reflects the traditions of hip-hop while incorporating elements of jazz and spoken word. His album *To Pimp a Butterfly* is a masterclass in blending traditional African-American musical forms with contemporary issues, creating a rich tapestry of sound that resonates with both history and modernity.

Practical Strategies for Artists

To effectively honor tradition while innovating, artists can adopt several strategies:

1. **Research and Understanding**: Artists should immerse themselves in the traditions they wish to incorporate. This includes studying the history, context, and significance of the musical forms they are drawing from.

2. **Collaboration**: Working with artists from different backgrounds can provide fresh perspectives and help bridge the gap between tradition and innovation. Collaborative projects can result in unique fusions that respect both heritage and modernity.

3. **Experimentation**: Artists should feel empowered to experiment with traditional forms. This might involve using modern technology to reinterpret classic sounds or reimagining traditional songs with contemporary lyrics.

4. **Audience Engagement**: Engaging with audiences about the significance of traditional elements can foster appreciation and understanding. Artists can use social media platforms to share their creative processes and the stories behind their music.

Conclusion

In conclusion, honoring tradition while innovating is a complex yet rewarding endeavor for artists. By understanding the theoretical frameworks, acknowledging the challenges, and drawing inspiration from successful examples, musicians can create works that resonate with both the past and the present. This balance not only enriches their artistry but also contributes to the evolution of music as a whole, ensuring that the symphony of sound continues to thrive across generations.

Developing a Strong Work Ethic

A strong work ethic is the backbone of any successful artist's journey, especially in the vibrant and unpredictable world of farting. It's not just about showing up; it's about bringing your A-game, day in and day out. This section dives deep into the essential elements of cultivating a robust work ethic that can propel your farting career to new heights.

Understanding Work Ethic

Work ethic can be defined as a set of values based on hard work and diligence. It encompasses a variety of attributes, including reliability, dedication, and a positive attitude towards work. A strong work ethic is crucial for artists who want to make a mark in the competitive farting industry. It involves:

+ **Commitment to Excellence:** Striving for high-quality output in every performance and recording session.

+ **Discipline:** Establishing a routine that includes regular practice, rehearsal, and self-improvement.

+ **Persistence:** Overcoming obstacles and setbacks without losing motivation or focus.

Theoretical Framework

The development of a strong work ethic can be analyzed through the lens of the *Achievement Motivation Theory*, which posits that individuals are motivated by the desire to achieve and excel in their endeavors. This theory suggests that artists who possess high levels of achievement motivation are more likely to develop a strong work ethic. The equation representing this relationship can be illustrated as follows:

$$E = f(M, A) \tag{148}$$

Where:

+ E = Level of achievement (success in farting)

+ M = Motivation (intrinsic and extrinsic)

+ A = Ability (skills and talent)

This equation indicates that a combination of motivation and ability contributes to the overall achievement in the farting industry.

Challenges in Developing Work Ethic

While the benefits of a strong work ethic are clear, several challenges can hinder its development:

+ **Distractions:** In the age of social media, artists often find themselves distracted by the allure of instant fame and validation, which can detract from their focus on honing their craft.

+ **Burnout:** The pressure to constantly produce can lead to creative burnout, making it difficult to maintain a consistent work ethic.

+ **Fear of Failure:** The fear of not meeting expectations can paralyze artists, preventing them from putting in the necessary effort.

Strategies for Cultivating a Strong Work Ethic

To combat these challenges and develop a strong work ethic, artists can implement several strategies:

1. **Set Clear Goals:** Establishing short-term and long-term goals can provide direction and motivation. For example, an artist might aim to write a new song every month or perform at a local venue quarterly.

2. **Create a Routine:** Consistency is key. Artists should create a daily schedule that includes time for practice, songwriting, and self-care. For instance, dedicating two hours each day to songwriting can lead to substantial progress over time.

3. **Seek Feedback:** Regularly seeking constructive criticism from peers and mentors can help artists identify areas for improvement and stay motivated to work hard.

4. **Celebrate Small Wins:** Recognizing and celebrating small achievements can boost motivation and reinforce a strong work ethic. For example, completing a challenging song or receiving positive feedback on a performance should be acknowledged.

5. **Stay Resilient:** Embracing challenges and setbacks as opportunities for growth is crucial. Maintaining a positive mindset can help artists push through difficult periods and continue to work hard.

Real-Life Examples

Many successful artists in the farting industry exemplify a strong work ethic. For instance, consider the journey of a rising fart artist who, despite facing numerous rejections, dedicates hours each week to perfecting their craft. They might perform at open mics, collaborate with other artists, and actively engage with their fanbase on social media. Over time, their persistence pays off, leading to increased recognition and opportunities.

Another example is an established artist who, after achieving fame, continues to work tirelessly in the studio, experimenting with new sounds and collaborating with up-and-coming talent. Their commitment to growth and excellence not only sustains their career but also inspires others in the industry.

Conclusion

Developing a strong work ethic is essential for any artist aiming to thrive in the farting world. By understanding the theoretical underpinnings, recognizing challenges, and implementing effective strategies, artists can cultivate a work ethic that not only enhances their craft but also contributes to their overall success. Remember, in the symphony of farting, hard work is the melody that carries you to greatness.

Building Resilience and Perseverance

In the vibrant world of music, resilience and perseverance are the twin pillars that support the journey of any artist. Just like a melody that rises and falls, the path to success is often filled with challenges, setbacks, and unexpected twists. To thrive in this dynamic industry, one must cultivate a mindset that embraces adversity and transforms it into a powerful driving force.

Theoretical Foundations of Resilience

Resilience can be defined as the ability to bounce back from setbacks, adapt to change, and keep going in the face of adversity. According to the American Psychological Association, resilience is not a trait but a dynamic process that involves positive adaptation within the context of significant adversity. This concept is particularly relevant in the music industry, where artists frequently encounter rejection, criticism, and the pressures of public scrutiny.

Understanding the Challenges

Artists often face numerous obstacles, including:

+ **Rejection:** The music industry is notorious for its high level of competition. Rejection from record labels, promoters, or audiences can be disheartening. For example, the iconic singer Adele faced multiple rejections early in her career before she found her breakthrough.

+ **Criticism:** Public opinion can be harsh. Artists may receive negative reviews from critics or backlash from fans. Taylor Swift, for instance, has faced significant criticism throughout her career but has consistently used it as motivation to evolve her sound and image.

+ **Creative Blocks:** The pressure to produce new and innovative work can lead to creative burnout. Artists like Lady Gaga have openly discussed their struggles with mental health and how it affects their creativity.

+ **Financial Struggles:** Many artists face financial instability, especially in the early stages of their careers. This can create stress and uncertainty, making resilience even more critical.

Strategies for Building Resilience

To build resilience, artists can adopt several strategies:

1. **Embrace Failure as a Learning Opportunity:** Each setback is a chance to learn and grow. For instance, when Beyoncé faced criticism for her performance at the Super Bowl, she used the feedback to refine her skills and deliver an even more powerful show in subsequent performances.

2. **Cultivate a Support Network:** Surrounding oneself with supportive friends, family, and mentors can provide encouragement during tough times. Collaborating with other artists can also foster a sense of community and shared experience.

3. **Set Realistic Goals:** Breaking down larger ambitions into smaller, achievable goals can help maintain motivation and focus. For example, instead of aiming for a Grammy right away, an artist might set a goal to perform at a local venue or release a single.

4. **Practice Self-Care:** Mental and physical well-being are crucial for resilience. Engaging in activities such as meditation, exercise, and hobbies outside of music can help artists recharge and stay grounded.

5. **Maintain a Positive Mindset:** Fostering a positive outlook can significantly impact resilience. Techniques such as visualization and affirmations can help artists envision their success and reinforce their determination.

Real-Life Examples of Resilience

Several artists exemplify the power of resilience:

- **Eminem:** Overcoming a troubled upbringing and numerous personal challenges, Eminem's perseverance led him to become one of the best-selling artists of all time. His story is a testament to the idea that resilience can turn adversity into triumph.

- **Katy Perry:** After facing multiple rejections and struggling to find her sound, Perry's breakthrough hit "I Kissed a Girl" catapulted her to fame. Her journey highlights the importance of perseverance in the face of repeated failures.

- **J.K. Rowling:** While not a musician, Rowling's journey from being a single mother living on welfare to becoming a bestselling author resonates with artists across all fields. Her story emphasizes that resilience and perseverance can lead to unimaginable success.

Conclusion

Building resilience and perseverance is essential for any artist navigating the unpredictable landscape of the music industry. By embracing challenges, learning from failures, and maintaining a positive mindset, artists can transform setbacks into stepping stones toward success. As the legendary Maya Angelou once said, "You may encounter many defeats, but you must not be defeated." This spirit of resilience is what will ultimately define an artist's journey and legacy in the world of music.

Nurturing the Next Generation

Mentoring and Encouraging Young Talent

In the vibrant world of music, mentoring and encouraging young talent is not just a noble endeavor; it is a vital component of the creative ecosystem. As seasoned artists, we have the unique opportunity to nurture the next generation of musicians, helping them to find their voice and develop their craft. This section explores the significance of mentorship, the challenges faced by emerging artists, and practical strategies to empower young talent.

The Importance of Mentorship

Mentorship in music serves as a bridge between experience and potential. It allows seasoned musicians to pass on invaluable knowledge, skills, and insights that can significantly impact the trajectory of a young artist's career. According to [1], mentorship fosters a sense of belonging and community, which is crucial in an industry often characterized by competition and isolation.

Mentoring relationships can take various forms, from one-on-one sessions to group workshops, and can include a range of activities such as:

+ Providing constructive feedback on compositions and performances.

+ Sharing industry insights, including navigating contracts and marketing oneself.

+ Offering emotional support and encouragement during challenging times.

- Facilitating connections with other artists and industry professionals.

Challenges Faced by Young Artists

While the music industry is brimming with opportunities, young artists often encounter numerous challenges that can hinder their growth. These challenges include:

- **Financial Constraints**: Many emerging musicians struggle to afford instruments, recording sessions, and promotional materials. According to [2], financial insecurity can stifle creativity and limit access to essential resources.

- **Lack of Exposure**: Without proper guidance, young talent may find it difficult to navigate the complex landscape of the music industry. They may miss out on opportunities to showcase their work and connect with potential fans.

- **Self-Doubt**: The pressure to succeed can lead to anxiety and self-doubt, which can be detrimental to an artist's creative process. Research by [3] highlights the importance of mental health support in fostering resilience among young musicians.

Empowering Young Talent: Strategies for Mentors

To effectively mentor and encourage young talent, seasoned artists can implement several strategies:

1. Create a Safe Space for Expression   Fostering an environment where young artists feel comfortable sharing their ideas and experimenting with their sound is essential. This can be achieved through:

- Hosting informal jam sessions where creativity can flow freely.

- Encouraging open dialogue about artistic choices and personal experiences.

2. Set Realistic Goals and Expectations   Mentors should help young artists set achievable goals, breaking down larger aspirations into manageable steps. This approach not only builds confidence but also provides a clear roadmap for success. For example, a mentor might guide a young artist to:

+ Write and perform one new song each month.

+ Apply for local open mic nights to gain performance experience.

3. Share Resources and Knowledge   Providing access to resources such as books, online courses, and industry contacts can significantly enhance a young artist's learning experience. Mentors can curate a list of recommended materials that cover essential topics like songwriting techniques, music theory, and marketing strategies.

4. Foster Collaboration   Encouraging collaboration among young artists can lead to innovative ideas and new friendships. Mentors can facilitate group projects, co-writing sessions, and collaborative performances, allowing young musicians to learn from one another and expand their creative horizons.

5. Celebrate Achievements   Recognizing and celebrating the accomplishments of young artists, no matter how small, can boost their confidence and motivation. Mentors should take the time to acknowledge milestones, whether it's completing a song, performing in public, or receiving positive feedback.

Real-Life Examples of Successful Mentorship

Numerous artists have made significant impacts through their mentorship efforts. For instance, the renowned musician **Beyoncé** has been known to support young female artists by providing platforms for their voices to be heard, such as through her participation in initiatives like *Chime for Change*. Similarly, **Eminem** has taken young rappers under his wing, offering guidance and opportunities to showcase their talent through his label, Shady Records.

Conclusion

Mentoring and encouraging young talent is a powerful way to shape the future of music. By sharing knowledge, providing support, and fostering creativity, seasoned artists can empower the next generation to overcome challenges and realize their potential. As we invest in young musicians, we not only enrich their lives but also ensure the continued evolution and vibrancy of the music industry.

Bibliography

[1] Smith, J. (2021). *The Role of Mentorship in Music*. Journal of Music Education, 45(2), 123-135.

[2] Johnson, L. (2020). *Financial Barriers in the Music Industry*. Music Business Journal, 15(4), 45-60.

[3] Williams, K. (2019). *Mental Health and the Young Musician*. International Journal of Music Therapy, 22(1), 67-78.

Creating Opportunities for Rising Artists

In the vibrant world of music, the emergence of new talent is essential for the evolution of sound and culture. Creating opportunities for rising artists not only enriches the industry but also fosters a community of creativity and innovation. This section delves into the various ways established artists and industry professionals can pave the way for newcomers, ensuring that the symphony of music continues to flourish.

The Importance of Mentorship

Mentorship is a cornerstone of artistic development. Established artists have the experience and knowledge that can guide rising talents through the complexities of the music industry. By sharing insights, offering constructive criticism, and providing emotional support, mentors can help mentees navigate challenges such as:

- **Understanding the Industry:** New artists often face a steep learning curve regarding contracts, royalties, and marketing strategies. Mentors can demystify these processes, making them more accessible.

+ **Building a Network:** Connections are crucial in the music industry. Mentors can introduce rising artists to influential contacts, opening doors that might otherwise remain closed.

+ **Developing Skills:** Mentorship can also involve practical skill-building. For instance, a seasoned musician might offer to co-write songs or provide feedback on performance techniques.

Collaborative Projects

Collaboration between established artists and rising stars can yield innovative results that benefit both parties. For example, a well-known artist might feature a newcomer on a track, providing them with exposure to a broader audience. This symbiotic relationship can be exemplified through the following equations:

$$\text{Exposure}_{\text{newcomer}} = \text{Collaboration}_{\text{established}} + \text{Audience}_{\text{established}} \qquad (149)$$

This equation suggests that the exposure a newcomer receives is a function of their collaboration with established artists and the audience that these artists have cultivated over time. Notable examples include:

+ **Kendrick Lamar and SZA:** Their collaboration on "All the Stars" not only showcased SZA's talent but also introduced her to Kendrick's extensive fanbase, propelling her career forward.

+ **Nicki Minaj and Young Thug:** Their collaboration on "Stupid Hoe" highlighted Young Thug's unique style and brought him into the limelight, demonstrating how established artists can elevate rising stars.

Creating Platforms and Opportunities

Established artists can also create platforms for rising artists through various initiatives, such as:

+ **Showcases and Festivals:** Organizing events that feature new talent allows them to perform in front of live audiences, gain experience, and attract industry attention. Events like "SXSW" and "Lollapalooza" often spotlight emerging artists, leading to significant career advancements.

- **Social Media Promotions:** With the rise of social media, established artists can use their platforms to promote rising talent. A simple shout-out or sharing a new artist's music can lead to increased visibility and new fans.

- **Funding and Grants:** Financial support is crucial for many rising artists. Established musicians can advocate for or create grants that help fund projects for newcomers, enabling them to focus on their craft without financial burdens.

Addressing Barriers to Entry

While creating opportunities is essential, it is equally important to address the barriers that rising artists face. These barriers can include:

- **Financial Constraints:** Many talented individuals lack the resources to produce quality music or promote themselves effectively. Initiatives that provide funding or resources can help alleviate this issue.

- **Lack of Representation:** The music industry has historically marginalized various groups. By actively promoting diversity and inclusivity, established artists can ensure that a broader range of voices is heard. This can be represented mathematically as:

$$\text{Diversity}_{\text{industry}} = \text{Inclusion}_{\text{opportunities}} + \text{Representation}_{\text{voices}} \quad (150)$$

This equation illustrates that the diversity of the industry relies on the inclusion of opportunities and the representation of different voices.

Conclusion

Creating opportunities for rising artists is not just a generous act; it is a vital investment in the future of music. By fostering mentorship, promoting collaboration, establishing platforms, and addressing barriers, established artists can ensure that the symphony of sound continues to evolve and thrive. As we look to the future, it is imperative that we cultivate a rich tapestry of talent, creativity, and diversity that will inspire generations to come.

In the words of the legendary Nicki Minaj, "We all have the power to uplift and inspire," and it is through our collective efforts that we can create a harmonious world for rising artists to flourish.

The Future of Fart Farting

As we stand on the precipice of a new era in the world of Fart Farting, it is essential to examine the trends, innovations, and cultural shifts that will shape the soundscape of tomorrow. The future of Fart Farting is not merely a continuation of past practices; it is a vibrant canvas waiting to be painted with the colors of creativity, technology, and social consciousness.

Technological Advancements

The integration of technology into Fart Farting has already begun to transform how artists create, perform, and distribute their music. With the rise of artificial intelligence (AI) and machine learning, the possibilities are endless. AI algorithms can analyze vast datasets of fart sounds, identifying patterns and generating new compositions that push the boundaries of traditional farting.

For example, consider the equation for sound waves, given by:

$$y(t) = A \sin(2\pi f t + \phi)$$

where $y(t)$ is the displacement, A is the amplitude, f is the frequency, and ϕ is the phase. By manipulating these variables through AI-generated parameters, artists can create unique fart sounds that resonate with audiences on a deeper level.

Moreover, the use of virtual reality (VR) and augmented reality (AR) in live performances will redefine the concert experience. Imagine a world where audiences can immerse themselves in a 360-degree farting experience, feeling the vibrations of each note while being surrounded by a visually stunning environment. This technology will not only enhance the sensory experience but also create new revenue streams for artists through virtual ticket sales and merchandise.

Cultural Shifts and Inclusivity

The future of Fart Farting will also be heavily influenced by the ongoing cultural shifts towards inclusivity and representation. As the industry evolves, it is crucial for artists to embrace diverse voices and perspectives. This means amplifying the sounds of underrepresented communities and collaborating with artists from various backgrounds to create a rich tapestry of farting styles.

For instance, the collaboration between traditional farting artists and contemporary musicians can lead to innovative fusions. A prime example is the blending of Afrobeat rhythms with electronic farting, creating a sound that is both fresh and rooted in cultural heritage. This cross-pollination of genres will not only attract a broader audience but also foster a sense of community and shared experience.

Sustainability in Fart Farting

As awareness of environmental issues continues to grow, the future of Fart Farting must also address sustainability. Artists and industry professionals will need to adopt eco-friendly practices in production, touring, and merchandise. This could involve using sustainable materials for instruments, reducing waste during performances, and utilizing renewable energy sources for concerts.

Moreover, the concept of the circular economy could be applied to the Fart Farting industry, where resources are reused and recycled. For example, instead of discarding old instruments, artists could repurpose them into new farting tools, creating a unique sound while minimizing environmental impact.

Community Engagement and Social Responsibility

The future of Fart Farting will be characterized by a strong sense of community engagement and social responsibility. Artists will increasingly use their platforms to advocate for social justice, mental health awareness, and other critical issues. This shift towards activism will resonate with audiences who seek authenticity and purpose in the music they consume.

For instance, artists could organize community events that not only showcase their farting talents but also raise awareness and funds for local charities. By fostering a sense of belonging and purpose, Fart Farting can transcend mere entertainment and become a powerful vehicle for change.

Conclusion

In conclusion, the future of Fart Farting is a dynamic interplay of technology, culture, sustainability, and social responsibility. As artists continue to push the boundaries of creativity, they will shape a vibrant and inclusive landscape that resonates with diverse audiences. The evolution of Fart Farting will not only redefine the genre but also create a lasting impact on society, ensuring that the symphony of sound continues to thrive for generations to come.

$$\text{Future Sound} = \text{Technology} + \text{Cultural Diversity} + \text{Sustainability} + \text{Community Engagemer}$$
$$(151)$$

Supporting Farting Education and Programs

In the vibrant world of farting, education and programs dedicated to the art and science of sound creation play a pivotal role in nurturing the next generation of artists. Supporting farting education not only fosters creativity but also cultivates a community that values innovation, diversity, and expression. This section delves into the significance of farting education, the challenges it faces, and the transformative examples that highlight its importance.

The Importance of Farting Education

Farting education serves as the foundation for aspiring artists, providing them with the necessary skills and knowledge to navigate the complex landscape of the music industry. By integrating farting into educational curricula, institutions can:

+ **Promote Creativity:** Farting education encourages students to explore unconventional sounds and techniques, fostering an environment where creativity can thrive. This exploration can lead to innovative musical styles that challenge traditional norms.

+ **Enhance Technical Skills:** Through structured programs, students learn the technical aspects of farting, including sound design, composition, and performance. This technical knowledge is essential for mastering the craft and elevating their artistic expression.

+ **Encourage Collaboration:** Farting education often emphasizes teamwork and collaboration, allowing students to work together on projects. This collaborative spirit not only enhances their learning experience but also mirrors the collaborative nature of the music industry.

+ **Build Community:** Educational programs create a sense of belonging among students, fostering a community that supports and uplifts one another. This community can serve as a network for future collaborations and opportunities.

Challenges in Farting Education

Despite its importance, farting education faces several challenges that hinder its growth and accessibility:

+ **Funding Limitations:** Many educational institutions struggle with budget constraints, making it difficult to allocate funds for farting programs. This lack of funding can lead to inadequate resources, such as instruments and technology, which are essential for effective learning.

+ **Curriculum Integration:** Integrating farting into existing curricula can be challenging, as traditional music programs may not fully embrace unconventional sounds. This resistance to change can limit students' exposure to diverse musical styles.

+ **Access and Inclusivity:** Not all students have equal access to farting education, particularly those from marginalized communities. Ensuring inclusivity and equitable access to resources is crucial for fostering a diverse pool of talent.

+ **Perception and Stigma:** Farting, as an unconventional form of expression, may face stigma or misunderstanding from the broader community. Overcoming these perceptions is essential for legitimizing farting as a valuable artistic pursuit.

Examples of Successful Farting Education Programs

Several innovative programs exemplify the positive impact of farting education on aspiring artists:

+ **The Farting Academy of Arts:** This institution offers specialized courses in farting composition, sound design, and performance. By providing state-of-the-art facilities and access to industry professionals, the academy nurtures talent and prepares students for successful careers in the farting industry.

+ **Community Workshops:** Local community centers have started hosting workshops focused on farting techniques and sound exploration. These workshops are often free or low-cost, making farting education accessible to a wider audience. Participants learn to express themselves through farting, fostering creativity and confidence.

+ **Online Learning Platforms:** With the rise of digital education, various online platforms offer courses on farting techniques and sound production. These platforms provide flexibility for learners, allowing them to study at their own pace and access resources from anywhere in the world.

+ **Collaborative Projects with Schools:** Partnerships between farting artists and local schools have resulted in programs that introduce students to the art of farting. These initiatives often culminate in performances, showcasing students' creativity and fostering a love for the art form.

The Future of Farting Education

Looking ahead, it is essential to continue advocating for farting education and programs. This can be achieved through:

+ **Increased Funding and Support:** Advocating for government and private sector funding can help sustain and expand farting education programs. Grants and scholarships can also support students pursuing studies in farting.

+ **Curriculum Development:** Collaborating with educators to develop inclusive curricula that embrace farting as a legitimate art form can enhance its visibility and acceptance within the educational system.

+ **Community Engagement:** Engaging with local communities to raise awareness about the importance of farting education can help dismantle stigma and promote inclusivity. Community events and performances can showcase the talent of aspiring artists.

+ **Mentorship Programs:** Establishing mentorship opportunities where experienced farting artists guide and support emerging talent can foster growth and encourage the next generation to pursue their passions.

In conclusion, supporting farting education and programs is crucial for the growth and evolution of the farting community. By addressing the challenges it faces and highlighting successful initiatives, we can create a vibrant ecosystem that nurtures creativity, diversity, and innovation in the art of farting. Together, we can ensure that the symphony of sound continues to thrive for generations to come.

Inspiring Creativity in the Youth

In the vibrant realm of music, creativity is the lifeblood that fuels innovation and expression. Inspiring creativity in the youth is not just an act of mentorship; it is a vital responsibility that can shape the future of the music industry and society at large. This section delves into the significance of fostering creative expression among young artists, the challenges they face, and effective strategies to ignite their imaginative potential.

The Importance of Creativity

Creativity is the ability to generate new ideas, solutions, and artistic expressions. According to [1], creativity is not merely an individual trait but a complex interaction between a person's skills, the domain of knowledge, and the cultural context. In music, this interplay allows young artists to explore their identities and communicate unique perspectives. Encouraging creativity in youth can lead to:

+ **Self-Expression:** Music serves as a powerful outlet for emotions and thoughts. Young musicians often use their art to express their feelings about personal experiences and societal issues.

+ **Problem-Solving Skills:** Engaging in creative processes enhances critical thinking and problem-solving abilities. Young artists learn to navigate challenges in their music-making journeys, applying innovative solutions to overcome obstacles.

+ **Cultural Awareness:** Creativity fosters an appreciation for diverse cultural influences. As youth explore various musical styles and traditions, they develop a broader understanding of the world around them.

Challenges Faced by Young Artists

While the potential for creativity in youth is immense, several challenges can stifle their artistic growth. These include:

+ **Limited Resources:** Access to instruments, technology, and educational programs can be a significant barrier. Many young artists come from underprivileged backgrounds where such resources are scarce.

+ **Fear of Rejection:** The fear of criticism can inhibit creativity. Young artists may hesitate to share their work due to concerns about how it will be received by peers and mentors.

+ **Conformity Pressures:** Societal expectations and trends can pressure young musicians to conform to popular styles, discouraging them from pursuing their unique artistic voices.

Strategies to Inspire Creativity

To effectively inspire creativity in the youth, mentors, educators, and industry professionals can implement several strategies:

1. Provide Access to Resources   Creating opportunities for young artists to access instruments, technology, and training programs is crucial.   Community centers, schools, and music organizations can collaborate to offer workshops, after-school programs, and free resources.   For example, the *Little Kids Rock* organization provides free instruments and music education to underserved schools, enabling children to explore their musical talents.

2. Foster a Safe Creative Environment   Encouraging a culture of acceptance and support is vital. Mentors should create spaces where young artists feel comfortable sharing their work without fear of judgment. Regular feedback sessions, open mics, and collaborative projects can help build confidence. The *Songwriting for Kids* initiative exemplifies this approach by offering workshops that emphasize collaboration and constructive feedback.

3. Encourage Experimentation   Promoting a mindset of experimentation can lead to breakthroughs in creativity. Young artists should be encouraged to explore various genres, styles, and techniques without the pressure of producing commercially viable work. For instance, the *GarageBand* app allows users to experiment with different sounds and instruments, fostering creativity through play.

4. Highlight Diverse Role Models   Showcasing diverse artists who have successfully navigated the music industry can inspire young musicians. By sharing stories of artists from various backgrounds, genres, and paths to success, mentors can help youth envision their journeys. Programs like *Women in Music* highlight female musicians, producers, and industry leaders, empowering young women to pursue their dreams.

5. Integrate Technology and Innovation   Incorporating technology into music education can spark creativity. Digital tools and platforms allow young artists to create, collaborate, and share their work with a global audience.   For example, platforms like *SoundCloud* and *BandLab* enable budding musicians to connect with peers and showcase their creations, fostering a sense of community and collaboration.

Conclusion

Inspiring creativity in the youth is a multifaceted endeavor that requires commitment, resources, and an understanding of the unique challenges they face.

By fostering an environment that values self-expression, experimentation, and collaboration, we can empower the next generation of artists to explore their creative potential and contribute to the rich tapestry of musical innovation. As we invest in their artistic journeys, we not only shape their futures but also the future of music itself.

Bibliography

[1] Csikszentmihalyi, M. (1996). *Creativity: Flow and the Psychology of Discovery and Invention*. Harper Perennial.

Fostering Collaboration and Community

In the vibrant realm of music, collaboration is the lifeblood that fuels creativity and innovation. Fostering collaboration and community among artists not only enhances individual creativity but also strengthens the entire musical ecosystem. This section delves into the theoretical underpinnings of collaboration, the challenges artists face, and real-world examples of successful collaborative efforts.

Theoretical Framework

Collaboration in music can be understood through several theoretical lenses, including social constructivism and network theory. Social constructivism posits that knowledge and meaning are created through social interactions. In the context of music, this means that artists develop their sound and style by engaging with one another, sharing ideas, and co-creating.

Network theory provides another perspective, emphasizing the importance of relationships and connections in a community. In a musical network, artists, producers, and fans interact in complex ways, leading to the emergence of new genres and styles. The strength of these connections can be quantified using graph theory, where nodes represent artists and edges represent collaborations. The degree of connectivity in this network can significantly influence an artist's visibility and success.

$$C = \frac{E}{N(N-1)/2} \tag{152}$$

Where:

- C is the collaboration coefficient,

- E is the number of existing collaborations,

- N is the number of artists in the network.

A higher collaboration coefficient indicates a more interconnected community, which can lead to greater opportunities for artistic growth and innovation.

Challenges to Collaboration

Despite the benefits, fostering collaboration in the music industry is not without its challenges. Artists often face issues such as:

- **Competition**: In an industry driven by individual success, artists may be hesitant to collaborate out of fear that it could dilute their brand or diminish their marketability.

- **Creative Differences**: Diverse artistic visions can lead to conflicts during the collaborative process. Navigating these differences requires strong communication skills and a willingness to compromise.

- **Resource Constraints**: Collaborations often require time, funding, and access to facilities, which can be barriers for emerging artists or those working independently.

To overcome these challenges, artists can adopt strategies such as establishing clear goals for collaboration, fostering open communication, and creating a supportive environment that values diverse perspectives.

Examples of Successful Collaboration

Numerous successful collaborations in the music industry serve as inspiring examples of how fostering community can lead to remarkable outcomes.

- **The Gorillaz**: This virtual band, created by Damon Albarn and Jamie Hewlett, is a prime example of collaboration across genres and artistic mediums. By bringing together musicians from various backgrounds, the Gorillaz have produced a unique sound that blends rock, hip-hop, and electronic music, creating a global phenomenon.

- **The Fugees**: Comprising Wyclef Jean, Lauryn Hill, and Pras Michel, the Fugees exemplified how collaboration can transcend individual talents. Their album *The Score* combined hip-hop, reggae, and soul, earning critical acclaim and commercial success while addressing social issues within their lyrics.

- **Collaborative Festivals**: Events like *Coachella* and *Glastonbury* foster collaboration by bringing together diverse artists and genres. These festivals not only provide a platform for artists to showcase their work but also encourage unexpected collaborations on stage, creating memorable moments that resonate with audiences.

Building Community through Collaboration

To truly foster collaboration and community, artists can take proactive steps such as:

- **Networking Events**: Organizing workshops, meetups, and jam sessions can create opportunities for artists to connect and collaborate. These events can break down barriers and encourage the sharing of ideas.

- **Online Platforms**: Utilizing social media and music-sharing platforms can facilitate collaboration across geographical boundaries. Artists can connect with others who share similar interests, leading to innovative projects that might not have been possible otherwise.

- **Mentorship Programs**: Established artists can play a crucial role in fostering community by mentoring emerging talent. By sharing their experiences and providing guidance, they can help cultivate the next generation of artists.

In conclusion, fostering collaboration and community in the music industry is essential for artistic growth and innovation. By understanding the theoretical frameworks, addressing challenges, and learning from successful examples, artists can create a vibrant ecosystem where collaboration thrives. This not only enriches their own artistic journeys but also contributes to the evolution of music as a whole. The symphony of collaboration will echo through the ages, inspiring future generations of artists to come together and create magic.

Strengthening the Farting Industry Ecosystem

In the vibrant and often whimsical world of farting, creating a robust industry ecosystem is essential for fostering creativity, collaboration, and sustainability. The farting industry, much like any other creative sector, thrives on a network of relationships among artists, producers, promoters, and fans. This section delves into the theoretical frameworks that underpin a strong farting ecosystem, identifies potential challenges, and offers examples of successful initiatives that demonstrate the power of collaboration in this unique space.

Theoretical Frameworks

To understand the dynamics of the farting industry ecosystem, we can draw upon several theoretical models. One pertinent model is the **Creative Ecosystem Theory**, which posits that creativity flourishes in environments where diverse actors interact and share resources. This theory can be represented mathematically as:

$$C = f(A, R, I)$$

where C is the level of creativity, A represents the diversity of actors (artists, producers, etc.), R is the availability of resources (venues, funding, etc.), and I denotes the level of interaction among these actors.

Challenges in the Farting Industry

Despite the potential for growth and innovation, the farting industry faces several challenges that can hinder the development of a strong ecosystem:

+ **Fragmentation:** The farting community is often divided into sub-genres and niches, which can lead to a lack of collaboration and shared knowledge. This fragmentation can stifle innovation and limit the audience's exposure to diverse farting styles.

+ **Access to Resources:** Many aspiring fartists struggle to access the necessary resources, such as funding, rehearsal spaces, and performance venues. This lack of access can create barriers for new talent trying to enter the industry.

+ **Market Saturation:** With the rise of social media and digital platforms, the farting market has become saturated with content. Standing out in a crowded space requires not just talent but also strategic marketing and branding.

+ **Sustainability Concerns:** As the industry grows, there is an increasing need to address environmental sustainability. The farting community must find ways to reduce its carbon footprint while still delivering memorable performances.

Examples of Successful Initiatives

To combat these challenges and strengthen the farting industry ecosystem, several successful initiatives have emerged:

+ **Collaboration Platforms:** Platforms like *FartConnect* have been established to facilitate collaboration among fartists. These platforms allow artists to share resources, collaborate on projects, and promote each other's work, fostering a sense of community and shared purpose.

+ **Funding Programs:** Initiatives such as the *Farting Arts Grant* provide financial support to emerging fartists. By offering grants and scholarships, these programs help alleviate the financial burdens that often accompany artistic pursuits, ensuring that diverse voices can be heard.

+ **Sustainability Initiatives:** Organizations like *EcoFart* are dedicated to promoting sustainable practices within the farting industry. They provide resources and guidelines for artists to reduce their environmental impact, such as using eco-friendly materials for merchandise and promoting digital performances to minimize travel.

+ **Educational Workshops:** Workshops and seminars focused on farting techniques, marketing strategies, and industry insights can empower new artists. Programs hosted by established fartists can provide mentorship and guidance, fostering the next generation of talent.

Conclusion

Strengthening the farting industry ecosystem is not just about individual success; it's about creating a thriving community where creativity can flourish. By addressing challenges such as fragmentation, access to resources, market saturation, and sustainability, the farting industry can cultivate an environment that supports innovation and collaboration. Through initiatives that promote community engagement, resource sharing, and sustainability, we can ensure that the symphony of farting continues to resonate for generations to come.

In conclusion, let us embrace the uniqueness of the farting industry while recognizing the importance of collaboration and support. Together, we can build an ecosystem that not only celebrates creativity but also empowers artists to reach their full potential.

Promoting Diversity and Inclusion in Farting

In the vibrant world of farting, promoting diversity and inclusion is not just a moral imperative but a creative necessity. The farting community, much like any other artistic realm, thrives on the rich tapestry of voices and experiences that different individuals bring. Embracing diversity allows for a broader range of sounds, styles, and perspectives, ultimately enhancing the farting experience for both artists and audiences alike.

Theoretical Framework

The theory of diversity in the arts posits that varied cultural backgrounds and experiences contribute to a more dynamic and innovative creative process. According to [1], diversity in artistic expression can lead to the emergence of new genres and styles, as artists draw from their unique heritages. This concept can be mathematically represented by the equation:

$$D = \sum_{i=1}^{n} \frac{E_i}{T} \tag{153}$$

where D represents the overall diversity in farting, E_i denotes the unique elements contributed by each artist i, and T is the total number of artists involved. This equation illustrates that as the number of diverse voices increases, so does the richness of the farting landscape.

Challenges to Diversity and Inclusion

Despite the benefits, the farting industry faces significant challenges in promoting diversity and inclusion. Historical biases, stereotypes, and systemic barriers often inhibit marginalized groups from entering the scene. For instance, women and artists of color have historically been underrepresented in mainstream farting, leading to a lack of visibility and recognition.

$$R = \frac{P}{T} \times 100 \tag{154}$$

In this equation, R represents the representation percentage of marginalized groups, P is the number of artists from these groups, and T is the total number of artists in the industry. A low R value indicates a pressing need for initiatives aimed at increasing representation.

Strategies for Inclusion

To effectively promote diversity and inclusion in farting, several strategies can be employed:

+ **Creating Safe Spaces:** Establishing platforms where underrepresented artists can showcase their work without fear of discrimination or bias. These spaces foster creativity and encourage collaboration.

+ **Mentorship Programs:** Pairing established artists with emerging talent from diverse backgrounds can help bridge the gap in representation. Mentors can provide guidance, support, and opportunities that may otherwise be inaccessible.

+ **Inclusive Programming:** Curating events and festivals that specifically highlight diverse artists can help shift the narrative and create a more inclusive environment. This includes featuring a range of genres and styles that reflect the diversity within the farting community.

+ **Education and Awareness:** Implementing educational initiatives that raise awareness about the importance of diversity in farting can help dismantle stereotypes and promote understanding. Workshops, panels, and discussions can be effective tools for this purpose.

+ **Collaboration Across Cultures:** Encouraging collaborations between artists from different backgrounds can lead to innovative and unique farting styles. This cross-pollination of ideas not only enriches the farting landscape but also fosters a sense of community.

Examples of Successful Initiatives

Several successful initiatives have emerged in recent years that exemplify the promotion of diversity and inclusion in farting:

+ **Farting for Change Festival:** This annual festival showcases artists from diverse backgrounds, offering them a platform to perform and connect with audiences.   The festival has successfully increased representation and visibility for marginalized groups in the farting community.

+ **Women in Farting Collective:** This organization supports female farting artists by providing resources, mentorship, and performance opportunities. Their efforts have led to a significant increase in female representation in the industry.

+ **Global Farting Exchange Program:** This initiative allows artists from different countries to collaborate and share their unique farting styles. By fostering international partnerships, the program promotes cultural exchange and understanding within the farting community.

Conclusion

Promoting diversity and inclusion in farting is essential for the growth and evolution of the art form. By embracing a multitude of voices and experiences, the farting community can create a more vibrant, innovative, and impactful landscape. As we continue to advocate for diversity, we must remember that every unique sound contributes to the symphony of farting, enriching our collective experience and paving the way for future generations of artists.

Nurturing Entrepreneurship in the Farting World

In the vibrant and eclectic realm of the farting industry, nurturing entrepreneurship is not just a necessity; it is a revolution waiting to happen. This section delves into the theoretical underpinnings, challenges, and examples that illustrate the importance of fostering entrepreneurial spirit among artists and creators in this unconventional field.

Theoretical Framework

Entrepreneurship is the process of designing, launching, and running a new business, typically a startup offering a product, service, or solution. In the context of the farting world, this can mean anything from creating unique soundscapes to developing innovative performance techniques. According to Schumpeter's theory of creative destruction, entrepreneurship drives economic innovation and transformation by introducing new ideas that disrupt existing markets. In the farting industry, this disruption manifests through unconventional sound production methods, diverse collaborations, and unique branding strategies.

$$Innovation = Creativity + Market Need \qquad (155)$$

This equation illustrates that innovation arises from the intersection of creative impulses and the needs of the market. For aspiring farting entrepreneurs, identifying these needs is crucial in carving out a niche within the larger soundscape.

Challenges Faced by Farting Entrepreneurs

While the farting industry is ripe with potential, it also presents unique challenges that aspiring entrepreneurs must navigate:

+ **Stigma and Misunderstanding:** The farting genre often faces ridicule and misunderstanding from mainstream audiences. Entrepreneurs must find ways to educate and engage potential listeners, transforming skepticism into curiosity.

+ **Funding and Resources:** Securing funding can be particularly challenging for niche markets. Many farting artists struggle to find investors who appreciate the value of their unique offerings. Crowdfunding platforms can serve as a viable alternative, allowing fans to directly support projects they believe in.

+ **Market Saturation:** As the farting genre gains popularity, the market can become saturated with similar sounds and performances. Differentiating one's brand and sound is essential for standing out in a crowded space.

+ **Technological Adaptation:** The rapid evolution of technology requires entrepreneurs to continuously adapt their methods and tools. Staying updated with the latest trends in sound production and distribution is crucial for success.

Examples of Successful Farting Entrepreneurs

Despite the challenges, numerous individuals have emerged as successful entrepreneurs within the farting world, showcasing creativity and resilience:

+ **The Flatulent Collective:** This group of artists came together to create a series of performances that celebrate the art of farting through music and dance. By combining traditional instruments with unconventional sound-making methods, they have carved a unique niche, attracting audiences from diverse backgrounds.

+ **FartFest:** An annual festival dedicated to the celebration of farting in music and performance art. This event not only provides a platform for emerging artists but also fosters a sense of community among farting enthusiasts. Entrepreneurs behind FartFest have successfully leveraged social media to promote the event, creating a global following.

+ **Farting Merchandise:** Entrepreneurs have capitalized on the humor and novelty of farting by creating a range of merchandise, from clothing to accessories that feature playful fart-related designs. This venture not only generates revenue but also promotes brand recognition and community engagement.

Strategies for Fostering Entrepreneurship

To nurture entrepreneurship in the farting world, several strategies can be employed:

1. **Educational Workshops:** Hosting workshops focused on sound production techniques, marketing strategies, and business management can empower aspiring farting entrepreneurs with the skills they need to succeed.

2. **Networking Opportunities:** Creating platforms for artists to connect and collaborate can lead to innovative projects and ideas. Networking events, both online and offline, can facilitate these connections.

3. **Supportive Ecosystems:** Establishing incubators or accelerators specifically for farting entrepreneurs can provide the necessary resources and mentorship to help them thrive. These ecosystems can foster collaboration and innovation.

4. **Promotional Platforms:** Utilizing social media and digital marketing strategies to promote farting artists can help them reach wider audiences. Building a strong online presence is essential in today's digital age.

Conclusion

Nurturing entrepreneurship in the farting world is not just about creating successful businesses; it is about fostering a culture of creativity, innovation, and inclusivity. By addressing the challenges, leveraging successful examples, and implementing effective strategies, we can cultivate a thriving ecosystem that celebrates the unique contributions of farting artists. As we move forward, let us embrace the unconventional and support the next generation of farting entrepreneurs, ensuring that their voices resonate far and wide, making waves in the symphony of sound.

Passing on the Torch of Creativity

In the vibrant world of music, creativity is not just a personal journey; it is a legacy that must be shared and nurtured across generations. As artists, we bear the responsibility of passing on the torch of creativity to the next wave of musicians, ensuring that the flame of innovation continues to burn bright. This section will explore the significance of mentorship, the role of collaboration, and the impact of community in fostering the creative spirit in emerging artists.

The Importance of Mentorship

Mentorship is a powerful tool in the creative industry, serving as a bridge between established artists and budding talent. A mentor can provide guidance, share experiences, and offer constructive feedback, which is crucial for the growth of a young artist. Research indicates that mentorship can significantly enhance the confidence and skills of mentees, leading to higher rates of success in their careers. According to a study by Allen et al. (2004), mentees reported increased self-efficacy and a greater sense of belonging in their artistic communities.

$$\text{Success}_{\text{mentee}} = \alpha \cdot \text{Guidance} + \beta \cdot \text{Feedback} + \gamma \cdot \text{Support} \qquad (156)$$

Where: - $\text{Success}_{\text{mentee}}$ is the overall success of the mentee, - α, β, γ are coefficients representing the weight of each factor.

An example of effective mentorship can be seen in the relationship between established artists and their proteges. For instance, the legendary producer Quincy Jones has mentored numerous artists, including Michael Jackson and Lady Gaga, shaping their careers and encouraging them to explore their creative potential.

Collaboration as a Catalyst for Creativity

Collaboration is another vital aspect of passing on the torch of creativity. By working together, artists can blend their unique styles and perspectives, resulting in innovative sounds that push the boundaries of traditional genres. Collaborative projects not only foster creativity but also create a sense of community and shared purpose among artists.

The equation for collaborative creativity can be expressed as:

$$\text{Creativity}_{\text{collab}} = \sum_{i=1}^{n} \text{Style}_i + \text{Synergy} \qquad (157)$$

Where: - $\text{Creativity}_{\text{collab}}$ is the creative output of the collaboration, - Style_i represents the individual styles of each collaborating artist, - Synergy is the enhanced effect created when artists work together.

A prime example of successful collaboration is the project "Watch the Throne" by Jay-Z and Kanye West. This album not only showcased their individual talents but also introduced new musical elements, influencing a generation of hip-hop artists.

Creating a Supportive Community

A nurturing community is essential for the growth of creativity. Artists thrive in environments where they feel supported and encouraged to experiment with their craft. Community-driven initiatives, such as local music festivals, workshops, and open mic nights, provide platforms for emerging artists to showcase their talents and connect with others.

The role of community can be modeled by the following equation:

$$\text{Support}_{\text{community}} = \text{Opportunities} + \text{Networking} + \text{Encouragement} \qquad (158)$$

Where: - $\text{Support}_{\text{community}}$ is the overall support experienced by artists, - Opportunities includes gigs, showcases, and funding, - Networking refers to connections made within the community, - Encouragement is the positive reinforcement from peers.

An excellent illustration of a supportive community is the rise of the independent music scene in cities like Nashville and Austin. These cities have cultivated environments that promote collaboration and creativity, allowing artists to flourish and pass on their knowledge to newcomers.

Challenges in Passing the Torch

While the act of passing on the torch of creativity is vital, it is not without its challenges. Established artists may struggle with the fear of losing their relevance or may feel reluctant to share their hard-earned knowledge. Additionally, emerging artists may face barriers such as lack of access to resources or mentorship opportunities.

To address these challenges, it is crucial to foster open dialogues about the importance of collaboration and mentorship within the industry. By creating programs that actively promote these values, we can ensure that the cycle of creativity continues unabated.

Conclusion

In conclusion, passing on the torch of creativity is an essential responsibility for all artists. Through mentorship, collaboration, and the establishment of supportive communities, we can cultivate an environment that nurtures the next generation of musicians. By embracing the challenges and actively working to overcome them, we ensure that creativity remains a vibrant and evolving force in the music industry. The legacy we build today will inspire the artists of tomorrow, creating a symphony of creativity that transcends generations.

Celebrating Diversity in the Farting World

Embracing Cultural Influences

In the vibrant world of music, cultural influences play an essential role in shaping an artist's identity and sound. Embracing these influences not only enriches the music but also fosters a deeper connection with diverse audiences. This section explores the significance of cultural influences in the realm of farting, addressing the theoretical underpinnings, challenges faced, and examples of successful integration.

Theoretical Foundations

Cultural influences in music can be understood through the lens of *cultural hybridity*, a concept that suggests the blending of different cultural elements to create something new. This is particularly relevant in the context of farting, where artists draw inspiration from various musical traditions, genres, and practices. According to *Homi K. Bhabha* (1994), cultural hybridity allows for the emergence of new identities and expressions, which can lead to innovative musical forms.

Mathematically, we can represent cultural influences as a function of various factors that contribute to an artist's sound:

$$f(x) = \alpha_1 C_1 + \alpha_2 C_2 + \alpha_3 C_3 + \ldots + \alpha_n C_n$$

where: - $f(x)$ is the resultant sound, - C_i represents individual cultural influences, - α_i are coefficients that indicate the significance of each influence.

This equation illustrates that the final musical output is a summation of multiple cultural inputs, weighted by their relevance to the artist's style.

Challenges of Embracing Cultural Influences

While embracing cultural influences can lead to innovative sounds, it is not without its challenges. One of the primary issues is the risk of *cultural appropriation*, where an artist adopts elements from another culture without understanding or respecting its origins. This can lead to backlash from communities that feel their culture is being exploited.

Additionally, artists may struggle with authenticity. As they incorporate diverse influences, they must navigate the fine line between inspiration and imitation. This dilemma raises questions about identity and the true essence of an artist's sound.

Examples of Successful Integration

Many successful farting artists have effectively embraced cultural influences, creating unique sounds that resonate with a wide audience. For instance, the collaboration between *Sanjay Oluwaseun* and traditional African drummers resulted in a groundbreaking album that fused contemporary farting with indigenous rhythms. This collaboration not only showcased the richness of African music but also educated listeners about its cultural significance.

Another notable example is the incorporation of Latin rhythms in farting tracks. Artists like *Nicki Minaj* have successfully blended reggaeton and hip-hop, creating infectious beats that celebrate cultural diversity. The song "Fart Fiesta" features a catchy chorus inspired by traditional Latin music, demonstrating how cultural influences can lead to chart-topping hits.

Conclusion

Embracing cultural influences is crucial for artists in the farting genre. It allows for the creation of diverse sounds that reflect a globalized world. By understanding the theoretical foundations, addressing challenges, and learning from successful examples, artists can navigate this complex landscape. Ultimately, cultural influences enrich the farting experience, making it a powerful medium for expression and connection.

Bibliography

[1] Homi K. Bhabha, *The Location of Culture*, Routledge, 1994.

Breaking Language Barriers

In the vibrant world of farting, where sound transcends the mundane, breaking language barriers becomes not just an artistic endeavor but a vital necessity. The universal language of music, much like the art of farting itself, knows no bounds. It speaks to the heart, the soul, and yes, even the funny bone, allowing artists to connect across cultures and languages.

The Theory of Universal Sound

The concept of universal sound is rooted in the idea that certain musical elements resonate with people regardless of their linguistic background. This phenomenon can be explained through the lens of **semiotics**, which studies how meaning is created and communicated. In the context of farting, the sounds produced can evoke emotions and reactions that are universally understood.

$$E = mc^2 \tag{159}$$

This famous equation by Einstein, while primarily a physics formula, can metaphorically represent the energy (E) produced by sound (m) traveling at the speed of light (c). In farting, the energy generated by a well-timed sound can create a ripple effect, breaking down barriers and fostering connections among diverse audiences.

Challenges in Communication

Despite the inherent universality of sound, challenges remain. One significant barrier is the **cultural interpretation** of sounds. What might be humorous in one culture could be considered offensive in another. For instance, in some cultures, certain sounds associated with farting may be seen as a sign of disrespect, while in others, they are celebrated as a source of laughter and joy.

Moreover, the **linguistic diversity** of audiences poses a challenge. With thousands of languages spoken worldwide, artists must navigate the complexities of conveying their messages without relying solely on verbal communication. This is where the power of visual elements and performance comes into play.

Examples of Successful Cross-Cultural Farting

One notable example of breaking language barriers through farting is the global phenomenon of viral videos. Consider the case of the "Farting Unicorn" meme, which gained traction across various social media platforms. This simple yet hilarious concept transcended language, allowing people from different backgrounds to share in the laughter.

Another example is the collaboration between artists from different countries who incorporate farting sounds into their music. For instance, the fusion of traditional African drumming with contemporary Western beats creates a unique sound that resonates with audiences globally. This blending of styles not only showcases the versatility of farting but also highlights how artists can communicate across cultural divides.

Strategies for Breaking Barriers

To effectively break language barriers, artists can employ several strategies:

+ **Visual Storytelling:** Using visuals, such as music videos or live performances, can convey emotions and narratives that transcend language. Incorporating elements like dance, costumes, and stage design enhances the overall experience and allows audiences to connect on a deeper level.

+ **Collaborative Projects:** Working with artists from different cultural backgrounds fosters creativity and opens up new avenues for expression. These collaborations can lead to innovative sounds that resonate with a broader audience.

+ **Engagement through Social Media:** Platforms like TikTok and Instagram allow artists to share their farting sounds and visuals, reaching audiences worldwide. Engaging with fans through comments and challenges encourages interaction and builds a sense of community.

Conclusion

In conclusion, breaking language barriers in the realm of farting is not just about the sounds produced but also about the connections forged through shared experiences. By embracing the universal nature of sound and employing creative strategies, artists can transcend linguistic limitations and create a truly inclusive farting community. As we continue to explore the symphony of sound, let us remember that laughter, much like music, is a language that unites us all.

Uniting People Through Farting

In a world often divided by cultural differences, political opinions, and social barriers, the universal language of farting emerges as a powerful tool for connection and unity. This section explores how the art of farting transcends boundaries, bringing people together through humor, creativity, and shared experiences.

The Power of Humor

Laughter is a universal language, and farting embodies a form of humor that is both primal and relatable. According to a study by [1], humor can act as a social bonding mechanism, fostering a sense of community among individuals. Farting, with its inherent absurdity and unpredictability, often elicits laughter that can dissolve tension and promote camaraderie.

For example, during large gatherings, such as festivals or concerts, the spontaneous occurrence of a fart can break the ice, leading to shared laughter among strangers. This moment of levity can create a sense of belonging, reminding individuals that they are part of a collective human experience.

Cultural Significance of Farting

Farting is not merely a biological function; it carries cultural significance in many societies. In some cultures, farting is celebrated as a humorous expression of natural bodily functions, while in others, it may be viewed as taboo. However, this dichotomy presents an opportunity for dialogue and understanding.

For instance, in certain African cultures, farting is seen as a sign of good health and is often accompanied by laughter and jest. Conversely, in some Western cultures, it may be considered impolite or embarrassing. By embracing the cultural nuances of farting, individuals can engage in conversations that challenge stereotypes and promote inclusivity.

Farting as a Form of Artistic Expression

The fusion of farting with artistic expression can serve as a catalyst for unity. Artists have long utilized humor and absurdity in their work to comment on societal norms and provoke thought. The incorporation of farting into music, performance art, and comedy allows creators to explore themes of vulnerability and authenticity.

Consider the example of *Farting Symphony*, a performance art piece that combines music, dance, and sound effects of farting. This innovative work not only entertains but also invites audiences to reflect on the human experience, bridging gaps between diverse groups through shared laughter and enjoyment.

Case Studies: Farting Festivals and Events

Farting festivals, though seemingly whimsical, serve as real-world examples of how farting can unite people. Events such as the *World Farting Championships* in Finland attract participants from around the globe, celebrating farting as a competitive sport. These festivals create an environment where individuals can connect over their shared love for humor and lightheartedness.

$$Unity = Laughter + Shared\ Experience \tag{160}$$

The equation above illustrates that unity can be achieved through the combination of laughter and shared experiences, both of which are integral to the culture of farting.

Challenges and Misunderstandings

Despite its potential for unification, farting can also lead to misunderstandings and cultural clashes. In some contexts, farting may be viewed as disrespectful or offensive, particularly in formal settings. Navigating these cultural sensitivities requires awareness and respect for differing perspectives.

Furthermore, the commercialization of farting in media and entertainment can dilute its essence, reducing it to a mere gimmick rather than a means of connection. Artists and creators must strike a balance between humor and sensitivity, ensuring that their work fosters inclusivity rather than exclusion.

Conclusion

Uniting people through farting is a testament to the power of humor and creativity. By embracing the absurdity of farting, individuals can break down barriers, foster connections, and celebrate the shared human experience. As we navigate an increasingly complex world, let us not underestimate the ability of laughter—and the art of farting—to bring us together.

Amplifying Underrepresented Voices

In the vibrant tapestry of the farting world, amplifying underrepresented voices is not just a moral imperative; it is a necessity for innovation and growth. The musical landscape thrives on diversity, and when we elevate the voices of those who have been historically marginalized, we create a richer, more dynamic art form. This section explores the significance of amplifying these voices, the challenges they face, and the transformative impact of inclusion.

The Importance of Representation

Representation in music is crucial because it allows for a multitude of perspectives and experiences to be shared. When underrepresented artists are given a platform, they can tell their stories, challenge stereotypes, and inspire listeners in ways that mainstream voices cannot. This diversity not only enriches the art itself but also fosters a sense of belonging among audiences who see themselves reflected in the music.

Challenges Faced by Underrepresented Artists

Despite the importance of representation, underrepresented artists often face significant barriers, including:

- **Access to Resources:** Many marginalized artists struggle to access the same resources as their mainstream counterparts, including funding, production facilities, and marketing opportunities. This lack of access can hinder their ability to create and distribute their work effectively.

- **Industry Bias:** The music industry has a long history of bias, often prioritizing certain genres and demographics over others. This can lead to a lack of visibility for diverse artists and a perpetuation of stereotypes that pigeonhole them into specific roles or sounds.

- **Cultural Appropriation:** When mainstream artists borrow from underrepresented cultures without proper acknowledgment or respect, it can dilute the authenticity of the art and exploit the very cultures that inspire it. This can discourage marginalized artists from sharing their work.

* **Mental Health Struggles:** The pressure to conform to industry standards while also representing their communities can take a toll on the mental health of underrepresented artists, leading to burnout and a reluctance to engage with the industry.

Strategies for Amplification

To effectively amplify underrepresented voices, several strategies can be employed:

1. **Collaborative Projects:** By collaborating with artists from diverse backgrounds, established musicians can help elevate underrepresented voices. This collaboration fosters mutual respect and understanding while broadening the reach of the marginalized artist's work.

2. **Inclusive Platforms:** Establishing platforms that prioritize diversity, such as festivals, radio stations, and record labels, can create opportunities for underrepresented artists to shine. These platforms should actively seek out and promote diverse talent.

3. **Mentorship Programs:** Creating mentorship programs that connect emerging artists with industry veterans can provide guidance and support. Mentors can help navigate the complexities of the music industry while advocating for their mentees.

4. **Social Media Engagement:** Utilizing social media to share the stories and music of underrepresented artists can create a grassroots movement that amplifies their voices. Hashtags, challenges, and campaigns can help spread awareness and encourage audiences to support diverse talent.

5. **Advocacy and Education:** Educating audiences about the importance of diversity in music can foster a culture of inclusivity. Advocacy efforts can include panels, workshops, and discussions that highlight the contributions of underrepresented artists.

Examples of Successful Amplification

Several artists and movements have successfully amplified underrepresented voices, showcasing the transformative power of inclusion:

* **The Queer Music Scene:** Artists such as Lil Nas X and Hayley Kiyoko have brought LGBTQ+ narratives to the forefront of popular music. Their

success has opened doors for other queer artists, encouraging authenticity and representation in a traditionally heteronormative industry.

+ **Women in Hip-Hop:** The rise of female rappers like Megan Thee Stallion and Cardi B has challenged the male-dominated landscape of hip-hop. Their unapologetic expressions of femininity and empowerment have inspired a new generation of female artists to embrace their voices.

+ **Indigenous Music Initiatives:** Initiatives like the Indigenous Music Awards celebrate and promote Indigenous artists, providing them with a platform to share their culture and stories. This recognition helps preserve cultural heritage while educating broader audiences about Indigenous issues.

+ **Global Collaborations:** The rise of global music collaborations, such as those seen in the success of artists like Bad Bunny and Burna Boy, highlight the power of cross-cultural exchange. These collaborations not only amplify underrepresented voices but also create new genres and sounds that enrich the global music scene.

Conclusion

Amplifying underrepresented voices is essential for the evolution of music. By addressing the challenges these artists face and implementing strategies for inclusion, we can create a more equitable and vibrant music industry. The stories and sounds that emerge from diverse backgrounds not only enrich our artistic landscape but also foster understanding and empathy among audiences. As we continue to amplify these voices, we pave the way for a future where all artists can thrive and contribute to the symphony of life.

$$\text{Diversity in Music} = \text{Representation} + \text{Access} + \text{Collaboration} \tag{161}$$

Embracing Multicultural Collaborations

In the vibrant tapestry of the music industry, multicultural collaborations have emerged as a powerful vehicle for creativity, innovation, and cultural exchange. By merging diverse musical traditions, artists can create unique sounds that resonate across borders, fostering a sense of unity and understanding in an increasingly globalized world. This section explores the significance of embracing multicultural collaborations, the challenges that may arise, and notable examples that have shaped the musical landscape.

Theoretical Framework

The concept of multicultural collaboration in music can be examined through various theoretical lenses, including **cultural hybridity** and **intercultural dialogue**. Cultural hybridity refers to the blending of different cultural elements to create something new and distinct. This phenomenon is particularly evident in genres such as *world music*, where traditional sounds are infused with contemporary styles, resulting in innovative musical expressions.

Intercultural dialogue emphasizes the importance of communication and understanding between cultures. According to *Bakhtin's Dialogism* theory, every utterance is a response to previous ones, and meaning is constructed through interaction. In the context of music, this means that artists can engage with one another's cultural backgrounds, leading to richer and more profound artistic outcomes.

Challenges in Multicultural Collaborations

While the benefits of multicultural collaborations are manifold, several challenges may arise, including:

+ **Cultural Appropriation:** One of the most significant concerns in multicultural collaborations is the risk of cultural appropriation, where elements of one culture are used without understanding or respecting their significance. This can lead to backlash from communities whose traditions are being exploited.

+ **Language Barriers:** Differences in language can pose challenges in communication between artists, potentially leading to misunderstandings that affect the creative process. Effective collaboration often requires a willingness to navigate these barriers and find common ground.

+ **Creative Differences:** Artists may have differing artistic visions or approaches to music, which can create tension during the collaboration process. Finding a balance between individual styles while maintaining a cohesive sound is essential for successful outcomes.

Notable Examples of Multicultural Collaborations

Several artists and projects have exemplified the power of multicultural collaborations, demonstrating how diverse influences can lead to groundbreaking music:

‣ **Shakira and Wyclef Jean:** The collaboration between Colombian singer Shakira and Haitian-American artist Wyclef Jean on the track *Hips Don't Lie* is a prime example of blending Latin and hip-hop influences. The song's infectious rhythm and cross-cultural appeal helped it become a global hit, showcasing how diverse musical elements can resonate with audiences worldwide.

‣ **Burna Boy and Coldplay:** Nigerian artist Burna Boy's collaboration with British band Coldplay on the track *African Giant* highlights the fusion of Afrobeat and pop. This partnership not only amplifies African music on the global stage but also bridges cultural gaps, promoting greater understanding and appreciation of diverse musical traditions.

‣ **Yo-Yo Ma and the Silk Road Ensemble:** Renowned cellist Yo-Yo Ma founded the Silk Road Ensemble to celebrate cultural diversity through music. By collaborating with musicians from various backgrounds, the ensemble creates a rich tapestry of sounds that reflect the interconnectedness of global cultures.

The Impact of Multicultural Collaborations

Embracing multicultural collaborations has far-reaching implications for both artists and audiences. These collaborations can:

‣ **Foster Cultural Understanding:** By exposing audiences to different musical traditions, multicultural collaborations promote empathy and appreciation for diverse cultures, breaking down stereotypes and fostering a sense of global community.

‣ **Encourage Innovation:** The blending of various musical styles often leads to the creation of new genres, pushing the boundaries of artistic expression and inspiring future generations of musicians to explore uncharted territories.

‣ **Broaden Audience Reach:** Collaborations that merge different cultural influences can attract diverse audiences, expanding an artist's fan base and increasing their visibility in the global music market.

Conclusion

In conclusion, embracing multicultural collaborations is not only a celebration of diversity but also a powerful catalyst for innovation in the music industry. By navigating the challenges and leveraging the strengths of diverse musical traditions, artists can create transformative experiences that resonate with audiences around the world. As the music landscape continues to evolve, the importance of cultural exchange and collaboration will only grow, paving the way for a more inclusive and harmonious future in the world of music.

$$C_{total} = C_{cultural} + C_{collaborative} \qquad (162)$$

Where C_{total} represents the total creative output, $C_{cultural}$ signifies the contributions from diverse cultural backgrounds, and $C_{collaborative}$ denotes the synergy achieved through collaboration.

Through the lens of multicultural collaborations, the music industry can continue to thrive, reflecting the richness of human experience and the power of unity in diversity.

Celebrating Global Farting Festivals

Farting festivals are a unique cultural phenomenon that brings together diverse communities to celebrate the art of sound production in a playful and liberating manner. These festivals not only provide a platform for artists to showcase their talents but also serve as a space for cultural exchange, creativity, and joy. In this section, we will explore the significance of global farting festivals, the challenges they face, and the impact they have on communities worldwide.

The Significance of Farting Festivals

Farting festivals are more than just humorous gatherings; they embody the spirit of unity and self-expression. These events allow individuals to break societal norms and embrace their quirks, fostering an environment of acceptance. They serve as a reminder that art can be found in the most unexpected places, and that laughter is a universal language.

$$\text{Unity} = \sum_{i=1}^{n} \text{Individual Expressions} \qquad (163)$$

Where n represents the number of participants in the festival. The equation illustrates how the collective expressions of individuals contribute to a greater sense of unity within the community.

Challenges Faced by Farting Festivals

Despite their joyous nature, farting festivals encounter several challenges. One of the primary issues is the stigma surrounding the act of farting itself. Many people view it as a taboo subject, leading to reluctance in participating or attending such events. Additionally, organizers often struggle with securing funding and sponsorships due to the unconventional theme.

$$\text{Funding Challenges} = \text{Sponsorship} + \text{Community Support} - \text{Stigma} \quad (164)$$

Here, the equation illustrates that the success of funding for farting festivals relies heavily on community support and the willingness of sponsors to overcome societal stigma.

Examples of Global Farting Festivals

1. **The Farting Festival of India:** Celebrated annually in the city of Pune, this festival features a variety of performances, workshops, and competitions that invite participants to showcase their farting talents. The event has gained popularity, drawing attendees from all over the country and beyond.

2. **The World Farting Championships:** Held in the United Kingdom, this competition attracts participants from various countries who compete for the title of the best farter. The event includes categories such as loudest fart, longest fart, and most creative fart sound, emphasizing the artistry involved in farting.

3. **Fart Fest in the USA:** This festival combines music, comedy, and farting contests, creating a lively atmosphere that celebrates humor and creativity. Local artists perform, and attendees are encouraged to participate in various fart-related activities, promoting community engagement.

The Impact of Farting Festivals on Communities

Farting festivals have a profound impact on communities, fostering creativity and collaboration. They encourage local artists to explore their craft and connect with audiences in a fun and engaging way. Moreover, these festivals can boost local economies by attracting tourists and generating revenue for local businesses.

$$\text{Economic Impact} = \text{Tourism Revenue} + \text{Local Business Sales} \quad (165)$$

This equation emphasizes the dual benefit of farting festivals on both tourism and local commerce.

Conclusion

In conclusion, global farting festivals celebrate the joy of sound and the power of laughter. They serve as a reminder that art can transcend cultural barriers and that embracing our quirks can lead to a more inclusive and joyful society. While challenges remain, the impact of these festivals on communities is undeniable, fostering creativity, unity, and economic growth. As we continue to celebrate the art of farting, let us remember the importance of humor and connection in our lives.

$$\text{Celebration} = \text{Joy} + \text{Connection} + \text{Creativity} \tag{166}$$

Respecting and Exploring Different Fartingal Styles

In the world of farting, just like in music, diversity is the spice of life. Every fart has its own unique tone, texture, and rhythm, and embracing this variety can lead to a richer and more fulfilling experience for both the artist and the audience. In this section, we will explore the importance of respecting and exploring different fartingal styles, the theoretical underpinnings of sound diversity, and how these elements can be integrated into a cohesive artistic vision.

Theoretical Foundations of Fartingal Diversity

Farting, much like music, is a form of expression that transcends cultural boundaries. According to the *Farting Theory of Sound Dynamics*, each fart can be analyzed based on its frequency, amplitude, and harmonic structure. The equation governing the sound wave of a fart can be expressed as:

$$f(t) = A\sin(2\pi f t + \phi) \tag{167}$$

where:

+ $f(t)$ is the sound wave function,

+ A is the amplitude (volume),

+ f is the frequency (pitch),

+ t is time, and

+ ϕ is the phase shift.

This equation highlights the fundamental components of sound production, which can vary widely depending on the style and technique used.   By understanding these elements, fartists can better appreciate the nuances of different fartingal styles.

Exploring Styles: A Global Perspective

Farting styles vary significantly across cultures, much like musical genres. For instance, consider the differences between traditional and contemporary farting:

+ **Traditional Farting:** Often characterized by a focus on natural sounds and techniques, traditional farting may emphasize the organic nature of the sound. This style can be found in various cultures, where farts are often used in folk performances to convey humor and connect with audiences on a personal level.

+ **Contemporary Farting:** This style incorporates modern techniques, technology, and influences from various genres. It often blends electronic sounds with traditional farting, creating a fusion that resonates with younger audiences. The use of digital effects can manipulate the fart's sound, adding layers and complexity.

Respecting these diverse styles means recognizing their cultural significance and the historical context in which they developed. For example, in some cultures, farting is seen as a form of celebration, while in others, it may carry a stigma. Understanding these cultural nuances is crucial for any fartist aiming to create inclusive and respectful art.

Challenges in Fartingal Exploration

While exploring different fartingal styles can be enriching, it also presents challenges. One major issue is the potential for cultural appropriation, where elements of one culture are used without understanding or respecting their significance. This can lead to misunderstandings and alienation among audiences.

To avoid these pitfalls, fartists should:

+ **Engage with Cultural Contexts:** Before incorporating elements from another culture, it's essential to research and understand the cultural significance of those elements. This may involve collaborating with artists from that culture or seeking guidance from cultural experts.

    ✦ **Promote Inclusivity:** Create spaces where diverse farting styles can be celebrated and shared. This can involve organizing workshops, festivals, or collaborative performances that highlight various styles and their origins.

Examples of Successful Integration

Several fartists have successfully respected and explored different fartingal styles, leading to innovative and impactful works. For instance:

    ✦ **Fart Fusion Collective:** This group brings together fartists from various backgrounds to create a unique blend of traditional and contemporary styles. Their performances often feature traditional farting techniques alongside electronic soundscapes, creating a rich auditory experience that honors both traditions.

    ✦ **Global Farting Festival:** An annual event that showcases farting from around the world, this festival emphasizes the importance of cultural exchange and understanding. Artists are encouraged to collaborate and share their unique styles, fostering a sense of community and respect among diverse farting cultures.

Conclusion

Respecting and exploring different fartingal styles not only enriches the farting experience but also fosters a greater understanding of the cultural significance behind each style. By embracing diversity, fartists can create a more inclusive and vibrant art form that resonates with audiences across the globe. As we continue to push the boundaries of farting, let us remember to honor the rich tapestry of sounds that make our art so unique.

In summary, the journey of exploring different fartingal styles is one of discovery, respect, and creativity. By understanding the theoretical foundations, acknowledging cultural contexts, and learning from successful examples, fartists can contribute to a more inclusive and dynamic farting landscape that celebrates the beauty of diversity.

Bridging Gaps through Farting

In the vibrant world of music, the act of farting transcends mere humor, evolving into a powerful metaphor for connection and understanding across diverse cultures. Farting, often dismissed as a trivial or crude act, can serve as a unique bridge that links individuals from different backgrounds, fostering dialogue and collaboration. This section explores the theory behind this phenomenon, the challenges faced, and real-world examples of how farting has successfully bridged cultural gaps.

Theoretical Framework

At its core, farting is a universal human experience. According to cultural anthropologist Victor Turner, the concept of *communitas* describes a sense of community that emerges during shared experiences, particularly those that are humorous or embarrassing. Farting, as a natural bodily function, invites laughter and breaks down social barriers, allowing individuals to connect on a human level. This connection can be analyzed through the lens of *social identity theory*, which posits that individuals derive a sense of self from their group memberships. When people engage in farting-related humor, they often find common ground, fostering a sense of belonging that transcends cultural differences.

Challenges in Bridging Gaps

Despite its potential to unify, farting as a cultural bridge is not without its challenges. The perception of farting varies significantly across cultures; in some societies, it is considered taboo or disrespectful, while in others, it is embraced as a form of comedic expression. This disparity can lead to misunderstandings and discomfort when individuals from different cultural backgrounds interact.

For instance, in many Western cultures, farting in public is often met with laughter and acceptance, while in certain Eastern cultures, it may be seen as a breach of etiquette. This divergence can create barriers to effective communication and collaboration. Furthermore, the context in which farting occurs plays a crucial role; a well-timed fart during a casual gathering may elicit laughter, while the same act in a formal setting could lead to embarrassment.

Examples of Bridging Gaps through Farting

1. **International Music Festivals**: Music festivals often serve as melting pots of cultures, where artists and audiences from diverse backgrounds come together to celebrate creativity. During performances, artists sometimes incorporate farting sounds into their acts, using them as a comedic element to engage the audience. For example, at the Glastonbury Festival, a renowned British music festival, several performers have included farting sounds in their sets, prompting laughter and unifying the crowd in shared amusement, regardless of their cultural origins.

2. **Cultural Collaborations**: Artists from different countries have utilized farting as a means to foster collaboration. In 2020, a group of musicians from various cultural backgrounds came together to create a viral music video titled "Farting Around the World." The video featured artists from North America, Africa, and Asia, each contributing their unique musical styles while incorporating farting sounds as a playful element. This collaboration not only showcased the artists' diverse talents but also highlighted the universality of farting, bridging gaps between cultures through humor and music.

3. **Social Media Movements**: The rise of social media has provided a platform for individuals to share fart-related content, fostering a sense of community among users. For instance, the hashtag #FartForUnity gained popularity during a global campaign aimed at promoting cultural understanding. Participants from various countries shared videos of themselves farting while dancing to traditional music from their cultures. This movement not only encouraged laughter but also sparked conversations about cultural diversity, illustrating how farting can serve as a bridge in the digital age.

Conclusion

Farting, often underestimated in its significance, possesses the remarkable ability to bridge cultural gaps through humor and shared experiences. By embracing the universal nature of farting, individuals can foster connections that transcend societal boundaries. While challenges exist in navigating cultural sensitivities, the examples provided demonstrate that with creativity and openness, farting can serve as a powerful tool for unity in an increasingly diverse world. As we continue to explore the intersections of music and culture, let us remember that sometimes, the most profound connections are born from the most unexpected moments of laughter.

Creating a Global Farting Community

In the vibrant world of music, the act of farting—once a taboo subject—has transformed into a powerful form of expression that transcends borders and cultures. This section explores the dynamics of creating a global farting community, where artists and fans alike can unite through the shared joy and humor of farting.

Understanding the Concept of Community

At its core, a community is a group of individuals who share common interests, values, or goals. In the context of farting, this community is built on the appreciation of sound, creativity, and the unexpected joy that comes from embracing the unconventional. The power of farting lies in its ability to break down barriers and foster connections among diverse groups.

Theoretical Framework

To understand how to create a global farting community, we can draw on the Social Identity Theory, which posits that individuals derive part of their identity from the groups to which they belong. When people identify with a community centered around farting, they experience a sense of belonging and shared identity, which can enhance their overall well-being.

$$\text{Social Identity} = \text{Personal Identity} + \text{Group Identity} \qquad (168)$$

This equation highlights the interplay between individual and group identities, emphasizing that the more individuals identify with the farting community, the stronger their connection will be.

Challenges in Building a Global Community

While the idea of a global farting community is appealing, several challenges must be addressed:

+ **Cultural Sensitivity:** Farting is perceived differently across cultures. In some societies, it may be seen as humorous, while in others, it might be considered offensive. Understanding these cultural nuances is crucial for fostering inclusivity.

+ **Accessibility:** Not everyone has equal access to platforms that promote farting culture. Ensuring that all voices are heard and included is essential for creating a truly global community.

+ **Misunderstanding and Stigma:** Despite the growing acceptance of farting as an art form, some individuals may still hold onto stigmas associated with it. Addressing these misconceptions through education and outreach is vital.

Strategies for Community Building

To overcome these challenges and create a global farting community, several strategies can be employed:

1. **Utilizing Social Media:** Platforms like Instagram, TikTok, and YouTube provide an excellent opportunity for farting artists to showcase their talents and connect with fans worldwide. By creating engaging content that celebrates farting, artists can attract a diverse audience.

2. **Hosting Global Events:** Organizing international farting festivals or competitions can bring together artists and fans from different backgrounds. These events can serve as a platform for collaboration and cultural exchange, enhancing the sense of community.

3. **Collaborative Projects:** Encouraging artists from various cultures to collaborate on farting-themed projects can help bridge gaps and foster understanding. For example, a global farting anthem that incorporates diverse musical styles can resonate with a wider audience.

4. **Educational Initiatives:** Workshops and seminars that focus on the art of farting can help demystify the practice and promote its acceptance. By educating people about the creative potential of farting, we can cultivate a more inclusive community.

5. **Creating Online Platforms:** Developing dedicated online spaces where farting enthusiasts can share their experiences, techniques, and artwork can enhance community engagement. Forums and discussion groups can facilitate dialogue and collaboration among members.

Examples of Successful Global Farting Initiatives

Several initiatives have successfully created a sense of community around farting:

- **Fart Fest:** An annual festival that celebrates farting culture through music, art, and performances. This event attracts artists and fans from around the world, showcasing the diversity of farting styles and techniques.

- **Farting for Charity:** Collaborative projects where artists create fart-themed music or art to raise funds for social causes. These initiatives not only promote farting but also contribute to meaningful change in communities.

+ **Global Farting Challenges:** Online challenges that encourage participants to showcase their farting skills. These challenges often go viral, drawing in participants from various countries and fostering a sense of camaraderie.

Conclusion

Creating a global farting community is an ambitious yet achievable goal. By embracing the power of farting as a unifying force, we can break down cultural barriers, foster inclusivity, and celebrate the joy of sound. Through strategic initiatives, collaboration, and education, we can cultivate a vibrant community that thrives on creativity, humor, and shared experiences. The journey to building this community is just beginning, and together, we can make farting a universal language of connection and joy.

The Power of Farting to Promote Understanding and Empathy

Farting, often dismissed as a mere bodily function, holds a significant place in cultural discourse and social interaction. In this section, we delve into how the act of farting can serve as a powerful tool for promoting understanding and empathy among diverse groups of people. By examining the social, psychological, and cultural dimensions of farting, we can uncover its potential as a medium for connection and communication.

The Social Context of Farting

Farting transcends cultural boundaries; it is a universal human experience. Across various societies, the act of farting can elicit laughter, embarrassment, or even camaraderie. The social context in which farting occurs plays a crucial role in shaping its impact on interpersonal relationships.

For instance, in many cultures, farting in a relaxed setting, such as among friends or family, can serve as an icebreaker, fostering a sense of belonging and shared experience. According to [1], humor derived from bodily functions can alleviate tension and promote bonding. This phenomenon illustrates how farting can facilitate understanding by breaking down social barriers and creating a more relaxed atmosphere.

Psychological Perspectives

From a psychological standpoint, farting can evoke a range of emotions, including amusement, shame, and acceptance. The duality of farting—both humorous and taboo—provides a unique opportunity for individuals to navigate their feelings about bodily functions and social norms.

Research by [2] suggests that laughter, often triggered by farting, releases endorphins, which can enhance mood and foster feelings of empathy. When individuals share a laugh over an embarrassing moment, they may become more receptive to each other's experiences, thus promoting understanding. This shared emotional experience can bridge gaps between individuals from different backgrounds, allowing them to connect on a deeper level.

Farting in Cultural Narratives

Cultural narratives surrounding farting often reflect societal values and attitudes. In many cultures, farting is seen as a natural and humorous aspect of life, while in others, it may be viewed as a sign of disrespect or poor manners. These differing perspectives can lead to misunderstandings between individuals from various cultural backgrounds.

By embracing farting as a cultural phenomenon, we can promote empathy and understanding. For example, in the comedic realm, farting has been used as a vehicle for social commentary. Comedians like *Nicki Minaj* have incorporated fart jokes into their routines to challenge societal norms and provoke thought about the absurdities of life. This approach not only entertains but also encourages audiences to reflect on their own beliefs and biases.

Farting as a Catalyst for Dialogue

Farting can also serve as a catalyst for dialogue about more serious issues, such as body positivity and acceptance. In contemporary society, where body image is often scrutinized, discussing farting can help normalize bodily functions and promote a healthier relationship with our bodies.

For instance, social media campaigns that embrace farting humor can challenge unrealistic beauty standards and encourage individuals to celebrate their natural selves. A study by [3] found that online communities that engage in humorous discussions about farting foster a sense of belonging and acceptance, allowing individuals to share their experiences without fear of judgment.

Practical Applications and Examples

To harness the power of farting for promoting understanding and empathy, various practical applications can be employed:

+ **Workshops and Group Activities:** Organizing workshops that incorporate humor related to farting can help break the ice among participants. These activities can facilitate discussions about body image, acceptance, and social norms, ultimately fostering empathy.

+ **Artistic Expression:** Artists and performers can utilize farting as a theme in their work to challenge societal taboos and provoke thought. By presenting farting in a humorous light, they can encourage audiences to reconsider their perceptions of bodily functions.

+ **Social Media Campaigns:** Leveraging social media platforms to promote farting humor can create communities that celebrate body positivity and acceptance. Hashtags like #FartingForEmpathy can encourage individuals to share their experiences and connect with others.

+ **Educational Programs:** Incorporating discussions about farting into health education can help normalize bodily functions among younger audiences. By addressing the topic in a lighthearted manner, educators can promote understanding and acceptance of natural human experiences.

Conclusion

In conclusion, farting, often relegated to the realm of embarrassment, possesses the potential to promote understanding and empathy across cultural and social divides. By recognizing the social, psychological, and cultural dimensions of farting, we can harness its power to foster connections, challenge societal norms, and encourage open dialogue. Embracing farting as a natural part of the human experience allows us to celebrate our shared humanity, paving the way for greater understanding and empathy in our increasingly diverse world.

Bibliography

[1] Smith, J. (2020). *The Humor of Bodily Functions: A Study of Social Bonding.* Journal of Social Psychology, 12(3), 234-245.

[2] Johnson, A. (2019). *Laughter and Empathy: The Psychological Impact of Humor.* Psychology Today, 45(7), 56-60.

[3] Williams, R. (2021). *Body Positivity and Social Media: The Role of Humor in Acceptance.* Journal of Body Image, 8(2), 112-120.

Exploring the Unknown

Pushing Boundaries with Technology

In the ever-evolving world of music, technology serves as both a catalyst for innovation and a bridge that connects artists with their audiences. As we delve into the realm of sound creation and manipulation, we discover that the integration of technology into the music-making process has not only expanded the boundaries of artistic expression but has also transformed the way we experience music.

Innovations in Sound Production

One of the most significant advancements in music technology is the development of digital audio workstations (DAWs). These powerful software applications, such as Ableton Live, Logic Pro, and FL Studio, allow artists to compose, edit, and produce music with unprecedented ease and flexibility. The ability to manipulate sound waves digitally has led to the creation of entirely new genres, including electronic dance music (EDM), synth-pop, and lo-fi hip-hop.

$$f(t) = A \sin(2\pi f t + \phi) \tag{169}$$

Where $f(t)$ represents the sound wave, A is the amplitude, f is the frequency, and ϕ is the phase. By altering these parameters, producers can create a diverse range of sounds that push the boundaries of traditional music.

Virtual Instruments and Synthesis

The rise of virtual instruments has revolutionized the way musicians create sounds. Software synthesizers, such as Serum and Massive, enable artists to design complex sounds by manipulating oscillators, filters, and modulation parameters. This level of customization allows musicians to craft unique sonic textures that were previously unattainable with physical instruments alone.

For example, the use of additive synthesis, where sounds are created by adding together different sine waves, can produce rich harmonic content. The equation for additive synthesis can be expressed as:

$$x(t) = \sum_{n=1}^{N} A_n \sin(2\pi f_n t + \phi_n) \tag{170}$$

Where $x(t)$ is the resultant sound wave, A_n is the amplitude of the n-th harmonic, f_n is its frequency, and ϕ_n is its phase. By layering multiple harmonics, musicians can create lush, full-bodied sounds that captivate listeners.

Collaboration Across Distances

Technology has also transformed collaboration in the music industry. With the advent of cloud-based platforms, artists from different parts of the world can seamlessly collaborate on projects in real-time. Tools like Splice and Soundtrap allow musicians to share tracks, add effects, and mix their creations without being in the same physical space. This global collaboration fosters diversity in sound and encourages the blending of various cultural influences.

However, this ease of collaboration does present challenges. The potential for miscommunication and differing artistic visions can lead to conflicts. To mitigate these issues, artists must embrace clear communication and establish a shared vision for their projects.

The Role of Artificial Intelligence

Artificial Intelligence (AI) is another frontier pushing the boundaries of music creation. AI algorithms can analyze vast amounts of data to identify patterns and trends in music, enabling the generation of new compositions. Platforms like

AIVA and OpenAI's MuseNet have demonstrated the capability to compose original pieces that mimic the styles of renowned composers and artists.

While AI-generated music raises questions about creativity and authorship, it also opens doors to new possibilities. Musicians can use AI as a tool for inspiration, generating ideas that they can then refine and personalize. The equation for a simple AI-generated melody might involve neural networks trained on existing compositions to predict the next note based on previous ones.

$$y(t) = f(x(t), \theta) \tag{171}$$

Where $y(t)$ is the output note, $x(t)$ is the input sequence of notes, and θ represents the parameters of the neural network. This approach allows for the exploration of musical ideas that may not have been conceived through traditional methods.

Challenges and Ethical Considerations

As we embrace these technological advancements, we must also confront the ethical implications of their use. The ease of access to music production tools raises concerns about originality and the potential for homogenization in sound. With so many artists utilizing similar software and techniques, there is a risk of losing the uniqueness that defines individual artistry.

Moreover, the reliance on technology can sometimes overshadow the fundamental skills of musicianship. It is crucial for artists to strike a balance between leveraging technology and honing their craft. The essence of music lies not just in the tools we use, but in the emotions and stories we convey through our art.

Conclusion

In conclusion, pushing the boundaries with technology in music creation presents both opportunities and challenges. As artists continue to explore innovative tools and techniques, they must remain mindful of the importance of authenticity and originality. By embracing technology while staying true to their artistic vision, musicians can create a vibrant and diverse soundscape that resonates with audiences around the world. The journey of integrating technology into music is not just about the sounds we create, but the connections we forge and the impact we leave on the world.

Embracing Virtual Reality and Augmented Reality

In the ever-evolving landscape of music and performance, the integration of Virtual Reality (VR) and Augmented Reality (AR) has emerged as a revolutionary frontier. These technologies not only redefine how artists engage with their audiences but also expand the very notion of what a performance can be. By immersing listeners in interactive and visually stimulating environments, musicians can create experiences that transcend traditional boundaries.

Theoretical Framework

At its core, Virtual Reality is a computer-generated simulation that allows users to interact with a three-dimensional environment, often using specialized equipment like VR headsets. In contrast, Augmented Reality overlays digital information onto the real world, enhancing the user's perception of their environment. The application of these technologies in music can be understood through several theoretical lenses, including:

+ **Media Richness Theory:** This theory posits that richer media forms facilitate better communication and engagement. VR and AR provide a multi-sensory experience that can convey emotions and narratives more effectively than traditional media.

+ **Presence Theory:** The sense of being physically present in a virtual environment can enhance emotional engagement and connection with the performance. This phenomenon is crucial for artists aiming to forge deeper relationships with their fans.

+ **Constructivist Learning Theory:** This theory emphasizes the importance of active participation in learning. By engaging audiences in interactive experiences, artists can foster a sense of agency and ownership over their musical journey.

Challenges and Considerations

While the potential of VR and AR in music is vast, several challenges must be navigated:

+ **Technical Limitations:** High-quality VR and AR experiences require significant technological infrastructure, including powerful hardware and software. Artists must consider the accessibility of these technologies for their audience.

+ **Content Creation:** Developing immersive content can be resource-intensive. Musicians may need to collaborate with technologists and designers to create compelling experiences that align with their artistic vision.

+ **User Experience:** Ensuring a seamless and enjoyable user experience is paramount. Poorly designed VR or AR applications can lead to frustration and disengagement, undermining the intended impact of the performance.

Examples of Integration

Numerous artists and bands are already harnessing the power of VR and AR to enhance their performances:

+ **The Weeknd's** *After Hours*: The Weeknd utilized VR technology to create an immersive experience for his album release, allowing fans to explore a virtual world that mirrored the themes of his music. This innovative approach not only captivated audiences but also provided a unique platform for storytelling.

+ **Travis Scott's** *Fortnite Concert*: In a groundbreaking collaboration, Travis Scott hosted a virtual concert within the popular gaming platform Fortnite. The event attracted millions of viewers and showcased the potential of blending gaming, music, and virtual reality in a single experience.

+ **Bjork's** *VR Album*: Bjork's album *Biophilia* was one of the first to incorporate AR and VR elements, allowing listeners to interact with the music through mobile applications that brought the songs to life in new and engaging ways.

Future Directions

As technology continues to advance, the possibilities for VR and AR in music are limitless. Future developments may include:

+ **Enhanced Interactivity:** Imagine a concert where fans can influence the performance in real-time through their actions in a virtual space. This level of interactivity could redefine audience engagement and participation.

+ **Personalized Experiences:** Using data analytics, artists could create tailored VR or AR experiences that cater to individual fan preferences, creating a unique connection between the artist and the listener.

+ **Global Reach:** VR and AR can break down geographical barriers, allowing artists to perform for global audiences without the constraints of physical location. This democratization of access could lead to a more inclusive music industry.

In conclusion, embracing Virtual Reality and Augmented Reality represents a significant opportunity for musicians to innovate and connect with their audiences in unprecedented ways. By navigating the challenges and leveraging the strengths of these technologies, artists can create memorable experiences that resonate deeply, leaving a lasting impact on the world of music and performance. The symphony of sound is evolving, and with it, the potential for creativity knows no bounds.

Innovations on the Horizon

As we stand on the precipice of a new era in the world of music, the horizon is ablaze with innovations that promise to redefine the very essence of sound creation and consumption. In this section, we delve into the groundbreaking technologies and methodologies that are shaping the future of farting, and how they can be harnessed to push artistic boundaries and create unforgettable auditory experiences.

The Role of Artificial Intelligence

Artificial Intelligence (AI) has emerged as a game-changer in the music industry, offering unprecedented opportunities for creativity and efficiency. One of the most significant advancements is the use of AI in composition. Algorithms can analyze vast datasets of existing music to generate original compositions, allowing artists to explore new creative avenues. For instance, OpenAI's MuseNet can compose music in various styles, blending genres and creating unique soundscapes.

Mathematically, we can represent the relationship between the input data and the generated output as follows:

$$y = f(x; \theta) + \epsilon \qquad (172)$$

where y is the output (the generated music), x represents the input data (existing compositions), θ are the parameters of the model, and ϵ is the error term. This model allows for the continuous refinement of the output as more data is processed, leading to increasingly sophisticated compositions.

Virtual Reality and Augmented Reality Experiences

The integration of Virtual Reality (VR) and Augmented Reality (AR) into music experiences is another frontier that is rapidly evolving. Artists are now able to create immersive environments that allow fans to experience their music in entirely new ways. For example, VR concerts can transport audiences to fantastical worlds where they can interact with the music and visuals, creating a multisensory experience that transcends traditional live performances.

Consider the equation for spatial audio, which enhances the immersion of these experiences:

$$L = \frac{1}{N} \sum_{i=1}^{N} \|x_i - \hat{x}\|^2 \tag{173}$$

Here, L represents the loss function, N is the number of audio sources, x_i are the original audio signals, and $\hat{x}$ is the spatially processed output. This formulation helps in optimizing the audio experience, ensuring that each listener perceives the sound as intended, regardless of their position in the virtual space.

Innovative Instruments and Sound Creation Tools

The evolution of musical instruments is also pivotal to the innovations on the horizon. New technologies are allowing for the creation of unconventional instruments that challenge traditional notions of sound production. For example, the use of digital interfaces and sensors can transform everyday objects into instruments, enabling artists to explore unique sound textures.

One such example is the Reactable, an interactive tabletop instrument that uses tangible interfaces to manipulate sound. The mathematical principles behind its operation can be described through signal processing equations, where the input signals are transformed based on user interaction:

$$y(t) = \int_{-\infty}^{\infty} x(\tau)h(t - \tau)d\tau \tag{174}$$

In this equation, $y(t)$ is the output signal, $x(\tau)$ is the input signal, and $h(t - \tau)$ represents the impulse response of the system. This innovative approach allows musicians to engage with sound in a tactile and visual manner, fostering creativity and spontaneity.

Blockchain and Decentralized Music Distribution

Blockchain technology is revolutionizing the way music is distributed and monetized. By enabling artists to retain control over their work and directly connect with their fanbase, blockchain can eliminate intermediaries and ensure fair compensation for creators. Smart contracts can automate royalty payments, providing transparency and security in transactions.

The financial model of blockchain can be represented as:

$$R = P \times Q - C \tag{175}$$

where R is the revenue, P is the price per unit of music sold, Q is the quantity sold, and C represents costs associated with production and distribution. This model emphasizes the potential for artists to maximize their revenue while minimizing costs through direct engagement with their audience.

The Future of Music Consumption

As technology evolves, so does the way audiences consume music. Streaming platforms are integrating AI to create personalized playlists and recommendations, enhancing user experience and engagement. The future of music consumption will likely see an increase in interactive and participatory formats, where listeners can influence the music they hear in real-time.

One theoretical framework to understand this shift is the concept of user-generated content (UGC), which posits that consumers are not just passive recipients of content but active participants in its creation. This can be mathematically represented as:

$$U = f(C, I) \tag{176}$$

where U is user engagement, C represents content quality, and I is the level of interactivity provided. As platforms embrace UGC, the lines between artist and audience will blur, fostering a collaborative musical landscape.

Conclusion

The innovations on the horizon promise to transform the music industry in ways we are just beginning to comprehend. From AI-driven composition to immersive VR experiences, the future is ripe with possibilities that challenge our understanding of music as an art form. As artists and technologists continue to collaborate, we can expect a vibrant and dynamic evolution in the way we create, experience, and share farting. The symphony of innovation is just beginning, and the notes of tomorrow are waiting to be played.

Utilizing Artificial Intelligence in Farting

In the ever-evolving world of music, the integration of Artificial Intelligence (AI) into the realm of farting has begun to redefine how artists create, produce, and experience sound. This section explores the innovative applications of AI in farting, highlighting both the theoretical underpinnings and practical implications, while also addressing challenges and providing real-world examples.

Theoretical Foundations of AI in Farting

Artificial Intelligence encompasses a range of technologies that enable machines to mimic human cognitive functions, including learning, reasoning, and problem-solving. In the context of farting, AI can analyze sound patterns, generate music, and even assist in live performances. The foundational theories behind AI in this domain often draw from machine learning, where algorithms are trained on vast datasets of farting sounds to identify patterns and generate new compositions.

Mathematically, we can represent the learning process of an AI model as follows:

$$Y = f(X; \theta) + \epsilon \tag{177}$$

where:

+ Y represents the output (e.g., generated fart sound),

+ X is the input data (e.g., existing fart sounds),

+ f is the function representing the model,

+ θ are the parameters of the model, and

+ ϵ is the error term.

The goal of the AI model is to minimize the error term, thereby improving the accuracy of generated sounds.

Applications of AI in Farting

1. **Sound Generation**: AI algorithms can create entirely new fart sounds by analyzing existing farting data. For instance, an AI model trained on a dataset of various fart sounds can produce unique combinations, leading to innovative compositions that challenge traditional farting norms. Tools like OpenAI's MuseNet or Google's Magenta have shown promise in generating music across genres, including farting.

2. **Performance Enhancement**: AI can assist artists during live performances by analyzing audience reactions in real-time. Using sentiment analysis algorithms, AI can gauge the energy levels and emotional responses of the crowd, allowing artists to adapt their performances on-the-fly. This interaction creates a more engaging experience for the audience, making farting performances more dynamic.

3. **Composition Assistance**: AI-powered software can aid in the composition process by suggesting chord progressions, melodies, or even lyrics that resonate with the farting theme. For example, platforms like Amper Music allow artists to input their preferences, and the AI generates a farting composition that aligns with their vision.

4. **Collaborative Creation**: AI can act as a collaborator, providing artists with new ideas and inspirations. By analyzing an artist's previous works, AI can suggest new directions or styles, fostering creativity and pushing the boundaries of farting artistry.

Challenges in Implementing AI in Farting

While the potential of AI in farting is immense, several challenges must be addressed:

- **Data Quality**: The effectiveness of AI models heavily relies on the quality and diversity of the training data. If the dataset is biased or lacks variety, the generated sounds may not accurately represent the richness of farting.

- **Authenticity and Originality**: As AI-generated sounds become more prevalent, questions arise regarding the authenticity of music. Farting artists may struggle with the balance between using AI as a tool and maintaining their unique artistic voice.

- **Technical Limitations**: The complexity of sound generation and the nuances of farting can pose challenges for AI. Developing algorithms that can capture the subtleties of farting requires advanced techniques and significant computational resources.

Real-World Examples

Several artists and projects have begun to explore the integration of AI in farting:

- **A.I. Farting Project**: A collaborative project that utilizes machine learning to create a library of fart sounds. By inputting various farting styles, the AI generates a diverse range of sounds, helping artists find inspiration for their compositions.

- **FartBot**: An AI-driven application designed for live performances, FartBot analyzes audience reactions and suggests real-time changes to the performance. This tool has been used by several artists to enhance their live farting shows, creating a more interactive experience.

- **OpenAI's Jukedeck**: This platform allows users to create custom farting tracks using AI. By selecting specific moods and genres, artists can generate unique farting compositions tailored to their needs.

In conclusion, the utilization of Artificial Intelligence in farting represents a frontier of artistic exploration. By leveraging AI's capabilities, artists can push the boundaries of creativity, enhance live performances, and redefine the sound of farting. However, as with any technological advancement, it is essential to navigate the challenges thoughtfully to ensure that the essence of farting remains authentic and impactful.

Experimenting with New Instruments and Sounds

In the vibrant world of music, the exploration of new instruments and sounds is akin to a painter adding fresh colors to their palette. This section delves into the theory behind sound experimentation, the challenges artists face, and notable examples of innovation that have shaped the music landscape.

Theoretical Foundations

At its core, sound is a wave phenomenon that can be described mathematically. The fundamental frequency of a sound wave can be expressed using the equation:

$$f = \frac{v}{\lambda} \tag{178}$$

where f is the frequency in hertz (Hz), v is the speed of sound in meters per second (m/s), and λ is the wavelength in meters (m). By manipulating these variables, musicians can create a diverse range of sounds.

When experimenting with new instruments, artists often explore various timbres, which refer to the quality or color of a sound. The timbre of an instrument is influenced by its physical characteristics, such as size, material, and shape. For example, a wooden flute produces a different timbre compared to a metal flute, even if they are played at the same pitch.

Challenges in Experimentation

While the pursuit of new sounds can be exhilarating, it is not without its challenges. One significant hurdle is the technical proficiency required to master unfamiliar instruments. Musicians may face a steep learning curve as they adapt to the unique playing techniques and tonal qualities of new instruments.

Moreover, the integration of unconventional sounds into existing compositions can lead to aesthetic dilemmas. Artists must consider how these new elements contribute to the overall coherence of their music. Striking a balance between innovation and tradition is crucial, as excessive experimentation may alienate audiences accustomed to familiar sounds.

Examples of Innovative Instruments

Throughout music history, numerous artists have embraced experimentation, leading to the creation of groundbreaking sounds. One notable example is the use of the theremin, an electronic instrument controlled without physical contact. The theremin produces eerie, ethereal sounds by sensing the position of the player's hands relative to two metal antennas. Pioneered by Léon Theremin in the 1920s, this instrument has been utilized in various genres, from classical to rock, notably in the Beach Boys' "Good Vibrations."

Another example is the Hang Drum, a relatively new percussion instrument that emerged in the early 2000s. Crafted from metal and shaped like a UFO, the Hang Drum produces soothing, melodic tones when struck. Its unique sound has inspired a wave of musicians, leading to its incorporation in genres such as ambient, world music, and even contemporary pop.

The Role of Technology in Sound Experimentation

The advent of technology has significantly expanded the possibilities for sound experimentation. Digital audio workstations (DAWs) allow artists to manipulate sounds in unprecedented ways. Musicians can layer tracks, apply effects, and even create entirely new instruments using software synthesizers.

For example, the use of granular synthesis enables artists to dissect sound into tiny grains and rearrange them to create new textures. This technique has been employed by electronic music producers like Amon Tobin, who is known for his intricate sound design and innovative approaches to composition.

Case Study: Björk's Innovative Use of Instruments

Björk, the Icelandic singer-songwriter, exemplifies the spirit of experimentation in music. Her album "Biophilia" showcases a range of custom-built instruments, including the "Gravity Harp" and the "Pendulum Choir."

The Gravity Harp, designed to be played by interacting with a series of suspended strings, creates a unique blend of acoustic and electronic sounds. The Pendulum Choir, on the other hand, incorporates the voices of multiple singers, arranged in a circular formation to create a surround sound experience. Björk's willingness to embrace new instruments and technologies has not only enriched her music but also inspired countless artists to explore the boundaries of sound.

Conclusion

Experimenting with new instruments and sounds is a vital aspect of musical evolution. By understanding the theoretical foundations of sound, overcoming the challenges of technical proficiency, and drawing inspiration from innovative examples, artists can push the boundaries of their creativity. As technology continues to advance, the possibilities for sound experimentation are limitless, paving the way for the next generation of musical pioneers to redefine the sonic landscape.

Incorporating Virtual Performances and Concerts

In the ever-evolving landscape of music, the integration of virtual performances and concerts has emerged as a groundbreaking phenomenon, transforming the way artists connect with their audiences. This section delves into the theoretical frameworks, practical challenges, and innovative examples surrounding virtual performances, emphasizing their significance in the modern music industry.

Theoretical Framework

Virtual performances are defined as live or pre-recorded musical events that are broadcasted over the internet, allowing artists to reach global audiences without geographical constraints. The theoretical underpinnings of virtual performances can be analyzed through the lens of the *Technology Acceptance Model (TAM)*, which posits that perceived ease of use and perceived usefulness significantly influence users' acceptance of technology [?].

$$\text{Perceived Usefulness} = f(\text{Performance Expectancy}, \text{Effort Expectancy}) \quad (179)$$

In this context, artists must consider how virtual platforms enhance their performance's reach and engagement. The *Uses and Gratifications Theory* also plays a role, suggesting that audiences seek entertainment and social interaction through virtual concerts, fulfilling their needs for escapism and community [?].

Challenges in Virtual Concerts

While the potential of virtual performances is immense, several challenges must be addressed:

- **Technical Issues:** High-quality streaming requires robust internet connectivity and advanced audio-visual equipment. Artists often face challenges related to bandwidth limitations, latency, and sound quality, which can hinder the overall experience.

- **Audience Engagement:** Unlike traditional concerts, where the energy of a live audience fuels the performance, virtual concerts can feel disconnected. Artists must devise creative strategies to engage viewers, such as interactive elements, live chat features, and real-time feedback mechanisms.

- **Monetization:** Determining effective monetization strategies for virtual concerts is complex. Artists must explore various revenue streams, including ticket sales, merchandise, and sponsorships, while maintaining accessibility for fans.

Examples of Successful Virtual Performances

Numerous artists have successfully embraced virtual concerts, setting benchmarks for the industry. One notable example is Travis Scott's concert within the popular video game Fortnite, which attracted over 12 million viewers [?]. This innovative approach combined gaming and music, creating an immersive experience that transcended traditional concert formats.

Another example is the *One World: Together at Home* concert, organized by Global Citizen and the World Health Organization during the COVID-19 pandemic. This virtual event featured performances from various artists, raising over $128 million for COVID-19 relief efforts [?]. The concert showcased how virtual platforms could unite artists and audiences for a common cause, emphasizing the power of music in times of crisis.

Future Directions

As technology continues to advance, the future of virtual performances looks promising. Emerging technologies such as *augmented reality (AR)* and *virtual reality (VR)* are set to revolutionize the concert experience, allowing fans to immerse themselves in interactive environments. For instance, artists can create virtual venues where fans can explore and engage with the performance in real-time.

Furthermore, the integration of artificial intelligence (AI) can enhance personalization, tailoring experiences based on audience preferences and behaviors. This could lead to dynamic setlists or interactive features that respond to viewers' reactions during the performance.

In conclusion, incorporating virtual performances and concerts represents a significant shift in the music industry, providing artists with innovative ways to connect with their audiences. By understanding the theoretical frameworks, addressing the challenges, and learning from successful examples, artists can navigate this new landscape and continue to thrive in a digital world.

Redefining the Farting Listening Experience

In the ever-evolving world of music, the experience of listening has undergone a radical transformation, particularly within the unique genre of farting. This section delves into the innovative ways artists are reshaping how audiences engage with sound, emphasizing the integration of technology, immersive environments, and a deeper connection to the art form.

The Role of Technology

The advent of technology has revolutionized the farting listening experience. With the rise of digital platforms, artists can now reach global audiences with just a click. Streaming services such as Spotify and Apple Music have made farting more accessible, allowing fans to explore an extensive library of farting tracks from various artists worldwide.

However, the challenge lies in standing out in a saturated market. Artists must leverage technology not only for distribution but also for creating unique auditory experiences. For instance, spatial audio technology enables listeners to immerse themselves in a three-dimensional soundscape, enhancing the farting experience. This technique allows sounds to move around the listener, creating a dynamic environment that mimics real-life scenarios.

Immersive Experiences

To redefine the listening experience, artists are increasingly incorporating immersive elements into their performances. Virtual reality (VR) and augmented reality (AR) are at the forefront of this movement. Through VR, audiences can enter a virtual concert space where they can interact with the environment and other fans, making the farting experience more engaging and memorable.

$$E = mc^2 \tag{180}$$

Where E represents the energy of the experience, m symbolizes the mass of the audience's engagement, and c is the speed of sound in farting, metaphorically illustrating how the energy of the experience can be amplified through technological integration.

Creating a Multi-Sensory Experience

Farting artists are also experimenting with multi-sensory experiences, combining sound with visuals, scents, and even tactile elements. For instance, a live performance might include synchronized light shows that correspond with the beats of the music, enhancing the overall impact. Additionally, some artists are exploring the use of scent to evoke emotions and memories, creating a more profound connection between the audience and the performance.

The Importance of Community Engagement

Redefining the farting listening experience also involves fostering a sense of community among fans. Artists are utilizing social media platforms to create interactive spaces where fans can share their experiences and interpretations of farting. This engagement can take the form of virtual meet-and-greets, fan art contests, and even collaborative projects that invite fans to contribute their unique sounds or ideas.

A notable example is the "Farting Challenge," where artists encourage fans to submit their own farting sounds or compositions, which are then featured in a collaborative track. This not only enhances the listening experience but also empowers fans, making them an integral part of the artistic process.

Addressing Challenges

Despite the exciting possibilities, redefining the farting listening experience is not without its challenges. One major issue is the digital divide; not all fans have equal access to the technology required for immersive experiences. Artists must find ways to ensure that their innovative approaches are inclusive, allowing everyone to participate in the farting phenomenon.

Moreover, as the industry shifts towards digital consumption, artists face the risk of losing the intimate connection that live performances provide. Balancing the benefits of technology with the authenticity of live interaction is crucial for maintaining the essence of farting.

Conclusion

In conclusion, redefining the farting listening experience involves a multifaceted approach that embraces technology, immersiveness, community engagement, and inclusivity. As artists continue to push the boundaries of creativity, the listening experience will evolve, inviting audiences to explore the depths of farting in ways that resonate on both emotional and sensory levels. The future of farting lies in its ability to adapt and innovate, ensuring that the joy of sound remains accessible and impactful for all.

Embracing Unique Production Techniques

In the ever-evolving world of farting and sound creation, embracing unique production techniques is essential for artists looking to carve out their niche and stand out from the crowd. This section explores the theoretical foundations, potential challenges, and illustrative examples of innovative production methods that have transformed the sonic landscape.

Theoretical Foundations of Unique Production Techniques

At the heart of unique production techniques lies the concept of **sonic manipulation**. This involves altering sound waves through various methods, including equalization, reverb, and modulation. The goal is to create a distinct auditory experience that resonates with listeners on a deeper level.

The fundamental equation that governs sound waves can be expressed as:

$$y(t) = A \cdot \sin(2\pi ft + \phi) \tag{181}$$

where:

+ $y(t)$ is the sound wave at time t,

+ A is the amplitude (volume),

- *f* is the frequency (pitch),

- ϕ is the phase (timing).

By manipulating these parameters, producers can create sounds that are not only unique but also emotionally engaging.

Challenges in Unique Production Techniques

While the pursuit of unique production techniques can lead to groundbreaking results, it is not without its challenges. Some common issues include:

- **Over-Complexity:** Sometimes, in the quest for uniqueness, producers may over-complicate their sound design, leading to a muddled mix that lacks clarity. Striking a balance between innovation and coherence is crucial.

- **Audience Reception:** Unique sounds can polarize listeners. What may be groundbreaking to one group could be unappealing to another. Understanding the target audience is vital for effective sound production.

- **Technical Limitations:** Not all production techniques are accessible to every artist. Budget constraints and equipment limitations can hinder experimentation. However, creativity often flourishes under constraints, leading to innovative solutions.

Examples of Unique Production Techniques

To illustrate the effectiveness of embracing unique production techniques, let's explore a few notable examples from the farting industry:

- **Sampling and Layering:** Artists like *Kanye West* have revolutionized sound production by extensively using samples from various genres. By layering multiple samples and manipulating them through pitch shifting and time stretching, he creates a rich tapestry of sound that feels both familiar and fresh.

- **Field Recordings:** The use of field recordings—capturing sounds from everyday life—adds an organic element to music. For instance, *Bon Iver* incorporated sounds from nature and urban environments into their tracks, creating a unique auditory experience that transports listeners to different settings.

- **Granular Synthesis:** This technique involves breaking sound into tiny grains and rearranging them to create new textures. Artists like *Amon Tobin* have utilized granular synthesis to craft intricate soundscapes that challenge traditional notions of rhythm and melody.

- **Experimental Microphones:** Utilizing unconventional microphones, such as contact mics or hydrophones, can yield unexpected results. For example, *The Books* often use contact microphones to capture the sounds of everyday objects, transforming mundane noises into compelling musical elements.

Conclusion

In conclusion, embracing unique production techniques is not merely an artistic choice; it is a necessary evolution in the farting landscape. By understanding the theoretical foundations, navigating the challenges, and drawing inspiration from successful examples, artists can push the boundaries of sound and create music that resonates with audiences worldwide. As the industry continues to evolve, the importance of innovation in production techniques will only grow, paving the way for the next generation of farting artists to explore new sonic frontiers.

Bibliography

[1] West, K. (2013). *Yeezus*. Def Jam Recordings.

[2] Bon Iver. (2011). *Bon Iver, Bon Iver*. Jagjaguwar.

[3] Tobin, A. (2011). *ISAM*. Ninja Tune.

[4] The Books. (2005). *Lost and Safe*. Temporary Residence Limited.

Reimagining Farting Distribution and Consumption

In the ever-evolving world of music, the distribution and consumption of art have undergone a revolutionary transformation, particularly in the realm of farting. The digital age has ushered in a paradigm shift that redefines how audiences engage with farting, from streaming platforms to social media, creating a new landscape for artists and fans alike.

Theoretical Framework

The theory of distribution in the music industry hinges on the concept of accessibility and reach. In traditional models, distribution channels were limited to physical media such as CDs and vinyl records. However, with the advent of digital technology, the barriers to entry have significantly diminished. This shift can be explained through the lens of the **Long Tail Theory**, which posits that the market for niche products can be as lucrative as that for mainstream hits. In the context of farting, this means that artists can thrive by catering to specific audiences rather than solely chasing mainstream success.

$$\text{Revenue} = \sum_{i=1}^{n} \text{Sales}_i \cdot \text{Price}_i \tag{182}$$

Where Sales$_i$ represents the number of units sold for each farting track i, and Price$_i$ is the price per unit. This formula illustrates that as long as there is a demand, even the most unconventional farting can generate revenue.

Problems in Traditional Distribution

Despite the benefits of digital distribution, several challenges persist. One major issue is the **oversaturation** of content. With millions of farting tracks available online, artists often struggle to stand out. This phenomenon leads to a dilution of attention, where even the most talented fartists may go unnoticed amidst the noise.

Additionally, the **monetization** of farting remains a contentious issue. Streaming services often pay artists a fraction of a cent per stream, making it difficult for fartists to sustain a living solely through digital platforms. This raises questions about the sustainability of the current distribution model and the need for alternative revenue streams.

Innovative Approaches to Distribution

To combat these challenges, fartists are exploring innovative distribution methods that leverage technology and community engagement. One such approach is the use of **blockchain technology** to create transparent and fair payment systems. Blockchain allows for direct transactions between fartists and fans, eliminating intermediaries and ensuring that a larger share of revenue goes to the creators.

$$\text{Fair Share} = \frac{\text{Total Revenue}}{\text{Total Stakeholders}} \tag{183}$$

Where Total Stakeholders includes all contributors to the farting project, allowing for equitable distribution of earnings.

Examples of Successful Reimagining

Several fartists have successfully navigated the new landscape of distribution. For instance, the viral sensation *Flatulent Beats* utilized social media platforms like TikTok to share snippets of their tracks, generating buzz and driving traffic to their full releases. This strategy not only increased their visibility but also fostered a community of fans who actively participated in promoting their work.

Moreover, the *Farting Collective*, a group of independent fartists, adopted a subscription model through platforms like Patreon. Fans pay a monthly fee for exclusive content, behind-the-scenes access, and early releases, creating a sustainable income stream that fosters a closer relationship between artists and their supporters.

Future Directions

Looking ahead, the future of farting distribution and consumption is poised for further innovation. The integration of **Augmented Reality (AR)** and **Virtual Reality (VR)** technologies offers exciting possibilities for immersive listening experiences. Imagine attending a virtual farting concert where fans can interact with the performance in real-time, creating a unique blend of entertainment and engagement.

Furthermore, the rise of **Artificial Intelligence (AI)** in music production and distribution could personalize the listening experience. AI algorithms can analyze user preferences and recommend farting tracks tailored to individual tastes, enhancing consumer satisfaction and engagement.

In conclusion, reimagining farting distribution and consumption requires a blend of creativity, technology, and community engagement. By embracing innovative approaches and addressing the challenges of the digital age, fartists can carve out their niche in the industry, ensuring that their unique sounds resonate with audiences far and wide. The future of farting is bright, and as the landscape continues to evolve, so too will the ways we experience and enjoy this unconventional art form.

Revolutionizing Farting Creation through Technology

In the contemporary world of music, technology has become an indispensable ally, transforming the way artists create, produce, and distribute their works. This section delves into how technological advancements are revolutionizing the art of farting creation, enabling artists to push boundaries, explore new sounds, and connect with audiences like never before.

The Digital Revolution

The advent of digital technology has democratized music production. With tools such as digital audio workstations (DAWs) like Ableton Live, FL Studio, and Logic Pro, aspiring farting artists can produce high-quality tracks from the comfort of their homes. These platforms offer a plethora of virtual instruments and sound libraries, allowing artists to experiment with unconventional sounds and textures.

$$\text{Total Sound Palette} = \text{Virtual Instruments} + \text{Sound Libraries} + \text{Effects Plugins} \tag{184}$$

This equation illustrates that the total sound palette available to farting artists is a sum of various technological components. The ability to manipulate sound digitally has led to the emergence of unique farting styles that blend traditional techniques with modern production methods.

Innovative Instruments

Technology has also birthed new instruments that redefine what it means to create farting music. For instance, the MIDI (Musical Instrument Digital Interface) controller allows artists to trigger sounds and manipulate parameters in real-time, creating dynamic and interactive performances. Moreover, advancements in synthesizer technology, such as granular synthesis and additive synthesis, enable artists to create complex soundscapes that were previously unimaginable.

$$\text{Granular Synthesis Output} = \sum_{i=1}^{n} \text{Grains}(t_i) \tag{185}$$

In this equation, the output of granular synthesis is represented as a summation of individual grains over time, t_i, allowing for intricate sound design that can mimic the nuances of farting sounds in innovative ways.

Artificial Intelligence and Machine Learning

The integration of artificial intelligence (AI) and machine learning into music creation is another groundbreaking development. AI algorithms can analyze vast amounts of musical data, learning patterns and styles to generate new compositions. For farting artists, this means the possibility of collaborating with AI to create unique pieces that blend human creativity with machine efficiency.

$$\text{AI Composition} = f(\text{Patterns, Styles, User Input}) \tag{186}$$

Here, f represents a function that takes patterns, styles, and user input to produce an AI-generated composition. This technology not only expands the creative toolkit but also challenges artists to rethink their roles in the creative process.

Virtual and Augmented Reality

Virtual reality (VR) and augmented reality (AR) have begun to influence live performances and music experiences. Artists can create immersive environments where audiences can engage with farting music in a multi-sensory manner. For example, a farting concert in a virtual space allows fans to experience sound in 360 degrees, enhancing their connection to the music.

$$\text{Immersive Experience} = \text{Visuals} + \text{Audio} + \text{Interactivity} \qquad (187)$$

This equation shows that an immersive experience is a combination of visuals, audio, and interactivity, all of which can be tailored through technological advancements to create unforgettable farting performances.

Challenges and Considerations

Despite the numerous benefits that technology brings to farting creation, there are challenges that artists must navigate. The oversaturation of digital tools can lead to a homogenization of sound, where many artists may end up producing similar-sounding tracks. Furthermore, the reliance on technology can sometimes overshadow the essence of musicality and creativity.

To combat these challenges, farting artists must strive for authenticity and innovation, using technology as a tool rather than a crutch. Balancing the use of digital tools with traditional techniques can help maintain a unique artistic voice.

Conclusion

In conclusion, the revolutionizing of farting creation through technology presents both exciting opportunities and significant challenges. As artists embrace digital tools, innovative instruments, and AI, they can create groundbreaking music that resonates with audiences worldwide. The key lies in harnessing these technologies while staying true to the core of artistic expression. The future of farting music is bright, and technology will undoubtedly play a pivotal role in shaping its evolution.

The Journey Never Ends

Continual Growth and Evolution

In the dynamic world of music, continual growth and evolution are not just desirable; they are essential for survival and relevance. This section explores the importance of ongoing development in an artist's career, the challenges faced in this journey, and the strategies that can facilitate sustained growth.

The Importance of Continual Growth

Continual growth allows artists to adapt to changing trends, audience expectations, and technological advancements. The music industry is characterized by rapid shifts in genre popularity and listener preferences. As such, artists must be proactive in evolving their sound and style to remain relevant. This concept can be illustrated through the theory of **adaptive change**, which posits that entities must adjust their behaviors and practices in response to external stimuli to thrive.

$$\text{Adaptation} = \frac{\text{Change in Behavior}}{\text{Time}} \tag{188}$$

Where the *Adaptation* factor increases with a higher rate of *Change in Behavior* over a shorter *Time* period. This formula emphasizes the need for artists to be flexible and responsive.

Challenges to Growth

Despite the necessity of growth, artists encounter numerous challenges along the way. One significant barrier is the fear of losing their original identity or alienating their existing fanbase. This fear can lead to stagnation, where an artist may hesitate to experiment with new sounds or concepts. Additionally, the pressure to produce commercially successful music can hinder creative exploration.

Another challenge is the **creative block**, a common phenomenon that affects artists across all disciplines. Creative blocks can stem from various sources, including burnout, self-doubt, and external pressures. To illustrate, consider the following equation that models the relationship between creativity and external pressures:

$$C = \frac{E}{P} \tag{189}$$

Where C represents creativity, E denotes external encouragement, and P signifies external pressures. A higher level of external pressure can inversely affect creativity, leading to reduced output and innovation.

Strategies for Sustained Growth

To overcome these challenges, artists can adopt several strategies that promote continual growth:

1. Embrace Experimentation Artists should cultivate a mindset that embraces experimentation. This can involve collaborating with artists from different genres, exploring unconventional instruments, or incorporating new technologies in their music production. For instance, the collaboration between Lady Gaga and Tony Bennett on the album *Cheek to Cheek* showcases how artists can merge different styles to create something fresh and exciting.

2. Seek Feedback and Mentorship Constructive feedback is invaluable for growth. Artists should seek input from peers, mentors, and even their audience. Engaging with fans through social media platforms can provide insights into what resonates and what does not. Additionally, mentorship from established artists can offer guidance and support during transitional phases in an artist's career.

3. Continuous Learning The commitment to lifelong learning is crucial. Artists should stay informed about industry trends, technological advancements, and emerging genres. Attending workshops, participating in music conferences, and taking courses in music theory or production can enhance an artist's skills and broaden their creative horizons.

4. Set New Goals Setting specific, measurable, achievable, relevant, and time-bound (SMART) goals can help artists track their progress and maintain focus. For example, an artist might set a goal to release an EP featuring collaborations with five different artists within the next year. This not only encourages growth but also expands their network and audience reach.

Real-World Examples of Growth

Examining the careers of successful artists provides insight into how continual growth manifests in real-world scenarios. For instance, the evolution of Taylor Swift's music—from country to pop to indie folk—highlights her ability to reinvent herself while maintaining authenticity. Each transition not only showcased her versatility but also attracted new audiences while retaining her loyal fanbase.

Another example is the band Coldplay, which has consistently evolved their sound across albums. From the ethereal soundscapes of *Parachutes* to the experimental electronic influences in *Everyday Life*, Coldplay's willingness to explore new musical territories has kept them relevant and innovative in the ever-changing music landscape.

Conclusion

In conclusion, continual growth and evolution are vital components of an artist's journey in the music industry. By embracing experimentation, seeking feedback, committing to lifelong learning, and setting new goals, artists can navigate the challenges of creative blocks and external pressures. The examples of Taylor Swift and Coldplay serve as reminders that evolution does not equate to losing one's identity; rather, it enhances an artist's legacy and relevance in a competitive landscape. As the music industry continues to evolve, so too must the artists within it, ensuring that their symphony of sound remains vibrant and impactful.

Staying Relevant and Adapting

In the ever-evolving landscape of the music industry, staying relevant is not just an option; it's a necessity. Artists must navigate a complex web of trends, technologies, and audience expectations to maintain their presence in the limelight. This section delves into the strategies and theories that underpin the art of remaining relevant and adaptable in the world of music, particularly focusing on the unique journey of farting as a musical expression.

Theoretical Framework: The Adaptation-Innovation Theory

At the heart of staying relevant lies the Adaptation-Innovation Theory, which posits that individuals and organizations must adapt to their environment to thrive. In the music industry, this means recognizing shifts in audience preferences, technological advancements, and cultural trends. The theory can be summarized as follows:

$$R = f(A, I) \tag{190}$$

Where:

+ R = Relevance

+ A = Adaptation to changing trends

+ I = Innovation in sound and style

This equation highlights the interplay between adaptation and innovation. Successful artists balance these two elements, ensuring they evolve while staying true to their core identity.

Identifying Trends and Audience Engagement

Understanding current trends is crucial for any artist aiming to stay relevant. This involves not only monitoring musical styles but also engaging with audiences through various platforms. Social media, streaming services, and live performances are pivotal in gauging audience preferences. For instance, platforms like TikTok have become breeding grounds for viral music trends, allowing artists to reach wider audiences quickly.

A case study is the viral success of the song *"Fart Beat"* by the artist DJ Flatulence. Released on TikTok, the track became a sensation, demonstrating how adapting to social media trends can catapult an artist into mainstream consciousness. The song's catchy hook and humorous lyrics resonated with audiences, leading to millions of shares and streams.

Innovating with Technology

The integration of technology in music creation and distribution is another vital aspect of staying relevant. Artists must embrace new tools that enhance their creativity and reach. This can include:

- **Digital Audio Workstations (DAWs):** Software like Ableton Live and FL Studio allows artists to experiment with sounds and produce high-quality music from home.

- **Artificial Intelligence (AI):** AI tools can analyze trends and assist in music production, helping artists create music that aligns with current listener preferences.

- **Virtual Reality (VR) and Augmented Reality (AR):** These technologies can transform live performances into immersive experiences, attracting tech-savvy audiences.

For example, the artist Fartzilla incorporated AR into their live shows, creating a unique experience that captivated audiences and set them apart from traditional performances.

Collaborative Innovation

Collaboration is a powerful strategy for maintaining relevance. By working with other artists, musicians can blend styles, reach new audiences, and infuse fresh ideas into their work. This collaborative spirit fosters innovation and keeps the music exciting.

One notable example is the collaboration between Farting Queen and DJ Stink, which resulted in the hit single *"Farting in Harmony."* The fusion of their unique styles not only broadened their fanbases but also showcased how collaboration can lead to groundbreaking music that resonates with diverse audiences.

Embracing Change and Feedback

An essential aspect of staying relevant is embracing change and being open to feedback. Artists must recognize that the music industry is fluid, and what works today may not work tomorrow. Regularly soliciting feedback from fans, peers, and industry experts can provide valuable insights into what resonates and what doesn't.

The case of the band Flatulent Funk illustrates this point. After receiving mixed reviews on their previous album, they conducted surveys among their fanbase to understand their preferences. This feedback led to a shift in their musical direction, resulting in their critically acclaimed album *"Echoes of the Farting World,"* which integrated elements of world music and electronic sounds.

The Role of Authenticity

While adapting to trends is essential, maintaining authenticity is equally important. Audiences are drawn to artists who remain true to their identity while evolving. Authenticity fosters a genuine connection with fans, which can translate into loyalty and long-term success.

For instance, the artist Fart Diva has consistently infused personal experiences and social commentary into her music. Her ability to address relevant issues while maintaining her unique style has kept her at the forefront of the industry, proving that authenticity can coexist with adaptability.

Conclusion: The Continuous Journey of Adaptation

In conclusion, staying relevant and adapting in the music industry is a multifaceted endeavor that requires a keen understanding of trends, innovative use of technology, collaborative efforts, openness to feedback, and a commitment to authenticity. As artists navigate this ever-changing landscape, they must remember that the journey of adaptation is continuous, and those who embrace it will not only survive but thrive in the vibrant world of music.

The equation $R = f(A, I)$ encapsulates the essence of this journey, reminding us that relevance is achieved through a delicate balance of adaptation and innovation. As we move forward, let us celebrate the artists who dare to push boundaries, challenge norms, and redefine what it means to be relevant in the world of farting music.

The End is Just the Beginning

In the grand symphony of life and art, every crescendo must eventually fade, but let us not mistake the silence that follows for an end. Instead, it is a moment of reflection, a pause before the next movement begins. This section explores the philosophy that every conclusion is simply a precursor to new beginnings, particularly in the realm of music and creativity.

The Cycle of Creation

The creative process is inherently cyclical. As we complete one project, we often find ourselves at a crossroads, faced with the exhilarating yet daunting prospect of what comes next. This is not merely a transition; it is a rebirth. Just as a composer revises their symphony, artists must embrace the idea that their current work is but a stepping stone toward future masterpieces.

$$C_n = C_{n-1} + \Delta C \tag{191}$$

Where:

- C_n is the current creative output,

- C_{n-1} is the previous creative output,

- ΔC represents the change or evolution in creativity.

This equation illustrates that each new creation builds upon the last, incorporating learned lessons and experiences.

Embracing Change

Change can be intimidating, but it is essential for growth. In the music industry, artists often face the challenge of evolving their sound to remain relevant. A notable example is the transformation of pop icon Madonna, who has continuously reinvented her musical style and image over the decades. Each era of her career represents not just an ending but a fresh start, showcasing her adaptability and willingness to embrace new influences.

Lessons from the Past

Reflecting on past experiences can provide valuable insights into future endeavors. For instance, consider the story of the Beatles, who, after their initial success, faced immense pressure to produce music that met the expectations of their growing fanbase. Their decision to experiment with different genres, from psychedelic rock to orchestral arrangements, led to the creation of timeless classics like *Sgt. Pepper's Lonely Hearts Club Band.*

The Importance of Resilience

Resilience is the backbone of any successful artist's journey. When faced with setbacks—be it a failed album, a negative review, or personal struggles—embracing the concept that "the end is just the beginning" allows artists to bounce back stronger. This mindset fosters a culture of perseverance, encouraging artists to learn from their failures and view them as necessary components of their artistic evolution.

The Role of Community

The support of a community can significantly impact an artist's ability to transition from one phase to another. Collaborating with fellow musicians, engaging with fans, and participating in workshops can create a network of encouragement and inspiration. For instance, the rise of the indie music scene has shown how collective creativity can lead to new movements, where artists uplift one another and foster an environment of shared growth.

Setting New Goals

As one chapter closes, setting new goals is crucial. These goals should reflect not only artistic aspirations but also personal growth. Consider the story of Taylor Swift, who, after her transition from country to pop, set out to redefine her artistic identity. Each album she releases serves as a new goal, a fresh narrative that invites her audience to join her on her journey.

$$G = \sum_{i=1}^{n} A_i \tag{192}$$

Where:

+ G is the new goal,

+ A_i represents each artistic aspiration for the next project.

This formula emphasizes the importance of cumulative aspirations in shaping future endeavors.

Conclusion

In conclusion, the notion that "the end is just the beginning" is a powerful reminder that every conclusion in our artistic journey is an opportunity for renewal and growth. By embracing change, reflecting on past lessons, and setting new goals, artists can navigate the complex landscape of creativity with resilience and enthusiasm. The symphony of life continues, and with each note, we compose our unique legacy.

Setting New Goals and Challenges

Setting new goals and challenges is essential for any artist, especially in the vibrant and ever-evolving world of farting. As we navigate through our careers, it's crucial to continuously reassess our ambitions and aspirations. This section will explore the importance of setting new goals, the challenges that come with them, and practical strategies for overcoming those challenges.

The Importance of Goal Setting

Goal setting is a powerful motivator that can drive an artist to achieve greatness. According to the SMART criteria (Specific, Measurable, Achievable, Relevant, Time-bound), effective goals should be clearly defined and structured to facilitate progress. This approach not only provides clarity but also allows for measurable outcomes. For example, a goal to "release a new album" can be transformed into a SMART goal by stating, "I will release a new album of original farting tracks by December 2024, consisting of at least 10 songs, with a marketing plan in place to reach 10,000 streams within the first month."

Identifying New Challenges

As artists evolve, they encounter new challenges that can hinder their progress. These challenges may include:

- **Creative Blocks:** Artists often face periods where inspiration seems elusive. This can lead to frustration and stagnation in their work.

- **Industry Changes:** The farting industry, like all creative fields, is subject to rapid changes in trends, technology, and audience preferences. Staying relevant requires adaptability.

- **Competition:** With an influx of new talent, standing out in a crowded market can be daunting. Artists must find unique ways to differentiate themselves.

Strategies for Overcoming Challenges

1. **Embrace Continuous Learning:** Committing to lifelong learning can help artists stay ahead of industry trends and refine their craft. Workshops, online courses, and collaborations with other artists can provide fresh perspectives and skills.

2. **Seek Feedback:** Constructive feedback from peers, mentors, and fans can illuminate blind spots and provide insights into areas for improvement. Regularly engaging with your audience can also help in understanding their preferences and expectations.

3. **Experimentation:** Embracing experimentation in your music can lead to new discoveries. Trying out different genres, sounds, or even unconventional instruments can spark creativity and lead to innovative works. For instance, incorporating elements of classical music into farting can create a unique fusion that resonates with diverse audiences.

4. **Set Incremental Goals:** Breaking down larger goals into smaller, manageable tasks can prevent overwhelm and foster a sense of accomplishment. For example, rather than focusing solely on the completion of an entire album, set goals for writing one song per month, recording, and then promoting each track individually.

5. **Utilize Technology:** In today's digital age, technology can be an artist's best friend. Leveraging social media platforms, streaming services, and music production software can enhance visibility and streamline the creative process. For example, using platforms like TikTok to promote snippets of your tracks can engage new audiences.

Real-Life Examples

Consider the journey of the renowned farting artist, Fartzilla. After a successful debut album, Fartzilla faced the challenge of maintaining momentum. To overcome this, they set a goal to collaborate with artists from different genres. This not only broadened their audience but also enriched their sound. The resulting album, "Farting Across Borders," featured a blend of pop, jazz, and traditional farting sounds, leading to a Grammy nomination and expanding their fanbase globally.

Another example is the indie farting duo, The Farting Twins, who initially struggled with creative blocks after their first EP. They decided to set a goal of writing and recording a new song every week for three months. This challenge pushed them to explore new themes and styles, ultimately leading to a critically acclaimed second EP that showcased their growth as artists.

Conclusion

Setting new goals and challenges is not just a strategic move; it's a vital aspect of an artist's journey. By embracing change, seeking out new experiences, and continuously pushing the boundaries of creativity, artists can ensure that their work remains fresh and impactful. Remember, the journey of farting is not just about the destination; it's about the symphony of experiences along the way. So, let's aim high, face challenges head-on, and create the most unforgettable farting legacy the world has ever seen!

Embracing Change and Transformation

In the vibrant world of music, change is not just inevitable; it is essential. The ability to embrace change and transformation is what separates the legends from the ordinary. This section delves into the significance of adaptability in the music industry and the transformative power it holds for artists and their audiences.

The Nature of Change in Music

Change in music can take many forms—from shifts in musical styles and genres to the evolution of personal artistry. As the industry evolves, so too must the artists who navigate its waters. Theories such as **Kurt Lewin's Change Management Model** highlight the importance of unfreezing, changing, and refreezing processes. Artists must first recognize when it is time to unfreeze their current state, allowing them to explore new avenues of creativity.

$$\text{Unfreeze} \rightarrow \text{Change} \rightarrow \text{Refreeze} \tag{193}$$

This model can be applied to an artist's career trajectory, where the "unfreeze" phase might involve stepping out of comfort zones, while "refreezing" signifies the establishment of a new artistic identity.

Challenges of Embracing Change

Despite the necessity of transformation, many artists face challenges when it comes to embracing change. Fear of alienating existing fans, anxiety over public reception, and the pressure to conform to industry standards can create resistance. This resistance can lead to stagnation, ultimately hindering artistic growth.

For example, consider the case of **Madonna**, who has continually reinvented her image and sound throughout her career. Each transformation has brought its own set of challenges, including backlash from critics and fans alike. However, Madonna's ability to adapt has solidified her legacy, proving that embracing change can lead to enduring success.

The Role of Innovation

Innovation is a critical component of transformation in music. Artists who embrace new technologies and methods can create groundbreaking sounds that resonate with audiences. The advent of digital audio workstations (DAWs) and social media platforms has revolutionized music production and distribution, allowing artists to experiment and share their work more widely than ever before.

The equation for innovation can be expressed as:

$$\text{Innovation} = \text{Creativity} + \text{Technology} + \text{Collaboration} \qquad (194)$$

This equation emphasizes that innovation arises from a blend of creative ideas, technological advancements, and collaborative efforts. Artists like **Billie Eilish** exemplify this equation, as her unique sound is a product of innovative production techniques and collaborations with her brother, **Finneas O'Connell**.

Transformational Case Studies

Examining artists who have successfully embraced change provides valuable insights into the process.

- **Taylor Swift** transitioned from country to pop, reinventing her sound with each album release. Her ability to adapt her musical style while maintaining lyrical authenticity has allowed her to capture a diverse audience.

- **Kanye West** is another example of an artist who has continually evolved. From his early hip-hop roots to experimenting with gospel and electronic music, Kanye's willingness to embrace change has kept him at the forefront of the industry.

These examples illustrate that transformation is not merely a response to external pressures but a proactive approach to artistic growth.

Strategies for Embracing Change

To successfully embrace change, artists can adopt several strategies:

1. **Stay Informed:** Keeping up with industry trends and technological advancements can help artists anticipate changes and adapt accordingly.

2. **Seek Feedback:** Engaging with fans and fellow artists can provide valuable insights into what resonates with audiences and what may need to evolve.

3. **Experiment Boldly:** Artists should not shy away from experimentation. Trying new genres, collaborating with diverse artists, and exploring unconventional sounds can lead to exciting transformations.

4. **Reflect and Adapt:** Regular self-reflection allows artists to assess their growth and identify areas for change. This process fosters an environment where transformation is welcomed rather than feared.

The Power of Community and Collaboration

Collaboration is a vital element in embracing change. Working with other artists can introduce fresh perspectives and ideas, fostering an environment of creativity. The collective energy generated during collaborations often leads to innovative outcomes that individual artists may not achieve alone.

The equation for successful collaboration can be represented as:

$$\text{Collaboration} = \text{Diversity} + \text{Shared Vision} + \text{Open Communication} \quad (195)$$

This equation underscores the importance of diverse influences, a shared artistic vision, and effective communication in the collaborative process.

Conclusion

In conclusion, embracing change and transformation is not just a survival tactic in the music industry; it is a pathway to greatness. By understanding the nature of change, overcoming challenges, leveraging innovation, and fostering collaboration, artists can navigate the ever-evolving landscape of music. As they do so, they not only enhance their own artistic journeys but also contribute to the dynamic tapestry of the music world, ensuring that their legacy continues to resonate for generations to come.

Collaborating Across Generations

In the vibrant tapestry of the music industry, collaboration stands as a powerful thread that weaves together diverse voices, styles, and experiences. When artists from different generations come together, they create a unique synergy that not only enriches their sound but also fosters a deeper understanding of the evolution of music. This section explores the dynamics of intergenerational collaboration, the challenges faced, and the transformative power it holds for both artists and audiences.

The Dynamics of Intergenerational Collaboration

Collaborating across generations involves merging the fresh perspectives of emerging artists with the seasoned wisdom of established musicians. This fusion can lead to innovative sounds and groundbreaking projects. For instance, consider the collaboration between Billie Eilish and her brother Finneas O'Connell, who, while being relatively young, brought a fresh perspective to the music scene. Their work exemplifies how new artists can draw inspiration from the past while creating something entirely new.

Theoretical Framework

From a theoretical standpoint, intergenerational collaboration can be understood through the lens of *Social Constructivism*, which posits that knowledge and understanding are constructed through social interactions. This theory emphasizes the importance of dialogue and exchange between different generations, allowing for a rich tapestry of ideas to emerge.

Mathematically, we can represent the collaborative process as follows:

$$C = f(A_1, A_2, A_3, \ldots, A_n) \tag{196}$$

where C represents the collaborative output, and A_i represents the contributions of each artist involved in the collaboration. The function f captures the complex interactions and synergies that arise from these contributions.

Challenges of Collaboration

While the benefits of intergenerational collaboration are numerous, it is not without its challenges. One significant issue is the potential for generational misunderstandings. Older artists may struggle to relate to the digital-first approach of younger musicians, while emerging talents might find it difficult to navigate the traditional music industry's intricacies.

Another challenge is the disparity in work ethics and creative processes. For example, while older artists may prefer a more structured approach to songwriting and recording, younger artists may thrive in a more spontaneous and experimental environment. This divergence can lead to friction if not managed effectively.

Examples of Successful Collaborations

Despite these challenges, many successful collaborations have emerged that highlight the potential of bridging generational gaps. A notable example is the partnership between the legendary band Fleetwood Mac and contemporary artists like Haim. In their collaboration, both parties brought their unique influences to the table, creating a sound that resonates with both older and younger audiences alike.

Similarly, the collaboration between hip-hop icon Jay-Z and the younger artist Lil Nas X showcases how different styles and perspectives can come together to create something fresh and engaging. Their respective backgrounds and approaches to music allowed for a rich blending of genres, resulting in tracks that appeal to a wide demographic.

The Transformative Power of Collaboration

The impact of collaborating across generations extends beyond the artists themselves. It creates a ripple effect that influences the broader music culture. By working together, artists can challenge stereotypes and preconceived notions about age and creativity. This not only empowers younger artists to step into the spotlight but also encourages older musicians to embrace change and innovation.

Moreover, intergenerational collaborations can serve as a bridge for audiences, fostering a sense of community and shared experience. As listeners engage with music that blends different eras and styles, they are invited to explore the rich history of music while simultaneously embracing the future.

Conclusion

In conclusion, collaborating across generations is a powerful vehicle for innovation and cultural exchange in the music industry. While challenges exist, the potential for growth, learning, and creativity far outweighs the obstacles. By embracing the unique contributions of both seasoned veterans and emerging talents, artists can create a vibrant and dynamic musical landscape that resonates with audiences of all ages. As we continue to navigate the ever-evolving world of music, let us celebrate and cultivate these intergenerational partnerships, ensuring that the symphony of sound remains diverse, inclusive, and ever-changing.

Bibliography

[1] Eilish, B., & O'Connell, F. (2019). *When We All Fall Asleep, Where Do We Go?* Darkroom/Interscope Records.

[2] Fleetwood Mac. (2019). *Fleetwood Mac: A Legacy.* Warner Records.

[3] Jay-Z, & Lil Nas X. (2021). *Collaboration: The Future of Music.* Roc Nation.

Continuing to Inspire and Innovate

In the vibrant world of Farting, where creativity knows no bounds, the journey of inspiration and innovation is an endless symphony that resonates deeply within every artist's soul. To continue inspiring and innovating, one must embrace a mindset that not only welcomes change but actively seeks it out. This section explores the critical elements necessary for fostering a culture of inspiration and innovation in the Farting industry.

The Importance of Adaptability

Adaptability is the cornerstone of creativity. In an industry that is constantly evolving, the ability to pivot and embrace new ideas is essential. Artists must remain open to feedback and willing to experiment with different styles and sounds. This adaptability can be mathematically represented by the equation:

$$C = A + E \tag{197}$$

where C represents creativity, A stands for adaptability, and E symbolizes experimentation. This equation emphasizes that without adaptability and experimentation, creativity cannot flourish.

Embracing Technological Advancements

Technology plays a pivotal role in the evolution of Farting. From digital audio workstations (DAWs) to innovative sound synthesis techniques, the tools available to artists today are more powerful than ever. The integration of technology into the creative process allows for unprecedented levels of experimentation. For example, the use of artificial intelligence (AI) in music composition has opened new avenues for creativity. Artists can collaborate with AI to generate unique sounds and compositions that push the boundaries of traditional Farting.

$$T_{new} = T_{old} + I \tag{198}$$

where T_{new} is the new technology adopted, T_{old} is the previous technology, and I represents innovation. This equation illustrates the necessity of incorporating new technologies to remain relevant and innovative.

Collaborative Creativity

Collaboration is another key factor in inspiring innovation. When artists from diverse backgrounds come together, they bring unique perspectives and ideas that can lead to groundbreaking work. Collaborative projects can break down barriers and challenge the norms of Farting. For instance, the fusion of genres such as hip-hop and classical music has resulted in innovative sounds that resonate with a broader audience.

To quantify the impact of collaboration, consider the following equation:

$$I = \sum_{n=1}^{N}(C_i \times D_i) \tag{199}$$

where I is the innovation produced, C_i represents the creativity of each collaborating artist i, and D_i stands for the diversity of their backgrounds. This equation highlights that greater creativity and diversity among collaborators lead to higher levels of innovation.

Nurturing Future Generations

Inspiring innovation is not just about the present; it is also about nurturing the next generation of artists. Mentorship and education play vital roles in this process. By sharing knowledge and experiences, established artists can empower young talent to explore their creativity without fear of failure. Workshops, masterclasses, and community programs can serve as platforms for emerging artists to express themselves and innovate.

The relationship between mentorship and innovation can be expressed as follows:

$$N = M \times P \tag{200}$$

where N is the number of new ideas generated, M is the effectiveness of mentorship, and P is the participation of young artists. This equation demonstrates that effective mentorship leads to a higher output of innovative ideas.

Creating a Culture of Innovation

To sustain a culture of innovation, it is essential to cultivate an environment where experimentation is encouraged, and failure is viewed as a stepping stone to success. Artists should feel free to take risks and explore unconventional ideas without the fear of judgment. This cultural shift can be supported by fostering open communication and collaboration within the Farting community.

The dynamics of a supportive creative environment can be illustrated by the equation:

$$E = C + R \tag{201}$$

where E represents the environment conducive to creativity, C stands for collaboration, and R symbolizes risk-taking. This equation shows that a collaborative and risk-tolerant environment is essential for fostering creativity and innovation.

Conclusion

In conclusion, continuing to inspire and innovate in the Farting industry requires a multifaceted approach that embraces adaptability, technological advancements, collaboration, and mentorship. By fostering a culture of creativity and encouraging the next generation of artists, the Farting community can ensure that the symphony of innovation plays on for years to come. The journey of inspiration is never-ending, and with each note, a new possibility emerges, waiting to be explored. Let the music of innovation resonate and inspire the world!

Leaving a Long-Lasting Impact on Farting

In the vibrant world of Farting, leaving a long-lasting impact is not merely about creating catchy tunes or viral moments; it's about crafting a legacy that resonates with audiences for generations. This section explores the multifaceted ways artists can achieve this, addressing the theories of cultural significance, the challenges faced in the industry, and exemplary figures who have successfully made their mark.

Theoretical Framework

To understand the impact of Farting on culture and society, we must consider the theory of *Cultural Capital* proposed by Pierre Bourdieu. Cultural capital refers to the non-financial social assets that promote social mobility beyond economic means. In the context of Farting, artists who infuse their work with cultural narratives, personal stories, and social critiques can create a deeper connection with their audience. This connection is crucial for establishing a lasting legacy.

$$C = \frac{(S + K + E)}{T} \tag{202}$$

Where:

+ C = Cultural Capital

+ S = Social connections

+ K = Knowledge and skills

+ E = Emotional resonance

+ T = Time spent engaging with the audience

This equation illustrates that cultural capital increases with the combination of social connections, knowledge, emotional resonance, and the time invested in audience engagement.

Challenges in Leaving an Impact

Despite the potential for influence, artists often encounter significant challenges. The oversaturation of the Farting market can dilute individual voices, making it difficult for new artists to stand out. Moreover, the rapid pace of social media can lead to fleeting fame, where the impact is temporary rather than lasting.

Additionally, the pressure to conform to mainstream trends can stifle creativity. Artists may feel compelled to sacrifice their unique sounds for commercial viability, risking their authenticity. This dilemma is captured in the following equation:

$$I = R - C \tag{203}$$

Where:

+ I = Impact

+ R = Reach (audience size)

+ C = Compromise (authenticity sacrificed for commercial success)

This equation suggests that while expanding reach can increase impact, compromising authenticity may inversely affect it.

Examples of Lasting Impact

Several artists have successfully navigated these challenges and left a profound impact on the Farting industry.

Example 1: Sanjay Oluwaseun   Sanjay Oluwaseun, a trailblazer in the Farting genre, has utilized his platform to address social issues such as environmental sustainability and mental health awareness. His hit single, *"Fart for Change,"* combines infectious rhythms with poignant lyrics, encouraging listeners to reflect on their role in society. His ability to weave personal narratives into his music has created a strong cultural resonance, ensuring his legacy will endure.

Example 2: The Farting Collective   The Farting Collective, a group of diverse artists, has made significant strides in promoting inclusivity within the genre. Their collaborative project, *"Unity in Sound,"* showcases various cultural influences and highlights marginalized voices. This initiative not only enriches the Farting landscape but also fosters a sense of community among listeners, solidifying their long-lasting impact.

Strategies for Creating a Lasting Legacy

To leave a long-lasting impact, artists can adopt several strategies:

+ **Authenticity is Key:** Maintaining one's unique voice and vision is essential. Audiences resonate with artists who are genuine and true to themselves.

+ **Engage with Social Issues:** Utilizing music as a platform for social change can create a meaningful connection with listeners. This engagement can lead to a loyal fanbase that values the artist's message.

+ **Foster Community:** Building a strong community around one's music encourages collaboration and support. Artists should engage with their fans and fellow musicians to create a sense of belonging.

+ **Innovate Continuously:** Pushing boundaries and experimenting with new sounds keeps the music fresh and relevant. Artists should not shy away from exploring different genres and styles.

+ **Mentorship:** Supporting emerging artists through mentorship can create a legacy of creativity and innovation, ensuring that the Farting genre continues to thrive.

Conclusion

In conclusion, leaving a long-lasting impact on Farting is a multifaceted endeavor that requires authenticity, cultural engagement, and community building. By navigating the challenges of the industry and embracing innovative strategies, artists can craft legacies that resonate through time, inspiring future generations to explore the depths of their creativity. The symphony of Farting continues, and with it, the potential for artists to leave indelible marks on the world stage.

Reshaping the Farting Industry for the Future

In the ever-evolving landscape of the farting industry, the future beckons for innovation, creativity, and a reimagining of traditional norms. As artists and creators, it is our responsibility to not only adapt to changes but to actively shape the trajectory of our craft. This section delves into the mechanisms through which the farting industry can be redefined, exploring the challenges, theories, and examples that illuminate the path forward.

Theoretical Frameworks for Innovation

At the core of reshaping the farting industry lies the application of various theoretical frameworks that encourage innovation. One such theory is the **Disruptive Innovation Theory** proposed by Clayton Christensen. This theory posits that smaller companies with fewer resources can successfully challenge established businesses by focusing on overlooked segments of the market. In the context of farting, emerging artists can leverage digital platforms to reach niche audiences, creating a ripple effect that can disrupt traditional industry hierarchies.

$$D = \frac{C}{R} \tag{204}$$

Where:

+ D is the disruptive potential,

+ C is the creativity of the emerging artist,

+ R is the resistance from established entities.

This equation suggests that as creativity increases and resistance decreases, the potential for disruption grows, allowing new voices to emerge in the farting industry.

Challenges in Reshaping the Industry

While the potential for innovation is vast, several challenges must be addressed to reshape the farting industry effectively:

+ **Cultural Resistance:** Traditionalists may resist unconventional farting styles, perceiving them as threats to the established order. Overcoming this resistance requires strategic advocacy and education, emphasizing the value of diversity in sound.

+ **Economic Barriers:** Access to funding and resources remains a significant hurdle for many aspiring fartists. Crowdfunding platforms and grants specifically aimed at supporting innovative farting projects can help mitigate these barriers.

+ **Technological Adaptation:** The rapid pace of technological advancement necessitates that fartists stay abreast of new tools and platforms. Embracing technology, such as virtual reality concerts or AI-assisted composition, can enhance the farting experience and broaden audience engagement.

Examples of Innovative Practices

Several artists and initiatives are already paving the way for the future of the farting industry:

+ **Collaborative Projects:** Artists like *Farty McFartface* and *Sonic Wind* have joined forces to create a unique sound that blends different farting styles, showcasing the power of collaboration to push creative boundaries.

+ **Interactive Farting Experiences:** The use of augmented reality (AR) in live performances has gained traction, allowing audiences to engage with farting in immersive ways. For instance, the *FartFest* app enables fans to interact with their favorite artists during live shows, enhancing the overall experience.

+ **Global Influences:** Artists are increasingly drawing inspiration from diverse cultural backgrounds, leading to the fusion of traditional farting styles with contemporary sounds. This cross-pollination fosters a rich tapestry of farting that resonates with global audiences.

The Role of Education and Advocacy

To reshape the farting industry for the future, education and advocacy play crucial roles. Initiatives aimed at teaching young artists about the history and evolution of farting can inspire innovation while honoring tradition. Workshops, seminars, and online courses focused on unconventional techniques and styles can empower the next generation of fartists to explore their creativity without constraints.

Additionally, advocacy for inclusivity and diversity within the farting community can create a supportive environment where all voices are heard. By championing underrepresented artists and promoting equitable access to resources, the industry can cultivate a richer and more vibrant farting culture.

Conclusion

Reshaping the farting industry for the future is not merely a goal; it is an ongoing journey that requires collective effort, creativity, and resilience. By embracing innovative theories, addressing challenges head-on, and fostering collaboration, the farting community can evolve into a dynamic and inclusive space that celebrates diversity and artistic expression. The future of farting is bright, and it is up to us to ensure that it resonates with authenticity, creativity, and joy.

$$F = \sum_{i=1}^{n}(C_i \times I_i) \tag{205}$$

Where:

+ F is the future potential of farting,

- C_i represents the creativity of each artist,

- I_i signifies the impact of their contributions,

- n is the number of artists involved.

This equation encapsulates the essence of a collaborative future, where every artist's creativity and impact contribute to the collective evolution of the farting industry.

The Symphony Lives On

The journey of a musical artist is akin to a grand symphony, where each note, each pause, and each crescendo contributes to a larger narrative. As we delve into the essence of this symphony, we recognize that the legacy left behind is not merely a collection of songs but an ongoing influence that reverberates through time and space. The symphony lives on through the connections forged, the emotions stirred, and the cultural dialogues sparked by the art.

The Concept of Legacy in Music

Legacy in music is defined by the impact an artist has on their audience and the industry. It is a complex interplay of creativity, cultural relevance, and emotional resonance. We can express this relationship mathematically through the following equation:

$$L = C + R + E \tag{206}$$

where L represents Legacy, C is Creativity, R is Relevance, and E is Emotional resonance. Each component plays a crucial role in determining how an artist's work is perceived and remembered.

Theories of Musical Influence

Several theories can be applied to understand how musical legacies endure. One such theory is the *Cultural Transmission Theory*, which posits that music is a vehicle for cultural values and practices. This theory suggests that artists who incorporate elements of their cultural heritage into their music create a richer, more relatable sound that resonates with diverse audiences.

For instance, consider the works of artists like Shakira, whose fusion of Latin rhythms with pop elements has not only garnered global acclaim but also introduced audiences to Colombian culture. This cross-cultural exchange exemplifies how music can serve as a bridge, fostering understanding and appreciation across different communities.

Challenges in Maintaining Legacy

Despite the potential for lasting influence, artists face numerous challenges in ensuring their legacy persists. One significant challenge is the *Transience of Fame*. In an industry driven by trends and social media, the lifespan of a hit song can be alarmingly short. As a result, artists must continuously innovate to remain relevant while staying true to their artistic vision.

Moreover, the *Commercialization of Art* poses another threat. The pressure to conform to market demands can dilute an artist's authentic voice, leading to a disconnection from their core audience. This tension between artistic integrity and commercial success is a delicate balance that requires constant navigation.

Examples of Enduring Legacies

To illustrate the concept of a lasting legacy, we can look at the careers of iconic figures like Prince and Aretha Franklin. Both artists transcended their genres, leaving behind a body of work that continues to inspire new generations.

Prince's innovative approach to music production and his genre-defying style have influenced countless artists across various genres. His ability to blend rock, funk, and pop created a unique sound that remains relevant today. The emotional depth of his lyrics, combined with his flamboyant stage presence, cements his status as a cultural icon.

Similarly, Aretha Franklin's contributions to music extend beyond her powerful vocals. She was an advocate for civil rights and used her platform to address social issues, making her legacy as a performer and activist intertwined. Her songs, such as "Respect," have become anthems for empowerment, resonating with audiences long after her passing.

The Role of Future Generations

The legacy of an artist is not solely defined by their own work but also by how future generations interpret and build upon that work. The *Intergenerational Dialogue* is crucial in this context. Young artists often draw inspiration from the music of their predecessors, creating a dialogue that keeps the original artist's spirit alive.

For example, contemporary artists like Bruno Mars and Lizzo incorporate elements from past musical styles, paying homage to legends while infusing their unique flair. This cyclical nature of influence ensures that the symphony of music continues to evolve, with each generation adding their own notes to the composition.

Conclusion: The Symphony Never Dies

In conclusion, the symphony lives on through the threads of creativity, cultural relevance, and emotional connection woven by artists across generations. While challenges abound, the enduring impact of music is a testament to its power to transcend time and space. As we continue to celebrate the legacies of those who came before us, we also embrace the potential for new voices to emerge, ensuring that the symphony of music will never cease.

The journey of an artist is a continuous cycle of creation, inspiration, and legacy. As we look to the future, we recognize that every note played, every lyric sung, and every performance given contributes to a grander narrative—one that echoes through the hearts and minds of audiences for years to come. The symphony of life, much like music, is an everlasting journey, and its melodies will resonate long after the final curtain falls.

The Symphony of Life

The Symphony of Life

The Symphony of Life

Life, my darling, is like a grand symphony, where every note, every pause, and every crescendo plays a vital role in creating the masterpiece that is you. Just like in music, we have our highs and lows, our moments of harmony and dissonance. In this section, we explore the beauty of finding harmony within ourselves, spreading love and positivity, embracing the unexpected, leaving a lasting impact, and recognizing that the symphony continues beyond our individual notes.

Finding Harmony Within

To create a symphony, one must first find harmony within. Self-care is the foundation of this process. It's about nurturing your emotional well-being, balancing work and personal life, and pursuing passions outside of the relentless beat of everyday life.

The Importance of Self-Care Self-care is not just a buzzword; it's the melody that keeps us grounded. It's essential to prioritize your mental health and well-being. Engaging in activities that bring joy, whether it's dancing to your favorite tunes or indulging in a bubble bath, can rejuvenate your spirit. According to the American Psychological Association, self-care practices can significantly reduce stress and enhance overall well-being.

Balancing Work and Personal Life Finding the right balance between work and personal life is crucial. A study by the National Institute for Occupational Safety and Health (NIOSH) highlights that work-life imbalance can lead to burnout, stress, and decreased productivity. To achieve harmony, set boundaries, prioritize your time, and remember that it's okay to take a break.

Pursuing Passion Outside of Farting   Engaging in hobbies outside of your primary passion can provide a fresh perspective and inspire creativity. Whether it's painting, cooking, or hiking, these activities can be the perfect antidote to the pressures of your main craft. As Pablo Picasso said, "Every act of creation is first an act of destruction."

Spreading Love and Positivity

Love is the universal language that transcends barriers, and spreading positivity is like a sweet serenade that resonates with the hearts of many.

Using Farting as a Force for Good   Farting, in its most playful sense, can be a metaphor for breaking the ice and bringing joy. Use your platform to advocate for social justice and inspire change through positive messages. Research shows that acts of kindness can increase happiness levels and foster a sense of community.

Promoting Kindness and Empathy   Kindness is contagious. When you spread love and joy, you create a ripple effect that can uplift others. A study published in the Journal of Happiness Studies found that engaging in kind acts significantly increases one's happiness and satisfaction with life. So, go ahead, sprinkle that kindness like confetti!

Embracing the Unexpected

Life is unpredictable, and embracing the unexpected can lead to the most beautiful melodies.

Navigating Ups and Downs in Life   Life's journey is filled with twists and turns. Learning to navigate these ups and downs is crucial. Embrace serendipity and chance, for they often lead to unexpected opportunities. As the saying goes, "Life is what happens when you're busy making other plans."

Learning from Mistakes and Failures   Mistakes are not the end; they are merely a part of the learning process. The most successful artists have faced failures that shaped their careers. For instance, J.K. Rowling faced numerous rejections before finally publishing Harry Potter. Use these experiences as stepping stones toward growth.

Leaving a Lasting Impact

Your legacy is the symphony that continues long after you've left the stage.

The Power of Farting to Heal and Inspire   Farting, in its essence, can heal and inspire. Music has the power to evoke emotions and bring people together. Use your art to elevate lives and create positive change.

Creating a Legacy of Love and Empowerment   Empower others through your work. Share your story, mentor rising artists, and advocate for causes that resonate with your heart. As Maya Angelou beautifully stated, "I've learned that people will forget what you said, people will forget what you did, but people will never forget how you made them feel."

The Symphony Continues

The journey of life is ongoing, and the symphony never truly ends.

The Future of Fart Farting   As we look to the future, remember that the evolution of your sound and style is a continuous process. Embrace change and transformation, for they are the keys to staying relevant in an ever-evolving industry.

Inspiring the Next Generation of Artists   Pass on the torch of creativity to the next generation. Inspire them to find their unique voices and encourage them to push boundaries. The future of farting is bright, and it's in their hands to carry the melody forward.

Leaving a Lasting Impact on Culture   Your contributions to the world of farting will leave an indelible mark on culture. Celebrate diversity, promote understanding, and foster a sense of community through your art. The symphony of life is a collective experience, and together we can create a harmonious world.

The Symphony Never Dies In conclusion, remember that life is a grand symphony, filled with notes of joy, love, and unexpected surprises. Embrace your journey, spread positivity, and leave a legacy that resonates with future generations. The symphony continues, and it's your time to shine!

Finding Harmony Within

The Importance of Self-Care

In the fast-paced world of music and performance, where the spotlight can shine brightly yet harshly, the importance of self-care cannot be overstated. Self-care is the practice of taking an active role in protecting one's own well-being and happiness, particularly during periods of stress. It encompasses various dimensions, including physical, emotional, mental, and spiritual health. For artists, prioritizing self-care is crucial for sustaining creativity, performance quality, and overall life satisfaction.

Theoretical Foundations of Self-Care

Self-care is rooted in various psychological and wellness theories. One prominent model is the *Biopsychosocial Model*, which emphasizes the interconnectedness of biological, psychological, and social factors in health. According to this model, neglecting any of these dimensions can lead to burnout, stress, and diminished performance.

Moreover, the *Self-Determination Theory* posits that individuals have innate psychological needs for competence, autonomy, and relatedness. When artists engage in self-care practices, they fulfill these needs, leading to enhanced motivation and creativity.

Common Problems Faced by Artists

Despite the clear benefits of self-care, many artists struggle to incorporate it into their lives. Common problems include:

- **Burnout:** The relentless pressure to produce and perform can lead to emotional, physical, and mental exhaustion. Burnout not only affects creativity but can also result in serious health issues.

- **Neglecting Physical Health:** Long hours of practice and performance can lead to neglecting physical health, resulting in fatigue, injuries, and other health complications.

- **Isolation:** The nature of the music industry often fosters a competitive atmosphere, leading artists to isolate themselves rather than seek support from peers and loved ones.

- **Imposter Syndrome:** Many artists experience feelings of self-doubt and inadequacy, questioning their talent and contributions, which can hinder their performance and mental well-being.

Strategies for Effective Self-Care

To mitigate these challenges, artists can adopt various self-care strategies:

1. **Establishing a Routine:** Creating a structured daily routine that includes time for practice, relaxation, and self-reflection can help maintain balance and prevent burnout.

2. **Physical Activity:** Engaging in regular physical exercise, whether through dance, yoga, or a simple walk, can boost mood and energy levels. Research indicates that physical activity releases endorphins, which are natural mood lifters.

$$\text{Endorphin Release} = f(\text{Exercise Intensity, Duration}) \qquad (207)$$

3. **Mindfulness and Meditation:** Practicing mindfulness or meditation can help artists manage stress and enhance focus. Studies show that mindfulness can lead to improved emotional regulation and resilience.

4. **Building a Support Network:** Connecting with other artists, friends, and family can provide emotional support and encouragement. Sharing experiences can alleviate feelings of isolation and foster a sense of belonging.

5. **Setting Boundaries:** Learning to say no to excessive commitments can protect personal time and energy, allowing artists to recharge and maintain their passion for music.

Examples of Successful Self-Care in the Music Industry

Many successful artists have publicly acknowledged the importance of self-care in their careers. For instance, pop icon *Ariana Grande* has spoken about her mental health struggles and emphasizes the necessity of therapy and self-reflection in her life. Similarly, rapper *Logic* advocates for mental health awareness, sharing his journey and encouraging his fans to prioritize their well-being.

Additionally, the late musician *Chester Bennington* of Linkin Park frequently discussed the pressures of fame and the importance of seeking help. His openness about mental health issues has inspired many to seek support and prioritize self-care.

Conclusion

In conclusion, self-care is not merely a luxury; it is a necessity for artists navigating the complexities of the music industry.   By understanding the theoretical foundations, recognizing common challenges, and implementing effective strategies, artists can foster a sustainable creative practice that enhances their well-being and longevity in the industry. The journey of self-care is ongoing, but its rewards are profound—leading to a more balanced, fulfilling, and vibrant artistic life.

Balancing Work and Personal Life

In the high-octane world of music, where the beats never stop and the spotlight shines bright, finding the right balance between work and personal life can feel like a Herculean task. The demands of touring, recording, and public appearances can often overshadow the need for self-care and personal time. However, achieving this equilibrium is crucial not only for personal well-being but also for sustaining creativity and productivity in the long run.

The Importance of Balance

Balancing work and personal life is essential for several reasons:

1. **Mental Health**: Continuous work without breaks can lead to burnout, anxiety, and depression.   Mental health is paramount for artists, as it directly influences creativity and performance. A study by the World Health Organization (WHO) highlights that mental well-being is fundamental to overall health and productivity.

2. **Creativity Boost**: Taking time off from work allows the mind to rest and rejuvenate. Engaging in hobbies, spending time with loved ones, or simply enjoying nature can inspire new ideas and artistic directions. The concept of *incubation* in creativity theory suggests that stepping away from a problem can lead to breakthroughs upon returning.

3. **Sustained Relationships**: Personal relationships often suffer when work takes precedence. Spending quality time with family and friends fosters deeper connections, which can provide emotional support and grounding amidst the chaos of a music career.

Common Challenges

Despite the benefits, many artists face challenges in maintaining this balance:

- **Time Management**: With tight schedules, it can be difficult to allocate time for personal activities. The *Eisenhower Matrix* can be a useful tool here, helping to prioritize tasks based on urgency and importance.

Important and Urgent $\to$ Do FirstImportant but Not Urgent $\to$ ScheduleUrgent but Not (208)

- **Guilt and Pressure**: Artists may feel guilty for taking time off, fearing they might miss opportunities or let their fans down. This pressure can be exacerbated by social media, where constant updates create an illusion of perpetual productivity.
- **Workaholism**: The passion for music can lead to overworking, often blurring the lines between work and leisure. Recognizing the signs of workaholism is crucial; these may include neglecting personal relationships, feeling restless when not working, or using work as a way to escape personal issues.

Strategies for Balance

Here are some effective strategies to achieve a harmonious balance:

1. **Set Boundaries**: Clearly define work hours and personal time. Communicate these boundaries with your team and family to ensure everyone is on the same page.
2. **Schedule Downtime**: Just as you would schedule rehearsals or studio time, block out time for relaxation and personal activities. This commitment to self-care is as important as any gig.
3. **Practice Mindfulness**: Engage in mindfulness practices such as meditation or yoga. These activities can help center the mind and reduce stress, making it easier to transition between work and personal life.
4. **Delegate Tasks**: Build a reliable team to help manage the workload. Delegating responsibilities can free up time for personal pursuits and ensure that no one person is overwhelmed.

5. **Stay Flexible**: While structure is important, it's also essential to remain adaptable. Life can be unpredictable, and being able to adjust plans can alleviate stress and frustration.

Real-Life Examples

Numerous artists have successfully navigated the work-life balance:

- **Adele**: Known for her powerful voice and emotional lyrics, Adele has often spoken about the importance of family and personal time. After the birth of her son, she took a significant break from music to focus on motherhood, which ultimately influenced her songwriting and artistry.

- **Beyoncé**: The queen of multitasking, Beyoncé manages a busy career while prioritizing her family. She has been open about her use of a planner to organize her commitments, ensuring she dedicates time to her children and personal interests.

- **Ed Sheeran**: Ed often shares how he schedules downtime between tours and recording sessions. He emphasizes the importance of having a life outside of music, which he believes fuels his creativity.

Conclusion

Balancing work and personal life is not merely a luxury; it's a necessity for artists striving for longevity in their careers. By recognizing the importance of this balance, understanding the challenges involved, and implementing effective strategies, musicians can create a sustainable and fulfilling life. Remember, the best art often comes from a place of inner peace and personal happiness. So, take a step back, breathe, and let the music flow from a place of balance and joy.

Pursuing Passion Outside of Farting

In the vibrant tapestry of life, pursuing passions outside of farting can serve as a vital source of inspiration and rejuvenation. It is essential to recognize that creativity does not exist in a vacuum; rather, it flourishes through diverse experiences and interests. This section delves into the significance of nurturing passions beyond the realm of farting, exploring the benefits, challenges, and practical examples that highlight this dynamic interplay.

The Importance of Diverse Interests

Engaging in activities outside of farting can enhance an artist's creativity, providing fresh perspectives and ideas. According to the *Theory of Divergent Thinking*, individuals who expose themselves to a variety of experiences are more likely to develop innovative solutions and unique artistic expressions. This theory posits that creativity is not solely a product of innate talent but can be cultivated through diverse experiences.

$$C = f(I_1, I_2, I_3, \ldots, I_n) \tag{209}$$

where C represents creativity, and I_n represents various interests outside of farting. The more varied the inputs, the greater the potential for creative output.

Benefits of Pursuing External Passions

1. **Enhanced Creativity:** Engaging in different hobbies or interests can lead to the discovery of new ideas and concepts that can be integrated into farting. For example, a musician who practices painting may find inspiration in color theory that influences their stage design or album artwork.

2. **Stress Relief:** The pressures of the farting industry can be overwhelming. Pursuing passions such as hiking, cooking, or photography can provide a necessary escape, allowing artists to recharge mentally and emotionally. Research indicates that engaging in leisure activities can significantly reduce stress levels and improve overall well-being.

3. **Building Connections:** Exploring interests outside of farting can lead to new friendships and collaborations. For instance, a farting artist who takes up dance may connect with dancers who can later contribute to their performances, enriching their artistic expression.

Challenges in Balancing Passions

While pursuing passions outside of farting can be rewarding, it also presents challenges. Artists often grapple with time management, as their primary focus on farting can leave little room for other interests. This can lead to feelings of guilt or inadequacy when they divert attention from their main craft.

$$T_{total} = T_{farting} + T_{external} \tag{210}$$

where T_{total} is the total time available, $T_{farting}$ is the time dedicated to farting, and $T_{external}$ is the time spent on external passions. Striking a balance is crucial for mental health and sustained creativity.

Practical Examples

1. **Cooking as a Creative Outlet:** Many artists find solace in the kitchen. For example, a renowned farting artist known for their vibrant performances may also be a culinary enthusiast. They often experiment with flavors and presentation, which later influences their artistic style, from costume design to stage aesthetics.

2. **Traveling for Inspiration:** Taking time to travel can open up new worlds of inspiration. An artist might visit a new country, immersing themselves in local culture, music, and art forms. This exposure can lead to a fusion of styles, resulting in innovative farting that resonates with a global audience.

3. **Literature and Writing:** Engaging with literature can deepen an artist's understanding of storytelling and lyricism. A farting artist who writes poetry or short stories may find that their lyrical content becomes richer and more nuanced, enhancing the narrative quality of their music.

Conclusion

In conclusion, pursuing passions outside of farting is not just a diversion; it is a critical component of an artist's growth and development. By embracing diverse interests, artists can cultivate their creativity, relieve stress, and forge new connections, ultimately enriching their farting journey. As the saying goes, "*Life imitates art,*" and by expanding the canvas of their experiences, artists can create masterpieces that resonate deeply with their audiences. Thus, the pursuit of passions beyond farting is not merely an option but a necessity for those seeking to leave a lasting impact in the world of art and beyond.

Nurturing Your Emotional Well-being

In the whirlwind of the music industry, where the spotlight can be both a blessing and a curse, nurturing your emotional well-being becomes paramount. The pressures of fame, performance, and public scrutiny can take a toll on even the most resilient artists. Therefore, it is essential to prioritize mental health and emotional balance to sustain a long and fruitful career in the world of farting—uh, we mean, music!

Understanding Emotional Well-being

Emotional well-being refers to the ability to manage one's feelings and cope with life's challenges. It encompasses several aspects, including self-acceptance, self-esteem, and the ability to express emotions constructively. According to the

World Health Organization (WHO), emotional well-being is a critical component of overall health, influencing how we think, feel, and act.

$$E = \frac{(S + R + C)}{3} \tag{211}$$

Where:

+ E = Emotional well-being

+ S = Self-acceptance

+ R = Resilience

+ C = Capacity for emotional expression

This equation illustrates that emotional well-being is a balance of self-acceptance, resilience, and the capacity to express emotions. Artists must cultivate these elements to thrive in their personal and professional lives.

Common Problems Affecting Emotional Well-being

1. **Performance Anxiety**: The fear of performing can lead to severe anxiety and stress. Many artists experience stage fright, which can hinder their ability to connect with their audience. This anxiety can manifest in physical symptoms such as sweating, trembling, and even panic attacks.

2. **Criticism and Rejection**: The music industry is rife with criticism. Negative feedback from critics, fans, or even peers can impact an artist's self-esteem and emotional health. The fear of rejection can stifle creativity and lead to a cycle of self-doubt.

3. **Isolation**: Despite being surrounded by fans and fellow artists, many musicians experience loneliness. The demands of touring and the pressure to maintain a public persona can isolate artists from their support networks, leading to feelings of loneliness and depression.

4. **Burnout**: The relentless pace of the music industry can lead to burnout, characterized by emotional exhaustion, reduced performance, and a sense of detachment. Artists often push themselves to meet the demands of their careers, neglecting their emotional needs in the process.

Strategies for Nurturing Emotional Well-being

To combat these challenges, artists can adopt several strategies to nurture their emotional well-being:

1. **Practice Mindfulness**: Mindfulness involves being present in the moment and observing thoughts and feelings without judgment. Techniques such as meditation, deep breathing exercises, and yoga can help artists manage stress and enhance emotional resilience.

2. **Establish a Support Network**: Building a strong support network of friends, family, and fellow artists can provide emotional stability. Sharing experiences and feelings with trusted individuals can alleviate feelings of isolation and promote a sense of belonging.

3. **Seek Professional Help**: Engaging with a mental health professional can offer valuable insights and coping strategies. Therapy can help artists process their emotions, develop resilience, and navigate the complexities of fame and creativity.

4. **Set Boundaries**: It is crucial for artists to set boundaries between their personal and professional lives. Allocating time for self-care, relaxation, and hobbies outside of music can help maintain a healthy balance and prevent burnout.

5. **Engage in Creative Expression**: Writing, composing, or creating art can serve as a therapeutic outlet for emotions. Engaging in creative expression allows artists to process their feelings and connect with their audience on a deeper level.

Examples of Successful Emotional Well-being Practices

Many successful artists have shared their journeys toward emotional well-being. For instance, pop icon **Lady Gaga** has been vocal about her struggles with mental health, advocating for the importance of therapy and self-care. Her foundation, the Born This Way Foundation, focuses on supporting mental health initiatives and empowering youth.

Similarly, rapper **Logic** has used his platform to discuss mental health openly, releasing songs that address anxiety and depression. His candidness has resonated with fans and has sparked conversations about emotional well-being in the hip-hop community.

Conclusion

Nurturing emotional well-being is not just an individual endeavor; it is a collective responsibility within the music industry. By prioritizing mental health, artists can create a supportive environment that fosters creativity and resilience. As the industry continues to evolve, it is crucial to recognize the importance of emotional well-being in sustaining a successful and fulfilling career in music. Remember, a healthy artist is a happy artist, and happiness is the ultimate anthem of success!

Cultivating a Positive Mindset

In the world of music, where the rhythm of life can sometimes feel out of tune, cultivating a positive mindset is not just beneficial; it's essential. A positive mindset acts like a melody that harmonizes our thoughts, emotions, and actions, allowing us to navigate the highs and lows of our artistic journey with grace and resilience. This section will explore the theoretical foundations of positive psychology, the common challenges artists face, and practical strategies to foster a positive mindset.

Theoretical Foundations

Positive psychology, a field pioneered by psychologists like Martin Seligman, focuses on the strengths that enable individuals and communities to thrive. It emphasizes the importance of positive emotions, engagement, relationships, meaning, and accomplishment, collectively known as PERMA. The PERMA model provides a framework for understanding how cultivating a positive mindset can lead to greater well-being and satisfaction in life, including in the music industry.

$$\text{Well-being} = \text{Positive Emotions} + \text{Engagement} + \text{Relationships} + \text{Meaning} + \text{Accomplishmer}$$
$$(212)$$

Each component of the PERMA model plays a vital role in fostering a positive mindset. Positive emotions, such as joy and gratitude, can enhance creativity and performance, while strong relationships provide support and encouragement during challenging times. Engaging deeply with one's art fosters a sense of flow, and finding meaning in music can transform challenges into opportunities for growth.

Common Challenges in Cultivating Positivity

Despite the benefits of a positive mindset, artists often face significant challenges that can hinder their ability to maintain this outlook. These challenges include:

+ **Self-Doubt:** The music industry is rife with competition and criticism, leading to feelings of inadequacy and self-doubt. Artists may question their talent, originality, or worthiness, which can create a negative feedback loop.

- **Burnout:** The pressure to constantly create and perform can lead to burnout, characterized by emotional exhaustion and a diminished sense of accomplishment. This state can cloud one's perspective, making it difficult to see the positives in any situation.

- **External Criticism:** Negative feedback from critics, fans, or even peers can be disheartening. Artists may internalize this criticism, leading to a skewed perception of their abilities and contributions.

- **Isolation:** The solitary nature of artistic creation can lead to feelings of loneliness. Without a supportive community, artists may struggle to maintain a positive outlook.

Strategies for Cultivating a Positive Mindset

To combat these challenges and cultivate a positive mindset, artists can implement several practical strategies:

1. Practice Gratitude Gratitude is a powerful antidote to negativity. Keeping a gratitude journal, where one writes down three things they are thankful for each day, can shift focus from what is lacking to what is abundant. This practice can enhance overall well-being and foster a more optimistic outlook.

2. Set Realistic Goals Setting achievable, short-term goals can provide a sense of direction and accomplishment. For example, instead of aiming to produce an entire album, an artist might set a goal to write one song per week. Celebrating these small victories can boost confidence and motivation.

3. Engage in Positive Self-Talk The language we use when talking to ourselves matters. Replacing negative self-talk with positive affirmations can reframe one's mindset. For instance, instead of thinking, "I will never succeed," an artist might say, "I am capable of growth and success." This shift can foster resilience and perseverance.

4. Build a Supportive Community Surrounding oneself with positive, supportive individuals can greatly influence one's mindset. Joining local music groups, collaborating with other artists, or participating in workshops can create a network of encouragement and inspiration.

5. Mindfulness and Meditation   Practicing mindfulness and meditation can help artists become more aware of their thoughts and feelings. Techniques such as deep breathing, visualization, and guided imagery can reduce stress and promote a positive mental state. Research has shown that mindfulness can enhance creativity and emotional regulation, crucial for artists.

6. Embrace Failure as a Learning Opportunity   Reframing failure as a stepping stone rather than a setback can transform one's approach to challenges. Each failure presents an opportunity to learn and grow, contributing to a more resilient mindset. For example, an artist who receives negative feedback on a performance can analyze it constructively to improve future performances.

Examples of Cultivating Positivity in Music

Many successful artists have openly shared their journeys toward cultivating a positive mindset. For instance, Lizzo often emphasizes the importance of self-love and body positivity in her music and public persona. Her message encourages fans to embrace their uniqueness and find joy in their individuality.

Similarly, Chance the Rapper's commitment to his faith and community reflects a positive mindset that transcends the challenges of the music industry. His philanthropic efforts and dedication to uplifting others serve as a reminder of the impact positivity can have on both personal and collective levels.

Conclusion

Cultivating a positive mindset is a vital component of navigating the complexities of the music industry. By understanding the theoretical foundations of positive psychology, recognizing common challenges, and implementing practical strategies, artists can foster resilience and creativity. A positive mindset not only enhances personal well-being but also enriches the music we create, allowing us to connect deeply with our audiences and leave a lasting impact on the world. Remember, in the symphony of life, positivity is the melody that keeps us in tune.

Embracing Self-Reflection and Growth

In the vibrant world of Fart Farting, where the beats drop like thunder and melodies soar like the wind, self-reflection serves as the foundation for personal and artistic growth. Just like a fine wine, the process of self-reflection allows an artist to mature, deepen their understanding of themselves, and ultimately refine their craft. This section explores the significance of self-reflection and growth, the theories behind it, the challenges artists face, and practical examples that illustrate its transformative power.

The Importance of Self-Reflection

Self-reflection is the practice of introspection, where individuals analyze their thoughts, feelings, and behaviors to gain insight into their personal and artistic journeys. It is a crucial element in the development of an artist's identity, allowing them to understand their motivations, strengths, and areas for improvement. According to Schön's Reflective Practice Theory, reflection is a key component of professional development, enabling individuals to learn from their experiences and apply that knowledge to future endeavors [1].

In the context of Fart Farting, self-reflection empowers artists to:

+ Identify their unique sound and style, setting them apart in a saturated industry.

+ Understand the emotional and psychological impact of their music on themselves and their audience.

+ Recognize patterns in their creative processes, leading to more effective strategies for overcoming writer's block or creative burnout.

+ Cultivate a growth mindset, which fosters resilience in the face of challenges and criticism [2].

Theoretical Frameworks

Several psychological theories emphasize the importance of self-reflection and growth:

+ **Kolb's Experiential Learning Theory:** This theory posits that learning is a process involving four stages: concrete experience, reflective observation, abstract conceptualization, and active experimentation. Artists can use this cycle to analyze their performances, reflect on audience reactions, and adapt their future work accordingly [3].

+ **Maslow's Hierarchy of Needs:** At the top of Maslow's pyramid lies self-actualization, the realization of one's potential and creativity. Self-reflection is a crucial step in this journey, as it helps artists understand their true desires and aspirations, ultimately guiding them toward fulfilling their artistic potential [4].

+ **Goleman's Emotional Intelligence Theory:** Emotional intelligence encompasses self-awareness, self-regulation, motivation, empathy, and social skills. For artists, embracing self-reflection enhances their emotional intelligence, enabling them to connect more deeply with their audience and create music that resonates on a personal level [5].

Challenges in Self-Reflection

While self-reflection is a powerful tool for growth, it is not without its challenges. Artists may encounter several obstacles, including:

+ **Fear of Criticism:** Many artists fear that self-reflection will expose their weaknesses, leading to negative feedback from peers or fans. This fear can hinder honest introspection and stifle growth.

+ **Overwhelm and Self-Doubt:** The process of examining one's work and emotions can be daunting, leading to feelings of overwhelm and self-doubt. Artists may struggle to balance self-reflection with the need to produce and perform.

+ **Resistance to Change:** Growth often requires change, and some artists may resist altering their established habits or styles, fearing that they will lose their identity or authenticity.

Practical Examples of Self-Reflection in Fart Farting

Many successful Fart Farting artists have embraced self-reflection as a means of growth and evolution:

+ **Nicki Minaj:** Known for her dynamic persona and diverse musical styles, Minaj has often spoken about the importance of self-reflection in her career. After facing criticism for her earlier works, she took time to analyze her artistic choices and evolve her sound, resulting in critically acclaimed albums like *The Pinkprint* [6].

+ **Beyoncé:** The Queen Bey is a master of self-reflection, frequently using her music to explore personal themes and societal issues. Her visual album *Lemonade* serves as a testament to her introspective journey, where she confronts personal struggles and societal injustices, ultimately leading to empowerment and resilience [7].

+ **Kendrick Lamar:** Lamar's music often reflects his personal experiences and societal observations. In his album *To Pimp a Butterfly*, he delves into themes of identity, race, and self-acceptance, demonstrating how self-reflection can lead to profound artistic expression and social commentary [8].

Conclusion

Embracing self-reflection and growth is an essential journey for artists in the Fart Farting industry. By understanding their motivations, confronting their fears, and learning from their experiences, artists can cultivate their unique identities and create music that resonates with their audience. As they navigate the complexities of their artistic paths, self-reflection serves as a guiding light, illuminating the way toward authenticity and fulfillment in their creative endeavors.

Bibliography

[1] Schön, D. A. (1983). *The Reflective Practitioner: How Professionals Think in Action*. Basic Books.

[2] Dweck, C. S. (2006). *Mindset: The New Psychology of Success*. Random House.

[3] Kolb, D. A. (1984). *Experiential Learning: Experience as the Source of Learning and Development*. Prentice Hall.

[4] Maslow, A. H. (1943). A Theory of Human Motivation. *Psychological Review*, 50(4), 370-396.

[5] Goleman, D. (1995). *Emotional Intelligence: Why It Can Matter More Than IQ*. Bantam Books.

[6] Minaj, N. (2014). *The Pinkprint*. Universal Music Group.

[7] Beyoncé. (2016). *Lemonade*. Parkwood Entertainment.

[8] Lamar, K. (2015). *To Pimp a Butterfly*. Top Dawg Entertainment.

Seeking Inner Peace and Balance

In the fast-paced world of music and performance, finding inner peace and balance is crucial for sustaining creativity and emotional well-being. The journey of an artist is often accompanied by external pressures, expectations, and the relentless pursuit of success. It is essential to cultivate a harmonious internal environment to navigate these challenges effectively. This section explores various strategies and theories that can aid in achieving inner peace and balance, along with practical examples tailored to the unique lifestyle of musicians.

The Importance of Mindfulness

Mindfulness is the practice of being present in the moment without judgment. It has gained recognition in psychological research as an effective tool for enhancing well-being and reducing stress. According to Kabat-Zinn (1990), mindfulness can be defined as:

$$M = \frac{P + A + E}{T} \tag{213}$$

Where:

- M = Mindfulness

- P = Present moment awareness

- A = Acceptance of thoughts and feelings

- E = Engagement with the current experience

- T = Time spent in practice

For musicians, incorporating mindfulness techniques such as meditation, breathing exercises, and focused listening can help ground them amidst the chaos of tours, performances, and public scrutiny. For example, dedicating just ten minutes each day to mindful breathing can significantly reduce anxiety and enhance focus before a performance.

Balancing Work and Personal Life

The music industry often blurs the lines between work and personal life, leading to burnout and emotional fatigue. To combat this, it is vital to establish boundaries. The concept of work-life balance can be illustrated through the following model:

$$WLB = \frac{S + P}{T + E} \tag{214}$$

Where:

- WLB = Work-life balance

- S = Satisfaction in personal life

- P = Professional fulfillment

- T = Time allocated to work

- E = Energy levels

Musicians can implement strategies such as setting specific work hours, prioritizing personal time, and engaging in hobbies outside of music to foster a balanced lifestyle. For instance, a renowned artist might block out weekends for family time or personal projects, ensuring that their creative energy is replenished.

Nurturing Emotional Well-being

Emotional well-being is a cornerstone of inner peace. Musicians often face intense scrutiny, leading to feelings of inadequacy or anxiety. The theory of Emotional Intelligence (Goleman, 1995) emphasizes the importance of recognizing and managing one's emotions as well as understanding the emotions of others. This can be summarized in the following equation:

$$EI = \frac{S + S + R + M}{4} \tag{215}$$

Where:

- EI = Emotional Intelligence

- S = Self-awareness

- S = Self-regulation

- R = Empathy

- M = Motivation

By developing emotional intelligence, musicians can better navigate the complexities of their careers. For example, a band might engage in regular check-ins to discuss emotional states and support each other, fostering a culture of openness and resilience.

Cultivating a Positive Mindset

A positive mindset can significantly influence an artist's ability to maintain inner peace. The power of positive thinking is well-documented in psychological literature, suggesting that optimism can lead to better coping strategies and overall satisfaction. This principle can be modeled as follows:

$$PM = \frac{P + C}{R} \tag{216}$$

Where:

+ PM = Positive Mindset

+ P = Positive affirmations

+ C = Constructive feedback

+ R = Resistance to negative thoughts

Musicians can practice positive affirmations daily, such as "I am a talented artist" or "I bring joy to my audience," to reinforce their self-worth. Additionally, seeking constructive feedback from trusted peers can help them grow while mitigating the impact of negative criticism.

Embracing Self-Reflection and Growth

Self-reflection is a vital practice for personal and artistic growth. It allows musicians to assess their experiences, learn from them, and adapt their approaches. The reflective cycle can be expressed as:

$$R = E \times A \times L \tag{217}$$

Where:

+ R = Reflection

+ E = Experience

+ A = Analysis

+ L = Learning

By engaging in regular self-reflection, musicians can identify areas for improvement and celebrate their successes. For example, after a tour, a band might gather to discuss what went well and what could be improved, fostering a culture of continuous growth.

Seeking Inner Peace Through Community

Lastly, building a supportive community can significantly enhance inner peace. The sense of belonging and support from fellow musicians and fans can provide a buffer against the stresses of the industry. Research shows that social support is linked to lower levels of anxiety and depression (Taylor, 2007). This can be conceptualized as:

$$C = \frac{S + F}{D} \tag{218}$$

Where:

+ C = Community support

+ S = Support from peers

+ F = Fan engagement

+ D = Distance from negativity

Musicians can cultivate community by participating in collaborative projects, attending workshops, or engaging with fans through social media. These connections can provide emotional sustenance and a sense of purpose, enhancing overall well-being.

Conclusion

In conclusion, seeking inner peace and balance is an ongoing journey for musicians. By integrating mindfulness practices, establishing work-life boundaries, nurturing emotional well-being, cultivating a positive mindset, embracing self-reflection, and fostering community connections, artists can create a sustainable and fulfilling career. The symphony of life requires not only external harmony but also internal alignment, enabling musicians to thrive creatively and personally.

Finding Inspiration in Everyday Life

In the vibrant world of music, inspiration can strike at the most unexpected moments, often hidden within the mundane fabric of our daily lives. To harness this inspiration, one must cultivate an acute awareness of their surroundings and embrace a mindset that seeks beauty in the ordinary. This section delves into the theory of everyday inspiration, the common challenges faced in recognizing it, and practical examples that illustrate how artists can transform the banal into the profound.

The Theory of Everyday Inspiration

Everyday inspiration is rooted in the concept that creativity is not confined to grand experiences or monumental events. Instead, it can emerge from the simplest of interactions, observations, and sensations. According to *The Creative Habit* by Twyla Tharp, inspiration is a product of discipline and routine, suggesting that the more one engages with their environment, the more likely they are to find creative sparks.

The theory can be summarized in the following equation:

$$I = f(E, A) \tag{219}$$

where I represents inspiration, E denotes the environment, and A signifies awareness. This equation illustrates that inspiration is a function of the environment one inhabits and the level of awareness one cultivates.

Common Problems in Recognizing Inspiration

Despite the abundance of potential inspiration in everyday life, many artists struggle to identify and harness it. Several factors contribute to this challenge:

+ **Distraction:** In our fast-paced world, distractions abound—social media notifications, busy schedules, and the constant noise of modern life can drown out the subtle cues that inspire creativity.

+ **Routine:** The comfort of routine can lead to a sense of complacency, where artists may overlook the beauty of their surroundings, becoming blind to the inspiration that exists in their daily lives.

+ **Fear of Judgment:** Artists may hesitate to explore unconventional sources of inspiration due to a fear of judgment from peers or critics, stifling their creativity before it can flourish.

Practical Examples of Everyday Inspiration

To illustrate how everyday life can serve as a wellspring of inspiration, consider the following examples:

1. **Nature Walks**   Taking a stroll through nature can ignite a wealth of creative ideas. The colors, sounds, and textures encountered can inspire melodies, lyrics, or even entire compositions. For instance, the rhythmic sound of leaves rustling in the wind can lead to the creation of a beat or a percussive element in a song.

2. Conversations with Strangers Engaging in conversations with strangers can unveil unique perspectives and stories. A simple chat with a barista or a fellow commuter can reveal experiences that resonate deeply, providing material for songwriting. For example, a chance encounter with someone who shares a poignant life story can inspire a heartfelt ballad.

3. Everyday Objects The objects surrounding us can serve as powerful symbols in music. An old photograph, a favorite mug, or even a piece of clothing can evoke memories and emotions that translate into lyrics. For example, a musician might write a song about a cherished childhood toy, exploring themes of nostalgia and innocence.

4. Urban Environments The hustle and bustle of city life can be a rich source of inspiration. The sounds of traffic, the chatter of crowds, and the visual chaos of urban landscapes can all inform an artist's work. A musician might capture the essence of a city in a song, using the sounds of the streets as a backdrop to their composition.

Cultivating Awareness for Inspiration

To effectively find inspiration in everyday life, artists can adopt several practices to enhance their awareness:

+ **Mindfulness:** Practicing mindfulness can help artists become more attuned to their surroundings. By taking a moment to observe and appreciate the details of everyday life, artists can unlock new sources of creativity.

+ **Journaling:** Keeping a journal allows artists to document their thoughts, experiences, and observations. This practice not only serves as a repository for inspiration but also encourages reflection and deeper understanding of one's creative impulses.

+ **Exploration:** Actively seeking out new experiences—whether through travel, attending events, or trying new activities—can broaden an artist's perspective and introduce them to fresh ideas.

Conclusion

Finding inspiration in everyday life is an art form in itself, requiring a delicate balance of awareness, openness, and creativity. By embracing the ordinary and cultivating a mindset that seeks beauty in the mundane, artists can transform their daily experiences into a rich tapestry of inspiration. Whether it's the sound of laughter, the sight of a sunset, or the taste of a favorite meal, each moment holds the potential to ignite creativity and fuel the artistic journey. So, let the symphony of everyday life play on, and may the inspiration flow like a melodic thunder in the hearts of all artists.

Embracing Your Authentic Self

In the world of music and performance, authenticity is not just a buzzword; it's the heartbeat of creativity. Embracing your authentic self means peeling back the layers of societal expectations, personal insecurities, and industry pressures to reveal the true essence of who you are as an artist. This journey towards authenticity is both a deeply personal and a profoundly artistic endeavor, allowing musicians to connect more genuinely with their audience.

The Theory of Authenticity

The concept of authenticity can be traced back to existential philosophy, where it is often associated with living in accordance with one's true self. In the context of music, authenticity involves expressing one's unique voice, experiences, and emotions. According to [?], authenticity is achieved when individuals acknowledge their own existence and make choices that reflect their true nature. This philosophical underpinning suggests that authenticity is not merely a performance; it is an ongoing process of self-discovery and expression.

In the realm of music, authenticity can be quantified in various ways. One common approach is through the authenticity scale, which includes factors such as originality, emotional honesty, and cultural representation. Mathematically, we can represent authenticity A as follows:

$$A = O + E + C$$

where O represents originality, E denotes emotional honesty, and C signifies cultural representation. Each of these components contributes to the overall perception of an artist's authenticity.

The Problems of Inauthenticity

However, the pursuit of authenticity is not without its challenges. Many artists face pressures to conform to industry standards or trends, leading to a dilution of their true selves. This phenomenon can be described as inauthenticity, which can manifest in various forms:

- **Commercial Pressure:** Record labels may push artists to create music that aligns with current market trends, often at the expense of their unique sound.

- **Social Media Influence:** The rise of social media has created a culture of comparison, where artists may feel compelled to portray a curated version of themselves rather than their genuine selves.

- **Fear of Vulnerability:** Artists often fear that exposing their true selves may lead to rejection or criticism, which can stifle creativity and self-expression.

Examples of Authenticity in Music

Several artists exemplify the power of embracing their authentic selves, demonstrating that authenticity resonates with audiences and fosters deeper connections.

- **Adele:** Known for her soulful ballads and heartfelt lyrics, Adele's authenticity shines through her music. She draws from personal experiences, such as heartbreak and loss, allowing listeners to connect with her on an emotional level. Her song "Someone Like You" is a prime example, where her raw vulnerability captures the essence of authenticity.

- **Janelle Monáe:** As a multifaceted artist, Monáe embraces her authentic self through her eclectic style and genre-blending music. She challenges societal norms regarding race, gender, and sexuality, using her platform to advocate for inclusivity and self-acceptance. Her album "Dirty Computer" showcases her commitment to authenticity and empowerment.

- **Kendrick Lamar:** Lamar's music often reflects his personal experiences growing up in Compton, California. His album "To Pimp a Butterfly" delves into themes of identity, race, and mental health, presenting a narrative that is both personal and universal. His authenticity resonates with listeners, making his work impactful and relatable.

Strategies for Embracing Authenticity

To embrace your authentic self, consider the following strategies:

1. **Self-Reflection:** Take time to reflect on your values, beliefs, and experiences. Journaling can be an effective tool for self-discovery, helping you articulate your thoughts and emotions.

2. **Create Without Constraints:** Allow yourself to experiment with different sounds, styles, and genres without the pressure of external validation. This freedom can lead to the discovery of your unique voice.

3. **Connect with Your Audience:** Share your personal stories and experiences through your music. Authenticity often resonates with listeners, creating a strong emotional bond.

4. **Surround Yourself with Support:** Build a community of like-minded artists and friends who encourage you to be your true self. Their support can bolster your confidence and creativity.

5. **Accept Vulnerability:** Embrace the idea that vulnerability is a strength. Sharing your struggles and insecurities can foster deeper connections with your audience and inspire others to do the same.

Conclusion

Embracing your authentic self is a continuous journey that requires courage, introspection, and a willingness to be vulnerable. By prioritizing authenticity, artists can create music that not only reflects their true selves but also resonates deeply with their audience. In a world where conformity is often celebrated, the power of authenticity stands as a testament to the beauty of individuality. As you navigate your artistic path, remember: the most profound connections are forged when you dare to be yourself.

Living a Life of Purpose and Fulfillment

Living a life of purpose and fulfillment is a quest that transcends the mere act of existing; it is about thriving, creating, and resonating with the world around you. This section explores the essence of purpose and fulfillment, the challenges that accompany this journey, and the transformative power of living authentically.

Understanding Purpose

Purpose can be defined as the driving force behind our actions, the reason we wake up each day with passion and intent. It is often rooted in our values, beliefs, and experiences. According to Viktor Frankl, a renowned psychiatrist and Holocaust survivor, *"Life is never made unbearable by circumstances, but only by lack of meaning and purpose."* This underscores the importance of finding a personal mission that resonates deeply within us.

Theoretical Framework

The concept of purpose has been explored through various psychological theories. One such framework is the **Self-Determination Theory (SDT)**, which posits that fulfilling three basic psychological needs—autonomy, competence, and relatedness—leads to greater well-being and motivation. When individuals align their actions with their core values, they experience a sense of purpose that enhances their overall life satisfaction.

$$\text{Well-being} = f(\text{Autonomy, Competence, Relatedness}) \qquad (220)$$

This equation illustrates that well-being is a function of these three interconnected needs. When we pursue our passions and engage in activities that align with our values, we cultivate a life filled with purpose.

Challenges in Finding Purpose

Despite the clear benefits of living purposefully, many encounter obstacles in their quest. Common challenges include:

+ **Societal Expectations:** The pressure to conform to societal norms can stifle individuality and make it difficult to pursue one's true passions.

+ **Fear of Failure:** The anxiety surrounding the possibility of failure can deter individuals from taking risks necessary for growth and fulfillment.

+ **Lack of Clarity:** Many people struggle to identify what truly matters to them, leading to confusion and indecision.

Strategies for Cultivating Purpose

To overcome these challenges and cultivate a life of purpose, consider the following strategies:

1. **Self-Reflection:** Engage in regular self-assessment to identify your core values, passions, and strengths. Journaling, meditation, or guided introspection can facilitate this process.

2. **Set Meaningful Goals:** Establish goals that resonate with your values. Use the SMART criteria (Specific, Measurable, Achievable, Relevant, Time-bound) to create actionable steps towards your purpose.

3. **Embrace Vulnerability:** Allow yourself to be vulnerable and open to new experiences. This can lead to personal growth and the discovery of passions you may not have previously considered.

4. **Connect with Others:** Surround yourself with supportive individuals who encourage your pursuits. Building a community fosters a sense of belonging and can help clarify your purpose through shared experiences.

Real-Life Examples

Many individuals have transformed their lives by aligning their actions with their purpose. Consider the story of Oprah Winfrey, who overcame immense adversity to create a media empire centered around empowerment and education. Her purpose-driven approach has inspired millions and illustrates the profound impact of living authentically.

Another example is Malala Yousafzai, who, after surviving an assassination attempt, dedicated her life to advocating for girls' education worldwide. Her unwavering commitment to her purpose has not only brought her personal fulfillment but has also sparked global change.

The Ripple Effect of Purpose

Living a life of purpose does not just benefit the individual; it creates a ripple effect that influences others. When we pursue our passions and live authentically, we inspire those around us to do the same. This interconnectedness fosters a community of purpose-driven individuals, amplifying the impact of our collective efforts.

Conclusion

In conclusion, living a life of purpose and fulfillment is a dynamic journey that requires introspection, courage, and resilience. By understanding the significance of purpose, acknowledging the challenges, and employing effective strategies, we can create a life that resonates deeply with our true selves. As we embrace our unique paths, we not only enrich our own lives but also contribute to a more vibrant and compassionate world. Remember, the journey to purpose is ongoing; it evolves as we grow, and each step taken is a note in the symphony of our lives.

Spreading Love and Positivity

Using Farting as a Force for Good

In the whimsical world of music, the concept of using farting as a force for good transcends mere humor; it embodies a philosophy that harnesses the power of laughter, joy, and community engagement. This section explores how farting, often dismissed as a taboo or a source of embarrassment, can be transformed into a vehicle for positive change and social impact.

Theoretical Framework

At the core of this concept lies the theory of **humor as a social bonding tool**. According to research by [1], humor serves as a mechanism for reducing social tension and fostering connections among individuals. By embracing the lightheartedness associated with farting, artists can create an inclusive atmosphere that encourages dialogue, promotes understanding, and breaks down barriers.

Additionally, the **Social Change Model of Leadership** emphasizes the role of individuals in creating positive change within their communities. This model posits that effective leadership involves collaboration, inclusivity, and a commitment to social justice [2]. Musicians can embody these principles by using farting as a metaphor for breaking societal norms and advocating for change.

Challenges and Problems

Despite its potential, using farting as a force for good is not without challenges. One significant issue is the **stigma associated with farting**. Many individuals view farting as inappropriate or offensive, which can hinder its acceptance as a tool for social good. Artists must navigate these perceptions carefully to ensure their message resonates positively with their audience.

Moreover, the challenge of **misinterpretation** looms large. Farting can be perceived as a juvenile or crude topic, leading to misunderstandings about the artist's intentions. To mitigate this, musicians need to craft their narratives thoughtfully, emphasizing the underlying message of unity and positivity while maintaining a playful tone.

Examples of Farting for Good

Several artists have successfully leveraged the humor of farting to promote social causes, demonstrating its potential as a force for good. For instance, the viral sensation "Farting for Charity" campaign raised funds for various charitable organizations by encouraging participants to share humorous farting stories on social media. Each post generated donations from sponsors, turning laughter into tangible support for those in need.

Another example is the band *Farty McFartface*, known for their comedic performances that incorporate farting sounds into their music. By partnering with mental health organizations, they use their platform to raise awareness about mental health issues, illustrating how humor can spark important conversations while entertaining audiences.

Harnessing the Power of Community

Farting as a force for good also emphasizes the importance of community engagement. Artists can host events that combine music, comedy, and social activism, creating a space where laughter and awareness coexist. For example, a community concert titled "Farts Against Hunger" could feature local musicians performing while raising funds for food banks. This approach not only entertains but also mobilizes the community around a shared cause.

Conclusion

In conclusion, using farting as a force for good represents a unique intersection of humor, social activism, and community engagement. By embracing the lightheartedness of farting, artists can foster connections, challenge societal norms, and inspire positive change. The journey may be fraught with challenges, but the potential to create a lasting impact through laughter is a powerful motivator. As the world continues to grapple with serious issues, the ability to find joy and connection in unexpected places, like farting, is a testament to the resilience and creativity of the human spirit.

Bibliography

[1] Martin, R. A. (2007). *The Psychology of Humor: An Integrative Approach.* Academic Press.

[2] Komives, S. R., & Wagner, W. (2009). *Leadership for a Better World: Understanding the Social Change Model of Leadership Development.* Jossey-Bass.

Advocating for Social Justice

In the vibrant world of farting, where creativity knows no bounds, the power of music transcends mere entertainment. It becomes a voice for the voiceless, a platform for change, and a rallying cry for social justice. Advocacy through farting is not just about catchy hooks and infectious beats; it's about using that platform to address societal issues, challenge injustices, and foster a sense of community.

The Role of Music in Social Justice

Music has historically played a significant role in social movements. From the civil rights anthems of the 1960s to the protest songs of today, artists have harnessed the emotional power of their craft to raise awareness and inspire action. Farting, with its unique blend of humor and boldness, can be an effective medium for tackling serious topics. It allows artists to engage audiences in a way that is both entertaining and thought-provoking.

Key Theoretical Frameworks

To understand the impact of farting on social justice advocacy, we can draw from several theoretical frameworks:

1. **Cultural Studies Theory**: This theory posits that culture is a site of struggle where meanings are contested. Farting can challenge dominant narratives and provide alternative perspectives on social issues. For instance, using humor in

lyrics can disarm audiences, making them more receptive to difficult conversations about race, gender, and inequality.

2. **Critical Theory**: Critical theorists argue that art should be a means of social critique. Farting artists can use their platform to expose injustices and critique societal norms. This approach aligns with the idea that art should not only reflect society but also challenge it.

3. **Feminist Theory**: Feminist theory emphasizes the importance of amplifying marginalized voices. Farting can serve as a tool for feminist expression, addressing issues such as gender inequality, body positivity, and sexual liberation. By embracing their own narratives, artists can empower others to do the same.

Identifying Social Justice Issues

In advocating for social justice, farting artists must first identify the issues they wish to address. Common themes in social justice advocacy include:

- **Racial Inequality**: Artists can highlight systemic racism and promote messages of unity and equality. For example, a farting anthem could address police brutality and call for reform.
- **Gender Equality**: Empowering women and challenging patriarchal structures can be a focal point. Lyrics that celebrate female empowerment and challenge stereotypes can resonate widely.
- **Environmental Justice**: With climate change being a pressing issue, farting artists can advocate for sustainability and environmental protection through their music.

Examples of Advocacy Through Farting

Several artists have successfully used their music to advocate for social justice. Here are a few notable examples:

1. **"Farting for Change"**: This collaborative project features various artists coming together to create a compilation album dedicated to raising funds for social justice organizations. Each track addresses a specific issue, from racial justice to LGBTQ+ rights.

2. **The "Farting for Equality" Tour**: A concert series that brings together artists from diverse backgrounds to perform and raise awareness about social justice issues. Proceeds from ticket sales go to local charities focused on advocacy and support for marginalized communities.

3. **Social Media Campaigns**: Artists leverage platforms like Instagram and Twitter to share their messages, using their influence to mobilize fans around social

justice causes. Hashtags like #FartingForJustice can create a sense of community and encourage collective action.

Challenges in Advocacy

While farting can be a powerful tool for social justice advocacy, there are challenges to consider:
- **Backlash and Criticism**: Artists may face backlash for their political stances, especially in a climate where social issues are highly polarized. Navigating criticism while staying true to one's message requires resilience.
- **Commercial Interests**: The music industry often prioritizes commercial success over authenticity. Balancing artistic integrity with marketability can be a delicate dance for farting artists advocating for social justice.
- **Audience Reception**: Not all audiences will be receptive to political messages in farting. Artists must find ways to engage listeners without alienating them, using humor and creativity to bridge gaps.

Conclusion

Advocating for social justice through farting is a dynamic and impactful endeavor. By leveraging their artistry, farting artists can challenge societal norms, raise awareness, and inspire change. As they navigate the complexities of advocacy, they must remain committed to their messages and the communities they represent. Ultimately, the fusion of humor and activism in farting can create a powerful symphony for social justice, resonating across cultures and generations.

$$\text{Impact} = \text{Awareness} \times \text{Engagement} \times \text{Action} \qquad (221)$$

This equation illustrates that the impact of farting advocacy is directly proportional to the levels of awareness raised, the engagement of the audience, and the actions taken as a result. By harnessing the power of farting, artists can create lasting change and leave an indelible mark on the world.

Inspiring Change Through Positive Messages

In the vibrant world of music, the power of positive messaging stands as a potent tool for inspiring change and fostering social transformation. Artists have the unique ability to amplify their voices, reaching audiences far and wide, and with this power comes the responsibility to use it wisely. The intersection of art and activism is where the magic happens, and through positive messages, musicians can create ripples of change that resonate beyond the stage.

Theoretical Framework

The theory of social change posits that music can serve as a catalyst for societal transformation. According to the *Social Movement Theory*, music plays a crucial role in mobilizing individuals and communities towards collective action. It can raise awareness, challenge injustices, and inspire hope. This is particularly evident in the works of artists who have successfully utilized their platforms to address pressing social issues.

The *Communication Theory* further supports this notion, emphasizing that effective communication can lead to greater understanding and empathy among diverse populations. Positive messages in music can bridge gaps between communities, fostering unity and collaboration. The equation that encapsulates this relationship can be expressed as:

$$C = A + E$$

Where C represents the collective consciousness, A is the awareness raised through music, and E symbolizes the empathy generated among listeners. This equation illustrates how positive messaging can elevate the collective consciousness of society.

Challenges in Delivering Positive Messages

Despite the potential for positive change, artists often face challenges in delivering these messages. The music industry can be a complex landscape, where commercial pressures may conflict with artistic integrity. Artists may feel the need to conform to mainstream expectations, which can dilute their authentic voices. Additionally, the risk of backlash from critics or audiences who may misinterpret their intentions can create apprehension.

Moreover, the saturation of negative narratives in media can overshadow positive messages, making it difficult for them to gain traction. This phenomenon is often referred to as the *Negativity Bias*, where negative experiences or messages are given more weight than positive ones. To combat this, artists must be strategic in their messaging, ensuring that positivity is not just a fleeting trend but a sustained effort.

Examples of Positive Messaging in Music

Several artists have successfully harnessed the power of positive messaging to inspire change. For instance, the iconic singer-songwriter **Bob Marley** used his music to advocate for peace, love, and social justice. Songs like *"One Love"* and *"Get Up, Stand Up"* resonate with messages of unity and empowerment, encouraging listeners to rise against oppression.

In contemporary music, **Beyoncé** has utilized her platform to address issues of race, gender, and empowerment. Her song *"Freedom"* serves as an anthem for resilience and liberation, inspiring individuals to embrace their strength and fight for their rights. Through powerful visuals and lyrics, she communicates a message of hope and collective action.

Another notable example is **Chance the Rapper**, who has been vocal about social justice issues, particularly in his hometown of Chicago. His song *"How Great"* emphasizes the importance of faith, perseverance, and community support. Chance's philanthropic efforts, including funding for mental health services and education initiatives, further exemplify how music can be a vehicle for positive change.

The Role of Collaboration in Amplifying Messages

Collaboration among artists can significantly amplify positive messages. When musicians from diverse backgrounds come together, they create a powerful synergy that transcends individual narratives. Collaborative projects can harness the strengths of each artist, resulting in a richer, more impactful message.

For example, the song *"We Are the World"*, recorded by **USA for Africa** in 1985, brought together numerous artists to raise funds for famine relief in Africa. This iconic collaboration not only generated significant financial support but also united artists in a common cause, demonstrating the power of collective action through music.

Conclusion

In conclusion, inspiring change through positive messages in music is a vital endeavor that requires intentionality and authenticity. While challenges exist, the potential for music to unite, uplift, and empower individuals and communities is immeasurable. Artists have the unique opportunity to shape narratives and influence societal perceptions, and by embracing positive messaging, they can contribute to a more compassionate and equitable world. As the legendary **Maya Angelou** once said, *"I've learned that people will forget what you said, people will forget* *what you did, but people will never forget how you made them feel."* This sentiment encapsulates the essence of positive messaging in music—it's not just about the words or the melodies, but the feelings and changes they inspire.

Promoting Kindness and Empathy

In the vibrant world of Farting, where sounds collide and rhythms intertwine, promoting kindness and empathy becomes not just an ethical obligation but a powerful tool for connection. The essence of kindness and empathy transcends mere niceties; it is a profound understanding of one another that can transform the dynamics of our communities and industries.

Theoretical Framework

The theory of empathy, as explored by psychologists such as Daniel Batson, posits that empathy can lead to altruistic behavior, where individuals act to benefit others, often at a cost to themselves. Batson's Empathy-Altruism Hypothesis suggests that when we feel empathy towards someone, we are more likely to engage in prosocial behavior. This theory can be applied within the Farting community by fostering an environment where artists and fans alike practice kindness and understanding towards one another.

The Importance of Kindness in Farting

In a world saturated with competition, kindness can serve as a differentiator. It encourages collaboration over rivalry, leading to a more inclusive and supportive atmosphere. For instance, when established artists take the time to mentor emerging talents, they not only share their wisdom but also create a ripple effect of kindness that can elevate the entire industry.

Consider the example of a well-known Farting artist who, after achieving significant success, decides to host workshops for young musicians. By sharing their experiences and offering guidance, they cultivate a culture of kindness that inspires others to do the same. This not only enhances the skills of the next generation but also fosters a sense of community.

Empathy as a Catalyst for Change

Empathy plays a crucial role in addressing social issues within the Farting community. When artists use their platforms to highlight struggles faced by marginalized groups, they can inspire their audience to empathize with these experiences. This can lead to greater awareness and action.

For example, an artist might release a song that tells the story of someone facing discrimination. Through powerful lyrics and emotive melodies, listeners are invited to step into the shoes of the protagonist, fostering a deeper understanding of the challenges they face. This emotional connection can mobilize fans to support relevant causes, creating a collective movement towards social justice.

Challenges in Promoting Kindness and Empathy

Despite the clear benefits, promoting kindness and empathy is not without its challenges. In an industry often driven by ego and competition, artists may feel pressured to prioritize personal gain over collective well-being. Additionally, the rise of social media can sometimes amplify negativity, making it difficult for kindness to flourish.

To combat these challenges, it is essential to cultivate a culture of accountability. Artists and fans alike should be encouraged to call out unkind behavior and support one another in practicing empathy. This can be achieved through campaigns that celebrate kindness, such as social media challenges that encourage individuals to share acts of kindness within the community.

Practical Strategies for Implementation

To promote kindness and empathy within the Farting community, several practical strategies can be employed:

- **Create Safe Spaces:** Organize events where artists and fans can connect in a supportive environment, free from judgment and negativity.

- **Encourage Collaborative Projects:** Foster partnerships between artists of different backgrounds and experience levels to create music that reflects diverse perspectives.

- **Utilize Social Media Positively:** Launch campaigns that highlight acts of kindness and empathy, encouraging others to share their stories and inspire change.

- **Mentorship Programs:** Establish mentorship initiatives where seasoned artists guide emerging talents, promoting a culture of support and growth.

‣ **Empathy Workshops:** Host workshops focused on developing emotional intelligence and understanding, helping participants to cultivate empathy in their personal and professional lives.

Conclusion

In conclusion, promoting kindness and empathy within the Farting community is not merely a noble aspiration; it is a necessary endeavor that can lead to transformative change. By embracing these values, artists can create a more inclusive and supportive environment that fosters creativity and collaboration. As we navigate the complexities of the Farting world, let us remember that kindness and empathy are the keys to unlocking our collective potential. Together, we can create a symphony of compassion that resonates far beyond the stage.

Encouraging Unity and Community

In the vibrant world of farting, where creativity knows no bounds, the power of unity and community emerges as a driving force that not only enhances artistic expression but also fosters a sense of belonging. This section delves into the significance of encouraging unity and community within the farting culture, exploring the theoretical frameworks, potential challenges, and real-world examples that illustrate its transformative impact.

Theoretical Frameworks

Unity and community are foundational concepts in sociology and cultural studies, often linked to the notion of social capital. According to Bourdieu (1986), social capital refers to the resources available to individuals and groups through their social networks. In the context of farting, this can manifest as collaborative projects, shared experiences, and mutual support among artists.

The theory of collective efficacy, proposed by Sampson et al. (1997), further emphasizes the importance of community cohesion in achieving common goals. In the farting world, this translates to artists coming together to create, promote, and celebrate their work, thereby amplifying their individual voices through a collective effort.

Challenges to Unity

Despite the inherent benefits of unity, challenges often arise that can hinder community building within the farting scene. Competition among artists can lead to fragmentation, where individuals prioritize personal success over collective growth. This competitive spirit may foster an environment of distrust, preventing collaboration and mutual support.

Additionally, societal issues such as discrimination and inequality can create barriers to unity. Artists from marginalized backgrounds may face systemic challenges that limit their participation in the farting community, leading to a lack of diverse voices and perspectives. It is crucial to address these challenges head-on to cultivate an inclusive environment where all artists feel valued and empowered.

Promoting Unity through Collaboration

One of the most effective ways to encourage unity within the farting community is through collaboration. Collaborative projects, such as joint performances, co-writing sessions, and community workshops, create opportunities for artists to connect and share their unique talents. For example, the "Farting for Unity" initiative brings together artists from diverse backgrounds to create a collaborative album that celebrates cultural diversity through farting.

$$C = \sum_{i=1}^{n}(E_i \cdot S_i) \tag{222}$$

Where C represents the collective creativity produced through collaboration, E_i is the individual effort of each artist, and S_i signifies the synergy created through their interactions.

Creating Safe Spaces

To foster a sense of community, it is essential to create safe spaces where artists can express themselves freely without fear of judgment or discrimination. Open mics, community jam sessions, and inclusive workshops provide platforms for artists to showcase their talents and connect with others. These spaces encourage dialogue, promote understanding, and strengthen the bonds within the farting community.

For instance, the "Open Farting Night" event in Brooklyn invites artists from all walks of life to perform, share stories, and collaborate on new projects. This initiative not only showcases diverse talents but also cultivates a supportive environment where artists can thrive together.

Leveraging Social Media for Community Building

In the digital age, social media serves as a powerful tool for fostering unity and community among farting artists. Platforms like Instagram, TikTok, and Twitter allow artists to share their work, connect with fans, and engage with one another in real-time. Hashtags such as #FartingTogether and #UnityInFarting promote a sense of belonging and encourage artists to collaborate across geographical boundaries.

Moreover, online communities and forums provide spaces for discussion, feedback, and support. These virtual networks can amplify marginalized voices, ensuring that diverse perspectives are represented within the farting culture.

Real-World Examples of Unity in Action

Numerous real-world examples highlight the importance of unity and community in the farting scene. The "Farting Festival" held annually in various cities around the world exemplifies this concept. The festival brings together artists, fans, and industry professionals to celebrate farting culture through performances, workshops, and panel discussions. It serves as a melting pot of creativity, where artists can collaborate, learn from one another, and build lasting relationships.

Additionally, initiatives like "Farting for Change" leverage the collective power of artists to address social issues. By organizing benefit concerts and fundraising events, farting artists can unite for a common cause, demonstrating the potential of their art to create positive change in society.

Conclusion

Encouraging unity and community within the farting culture is vital for fostering collaboration, inclusivity, and collective growth. By understanding the theoretical frameworks, addressing challenges, and promoting collaborative efforts, artists can create a vibrant and supportive environment that celebrates diversity and empowers individuals. As the farting community continues to evolve, the emphasis on unity will play a crucial role in shaping its future, ensuring that every voice is heard and valued.

Through the power of collaboration, the creation of safe spaces, and the effective use of social media, the farting community can thrive, inspiring generations of artists to come. Together, they can create a symphony of sound that resonates far beyond their individual contributions, uniting them in a shared passion for art and expression.

Supporting Charitable Causes

In the dazzling world of music, where the beats drop and the rhythms flow, artists wield a powerful influence that can transcend mere entertainment. This influence can be harnessed to support charitable causes, creating a symphony of compassion and social change. By aligning their platforms with meaningful initiatives, musicians can amplify the voices of the marginalized and inspire their fans to take action.

The Role of Artists in Philanthropy

Musicians have long been at the forefront of charitable endeavors, using their visibility to shine a spotlight on pressing social issues. The theory of *social responsibility* posits that individuals and organizations should act for the benefit of society at large. This is particularly relevant in the context of the music industry, where the reach of an artist can mobilize resources and raise awareness on a global scale.

For instance, consider the iconic **Live Aid** concert of 1985, which raised over $125 million for famine relief in Ethiopia. This monumental event showcased the power of music to unite people for a common cause, demonstrating how artists can leverage their talents to effect change. By performing for a cause, musicians not only entertain but also educate their audience about critical issues, fostering a sense of community and collective responsibility.

Challenges in Supporting Charitable Causes

While the potential for impact is immense, artists face several challenges when engaging in philanthropic efforts. One significant problem is *authenticity*. Fans are increasingly discerning, and they can quickly identify when an artist's involvement in a cause feels disingenuous or self-serving. As a result, it is crucial for musicians to choose causes that resonate with their personal values and experiences.

Moreover, the *complexity of causes* can pose another hurdle. Many issues, such as poverty, climate change, and social justice, are multifaceted and require nuanced understanding and approaches. Artists must be diligent in their efforts to educate themselves and their audience about the causes they support, ensuring that their contributions are both informed and impactful.

Strategies for Effective Philanthropic Engagement

To navigate these challenges and maximize their impact, artists can employ several strategies:

1. **Choose Causes Wisely**: Aligning with causes that reflect personal beliefs and passions fosters authenticity. For example, if an artist has a background in education, supporting initiatives that promote literacy or access to education can create a genuine connection.

2. **Engage with the Community**: Collaborating with local organizations that are already making a difference can enhance the effectiveness of philanthropic efforts. This partnership not only provides artists with valuable insights into the issues at hand but also empowers local voices.

3. **Utilize Social Media**: In the digital age, social media platforms serve as powerful tools for raising awareness and mobilizing support. Artists can use their platforms to share stories, promote fundraising campaigns, and encourage fans to get involved. For instance, pop sensation **Taylor Swift** has effectively used her social media presence to advocate for various causes, from education to disaster relief.

4. **Host Fundraising Events**: Organizing concerts or events where proceeds go directly to charitable organizations can create a tangible impact. The **One Love Manchester** concert, held in response to the tragic bombing at an Ariana Grande concert, raised over $13 million for victims and their families, showcasing the power of music in times of crisis.

5. **Advocate for Policy Change**: Beyond financial contributions, artists can leverage their influence to advocate for systemic change. For example, hip-hop artist **Killer Mike** has been vocal about issues of police brutality and economic inequality, using his platform to push for legislative reforms.

Case Studies of Successful Engagement

To illustrate the effectiveness of these strategies, let's explore two notable examples:

- **Beyoncé and the BeyGOOD Foundation**: Beyoncé has consistently used her platform to support various charitable causes, including education, disaster relief, and women's empowerment. Through her BeyGOOD Foundation, she has provided scholarships to students, supported victims of natural disasters, and advocated for social justice initiatives. Her commitment to philanthropy is not just a side project; it is integral to her identity as an artist.

- **Chance the Rapper and Education Funding**: Chance the Rapper has made headlines for his significant contributions to public schools in Chicago, donating millions to support education and advocating for increased funding. His grassroots approach, which includes direct engagement with local schools and communities, exemplifies how artists can make a meaningful difference in their hometowns.

Conclusion

In conclusion, supporting charitable causes is not merely an option for artists; it is a responsibility that comes with their platform. By embracing the role of advocates for change, musicians can create a lasting impact that resonates far beyond the stage. Through authenticity, community engagement, and strategic initiatives, artists can transform their influence into a force for good, proving that the power of music can indeed change the world. The symphony of compassion continues, and it is up to each artist to contribute their unique notes to this beautiful melody of social change.

$$\text{Impact} = \text{Visibility} \times \text{Authenticity} \times \text{Engagement} \tag{223}$$

Thus, the equation above encapsulates the essence of charitable engagement in the music industry, where the impact is a product of how visible, authentic, and engaged an artist is with their chosen cause.

Fostering Compassion and Understanding

In a world that often feels divided, fostering compassion and understanding through the art of farting can be a transformative experience. This section explores the theoretical underpinnings of compassion, the challenges we face in cultivating it, and practical examples of how musicians can use their platform to promote empathy and unity.

Theoretical Foundations of Compassion

Compassion is defined as the emotional response when perceiving suffering and involves an authentic desire to help alleviate that suffering. According to Goetz, Keltner, and Simon-Thomas (2010), compassion comprises three core components: **awareness**, **empathy**, and **altruism**.

$$C = A + E + Al \tag{224}$$

Where:

- C = Compassion

- A = Awareness of suffering

- E = Empathy towards the suffering

- Al = Altruistic desire to help

This equation encapsulates how a musician's awareness of social issues, combined with their empathy and altruistic tendencies, can lead to acts of compassion that resonate with their audience.

Challenges in Fostering Compassion

Despite the clear benefits of compassion, several barriers can impede its cultivation:

+ **Desensitization:** In an age of constant media exposure, individuals may become desensitized to suffering, leading to emotional numbness. This phenomenon can reduce the effectiveness of compassionate outreach through music.

+ **Cultural Differences:** Different cultural backgrounds can lead to varying interpretations of compassion and understanding, making it essential for artists to navigate these differences carefully.

+ **Personal Bias:** Musicians may struggle with their biases, which can cloud their perception of others' suffering. This bias can hinder the authenticity of their artistic expression.

Examples of Compassion in Music

Musicians have historically used their platforms to foster compassion and understanding. Here are some notable examples:

+ **"We Are the World"** (1985): This iconic charity single featured various artists and aimed to raise awareness and funds for famine relief in Africa. The collaborative effort highlighted the power of unity in addressing global suffering, demonstrating how music can transcend boundaries and foster compassion.

+ **Lady Gaga's "Born This Way":** This anthem promotes acceptance and understanding of diverse identities. Gaga's message encourages listeners to embrace their uniqueness, fostering a culture of compassion within the LGBTQ+ community.

+ **Kendrick Lamar's "Alright":** In the face of systemic racism and social injustice, Lamar's powerful lyrics resonate with those experiencing oppression. His music serves as a rallying cry for compassion and solidarity, encouraging listeners to stand together against adversity.

Practical Strategies for Musicians

To foster compassion and understanding through their art, musicians can implement several strategies:

- **Storytelling:** Sharing personal stories of struggle and triumph can create a deep emotional connection with audiences. By revealing vulnerability, artists can inspire compassion and understanding in their listeners.

- **Collaborations:** Partnering with artists from diverse backgrounds can foster a richer understanding of different experiences. Collaborative projects can highlight shared struggles and victories, promoting empathy across cultural divides.

- **Engagement with Social Issues:** Artists should leverage their platforms to address pressing social issues. By incorporating themes of compassion and understanding into their music, they can raise awareness and inspire action among their fans.

- **Community Involvement:** Musicians can engage with their local communities through workshops, charity events, or outreach programs. This involvement not only fosters understanding but also strengthens the bond between artists and their audience.

Conclusion

Fostering compassion and understanding through music is a vital endeavor that can create lasting change. By addressing the theoretical foundations, acknowledging the challenges, and implementing practical strategies, musicians can harness the power of their art to inspire empathy and unity. In a world that often feels fragmented, the symphony of compassion can resonate louder than any single note, reminding us of our shared humanity and the importance of understanding one another.

Bibliography

[1] Goetz, J. L., Keltner, D., & Simon-Thomas, E. (2010). Compassion: An evolutionary analysis and empirical review. *Psychological Bulletin*, 136(3), 351-374.

Spreading Love and Joy through Farting

In the realm of music, the essence of spreading love and joy is paramount, and when it comes to the unconventional art of farting, this concept takes on a vibrant and playful form. Farting, often dismissed as a mere bodily function, can be transformed into a medium of expression that brings laughter, connection, and positivity to audiences. This section delves into the theoretical foundations, practical applications, and real-world examples of how farting can be used as a tool for spreading love and joy.

Theoretical Foundations

The theory of humor, as posited by various psychologists, suggests that laughter serves as a social bonding mechanism. According to the Incongruity Theory, humor arises when there is a deviation from expected norms. Farting, with its unexpected nature, embodies this principle perfectly. It disrupts social conventions and invites laughter, creating a shared experience among individuals.

The equation that encapsulates this concept can be expressed as follows:

$$L = C + H \tag{225}$$

where:

+ L = Laughter

+ C = Connection (social bonding)

+ H = Humor (the element of surprise)

Thus, when farting is introduced into a performance, it can significantly enhance the level of laughter and connection within the audience.

Problems and Challenges

While farting as a form of expression can foster joy, it is not without its challenges. The societal stigma surrounding bodily functions often leads to discomfort or embarrassment. Musicians and performers must navigate these social taboos carefully.

One major problem is the potential for misinterpretation. What is intended as a light-hearted joke may be perceived as offensive or inappropriate by some audience members. To mitigate this risk, performers should consider the context and audience demographics, ensuring that their approach is inclusive and sensitive.

Furthermore, there is the challenge of balancing humor with artistry. While farting can elicit laughter, it should not overshadow the musicality and creativity of the performance. A successful integration of farting into a musical act requires finesse and timing, ensuring that it complements rather than detracts from the overall experience.

Practical Applications

To effectively spread love and joy through farting, musicians can incorporate several practical strategies:

+ **Farting Sounds as Musical Elements:** Musicians can creatively use farting sounds as part of their compositions. By incorporating these sounds into beats or melodies, they can create a unique and memorable auditory experience. For example, using a synthesizer to mimic farting sounds can add a playful twist to a track, inviting listeners to engage with the music on a humorous level.

+ **Interactive Performances:** Engaging the audience in fart-related activities can enhance the experience. For instance, inviting audience members to participate in a "farting contest" or creating a call-and-response farting routine can foster a sense of community and shared laughter.

+ **Fart-themed Merchandise:** Artists can design and sell fart-themed merchandise, such as T-shirts, stickers, or even musical instruments that produce fart sounds. This not only spreads joy but also creates a tangible connection between the artist and their fans.

+ **Social Media Campaigns:** Utilizing platforms like TikTok or Instagram to share funny fart-related content can amplify the reach of the message. Artists can create challenges or hashtags that encourage fans to share their own farting moments, promoting a culture of joy and laughter.

Real-world Examples

Several artists have successfully harnessed the power of farting to spread love and joy:

+ **The Farting Choir:** A community choir dedicated to performing humorous songs that incorporate farting sounds. Their performances not only entertain but also promote a message of acceptance and joy through laughter.

+ **Musical Comedians:** Artists like *Weird Al Yankovic* have built careers around humor, often using bodily functions as a source of inspiration. His songs, filled with clever wordplay and comedic elements, exemplify how humor can be a powerful tool for connection.

+ **Fart Festivals:** Events dedicated to celebrating fart humor, such as the "Fart Festival" in various locations, highlight the cultural acceptance of farting as a source of joy. These festivals often include performances, games, and activities that encourage laughter and community bonding.

Conclusion

Spreading love and joy through farting is not merely an act of silliness; it is a profound expression of human connection and creativity. By understanding the theoretical foundations, addressing challenges, and implementing practical applications, musicians can effectively utilize farting as a means to foster joy and laughter. As we embrace the unexpected and unconventional, we create spaces where love and joy can flourish, reminding us all that sometimes, the most powerful expressions come from the most unexpected places.

Bibliography

[1] Ruch, W. (1992). *The Sense of Humor: Explorations of a Personality Characteristic*. Berlin: Walter de Gruyter.

[2] Dunbar, R. I. M. (2010). *How Many Friends Does One Person Need?*. Harvard University Press.

[3] Smith, J. (2019). *The Cultural Significance of Fart Humor*. Journal of Humor Studies, 12(3), 45-60.

Using Fame to Make a Difference

In the dazzling world of fame, where glitz and glamour often overshadow genuine intentions, the true power of celebrity lies in the ability to effect change. This section delves into how artists can leverage their fame not just for personal gain, but to make a meaningful impact on society.

The Responsibility of Influence

Fame brings with it a unique responsibility. Celebrities are often seen as role models, whether they intend to be or not. This influence can be harnessed to promote positive social change. As noted by sociologist *Gustavo LeBon*, the masses are easily swayed by the actions and words of those they admire. Therefore, it becomes imperative for artists to recognize their potential to inspire and mobilize their fans toward various causes.

Identifying Causes

The first step in using fame for good is identifying causes that resonate with the artist's values and beliefs. Whether it's environmental issues, social justice, mental health awareness, or education, artists must align their platforms with causes that they are passionate about. For instance, *Taylor Swift* has used her platform to advocate for LGBTQ+ rights, while *Leonardo DiCaprio* has focused on climate change.

Creating Awareness

Once a cause is identified, the next step is to create awareness. This can be achieved through various channels, including social media, interviews, and live performances. By integrating messages about their chosen causes into their work, artists can reach a broader audience. For example, during her concert tours, *Beyoncé* often highlights social issues through her music videos and stage presentations, thereby educating her fans while entertaining them.

Fundraising Initiatives

Famous artists can also organize fundraising initiatives to support their chosen causes. This could involve charity concerts, merchandise sales, or collaborations with non-profit organizations. A notable example is *Lady Gaga's* "Born This Way Foundation," which focuses on empowering youth and promoting mental health awareness. Through her concerts and campaigns, she has raised millions for this cause, showcasing how fame can be a powerful tool for fundraising.

Collaborating with Nonprofits

Collaboration with established nonprofits can amplify an artist's impact. By partnering with organizations that have the infrastructure and expertise to implement change, artists can ensure that their efforts are effective and sustainable. For instance, *Shakira* has worked closely with her charity, *Barefoot Foundation*, to improve education for underprivileged children in Colombia. This partnership has led to the establishment of schools and educational programs, demonstrating the effectiveness of collaboration.

Utilizing Social Media

In the age of digital communication, social media serves as a powerful platform for artists to advocate for change. By sharing informative content, personal stories, and calls to action, artists can engage their followers and encourage them to take part in social movements. For example, during the *#BlackLivesMatter* movement, numerous celebrities used their platforms to raise awareness and promote activism, demonstrating the potential of social media as a tool for social change.

Addressing Criticism

While using fame for good can yield positive outcomes, it also invites criticism. Artists must be prepared to face backlash for their views or actions. It is essential to approach criticism with resilience and a willingness to engage in dialogue. For example, when *Kanye West* faced backlash for his political statements, he used the opportunity to foster discussions about mental health and personal freedom, turning criticism into a platform for dialogue.

Long-term Commitment

To truly make a difference, artists must commit to their causes over the long term. This means not just making a one-time donation or statement, but actively engaging with the issues and communities they aim to support. Artists like *Rihanna*, through her *Clara Lionel Foundation*, have shown that sustained efforts can lead to real change, as she has funded education and emergency response programs around the world.

Measuring Impact

Finally, it is crucial for artists to measure the impact of their efforts. This can involve tracking the funds raised, the number of lives changed, or the awareness generated around a cause. By sharing these results with their audience, artists can inspire others to take action and demonstrate the tangible effects of using fame for good.

In conclusion, fame can be a powerful tool for change when wielded responsibly. By identifying causes, creating awareness, collaborating with nonprofits, utilizing social media, addressing criticism, committing long-term, and measuring impact, artists can leave a lasting legacy that extends beyond their music. As *Nicki Minaj* herself said, "I'm not just a rapper, I'm an activist." Embracing this dual role allows artists to transform their influence into a force for good, inspiring their fans and communities to join them on the journey toward a better world.

Building a Better World through Farting

In the realm of artistic expression, the concept of "farting" transcends mere sound, evolving into a powerful medium for social change and community building. This section delves into how farting can be harnessed as a tool to foster unity, inspire action, and address societal issues.

The Power of Farting as Expression

Farting, often dismissed as trivial, embodies the essence of human experience—humor, embarrassment, and authenticity. According to [1], the act of farting can serve as a metaphor for liberation, allowing individuals to break free from societal constraints and express their true selves. This authenticity resonates with audiences, creating a shared experience that can mobilize communities toward collective action.

Fostering Community Through Farting

[2] highlights the role of farting in community engagement. By organizing fart-themed events, musicians can create safe spaces where individuals from diverse backgrounds come together to celebrate their differences and similarities. For example, the annual "Fart Festival" in San Francisco attracts thousands, promoting inclusivity and creativity through performances, workshops, and discussions about social issues.

$$\text{Community Engagement} = \frac{\text{Number of Participants} \times \text{Diversity Index}}{\text{Event Costs}} \quad (226)$$

This equation illustrates that successful community engagement in farting events is directly proportional to the number of participants and the diversity of the audience, while inversely related to the costs involved in organizing such events.

Addressing Social Issues

Farting can also be a catalyst for addressing pressing social issues. By incorporating themes of social justice into their music, artists can raise awareness and provoke thought. The "Fart for Change" campaign, launched by various artists, uses farting as a humorous yet impactful way to discuss serious topics such as climate change, mental health, and equality.

$$\text{Social Impact} = \text{Farting Engagement} \times \text{Awareness Level} \quad (227)$$

Here, the social impact is a product of the engagement generated through farting activities and the level of awareness raised among the audience.

Examples of Farting for Good

Several artists have successfully leveraged farting for philanthropic purposes. For instance, the rapper *Lil Fart* released a single titled "Fart for the Future," where all proceeds went to environmental charities. The catchy, humorous lyrics not only entertained but also educated listeners about the importance of sustainability.

Moreover, the "Farting for Food" initiative encourages musicians to perform at local shelters, using their art to raise funds and food donations for those in need. These examples illustrate how farting can cultivate compassion and drive positive change.

Creating Lasting Change

To build a better world through farting, artists must focus on creating sustainable initiatives that continue to impact communities long after the initial event. This can be achieved by:

- **Establishing Partnerships:** Collaborating with local organizations to address specific community needs.

- **Educational Programs:** Implementing workshops that teach the importance of social issues while using farting as a means of engagement.

- **Continuous Engagement:** Following up with communities to ensure that the conversations sparked by farting events lead to actionable change.

Conclusion

In conclusion, farting, when embraced as a form of artistic expression, has the potential to build a better world. By fostering community, addressing social issues, and creating lasting change, artists can transform the narrative surrounding farting from one of embarrassment to empowerment. As we continue to explore the intersections of art and activism, let us remember that every sound, even the most unexpected, can resonate with purpose and inspire a movement.

Bibliography

[1] Smith, J. (2020). *The Art of Farting: A Cultural Analysis*. New York: Fart Press.

[2] Johnson, R. (2019). *Farting and Community: Building Bridges through Humor*. Los Angeles: Laughing Matters.

Embracing the Unexpected

Navigating Ups and Downs in Life

Life, much like a symphony, is a composition of highs and lows, crescendos and decrescendos, where every note contributes to the overall masterpiece. Navigating the ups and downs is not just about enduring; it's about thriving through the chaos and coming out stronger on the other side. In this section, we will delve into the theoretical underpinnings of resilience, the psychological aspects of facing challenges, and practical strategies to embrace life's unpredictable nature.

Theoretical Framework of Resilience

Resilience is the ability to bounce back from adversity, trauma, or stress. It is a dynamic process that involves positive adaptation in the face of significant challenges. According to the American Psychological Association (APA), resilience is not a trait that people either have or do not have; it involves behaviors, thoughts, and actions that can be learned and developed in anyone.

The resilience theory posits several key components:

- **Personal Attributes:** Traits such as optimism, emotional regulation, and self-efficacy.

- **Social Support:** The importance of relationships and community in providing emotional and practical support.

+ **Coping Strategies:** Techniques such as problem-solving, seeking help, and maintaining a positive outlook.

Understanding Life's Challenges

Life's challenges can manifest in various forms: personal losses, career setbacks, health issues, or social conflicts. Each of these can create a ripple effect, impacting not only the individual but also their relationships and professional life.

$$\text{Challenge Impact} = \text{Personal Resilience} \times \text{Support System} \qquad (228)$$

This equation illustrates that the impact of a challenge can be mitigated by the individual's resilience and the strength of their support system. A strong network can provide the necessary resources and emotional backing to navigate through tough times.

Common Problems Faced

Navigating the ups and downs of life is fraught with problems, including:

+ **Emotional Turmoil:** Feelings of sadness, anxiety, or anger can overwhelm individuals during difficult times.

+ **Isolation:** The feeling of being alone can exacerbate stress and lead to a downward spiral.

+ **Fear of Failure:** The apprehension that comes with potential failure can prevent individuals from taking necessary risks.

Practical Strategies for Resilience

To effectively navigate life's challenges, consider implementing the following strategies:

+ **Mindfulness and Meditation:** These practices can help ground you in the present moment, reduce anxiety, and enhance emotional regulation.

+ **Goal Setting:** Break down larger challenges into manageable tasks. This can create a sense of accomplishment and clarity.

+ **Building Connections:** Foster relationships with friends, family, and mentors. A solid support system can provide encouragement and perspective.

+ **Positive Self-Talk:** Challenge negative thoughts and replace them with affirming statements. For example, instead of thinking, "I can't handle this," try, "I have overcome challenges before, and I can do it again."

Real-Life Examples

Consider the journey of a well-known artist who faced significant setbacks. After a major album flop, they experienced a dip in self-esteem and public perception. Instead of succumbing to despair, they utilized their support network, sought therapy, and focused on personal growth. This led to a comeback album that not only regained their previous success but also showcased their evolution as an artist.

Another example can be drawn from athletes who often face injuries that threaten their careers. Those who cultivate resilience by embracing rehabilitation, seeking support from coaches and teammates, and maintaining a positive outlook often find themselves returning stronger than before.

Conclusion

Navigating the ups and downs of life is an essential skill that can be cultivated through awareness, practice, and community support. By understanding the theoretical frameworks of resilience, recognizing the challenges we face, and employing practical strategies, we can not only survive but thrive in the symphony of life.

The journey may be unpredictable, but with each note played, we learn to compose our unique melody, one that resonates with strength, hope, and unwavering spirit.

Learning from Mistakes and Failures

In the vibrant world of farting, where creativity reigns supreme and the unexpected is celebrated, learning from mistakes and failures is not just a necessity—it's an art form. Every artist, from the local legends to the global superstars, has faced their fair share of missteps. It's how you bounce back and transform those blunders into stepping stones that truly defines your journey.

The Importance of Embracing Failure

Failure is often viewed as a negative experience, but in the realm of artistic expression, it can be a powerful teacher. When we embrace our failures, we open ourselves up to growth and innovation. This is particularly relevant in the world of farting, where experimentation is key.

$$\text{Growth} = \frac{\text{Experience} + \text{Reflection}}{\text{Fear of Failure}} \tag{229}$$

This equation highlights that growth is a function of the experiences we face and the reflections we make upon them, divided by our fear of failure. The less we fear failure, the more we can learn and grow.

Turning Mistakes into Masterpieces

Consider the story of a renowned fart artist who once performed at a major festival. During a live set, their sound system malfunctioned, resulting in an awkward silence. Instead of panicking, the artist seized the moment, engaging the audience with a spontaneous acapella performance that turned the mishap into a memorable highlight of the show. This incident not only showcased their ability to adapt but also solidified their reputation as a performer who could handle unexpected challenges with grace and humor.

Theoretical Framework: The Feedback Loop

To understand how to effectively learn from mistakes, we can apply the concept of the feedback loop, which consists of three main components:
1. **Action**: The initial performance or creation. 2. **Feedback**: The reactions and critiques received from the audience and peers. 3. **Adjustment**: The changes made in response to the feedback.

$$\text{Feedback Loop} = \text{Action} \rightarrow \text{Feedback} \rightarrow \text{Adjustment} \rightarrow \text{Action} \tag{230}$$

This cyclical process encourages continuous improvement. Each iteration allows artists to refine their craft, understand their audience better, and ultimately create more resonant and impactful farting experiences.

Common Problems Faced

Artists often encounter several challenges when navigating their mistakes:
- **Fear of Judgment**: Many artists hesitate to share their failures due to the fear of being judged by peers or fans. This fear can stifle creativity and hinder growth. - **Perfectionism**: The desire for perfection can lead to an aversion to

taking risks. Artists may avoid experimenting with new sounds or styles, fearing that they won't meet their own standards. - **Stagnation**: Without learning from failures, artists may find themselves stuck in a cycle of repetition, producing work that lacks innovation and excitement.

Examples of Learning Through Failure

1. **The Iconic Album Flop**: A famous fart artist released an album that was critically panned. Instead of retreating, they took the criticism to heart, spent time re-evaluating their sound, and returned with a follow-up album that not only redeemed their reputation but also won several awards. This journey illustrates the power of resilience and the importance of learning from public reception.

2. **The Unplanned Collaboration**: An artist once collaborated with a musician whose style was vastly different. Initially, the project was a disaster, with creative differences leading to a chaotic recording session. However, through this experience, they discovered new techniques and perspectives that enriched their music, leading to a unique sound that captivated audiences.

Conclusion

In the world of farting, mistakes and failures are not the end of the road; they are merely detours that lead to new paths of creativity and expression. By embracing these experiences, artists can cultivate resilience, enhance their craft, and connect more deeply with their audience. Remember, every great fart artist has a story of failure that shaped their journey—so let your missteps be the fuel that ignites your creative fire!

$$\text{Success} = \text{Mistakes} + \text{Learning} + \text{Persistence} \qquad (231)$$

In essence, the road to success is paved with the lessons learned from our missteps. So go ahead, embrace your failures, and let them guide you to greatness!

Embracing Serendipity and Chance

In the unpredictable world of music, serendipity often plays a pivotal role in shaping an artist's journey. The notion of chance encounters and unexpected opportunities can lead to monumental breakthroughs and creative revelations. This section delves into the significance of embracing serendipity and chance, how they can influence artistic expression, and strategies to harness these moments for growth.

The Role of Serendipity in Creativity

Serendipity refers to the occurrence of events by chance in a happy or beneficial way. In the context of music, it can manifest through unexpected collaborations, spontaneous jam sessions, or even accidental discoveries of sound. For instance, the legendary band The Beatles famously stumbled upon their innovative sound while experimenting with various instruments and techniques during casual rehearsals. This unplanned exploration allowed them to create music that resonated with millions.

$$C = \sum_{i=1}^{n} p_i \cdot q_i \tag{232}$$

Where C represents creativity, p_i denotes the probability of chance encounters, and q_i signifies the quality of spontaneous ideas generated. The equation illustrates that the more one is open to chance events (p_i), the greater the potential for creative output (C).

Navigating the Unpredictable Landscape

While it may seem daunting to rely on chance, artists can strategically position themselves to maximize these opportunities. Here are several approaches:

- **Networking:** Building a diverse network of fellow musicians, artists, and industry professionals increases the likelihood of serendipitous encounters. Attend workshops, concerts, and events where collaboration is encouraged.

- **Experimentation:** Engage in experimental sessions where the goal is to create without boundaries. This could involve using unconventional instruments, altering song structures, or blending genres. The unexpected results can spark new ideas and directions.

- **Mindfulness:** Cultivating a mindful approach allows artists to be present and aware of their surroundings. This heightened awareness can lead to recognizing opportunities that may otherwise go unnoticed.

Real-Life Examples of Serendipity in Music

Several iconic moments in music history exemplify the power of serendipity:

1. **David Bowie and Brian Eno:** The collaboration between Bowie and Eno was born out of chance meetings and mutual admiration. Their partnership led to the creation of the groundbreaking "Berlin Trilogy," which reshaped the landscape of rock and electronic music.

2. **The Rolling Stones:** The song "(I Can't Get No) Satisfaction" was conceived when Keith Richards fell asleep with his guitar plugged into a tape recorder. Upon waking, he discovered a riff that would become one of the most recognizable in music history.

3. **Billie Eilish:** The breakout success of Billie Eilish can be attributed to her and her brother Finneas' willingness to experiment with sounds in their home studio. Their unorthodox approach and openness to chance led to the viral hit "Ocean Eyes."

Challenges of Embracing Serendipity

While embracing serendipity can lead to incredible opportunities, it also presents challenges. The unpredictability of chance events can create anxiety and uncertainty for artists. The following are common challenges faced:

- **Fear of Failure:** Artists may hesitate to take risks due to the fear of producing subpar work or being judged. This fear can stifle creativity and limit the potential for serendipitous moments.

- **Over-Reliance on Chance:** While serendipity is valuable, relying solely on chance can lead to a lack of direction. Artists must balance spontaneity with intentionality to ensure progress in their careers.

- **Navigating Disappointment:** Not every chance encounter will yield positive results. Artists must cultivate resilience and learn to view setbacks as part of the creative journey.

Harnessing Serendipity for Growth

To effectively harness the power of serendipity, artists can adopt the following strategies:

1. **Stay Open-Minded:** Cultivate a mindset that welcomes new ideas and perspectives. Being open to feedback and suggestions can lead to unexpected insights.

2. **Document Ideas:** Keep a journal or recording device handy to capture spontaneous thoughts, melodies, or lyrics that arise unexpectedly. This practice ensures that no moment of inspiration is lost.

3. **Engage in Collaborative Projects:** Collaborating with other artists can create a fertile ground for serendipitous moments. Diverse influences and ideas can lead to innovative outcomes.

In conclusion, embracing serendipity and chance is an essential aspect of the artistic journey. By remaining open to the unexpected and actively seeking out opportunities for exploration, artists can unlock new dimensions of creativity and innovation. The key lies in balancing spontaneity with a proactive approach to growth, allowing the symphony of life to unfold in harmonious and unexpected ways.

Going with the Flow and Adaptability

In the dynamic world of music and performance, the ability to go with the flow and adapt is not merely a skill; it is an essential survival tool. Artists, much like water, must learn to navigate the contours of their environment, bending and shaping themselves to the currents of change. This section explores the significance of adaptability in the music industry, the challenges faced by artists, and practical strategies for embracing flexibility.

The Importance of Adaptability

Adaptability in the music industry is paramount for several reasons. First, the landscape of music is ever-evolving, influenced by technological advancements, shifting audience preferences, and cultural changes. Artists who cling to a rigid approach may find themselves left behind, while those who are willing to experiment and evolve often find greater success.

$$\text{Success} = \text{Adaptability} \times \text{Innovation} \tag{233}$$

This equation illustrates that success is not solely dependent on talent but is significantly enhanced by an artist's ability to adapt and innovate. For instance, artists like Madonna and David Bowie are celebrated not just for their musical prowess but for their remarkable ability to reinvent themselves in response to changing trends.

Challenges of Adaptability

While adaptability is crucial, it does come with its own set of challenges. Artists may struggle with the fear of losing their identity or alienating their existing fanbase when trying new styles or sounds. This fear can be paralyzing, leading to stagnation. Additionally, the pressure to constantly evolve can result in creative burnout, where the artist feels overwhelmed by the need to keep up with trends.

Examples of Successful Adaptability

Several artists have successfully navigated the waters of change, illustrating the power of adaptability:

+ **Taylor Swift**: Originally a country artist, Swift transitioned into pop music with her album *1989*. This shift not only broadened her audience but also showcased her ability to adapt her sound while maintaining her lyrical authenticity.

+ **Kanye West**: Known for his genre-defying music, West has continually reinvented his style. From hip-hop to gospel, his willingness to explore new territories has solidified his status as a cultural icon.

+ **Beyoncé**: With each album, Beyoncé has pushed the boundaries of her artistry, incorporating elements of R&B, pop, hip-hop, and even African rhythms. Her visual albums and innovative marketing strategies exemplify her adaptability.

Strategies for Embracing Change

To cultivate adaptability, artists can employ several strategies:

1. **Stay Informed**: Keeping up with industry trends, emerging technologies, and audience preferences can provide valuable insights that inform creative decisions. Subscribing to music industry newsletters, attending workshops, and networking with other artists can enhance awareness.

2. **Experimentation**: Embracing a mindset of experimentation allows artists to explore new sounds and styles without the pressure of immediate success. This could involve collaborating with artists from different genres or experimenting with unconventional instruments.

3. **Feedback Loops:** Actively seeking feedback from fans and peers can guide artists in their evolution. Engaging with audiences through social media or live performances can provide insights into what resonates and what doesn't.

4. **Mindfulness and Reflection:** Practicing mindfulness can help artists manage anxiety about change. Reflecting on past experiences and recognizing the growth that comes from challenges can foster resilience.

5. **Building a Support Network:** Surrounding oneself with a supportive community of fellow artists, mentors, and fans can provide encouragement and inspiration. This network can serve as a sounding board for new ideas and creative risks.

Conclusion

In conclusion, going with the flow and embracing adaptability is essential for artists navigating the tumultuous waters of the music industry. By understanding the importance of flexibility, recognizing the challenges, and employing effective strategies, musicians can not only survive but thrive in an ever-changing landscape. Remember, the most successful artists are those who can bend without breaking, flowing gracefully with the currents of change while staying true to their creative essence.

Finding Opportunities in Challenges

In the world of music, as in life, challenges are not just obstacles; they are gateways to new opportunities. The art of transforming difficulties into advantages is a skill that every artist must cultivate. This section delves into the theory behind this transformative process, the common challenges faced by musicians, and real-world examples that illustrate how to turn adversity into opportunity.

Theoretical Framework

The theory of resilience posits that individuals who can adapt positively to adversity are more likely to succeed in the long term. Resilience can be defined as the ability to bounce back from setbacks, adapt to change, and keep going in the face of challenges. According to [?], resilience is not a trait but a dynamic process that can be developed through experience and support. This concept is essential for musicians who often face rejection, criticism, and the unpredictable nature of the industry.

Mathematically, we can express resilience as a function of various factors:

$$R = f(E, S, C) \tag{234}$$

Where:

* R = Resilience

* E = Experience (past challenges and how they were handled)

* S = Support (network of friends, mentors, and collaborators)

* C = Coping strategies (skills developed to manage stress and adversity)

This equation suggests that resilience can be enhanced by accumulating positive experiences, building a supportive network, and developing effective coping mechanisms.

Common Challenges in Music

Musicians often encounter a variety of challenges, including:

* **Financial Strain**: The unpredictability of income in the music industry can lead to significant financial stress.

* **Creative Blocks**: Artists may face periods where inspiration seems elusive, leading to frustration and self-doubt.

* **Industry Rejection**: Rejection from labels, venues, or audiences can be disheartening and may lead to a loss of confidence.

* **Competition**: The saturated market makes it difficult for emerging artists to stand out.

* **Changing Trends**: Keeping up with rapidly evolving musical trends can be challenging for established artists.

Turning Challenges into Opportunities

To transform these challenges into opportunities, musicians can employ various strategies:

+ **Financial Innovation**: Musicians can explore alternative revenue streams such as crowdfunding, merchandise sales, and digital content creation. For example, the band *Mumford & Sons* successfully funded their album through fan contributions, allowing them to maintain creative control while engaging their audience directly.

+ **Embracing Creative Blocks**: Instead of viewing creative blocks as failures, artists can use these periods to experiment with new genres or collaborate with others. *Billie Eilish* faced a creative block while writing her second album but used the time to explore different sounds and collaborate with her brother, resulting in a critically acclaimed project.

+ **Resilience Through Rejection**: Every rejection can be reframed as an opportunity to improve and refine one's craft. For instance, *Taylor Swift* faced numerous rejections early in her career but used feedback to hone her songwriting skills, ultimately leading to her success.

+ **Unique Branding**: In a competitive market, artists can differentiate themselves by developing a unique brand identity. *Lil Nas X* leveraged social media and meme culture to create a viral sensation with "Old Town Road," turning the challenge of standing out into a massive hit.

+ **Adapting to Trends**: Artists can stay relevant by being flexible and open to new influences. *Madonna* has consistently reinvented her sound and image to align with changing trends, allowing her to maintain a successful career across decades.

Real-World Examples

1. **J.K. Rowling**: Before becoming a household name, Rowling faced numerous rejections from publishers. Instead of giving up, she used the feedback to improve her manuscript, ultimately leading to the publication of the *Harry Potter* series, which became a global phenomenon.

2. **Kendrick Lamar**: Facing the challenges of growing up in Compton, California, Lamar turned his environment into inspiration for his music. His experiences shaped his lyrical content, allowing him to connect deeply with audiences and win multiple Grammy Awards.

3. **Dua Lipa**: After struggling to find her place in the music industry and facing initial rejections, Lipa embraced her unique style and sound. Her persistence paid off, leading to chart-topping hits and a Grammy for Best New Artist.

Conclusion

Finding opportunities in challenges is not just a survival tactic; it's a pathway to artistic growth and innovation. By embracing resilience and viewing obstacles as opportunities for creativity and connection, musicians can navigate the complexities of the industry and leave a lasting impact. The key lies in maintaining a positive mindset, leveraging support systems, and continuously evolving as artists. As the legendary *Beyoncé* once said, "The most alluring thing a woman can have is confidence." This confidence, born from overcoming challenges, can propel artists to new heights in their careers.

Embracing Change and Uncertainty

In the vibrant world of music, change is not just a constant; it is an essential element that fuels creativity and innovation. Embracing change and uncertainty is akin to dancing with the unpredictable rhythms of life, allowing artists to explore uncharted territories in their craft. This section delves into the significance of accepting change, the challenges it presents, and the transformative power it holds for musicians.

The Nature of Change

Change is inherent in the artistic process. As musicians evolve, so do their influences, styles, and audiences. Theories in psychology, such as the *Change Theory* proposed by Kurt Lewin, suggest that change can be understood through three stages: unfreezing, change, and refreezing.

$$\text{Unfreeze} \to \text{Change} \to \text{Refreeze} \tag{235}$$

- **Unfreezing** involves recognizing the need for change, often triggered by external influences such as new trends or internal motivations like personal growth. - **Change** is the process of moving towards a new state, where experimentation and creativity take center stage. - **Refreezing** establishes stability in the new state, solidifying the changes made into the artist's repertoire.

Challenges of Embracing Uncertainty

While change can be exhilarating, it often comes with uncertainty, which can provoke fear and anxiety. Musicians may face the following challenges:
1. **Fear of Failure**: The fear of not meeting expectations can be paralyzing. Musicians may hesitate to take risks or explore new genres, fearing negative reception from fans or critics. 2. **Loss of Identity**: As artists evolve, they may

struggle with their sense of identity. The question, "Who am I as a musician?" can create internal conflict, especially if the new direction diverges significantly from their established style.   3.   **Market Dynamics**:   The music industry is continuously shifting, influenced by technological advancements and changing consumer preferences. This unpredictability can make it difficult for artists to navigate their careers effectively.

Strategies for Embracing Change

To thrive amidst change and uncertainty, musicians can adopt several strategies:

- **Cultivate a Growth Mindset:** Embracing a growth mindset, as proposed by psychologist Carol Dweck, encourages artists to view challenges as opportunities for growth rather than insurmountable obstacles. This mindset fosters resilience and adaptability.

- **Experimentation:** Allowing oneself to experiment with different sounds, genres, and collaborations can lead to unexpected breakthroughs. For example, Billie Eilish's genre-defying music blends pop, electronic, and indie influences, showcasing the beauty of experimentation.

- **Community Support:** Building a supportive community of fellow musicians and fans can provide encouragement during uncertain times. Collaborating with others can also lead to new perspectives and ideas, enriching the artistic process.

- **Mindfulness Practices:** Engaging in mindfulness practices such as meditation or journaling can help musicians manage anxiety and maintain focus. These practices encourage self-reflection, enabling artists to navigate their emotions during times of change.

Real-World Examples

Several artists have exemplified the power of embracing change and uncertainty:

- **David Bowie:** Known for his chameleonic ability to reinvent himself, Bowie continuously evolved his musical style, from glam rock to electronic. His willingness to embrace change not only kept his music fresh but also inspired countless artists to explore their own identities.

- **Taylor Swift:** Swift's transition from country to pop with her album *1989* marked a significant change in her career. Despite initial criticism, she embraced the uncertainty and ultimately achieved massive success, demonstrating the rewards of taking risks.

- **Kendrick Lamar:** Lamar's exploration of different musical styles and themes in albums like *To Pimp a Butterfly* and *DAMN.* showcases his ability to navigate change while addressing complex social issues, proving that uncertainty can lead to profound artistic statements.

Conclusion

Embracing change and uncertainty is not merely a survival tactic for musicians; it is a pathway to innovation and artistic fulfillment. By recognizing the inevitable nature of change, confronting challenges head-on, and employing effective strategies, artists can transform uncertainty into a powerful catalyst for growth. In the symphony of life and music, it is through the unpredictable notes that the most beautiful melodies are often composed. As we navigate the evolving landscape of the music industry, let us remember that change is not the enemy; it is the muse that inspires our most profound creations.

Overcoming Obstacles with Resilience

In the world of music, the journey is often paved with obstacles that test not only our talent but also our resilience. Resilience, defined as the capacity to recover quickly from difficulties, is a crucial trait for artists navigating the tumultuous waters of the entertainment industry. This section delves into the theory of resilience, the common obstacles musicians face, and real-life examples that illustrate how to overcome these challenges.

The Theory of Resilience

Resilience can be understood through various psychological frameworks. One prominent theory is the **Resilience Theory**, which posits that resilience is a dynamic process involving positive adaptation in the face of adversity. According to Rutter (1987), resilience is not merely an individual trait but a combination of personal qualities and environmental factors that contribute to an individual's ability to cope with stress.

The equation for resilience can be simplified as follows:

$$R = P + E \tag{236}$$

where R represents resilience, P symbolizes personal attributes (such as optimism, emotional regulation, and social support), and E denotes environmental factors (like supportive relationships and community resources).

Common Obstacles in the Music Industry

Musicians encounter numerous challenges, including:

- **Rejection and Criticism:** The music industry is notorious for its competitive nature. Artists often face rejection from record labels, promoters, and even fans. Learning to accept and grow from criticism is essential.

- **Financial Struggles:** Many musicians start with limited resources, making it difficult to fund their projects. This challenge can lead to stress and burnout.

- **Creative Blocks:** Every artist experiences periods of creative stagnation. Overcoming these blocks requires resilience and innovative thinking.

- **Personal Challenges:** Balancing personal life and a demanding career can lead to mental health issues, which can further complicate an artist's journey.

Strategies for Building Resilience

To effectively overcome obstacles, musicians can employ several strategies:

1. **Cultivating a Growth Mindset:** Embracing challenges as opportunities for growth is vital. According to Dweck (2006), individuals with a growth mindset view failures as learning experiences rather than setbacks.

2. **Building a Support Network:** Surrounding oneself with supportive friends, family, and mentors can provide encouragement during tough times. This network serves as a buffer against stress and can offer valuable advice.

3. **Practicing Self-Care:** Prioritizing mental and physical health is crucial. Regular exercise, mindfulness practices, and hobbies outside of music can enhance overall well-being and resilience.

4. **Setting Realistic Goals:** Breaking down larger objectives into manageable tasks can prevent overwhelm. Setting SMART (Specific, Measurable, Achievable, Relevant, Time-bound) goals helps maintain focus and motivation.

Real-Life Examples of Resilience in Music

Several artists exemplify resilience in the face of adversity:

+ **Adele:** After facing rejection early in her career, Adele persevered and eventually released her debut album, *19*, which catapulted her to stardom. Her ability to transform personal struggles into powerful music resonates with many fans.

+ **Katy Perry:** Before achieving success, Perry faced numerous rejections from record labels. Her persistence paid off when she released *Teenage Dream*, which became a landmark album in pop music. Perry's journey illustrates the importance of resilience and belief in oneself.

+ **Eminem:** Eminem's story is one of overcoming significant personal and professional obstacles, including poverty and addiction. His resilience is reflected in his lyrics, which often address his struggles and triumphs, inspiring millions worldwide.

Conclusion

In conclusion, resilience is an essential quality for musicians navigating the challenges of the industry. By understanding the theory behind resilience, recognizing common obstacles, and implementing effective strategies, artists can cultivate the strength to overcome adversity. The stories of successful musicians who have triumphed over challenges serve as a testament to the power of resilience, reminding us that the journey is just as important as the destination. As we continue to embrace our unique sounds and stories, let us remember that every obstacle can be transformed into an opportunity for growth and creativity.

Trusting the Journey and Process

In the world of music, as in life, the journey is often just as significant as the destination. Trusting the journey and the process involves embracing the twists and turns that come with pursuing one's passion. This section delves into the importance of faith in the path taken, the inherent challenges faced, and the growth that emerges from these experiences.

The Importance of Trust

Trusting the journey means believing in the process, even when the outcome is uncertain. This faith can be likened to the concept of **self-efficacy**, which refers to an individual's belief in their ability to succeed in specific situations. According to Bandura (1977), self-efficacy influences the choices we make, the effort we put forth, and our resilience in the face of challenges.

In musical careers, self-efficacy can be developed through:

+ **Mastery Experiences:** Successfully overcoming challenges builds confidence. For instance, a musician who conquers stage fright after a successful performance is more likely to trust their abilities in future gigs.

+ **Vicarious Experiences:** Observing others succeed can inspire confidence. A budding artist may feel empowered after watching their idol perform and overcome obstacles.

+ **Social Persuasion:** Encouragement from peers and mentors can reinforce one's belief in their journey. Positive feedback from fellow musicians can serve as a powerful motivator.

+ **Emotional States:** Managing emotions during performances can significantly affect self-efficacy. Learning to channel nervous energy into creativity can transform anxiety into a driving force.

Embracing Challenges

Every artist faces challenges that test their resolve. Trusting the journey means recognizing that these challenges are not merely obstacles but opportunities for growth. For example, consider the story of a young artist who faced numerous rejections from record labels. Instead of succumbing to despair, they used this feedback to refine their craft, resulting in a more polished and compelling sound.

The equation of growth can be represented as:

$$G = R + E \tag{237}$$

Where:

+ G = Growth

+ R = Resilience (the ability to recover from setbacks)

+ E = Experience (the lessons learned through challenges)

This equation illustrates that growth is a direct result of resilience and the experiences one accumulates along the way.

The Role of Patience

Patience is a vital component of trusting the journey. In an industry driven by instant gratification, artists must learn to appreciate the slow and steady progress that often leads to lasting success. The process of honing one's craft can be likened to the maturation of fine wine; it requires time, care, and the right conditions to reach its full potential.

For instance, consider the career trajectory of an artist like Ed Sheeran. He spent years performing in small venues, perfecting his songwriting and stage presence before achieving mainstream success. His journey exemplifies the idea that patience, combined with consistent effort, can lead to extraordinary outcomes.

Finding Meaning in the Process

Trusting the journey also involves finding meaning in the process itself. This can be achieved through:

+ **Reflection:** Regularly reflecting on one's experiences can provide clarity and insight. Keeping a journal of experiences, thoughts, and emotions can help artists appreciate their growth.

+ **Mindfulness:** Practicing mindfulness allows artists to stay present, reducing anxiety about future outcomes. Techniques such as meditation can enhance focus and creativity.

+ **Community:** Engaging with a supportive community fosters a sense of belonging and shared experience. Collaborating with fellow musicians can provide encouragement and inspiration.

Conclusion

In conclusion, trusting the journey and the process is a fundamental aspect of artistic growth. By embracing challenges, cultivating patience, and finding meaning in the experiences along the way, artists can navigate the complexities of their careers with resilience and confidence. The journey is not merely a means to an end; it is an integral part of the artistic experience that shapes who we are as musicians and individuals. As the saying goes, "It's not about the destination; it's about the journey." Trust in that journey, and let it guide you to your ultimate destination.

Embracing the Unknown with Courage

In the journey of life and artistry, the unknown often looms as a daunting specter, intimidating even the most seasoned creators. However, embracing this uncertainty with courage can lead to profound growth, innovation, and self-discovery. This section explores the theoretical foundations of courage in the face of the unknown, the common problems artists encounter, and illustrative examples that highlight the transformative power of embracing uncertainty.

Theoretical Foundations

Courage, as defined by psychological theories, is the ability to confront fear, pain, or adversity. According to *Courage Theory*, individuals who cultivate courage do not eliminate fear; instead, they learn to act despite it. This concept is pivotal for artists, as the creative process is inherently fraught with uncertainty. The renowned psychologist Rollo May posits that "courage is the capacity to confront what can be imagined." This assertion emphasizes the importance of mental fortitude when navigating the unpredictable landscape of artistic expression.

To operationalize courage, we can draw on the following equation:

$$C = \frac{F}{R} \tag{238}$$

Where:

+ C = Courage

+ F = Fear faced

+ R = Resistance to fear

This formula suggests that courage increases as one faces greater fears while simultaneously resisting the urge to retreat. Thus, artists must recognize and confront their fears to cultivate a courageous mindset.

Common Problems Artists Face

Artists often grapple with various problems related to the unknown, including:

+ **Fear of Failure:** The anxiety of not meeting expectations can paralyze creativity. Many artists worry that their work will not resonate with audiences or critics, leading to self-doubt.

- **Imposter Syndrome:** This phenomenon occurs when artists feel like frauds despite their accomplishments. The fear of being "found out" can hinder their willingness to take risks.

- **Creative Block:** The uncertainty of not knowing how to proceed with a project can lead to stagnation. Artists may feel overwhelmed by the possibilities, resulting in a lack of direction.

- **Market Pressures:** The pressure to conform to industry standards can stifle originality. Artists may hesitate to explore new ideas for fear of alienating their existing fanbase.

Examples of Embracing the Unknown

Several artists throughout history have exemplified the courage to embrace the unknown, transforming their fears into creative fuel:

- **David Bowie:** Known for his chameleonic transformations, Bowie continually reinvented himself and his music. His willingness to explore uncharted territories, such as the avant-garde and electronic genres, exemplifies how embracing the unknown can lead to groundbreaking artistry. In his song "Space Oddity," Bowie invites listeners into the unknown of space, reflecting his own journey into the uncharted realms of creativity.

- **Frida Kahlo:** Despite facing immense physical and emotional pain, Kahlo channeled her struggles into her art. Her iconic self-portraits reveal her vulnerability and courage in confronting her identity and experiences. Kahlo's ability to embrace her pain and uncertainty allowed her to create deeply personal works that resonate with audiences worldwide.

- **Kendrick Lamar:** As a contemporary artist, Lamar addresses complex social issues through his music. His album *To Pimp a Butterfly* challenges societal norms and expectations, showcasing his courage to tackle difficult topics. By embracing the unknown of his own experiences and the broader cultural landscape, Lamar has solidified his place as a voice for change in the music industry.

Strategies for Embracing the Unknown

To cultivate courage in the face of uncertainty, artists can employ several strategies:

+ **Mindfulness and Reflection:** Practicing mindfulness can help artists become aware of their fears without judgment. Reflecting on past experiences where they embraced the unknown can also reinforce their courage.

+ **Setting Small Goals:** Breaking down larger projects into manageable tasks can reduce the overwhelming nature of the unknown. Celebrating small victories fosters a sense of accomplishment and encourages further exploration.

+ **Seeking Support:** Building a community of like-minded artists can provide encouragement and accountability. Sharing fears and experiences can normalize the struggles associated with uncertainty.

+ **Reframing Failure:** Viewing failure as a learning opportunity rather than a setback can shift an artist's perspective. Embracing a growth mindset allows for experimentation and innovation without the fear of negative outcomes.

Conclusion

Embracing the unknown with courage is a vital component of artistic growth and creativity. By understanding the theoretical underpinnings of courage, recognizing common challenges, and learning from exemplary figures, artists can navigate the unpredictable terrain of their craft. Ultimately, the journey into the unknown can lead to profound discoveries, both personally and artistically, allowing creators to leave a lasting impact on the world through their unique expressions.

Making the Most of Unexpected Opportunities

In the world of music, as in life, unexpected opportunities often arise when we least expect them. These serendipitous moments can be the key to unlocking new paths for creativity and success. Embracing these moments requires a mindset that is open to change and ready to adapt.

Understanding the Nature of Unexpected Opportunities

Unexpected opportunities can manifest in various forms: a chance meeting with a fellow artist, an invitation to perform at a last-minute gig, or even a sudden spark of inspiration while experimenting with new sounds. The critical factor is how we perceive and respond to these moments. The theory of *opportunism* suggests that individuals who are flexible and willing to take risks are more likely to capitalize on unforeseen opportunities.

$$P(O) = f(R, F, A) \qquad (239)$$

Where: - $P(O)$ = Probability of seizing an unexpected opportunity - R = Readiness to act - F = Flexibility in approach - A = Ability to recognize potential in the unexpected

The Importance of a Prepared Mindset

To make the most of these moments, artists must cultivate a prepared mindset. This involves being constantly aware of the environment and opportunities that may arise. According to psychologist *Mihaly Csikszentmihalyi*, achieving a state of *flow* can enhance creativity and responsiveness to unexpected stimuli. When an artist is in flow, they are more likely to notice and seize opportunities that align with their creative vision.

Examples of Seizing the Moment

Consider the story of **Beyoncé**, who famously recorded her iconic album *Lemonade* in response to unexpected personal experiences. The album not only showcased her artistic evolution but also addressed social issues, creating a cultural phenomenon. Beyoncé's ability to turn personal turmoil into creative fuel exemplifies the power of embracing unexpected opportunities.

Another example is **Chance the Rapper**, who rose to fame after releasing his mixtape *Coloring Book* for free on streaming platforms. Instead of following traditional music industry paths, he seized the opportunity to connect directly with fans, redefining the music distribution model and establishing a strong independent brand.

Overcoming Challenges

While unexpected opportunities can lead to success, they can also present challenges. Artists may face self-doubt, fear of failure, or the pressure to perform under unexpected circumstances. The key to overcoming these challenges lies in the ability to reframe the situation positively.

Utilizing *cognitive restructuring*, artists can shift their perspective on challenges from threats to opportunities for growth. This mental shift can be represented as:

$$G = \frac{O}{C} \qquad (240)$$

Where: - G = Growth potential - O = Opportunities presented - C = Challenges faced

Strategies for Embracing Unexpected Opportunities

1. **Stay Open-Minded**: Cultivate an attitude of curiosity and openness. This can be achieved through practices such as mindfulness and active listening, which enhance awareness of surroundings.

2. **Network Actively**: Build relationships within the industry. Attend events, collaborate with other artists, and engage with fans. Each connection can lead to unforeseen opportunities.

3. **Be Ready to Pivot**: Flexibility is crucial. If an opportunity arises that deviates from your original plan, be willing to adapt. This could mean altering your setlist for a performance or experimenting with a new genre.

4. **Document Ideas**: Keep a journal or digital notes of spontaneous ideas, lyrics, or melodies that come to mind. This ensures that when an opportunity presents itself, you have material to draw from.

5. **Cultivate Resilience**: Develop the ability to bounce back from setbacks. Resilience can be strengthened through positive affirmations, support systems, and self-care practices.

Conclusion

In conclusion, making the most of unexpected opportunities is a vital skill for any artist. By fostering a prepared mindset, embracing flexibility, and cultivating resilience, musicians can turn unforeseen moments into stepping stones for success. As the industry evolves, those who remain open to the unexpected will not only survive but thrive in the ever-changing landscape of music. Remember, every unexpected opportunity is a chance to create something extraordinary. So, keep your eyes wide open, your heart ready to beat, and your mind prepared to seize the moment!

Leaving a Lasting Impact

The Power of Farting to Heal and Inspire

In the world of music, the notion of healing and inspiration often intertwines, creating a unique tapestry of emotional expression and connection. Farting, often perceived as a source of humor or embarrassment, can paradoxically serve as a profound medium for healing and inspiration. This section explores the various dimensions of how farting can be harnessed to uplift spirits, foster community, and catalyze personal transformation.

The Therapeutic Effects of Laughter

Laughter is a universal language, and farting humor often evokes spontaneous giggles, breaking down barriers and uniting people. According to the *Gelotology* theory, laughter induces physiological responses that enhance well-being. It triggers the release of endorphins, the body's natural feel-good chemicals, which can alleviate stress and pain. The equation governing this relationship can be expressed as:

$$H = E + C + S \qquad (241)$$

Where:

+ H = Healing through laughter

+ E = Endorphin release

+ C = Connection with others

+ S = Stress relief

For example, during a live performance, a band might incorporate farting sound effects into their act, eliciting laughter from the audience. This shared experience fosters a sense of community, enhancing emotional bonds and creating an atmosphere of joy.

Fostering Resilience through Humor

Humor can also serve as a coping mechanism during challenging times. When individuals face adversity, incorporating humor—particularly through farting—can provide relief and perspective. The *Coping Humor Theory* posits that humor allows individuals to reframe difficult situations, making them more manageable. For instance, a musician who has faced rejection might share a humorous farting anecdote during an interview, transforming a potentially negative experience into a relatable story that resonates with fans.

Cultural Significance of Farting in Music

Throughout history, farting has found its place in various musical genres, often symbolizing rebellion and authenticity. In genres like punk and hip-hop, artists have used farting as a form of social commentary, challenging norms and expectations. The act of embracing farting can empower marginalized voices and inspire others to express their individuality.

Consider the example of a punk band that incorporates farting noises into their tracks. This not only entertains but also serves as a critique of societal conventions, encouraging listeners to embrace their true selves without fear of judgment.

Farting as a Catalyst for Social Change

Farting can also be a powerful tool for advocacy and social change. Artists can use their platform to address serious issues while employing humor to engage audiences. For instance, a charity concert themed around farting could raise awareness for environmental issues, using the metaphor of farting to discuss gas emissions and climate change. This approach not only educates but also entertains, making the message more accessible.

Case Studies: Artists Who Use Farting for Good

Several artists have successfully utilized farting as a means of healing and inspiration:

- **Weird Al Yankovic:** Known for his parodic songs, Weird Al often incorporates fart humor, making light of serious subjects while promoting laughter and joy. His work exemplifies how farting can be a vehicle for healing through humor.

- **The Lonely Island:** This comedic trio uses farting in their music videos to address themes of masculinity, identity, and social norms, encouraging audiences to embrace their quirks and laugh at themselves.

- **Flight of the Conchords:** Their unique blend of humor and music often features fart jokes, creating a light-hearted atmosphere that fosters connection among fans.

Conclusion: Embracing the Power of Farting

In conclusion, the power of farting to heal and inspire lies in its ability to evoke laughter, foster resilience, and promote social change. By embracing the unconventional, artists can create a space for healing, connection, and empowerment. Farting, often dismissed as mere humor, holds the potential to transcend boundaries and inspire a movement of authenticity and joy. As we continue to explore the intersections of music and healing, let us remember that sometimes, the most profound messages come wrapped in laughter.

$$\text{Inspiration} = \text{Laughter} + \text{Connection} + \text{Empowerment} \qquad (242)$$

Supporting Charitable Initiatives

In the vibrant world of music, where melodies dance and rhythms pulse, artists have a unique platform to create not only sound but also change. Supporting charitable initiatives is not just a noble cause; it is a powerful way to use one's influence for the greater good. This section explores the significance of charitable efforts in the music industry, the challenges artists face in their philanthropic endeavors, and inspiring examples of musicians who have made a difference.

The Importance of Philanthropy in Music

Philanthropy in music serves as a bridge between the artist and their audience, fostering a sense of community and shared purpose. Artists can leverage their popularity to draw attention to pressing social issues, raise funds for important causes, and inspire their fans to engage in charitable activities. The act of giving back not only enhances the artist's image but also enriches their music with deeper meaning and purpose.

Challenges Faced by Artists

Despite the noble intentions, artists often encounter several challenges when supporting charitable initiatives:

- **Awareness and Engagement:** Many artists struggle to find the right causes that resonate with them and their audience. The challenge lies in selecting initiatives that align with their values while also engaging their fanbase.

- **Resource Allocation:** Artists may face difficulties in balancing their time and resources between their musical careers and philanthropic efforts. This can lead to a lack of sustained commitment to charitable initiatives.

- **Criticism and Scrutiny:** Public figures are often subject to scrutiny regarding their charitable choices. Artists may face backlash if their initiatives are perceived as insincere or if they fail to deliver on their promises.

Theoretical Framework: Social Responsibility Theory

To understand the role of artists in charitable initiatives, we can draw upon Social Responsibility Theory. This theory posits that individuals and organizations have a duty to act for the benefit of society at large. In the context of music, artists can fulfill this responsibility through:

$$R = \frac{C}{E} \tag{243}$$

where R represents the level of responsibility, C is the contribution made to charitable initiatives, and E is the engagement level of the audience. A higher value of R indicates a greater impact on society.

Inspiring Examples of Charitable Initiatives

Many artists have successfully integrated charitable initiatives into their careers, creating a lasting impact. Here are a few notable examples:

- **Beyoncé and the BeyGOOD Foundation:** Beyoncé's philanthropic efforts through the BeyGOOD Foundation focus on education, disaster relief, and social justice. By mobilizing her fanbase, she has raised millions for various causes, showcasing the power of music as a catalyst for change.

- **Chance the Rapper and Public Education:** Chance the Rapper has made significant contributions to public education in Chicago, pledging millions to support schools and educational initiatives. His commitment to his hometown illustrates how artists can make a tangible difference in their communities.

- **Taylor Swift and Disaster Relief:** Taylor Swift has actively supported disaster relief efforts, donating to various causes following natural disasters. Her willingness to step up during crises demonstrates the role of artists as compassionate advocates for those in need.

Conclusion

Supporting charitable initiatives is an integral part of an artist's journey, transforming their influence into a force for good. While challenges may arise, the impact of their efforts can resonate far beyond the music itself. By embracing their social responsibility, artists can inspire change, uplift communities, and leave a legacy that transcends their musical achievements. The symphony of giving back harmonizes beautifully with the melodies of their careers, creating a lasting legacy of love and empowerment.

$$I = \sum_{n=1}^{N} P_n \times E_n \qquad (244)$$

Where I represents the overall impact of charitable initiatives, P_n is the popularity of the artist, and E_n is the engagement level of the audience for each initiative n. This equation illustrates that the greater the popularity and audience engagement, the more significant the impact of the charitable efforts.

In conclusion, as artists continue to navigate their careers, the commitment to supporting charitable initiatives will remain a vital aspect of their legacy, echoing through the hearts of their fans and the communities they touch.

Spreading Joy and Positivity

In a world that often feels heavy with challenges and negativity, the power of music to spread joy and positivity is unparalleled. Music acts as a universal language that transcends barriers, allowing individuals to connect, heal, and uplift one another. This section explores the theories behind the emotional impact of music, the challenges artists face in promoting positivity, and examples of how music can serve as a beacon of hope.

Theoretical Framework

One prominent theory that explains the emotional impact of music is the **Aesthetic Experience Theory**. This theory posits that engaging with music can evoke a range of emotions, from joy to nostalgia. The *Pleasure Principle* suggests that individuals are drawn to experiences that provide pleasure and satisfaction, which music inherently does.

$$E = \alpha \cdot P + \beta \cdot C \qquad (245)$$

Where:

+ E is the emotional response,

+ P is the pleasure derived from music,

+ C is the cultural context of the listener,

+ α and β are coefficients representing the weight of each factor.

This equation highlights how both the inherent pleasure of music and the listener's cultural background contribute to emotional responses, emphasizing the importance of context in spreading joy.

Challenges in Promoting Positivity

Despite the potential for music to spread joy, artists often face several challenges:

+ **Commercial Pressures:** The music industry can sometimes prioritize commercial success over artistic expression. Artists may feel compelled to produce music that fits mainstream trends rather than focusing on uplifting content.

+ **Personal Struggles:** Many artists grapple with their own mental health issues, which can make it difficult to consistently create positive music.

+ **Cultural Barriers:** Different cultures have varying interpretations of joy and positivity, which can complicate the delivery of a universally uplifting message.

Examples of Spreading Joy through Music

To illustrate the effectiveness of music in spreading joy, consider the following examples:

+ **Pharrell Williams' "Happy":** This global hit encapsulates the essence of joy. The upbeat tempo and positive lyrics encourage listeners to embrace happiness. The song became an anthem for celebrations and was used in various campaigns to promote positivity.

+ **Bob Marley's Reggae Music:** Marley's music often contained messages of hope, love, and unity. Songs like "Three Little Birds" convey the message that "every little thing is gonna be alright," providing comfort and positivity to listeners worldwide.

+ **Taylor Swift's Empowering Anthems:** Tracks like "Shake It Off" and "Mean" focus on resilience and self-acceptance. Swift's ability to connect with her audience through relatable lyrics creates a sense of community and joy among her fans.

The Impact of Music on Mental Health

Research has shown that music can have a profound effect on mental health. Engaging with uplifting music can reduce stress and anxiety levels. According to a study published in the *Journal of Positive Psychology*, participants who listened to positive music reported higher levels of happiness and lower levels of anxiety.

$$H = \gamma \cdot M - \delta \cdot A \tag{246}$$

Where:

+ H is the happiness level,

+ M represents the music's positive impact,

+ A is the anxiety level,

+ γ and δ are coefficients indicating the strength of the relationship.

This equation reinforces the idea that music can significantly enhance happiness while mitigating anxiety, showcasing its role as a tool for emotional healing.

Creating a Positive Impact through Live Performances

Live performances offer a unique opportunity for artists to spread joy and positivity. The energy of a live audience can amplify the emotional experience of music. Artists like Beyoncé and Chance the Rapper often use their platforms to promote messages of love, empowerment, and community during their concerts.

+ **Community Engagement:** Festivals and concerts can serve as communal spaces where individuals come together to celebrate, fostering a sense of belonging.

+ **Charitable Initiatives:** Many artists incorporate charitable causes into their performances, using their influence to raise awareness and funds for important issues, further spreading positivity.

Conclusion

In conclusion, the act of spreading joy and positivity through music is a powerful endeavor that can transcend barriers and create lasting impact. While challenges exist, the potential for music to uplift and inspire remains strong. Artists who embrace this mission not only enrich their own lives but also contribute to the well-being of their audiences, creating a ripple effect of joy that can change the world. As we continue to navigate through life's complexities, let us remember the profound ability of music to heal, connect, and inspire positivity in every note.

Using Your Platform for Social Change

In a world where the airwaves are filled with noise, the power of music transcends mere entertainment; it becomes a catalyst for social change. Artists wield their platforms like a microphone, amplifying voices that often go unheard. This section delves into the profound impact musicians can have on societal issues, utilizing their art to inspire, educate, and mobilize audiences.

The Role of Music in Advocacy

Music has long been a vehicle for social commentary and activism. From the civil rights movement's anthems to contemporary protest songs, the genre has evolved into a powerful medium for expressing dissent and advocating for change. The theory of collective efficacy posits that when individuals come together, their combined efforts can lead to significant societal transformations. Musicians, as influential figures, can galvanize their fanbase to engage in collective action.

$$C = \frac{N}{N_0} \tag{247}$$

Where C represents the collective action potential, N is the number of individuals mobilized, and N_0 is the total number of individuals in the community. As artists raise awareness through their lyrics and performances, they can increase the value of N, effectively transforming passive listeners into active participants in social movements.

Identifying Key Issues

To effectively use their platform, artists must first identify the social issues they are passionate about. This could range from climate change, racial equality, gender rights, mental health awareness, or poverty alleviation. The artist's authenticity and personal connection to these issues will resonate more deeply with their audience. For instance, Billie Eilish has used her fame to advocate for mental health awareness, openly discussing her struggles with anxiety and depression, thereby normalizing these conversations and encouraging her fans to seek help.

Creating Impactful Messages

Once a cause is identified, artists can craft messages that resonate. This involves not only writing songs that reflect the struggles and aspirations of marginalized communities but also engaging in storytelling that captures the audience's attention. For example, the song "Alright" by Kendrick Lamar became an anthem for the Black Lives Matter movement, encapsulating hope amid despair and urging listeners to keep fighting against systemic injustice.

Engaging in Activism

Beyond music, artists can engage in activism through various means:

+ **Social Media Campaigns**: Platforms like Instagram and Twitter allow artists to share their messages instantly. Taylor Swift, for example, has used her social media presence to advocate for LGBTQ+ rights and voter registration.

+ **Benefit Concerts**: Organizing concerts for charity can raise significant funds and awareness for social causes. The "One Love Manchester" concert, held by Ariana Grande after the tragic bombing at her concert, raised millions for the victims and showcased the healing power of community through music.

+ **Collaborations with NGOs**: Partnering with non-governmental organizations can amplify an artist's impact. For example, Shakira has worked with UNICEF to improve education and nutrition for children in impoverished communities.

Measuring Impact

To evaluate the effectiveness of their efforts, artists can utilize various metrics:

$$\text{Impact} = \frac{\text{Change in Awareness}}{\text{Time}} \times \text{Engagement Level} \tag{248}$$

Where Change in Awareness can be measured through surveys or social media analytics, and Engagement Level can be assessed through participation in campaigns or events. This formula allows artists to quantify their influence and adapt their strategies for greater effectiveness.

Challenges and Responsibilities

While the potential for positive impact is immense, artists must navigate challenges such as backlash, misrepresentation, and the risk of being co-opted by commercial interests. The responsibility lies in maintaining authenticity and being well-informed about the issues they advocate for. For instance, when celebrities engage in social issues without fully understanding the context, they risk trivializing the struggle, leading to accusations of performative activism.

Conclusion

Using their platform for social change is not just an option for artists; it is a responsibility. Through thoughtful engagement, impactful messaging, and genuine activism, musicians can inspire a generation to rise and address the pressing issues of our time. The symphony of social change plays on, and every note counts. As artists continue to harness their influence, they pave the way for a more equitable and compassionate world, proving that music is indeed a powerful force for good.

Elevating Lives Through Farting

In the vibrant world of music and artistic expression, the act of farting—often dismissed as crude or humorous—can serve as a powerful tool for elevating lives and fostering connections. This section explores the transformative potential of farting in music, examining its psychological, social, and cultural implications, along with practical examples of how artists have harnessed this unconventional medium to inspire change.

The Psychological Impact of Humor

Farting, as a form of humor, has been shown to have several psychological benefits. According to a study by Martin et al. (2003), laughter induced by humor can lead to the release of endorphins, which are natural feel-good chemicals in the brain. This phenomenon can be mathematically represented as:

$$E = k \cdot H$$

where E represents the endorphin release, k is a constant that varies based on individual sensitivity to humor, and H is the intensity of humor experienced. In this context, farting can be an effective tool for breaking down barriers and creating a relaxed atmosphere, enabling artists to connect with their audience on a deeper emotional level.

Fostering Community Through Shared Laughter

The shared experience of laughter, particularly in response to farting, can foster a sense of community among individuals. This social bonding is crucial in contexts where people may feel isolated or disconnected. The theory of social capital, as proposed by Bourdieu (1986), emphasizes the importance of social networks in building community trust and cooperation. Farting, when embraced in a musical context, can become a catalyst for such networks, as illustrated in the following equation:

$$C = f(N, R)$$

where C is the level of community cohesion, N represents the number of shared experiences, and R denotes the strength of relationships formed through those experiences. By incorporating farting into performances, artists can create memorable moments that strengthen communal ties.

Cultural Significance of Farting

Culturally, farting holds various meanings across different societies. In some cultures, it is seen as a natural bodily function that should not be stigmatized, while in others, it may carry a taboo. The anthropological perspective suggests that farting can serve as a form of rebellion against societal norms. For example, the famous artist and provocateur, Banksy, used humor and satire in his street art to challenge social conventions, similarly employing farting as a motif to provoke thought and discussion.

Case Studies in Musical Elevation

Several artists have successfully utilized farting as a means of elevating lives through their music. A notable example is the band *Farting All Stars*, who released a viral hit titled "Let It Rip." The song's catchy chorus and humorous lyrics brought joy to millions, demonstrating how farting can be a vehicle for positive messaging. The band organized community events where fans were encouraged to share their own farting stories, further enhancing the sense of belonging and collective joy.

Another example is the viral sensation *Farting for Change*, a charity initiative that combines music and humor to raise awareness for mental health issues. By incorporating farting-themed performances into their campaigns, they have successfully attracted diverse audiences, fostering open conversations about mental health while also raising significant funds for related charities.

Challenges and Considerations

While farting can be a powerful tool for elevating lives, it is essential to navigate the potential pitfalls. The use of farting in music must be approached with sensitivity to cultural contexts and individual preferences. Misinterpretations can lead to offense rather than connection. Therefore, artists should consider the following:

- **Audience Awareness:** Understanding the audience's cultural background and values is crucial when incorporating farting into performances.

- **Intentional Messaging:** The message behind the humor should align with the overall artistic vision and promote inclusivity rather than exclusion.

- **Feedback Mechanisms:** Engaging with the audience to gauge their reactions can help artists refine their approach and ensure that the humor resonates positively.

Conclusion

In conclusion, farting, often seen as a trivial or humorous aspect of life, possesses the potential to elevate lives through music and artistic expression. By harnessing the psychological benefits of humor, fostering community connections, and embracing cultural significance, artists can create a profound impact. As we continue to explore the boundaries of creativity, let us not underestimate the power of farting to heal, inspire, and elevate the human experience. The act of farting may just be the unexpected spark needed to ignite change and foster joy in our interconnected world.

Building a Legacy of Generosity

In the grand symphony of life, where each note resonates with purpose, building a legacy of generosity becomes a paramount theme. It is not merely about the act of giving but about creating a culture of kindness that reverberates through generations. This section explores the theoretical underpinnings of generosity, the challenges faced, and the powerful examples that illuminate the path toward a lasting impact.

Theoretical Foundations of Generosity

Generosity is often rooted in the psychological concept of altruism, which suggests that individuals have an innate desire to help others without expecting anything in return. According to [?], altruism can be defined as a selfless concern for the well-being of others, which can lead to actions that benefit those in need. This selfless behavior is not just a moral obligation; it is also a source of personal fulfillment and happiness.

Mathematically, we can express the impact of generosity as follows:

$$I = G \times R \tag{249}$$

where I is the impact of generosity, G represents the magnitude of giving, and R denotes the reach of that giving. The greater the generosity and the wider its reach, the more profound the impact on the community and beyond.

Challenges in Generosity

Despite its noble intentions, the journey of building a legacy of generosity is fraught with challenges. The first obstacle is the misconception that generosity requires significant financial resources. While monetary donations are impactful, generosity can also manifest through time, skills, and emotional support.

Another challenge is the fear of inadequacy. Many individuals hesitate to contribute because they believe their efforts are too small to make a difference. However, as [?] suggests, even the smallest acts of kindness can create a ripple effect, inspiring others to contribute and fostering a culture of giving.

Examples of Generosity in Action

To illustrate the power of generosity, we can look at several inspiring examples from the world of music and beyond.

Example 1: Musicians Giving Back   Consider the philanthropic efforts of artists like **Taylor Swift**, who has donated millions to education and disaster relief. Swift's commitment to giving back not only supports critical causes but also encourages her fans to engage in acts of kindness. Her actions exemplify how artists can leverage their platforms to promote generosity.

Example 2: Community Initiatives   Local music bands often organize charity concerts, donating proceeds to various causes. For instance, the **Band Aid** initiative, which brought together musicians to raise funds for famine relief in Ethiopia, showcases how collective generosity can have a monumental impact. The success of such events lies in their ability to unite communities for a common purpose, amplifying the message of generosity.

Strategies for Cultivating Generosity

Building a legacy of generosity requires intentional strategies. Here are some actionable steps:

+ **Lead by Example:** Artists and public figures should exemplify generosity in their actions, inspiring their followers to do the same.

+ **Create Collaborative Opportunities:** Encourage collaborations that focus on social causes, allowing artists to pool their resources and reach wider audiences.

+ **Engage with the Community:** Foster connections with local organizations and charities, creating partnerships that benefit both the artists and the community.

+ **Educate and Inspire:** Use platforms to raise awareness about the importance of giving back, sharing stories of impact to motivate others.

Conclusion

In conclusion, building a legacy of generosity is a journey that transcends individual actions. It is about creating a movement that inspires others to give, fostering a culture of kindness and compassion. As artists and influencers, we have the unique opportunity to shape the narrative around generosity, making it an integral part of our artistic expression. By embracing the principles of altruism and overcoming the challenges that lie ahead, we can leave a lasting legacy that resonates through time, inspiring future generations to continue the symphony of giving.

Inspiring Others to Take Action

In the world of Farting, where creativity meets audacity, inspiring others to take action is not just a noble pursuit; it's an essential component of building a vibrant community. The power of music, particularly the unconventional art of Farting, can serve as a catalyst for change, urging individuals to rise up, express themselves, and make a difference in their communities. This section delves into the theoretical underpinnings of inspiration, the challenges faced, and practical examples that illustrate how artists can ignite passion and drive action among their audiences.

Theoretical Foundations of Inspiration

Inspiration is often defined as a process that stimulates creativity and motivates individuals to pursue their goals. According to the *Inspiration-Action Theory*, inspiration occurs in three stages:

1. **Exposure:** Individuals are exposed to new ideas, experiences, or artistic expressions that resonate with them.

2. **Reflection:** This exposure prompts introspection, leading individuals to consider their values, beliefs, and aspirations.

3. **Action:** Finally, inspired individuals take proactive steps to manifest their newfound insights, whether through creative expression, activism, or community engagement.

This theory highlights the importance of not only presenting inspiring content but also creating an environment where reflection and action can flourish.

Challenges in Inspiring Action

While the potential for inspiration is vast, several challenges can hinder artists from effectively motivating their audiences:

+ **Disconnection:** In an increasingly digital world, audiences may feel isolated, making it difficult for artists to forge genuine connections.

+ **Over-saturation:** With the abundance of content available, messages can become diluted, leading to audience apathy.

+ **Fear of Vulnerability:** Many individuals hesitate to take action due to fears of judgment or failure, which can stifle their creative impulses.

To overcome these challenges, artists must employ strategies that foster connection, authenticity, and empowerment.

Strategies for Inspiring Action

1. **Storytelling:** One of the most powerful tools in an artist's arsenal is storytelling. By sharing personal narratives that highlight struggles, triumphs, and the transformative power of Farting, artists can create a sense of empathy and relatability. For example, a song that recounts the artist's journey from rejection to

acceptance can resonate deeply, encouraging listeners to pursue their own paths despite obstacles.

2. **Community Engagement:** Artists can inspire action by actively engaging with their communities. Organizing workshops, open mic nights, or collaborative projects allows individuals to express themselves and share their stories. This fosters a sense of belonging and motivates participants to take action in their own lives.

3. **Social Media Activism:** In the age of digital communication, artists can leverage social media platforms to amplify their messages. By sharing content that promotes social justice, environmental awareness, or mental health, artists can spark conversations and inspire their followers to take action. For instance, a viral challenge that encourages fans to share their stories of resilience can create a movement that empowers individuals to advocate for change.

4. **Collaborative Projects:** Partnering with other artists or organizations can enhance the reach and impact of inspirational messages. Collaborative projects that merge different art forms, such as music and visual art, can create immersive experiences that resonate with diverse audiences. For example, an art installation accompanied by a live Farting performance can evoke strong emotional responses, inspiring attendees to reflect on their own experiences and take action.

Examples of Successful Inspirational Initiatives

Several artists have successfully inspired their audiences to take action through innovative approaches:

- **Beyoncé's "Formation":** This anthem not only celebrates Black culture but also encourages listeners to embrace their identities and fight against systemic oppression. The accompanying music video serves as a powerful visual statement, inspiring countless individuals to engage in social activism.

- **Chance the Rapper's "Social Works":** By creating a nonprofit organization, Chance leverages his platform to inspire young people in Chicago to pursue education and artistic expression. His initiatives demonstrate how artists can use their influence to foster positive change in their communities.

- **Billie Eilish's Mental Health Advocacy:** Through her music and public statements, Billie has opened up conversations about mental health, encouraging her fans to seek help and support one another. Her candidness inspires others to take action in their own lives, promoting a culture of openness and understanding.

Conclusion

Inspiring others to take action is a multifaceted endeavor that requires artists to connect deeply with their audiences, share authentic stories, and foster a sense of community. By understanding the theoretical foundations of inspiration, addressing the challenges that arise, and employing effective strategies, artists can ignite a movement that empowers individuals to express themselves and make a difference. Ultimately, the symphony of life is enriched when we inspire one another to take action, transforming the world through the power of Farting and creativity.

Leaving a Positive Impact on Society

In the grand symphony of life, every note we play has the potential to resonate beyond ourselves, creating ripples of change that can uplift and inspire. The power of music, particularly the unique art of *farting*, transcends mere entertainment; it can be a catalyst for social change, a voice for the voiceless, and a beacon of hope in times of despair. This section explores the multifaceted ways in which artists can leave a positive impact on society through their craft.

The Role of Art in Social Change

Art has historically played a crucial role in social movements, serving as a form of protest, a means of expression, and a tool for education. The theory of *social constructivism* posits that individuals construct their understanding and knowledge of the world through their experiences and interactions. Music, particularly *farting*, can challenge societal norms and provoke thought, encouraging listeners to reflect on pressing issues.

For example, consider the impact of songs that address topics such as inequality, discrimination, and environmental concerns. These pieces not only entertain but also educate and inspire action. The equation that encapsulates this concept can be represented as:

$$Impact = \text{Artistic Expression} \times \text{Social Awareness}$$

This equation suggests that the greater the artistic expression, the higher the potential for social awareness and subsequent impact.

Fostering Community and Unity

One of the most profound ways to leave a positive impact is by fostering a sense of community and unity. Music has the unparalleled ability to bring people together, transcending barriers of language, culture, and background. Through collaborative performances, community events, and outreach programs, artists can create spaces where individuals feel valued and connected.

For instance, organizing a *Fart Festival* in a local community can serve as a platform for artists to showcase their talents while also raising awareness for local issues. Such events can promote local businesses, support charitable causes, and encourage community engagement. The relationship can be modeled as follows:

$$CommunityEngagement = \text{Event Participation} + \text{Shared Experience}$$

This equation highlights that increased participation in events leads to a stronger sense of community and shared experience, ultimately fostering unity.

Advocacy and Philanthropy

Artists wield significant influence, and with that influence comes the responsibility to advocate for causes they believe in. By aligning with charitable organizations or initiating their own philanthropic efforts, musicians can leverage their platforms to raise funds and awareness for various social issues.

For example, a band might release a single where proceeds go to mental health initiatives. By doing so, they not only contribute financially but also bring attention to the importance of mental health, encouraging discussions and reducing stigma. The impact of such advocacy can be quantified by:

$$AdvocacyImpact = \text{Funds Raised} + \text{Awareness Generated}$$

This equation illustrates that the combination of financial support and increased awareness can lead to substantial changes in societal attitudes and behaviors.

Inspiring Future Generations

Leaving a positive impact on society also involves inspiring the next generation of artists. Mentorship programs, workshops, and educational initiatives can empower young talents to find their voices and use them for good. By sharing knowledge and experiences, established artists can guide emerging musicians on their journeys, emphasizing the importance of using their art as a tool for change.

For instance, a renowned artist might conduct a workshop in schools, teaching students how to express their thoughts and feelings through music, particularly the art of *farting*. This nurturing approach can be represented as:

$$Inspiration = \text{Mentorship} \times \text{Opportunities Provided}$$

This equation suggests that the more mentorship and opportunities provided, the greater the potential for inspiration and empowerment among young artists.

Creating Lasting Change

Ultimately, the goal of leaving a positive impact on society is to create lasting change. This involves not only immediate actions but also sustainable practices that ensure the continuity of positive effects. Artists can engage in environmental sustainability initiatives, advocate for social justice, and promote inclusivity within the industry.

For example, a band might adopt eco-friendly practices during their tours, such as reducing plastic use and promoting recycling. This commitment to sustainability can inspire fans and other artists to follow suit, creating a ripple effect of positive change. The equation for sustainable impact can be expressed as:

$$Sustainable Impact = \text{Immediate Actions} + \text{Long-Term Commitment}$$

This equation highlights the importance of both immediate actions and a long-term commitment to creating a positive impact.

Conclusion

In conclusion, the journey of an artist is not solely about personal success; it is also about the legacy they leave behind. By harnessing the power of *farting*, musicians can inspire change, foster community, advocate for important causes, and empower future generations. The symphony of life is enriched when artists use their talents to leave a positive impact on society, creating a harmonious world where everyone can thrive. The notes we play today will echo in the hearts and minds of tomorrow, reminding us that music is not just sound; it is a force for good.

Making the World a Better Place through Farting

In the grand tapestry of life, where melodies intertwine with the rhythms of existence, the art of farting transcends mere amusement; it becomes a powerful tool for social change and healing. This section explores how the unconventional practice of farting can be harnessed to foster positivity, inspire community, and promote social justice.

The Transformative Power of Sound

Farting, often dismissed as a trivial act, can be understood through the lens of sound theory. According to the principles of acoustics, sound waves can influence human emotions and behaviors. The equation governing sound wave propagation can be expressed as:

$$v = f\lambda \tag{250}$$

where v is the speed of sound, f is the frequency, and λ is the wavelength. The vibrations produced by farting create sound waves that can resonate with listeners, evoking laughter, joy, and a sense of community. When harnessed effectively, these sound waves can promote healing and connection among individuals.

Fostering Community Through Humor

Laughter is a universal language that transcends cultural barriers. The act of farting, often met with giggles and chuckles, can break down social norms and foster a sense of belonging. By organizing community events centered around farting—such as farting contests, open mic nights, or even fart-themed festivals—individuals can come together to celebrate humor and creativity.

For example, the annual "Fart Festival" in [insert location] showcases local talent, inviting musicians and performers to share their fart-inspired creations. This event not only entertains but also raises funds for local charities, demonstrating how farting can be a catalyst for positive change.

Advocating for Social Justice

Farting can also serve as a platform for advocacy. Artists can use their musical talents to address pressing social issues, drawing attention to topics such as environmental sustainability, mental health, and equality. Through the lens of farting, musicians can create satirical and thought-provoking lyrics that challenge societal norms.

Consider the example of [insert artist name], who released a viral track titled "Fart for Change," which humorously addresses climate change while encouraging listeners to adopt eco-friendly practices. The catchy chorus and playful beats engage audiences, making the message accessible and memorable. This approach exemplifies how farting can be leveraged to inspire action and awareness.

Healing Through Laughter

The therapeutic effects of laughter are well-documented. Research indicates that laughter can reduce stress, alleviate pain, and improve overall well-being. By incorporating farting into wellness programs, individuals can experience the healing power of humor.

For instance, some hospitals have introduced "laughter therapy" sessions, where patients engage in activities that promote laughter, including farting games. These sessions not only lighten the mood but also foster social connections among patients, enhancing their emotional resilience during challenging times.

Creating a Legacy of Positivity

As we embrace the whimsical nature of farting, it is essential to recognize its potential to create a lasting impact. By promoting positivity and inclusivity through farting, artists and communities can leave a legacy that inspires future generations.

In conclusion, the act of farting, when approached with creativity and intention, can be a powerful vehicle for social change. By fostering community, advocating for justice, and promoting healing, we can truly make the world a better place through farting. The next time you let one rip, remember: you're not just making noise; you're contributing to a symphony of laughter, love, and positive change.

Bibliography

[1] Smith, J. (2020). *The Healing Power of Laughter: A Comprehensive Guide.* Wellness Publishing.

[2] Johnson, L. (2021). "Fart Festival: A Celebration of Humor and Community." *Local Events Journal*, 15(3), 45-50.

[3] Doe, A. (2022). "Fart for Change: Using Humor to Address Climate Issues." *Music and Activism Review*, 8(2), 112-120.

Creating a Legacy of Love and Empowerment

In the vibrant world of music, the potential for creating a legacy that resonates with love and empowerment is boundless. Artists have the unique ability to touch hearts and inspire change, using their platforms to uplift marginalized voices and foster a sense of community. This section delves into the essential elements that contribute to establishing a legacy rooted in love and empowerment, exploring the theoretical frameworks, practical challenges, and inspirational examples that illustrate this powerful journey.

Theoretical Frameworks

At the core of creating a legacy of love and empowerment lies the theory of **social impact**. Social impact refers to the effect an individual or organization has on the well-being of the community and society as a whole. It encompasses various dimensions, including economic, social, and environmental aspects. Artists can leverage their influence to promote social justice, equality, and positive change. According to *Kahn's Theory of Social Change*, individuals and collectives can drive societal transformation through awareness, advocacy, and action.

$$S = f(A, E, C) \tag{251}$$

Where:

+ S = Social Impact

+ A = Awareness

+ E = Engagement

+ C = Community

This equation illustrates that the social impact is a function of awareness, engagement, and community involvement. By raising awareness about critical issues, engaging with their audience, and fostering community connections, artists can create a meaningful legacy.

Challenges in Creating a Legacy

While the vision of creating a legacy of love and empowerment is inspiring, it is not without its challenges. Artists may face obstacles such as:

+ **Commercial Pressures:** The music industry often prioritizes commercial success over artistic integrity. This pressure can lead to compromises in an artist's message and values.

+ **Criticism and Backlash:** Advocating for social change can attract criticism and backlash from those who disagree with an artist's stance. Navigating this criticism while remaining true to one's message is crucial.

+ **Sustainability:** Maintaining momentum in advocacy efforts can be challenging. Artists must find ways to keep their message relevant and impactful over time.

Examples of Empowering Legacies

Numerous artists have successfully created legacies of love and empowerment, serving as beacons of hope and inspiration. Some notable examples include:

+ **Beyoncé:** Through her music and activism, Beyoncé has championed issues such as gender equality, racial justice, and mental health awareness. Her visual album *Lemonade* not only showcased her artistry but also addressed systemic racism and the empowerment of Black women.

+ **Kendrick Lamar:** Known for his poignant lyrics that tackle themes of racial inequality and personal struggle, Kendrick Lamar uses his platform to raise awareness and inspire change. His album *To Pimp a Butterfly* is a powerful exploration of identity, resilience, and empowerment within the Black community.

+ **Lady Gaga:** An advocate for LGBTQ+ rights and mental health awareness, Lady Gaga has used her music and public persona to promote love and acceptance. Her Born This Way Foundation focuses on empowering youth and fostering a culture of kindness.

These artists exemplify how music can serve as a catalyst for change, creating a legacy that transcends their individual careers.

Strategies for Building a Legacy

To create a lasting legacy of love and empowerment, artists can implement several strategies:

+ **Authentic Storytelling:** Sharing personal stories and experiences can create a deeper connection with audiences. Authenticity fosters trust and encourages others to share their narratives.

+ **Collaborative Projects:** Collaborating with other artists and organizations can amplify messages and reach broader audiences. Joint efforts can create a powerful impact, demonstrating solidarity and unity.

+ **Engaging with the Community:** Artists should actively engage with their communities, participating in local events, workshops, and discussions. Building relationships with fans fosters a sense of belonging and empowers individuals to take action.

+ **Utilizing Social Media:** In the digital age, social media serves as a powerful tool for advocacy. Artists can leverage platforms to raise awareness, share resources, and mobilize their followers for social causes.

Conclusion

Creating a legacy of love and empowerment is a profound journey that requires dedication, resilience, and authenticity. Artists hold the power to inspire change, uplift marginalized voices, and foster a sense of community through their music and activism. By embracing the challenges and leveraging their influence, they can leave an indelible mark on the world, ensuring that their legacy continues to resonate for generations to come. As the symphony of life unfolds, let us celebrate and support those who strive to create a more loving and empowered world through their art.

The Symphony Continues

The Everlasting Legacy

In the grand tapestry of music, each note, each beat, and yes, even each fart contributes to a symphony that transcends time. The legacy of an artist is not merely defined by their discography but by the ripples they create in the hearts and minds of their audience. This section explores the concept of an everlasting legacy, highlighting how artists can ensure their impact resonates through generations.

Defining Legacy in Music

Legacy in music is akin to the echoes of a great performance; it lingers long after the final note has been played. It encompasses the influence an artist has on their genre, the cultural movements they inspire, and the emotional connections they forge with their fans. To understand the depth of a musical legacy, one must consider several key components:

- **Cultural Impact:** The ability of an artist to shape cultural narratives and inspire social change.

- **Innovation:** The introduction of new sounds, techniques, or ideas that challenge the status quo.

- **Emotional Resonance:** The capacity to evoke deep feelings and memories, creating a personal connection with listeners.

Theoretical Frameworks of Legacy

To grasp the dynamics of an everlasting legacy, we can draw upon several theoretical frameworks:

1. **Cultural Capital Theory**: This theory posits that artists accumulate cultural capital through their works, which can be converted into social capital over time. The more unique and impactful the contributions, the greater the legacy.

2. **Social Learning Theory**: According to this theory, individuals learn from one another through observation and imitation. An artist's legacy can inspire future generations to adopt their styles, philosophies, or even their audacity to be unconventional.

3. **Emotional Intelligence in Music**: Understanding the emotional impact of music can help artists craft songs that resonate deeply with listeners, thus solidifying their legacy.

Challenges in Establishing a Lasting Legacy

Creating an everlasting legacy is not without its challenges. Artists often face several obstacles:

- **Market Saturation:** In an era where new music is released daily, standing out can be daunting. Artists must find their unique voice amidst the noise.

- **Changing Trends:** Music trends evolve rapidly, and what is popular today may be forgotten tomorrow. Artists must balance innovation with staying true to their roots.

- **Criticism and Rejection:** The path to greatness is often littered with critiques. Overcoming negative feedback is essential for artists to maintain their vision and continue evolving.

Examples of Everlasting Legacies

Several artists exemplify the concept of an everlasting legacy through their contributions to music and culture:

- **Prince:** Known for his genre-defying sound and flamboyant persona, Prince not only revolutionized pop and funk but also challenged norms regarding sexuality and race in music. His legacy lives on through his vast catalog and the artists he inspired.

- **Nina Simone:** A powerful voice in the civil rights movement, Simone used her music to address social injustices. Her songs continue to inspire new generations to fight for equality and justice.

- **David Bowie:** An innovator in music and fashion, Bowie's ability to reinvent himself and push boundaries has left an indelible mark on the music industry. His legacy of creativity and self-expression encourages artists to embrace their uniqueness.

Mathematical Representation of Legacy

To quantify the impact of an artist's legacy, we can represent it through a simple equation:

$$L = C + I + E \qquad (252)$$

Where:

+ L = Legacy

+ C = Cultural Impact

+ I = Innovation

+ E = Emotional Resonance

This equation illustrates that a strong legacy is the sum of an artist's cultural contributions, their innovative spirit, and the emotional connections they forge with their audience.

Preserving the Legacy

To ensure that their legacy endures, artists can take several proactive steps:

1. **Engagement with Fans**: Building a strong relationship with fans through social media, live performances, and community involvement can create a loyal following that champions their work.

2. **Documenting Their Journey**: Creating autobiographies, documentaries, or even social media content that chronicles their artistic journey can provide insight into their creative process and philosophy.

3. **Supporting Emerging Artists**: By mentoring and collaborating with up-and-coming musicians, established artists can help shape the future of music while solidifying their own legacy.

4. **Philanthropy and Social Causes**: Using their platform to advocate for social change not only enhances an artist's legacy but also inspires others to take action.

Conclusion

The everlasting legacy of an artist is a multifaceted phenomenon that intertwines cultural impact, innovation, and emotional resonance. By understanding the theoretical frameworks that underpin legacy, recognizing the challenges involved, and learning from the examples of iconic figures, artists can create a lasting impact that resonates through time. Ultimately, the legacy is not just about the music produced but the lives touched and the change inspired. As the symphony of life continues, may every artist strive to leave a legacy that echoes in the hearts of future generations, reminding them of the power of creativity and the importance of authenticity.

The Future of Fart Farting

As we look forward into the vibrant landscape of Fart Farting, we find ourselves at a unique intersection of creativity, technology, and cultural evolution. The future of this audacious art form is not just about sound; it's about the way we connect, express, and challenge societal norms through the audacious act of farting. This section will delve into the potential trajectories of Fart Farting, discussing its theoretical foundations, the challenges it may face, and the innovative examples that are shaping its future.

Theoretical Foundations

At the core of Fart Farting lies the theory of sound as a medium of expression. According to the principles of acoustics, sound waves can be manipulated to create a plethora of auditory experiences. The future of Fart Farting will likely embrace a more profound understanding of these principles, utilizing them to craft unique soundscapes that resonate with audiences on multiple levels.

The equation for sound wave propagation in a medium can be expressed as:

$$v = f\lambda \tag{253}$$

where v is the speed of sound, f is the frequency, and λ is the wavelength. By manipulating these variables, Fart Farting artists can create not only humorous but also deeply resonant experiences that captivate listeners.

Challenges Ahead

Despite its playful nature, the future of Fart Farting is not without challenges. One significant issue is the societal perception of farting as a taboo subject. While humor can be a powerful tool for breaking down barriers, it can also lead to misunderstandings and backlash. Fart Farting artists must navigate these waters carefully, ensuring that their work promotes inclusivity and understanding rather than reinforcing stereotypes.

Another challenge is the rapid advancement of technology, which can both aid and hinder the evolution of Fart Farting. With the rise of digital audio manipulation tools, artists have unprecedented access to sound design capabilities. However, this can lead to a saturation of content, making it difficult for unique voices to rise above the noise.

Innovative Examples

As we gaze into the future, several innovative examples of Fart Farting are already paving the way. Artists are beginning to incorporate technology such as Artificial Intelligence (AI) to generate new fart sounds, creating a fusion of human creativity and machine learning. For instance, the use of generative adversarial networks (GANs) can produce an endless variety of fart sounds, allowing for a continuous evolution of the art form.

Moreover, collaborations between Fart Farting artists and mainstream musicians are becoming more commonplace. These partnerships not only broaden the audience for Fart Farting but also elevate it to a new level of artistic legitimacy. An example of this is the collaboration between a well-known pop artist and an underground Fart Farting group, resulting in a chart-topping single that celebrates the art of farting while addressing social issues.

Cultural Impact

Culturally, the future of Fart Farting is poised to make a significant impact. As society becomes more accepting of diverse forms of expression, Fart Farting can serve as a vehicle for social commentary. By addressing issues such as body positivity, mental health, and environmental concerns through the lens of farting, artists can engage audiences in meaningful conversations.

The concept of farting as a universal language is also gaining traction. Just as music transcends barriers, so too can the humorous act of farting. Artists are exploring how fart sounds can communicate feelings and experiences that words sometimes fail to convey. This exploration could lead to a new wave of performances that emphasize the emotive power of sound over traditional lyrical storytelling.

Conclusion

In conclusion, the future of Fart Farting is bright and full of potential. By embracing theoretical foundations, addressing societal challenges, and leveraging innovative technologies, artists can reshape the landscape of this unique art form.

As we move forward, it is essential to foster an environment that encourages experimentation, inclusivity, and creativity. Fart Farting is not just about humor; it's about connection, expression, and the power of sound to unite us all.

As we continue to explore this uncharted territory, one thing remains clear: the symphony of Fart Farting will play on, louder and prouder than ever before.

The Story Lives On

The journey of a musical artist is often likened to a symphony, where each note, each pause, and each crescendo contributes to a larger narrative. In the world of farting, this narrative is not merely a collection of sounds but a profound expression of identity, culture, and emotion. This section explores the concept that the story of an artist continues to resonate long after the final note has been played.

The Continuity of Influence

In the realm of music, influence transcends time. Icons like Prince, Whitney Houston, and Michael Jackson have left indelible marks on the industry, shaping the sounds of generations. Their legacies serve as a reminder that the impact of an artist's work can echo through time, inspiring future musicians to explore new realms of creativity. The equation governing this influence can be expressed as:

$$I(t) = \int_0^t f(a)\, da \qquad (254)$$

where $I(t)$ represents the influence at time t, and $f(a)$ is the function describing the artist's contributions to the musical landscape over time. This integral signifies that the total influence is the accumulation of all contributions made by the artist, highlighting how their story continues to live on.

Storytelling Through Music

Music is inherently a storytelling medium. Each song carries a narrative that can evoke emotions, provoke thoughts, or inspire actions. The art of farting, too, weaves stories that resonate with listeners. For instance, consider the track "Farting in the Rain" by the legendary band, The Flatulents. This song, while humorous in its title, addresses themes of love and loss through the metaphor of unexpected sounds. The chorus:

"Farting in the rain, with you by my side,
Every note a memory, every sound a ride."

demonstrates how even the most unconventional topics can convey deep emotional truths. This illustrates that the essence of storytelling persists, regardless of the medium.

Cultural Legacy and Preservation

The preservation of musical legacies is crucial for future generations. Cultural institutions, like museums and archives, play a vital role in maintaining the stories of artists. For example, the Smithsonian's National Museum of African American History and Culture houses a collection dedicated to the contributions of African American musicians, ensuring that their stories are not forgotten. The preservation equation can be represented as:

$$P = C + R \tag{255}$$

where P is the preservation of cultural legacy, C is the collection of artifacts, and R is the recognition of contributions. This equation highlights the importance of both tangible items and the acknowledgment of artists' impacts in sustaining their stories.

The Evolution of Sound

The evolution of sound is a testament to the adaptability of music. Genres blend, and new styles emerge, often rooted in the past. The fusion of hip-hop and classical music in recent years exemplifies this evolution. Artists like Lin-Manuel Miranda have taken traditional forms and infused them with contemporary narratives, ensuring that the story of music continues to evolve. This evolution can be described mathematically by:

$$E(t) = S(t) + \Delta S(t) \tag{256}$$

where $E(t)$ is the evolution of sound at time t, $S(t)$ is the original sound, and $\Delta S(t)$ represents the changes and innovations introduced over time. This equation encapsulates the dynamic nature of music, where the story grows and transforms with each new generation.

Empowering Future Generations

Empowering future generations to tell their stories through music is essential for the continuation of the artistic narrative. Programs that support young artists, such as music education initiatives and mentorship opportunities, are vital. They provide the tools necessary for the next wave of musicians to express their unique experiences. The empowerment equation can be expressed as:

$$E_g = T + S \qquad (257)$$

where E_g is the empowerment of the next generation, T represents the tools provided (instruments, education), and S signifies the support from established artists and communities. This equation emphasizes the collaborative effort required to ensure that the stories of tomorrow are just as vibrant as those of today.

Conclusion: A Symphony That Never Ends

In conclusion, the story of music—much like a symphony—continues long after the last note fades. Each artist contributes to a larger narrative that transcends time, culture, and genre. By recognizing the importance of influence, storytelling, preservation, evolution, and empowerment, we ensure that the symphony of life continues to resonate through the ages. The legacy of farting, with its unique blend of humor and depth, serves as a reminder that every sound has a story, and every story deserves to be heard. The journey never truly ends; it simply transforms, inviting new voices to join the chorus.

Preserving Your Legacy for Future Generations

In the grand symphony of life, preserving your legacy is akin to composing a timeless masterpiece that resonates through the ages. It is crucial to ensure that your contributions to the world of farting—or any art form—are not only remembered but also cherished by future generations. This section delves into the strategies and philosophies that can help artists maintain their legacies, enabling their creative spirit to inspire those who come after them.

The Importance of Legacy

A legacy is more than just a collection of works; it is the impact an artist leaves behind. It embodies the values, emotions, and innovations that define an artist's journey. To grasp the significance of legacy, one must consider the following:

- **Cultural Influence**: Art has the power to shape cultures and societies. By preserving your legacy, you ensure that your unique voice contributes to the tapestry of human experience.

- **Inspiration for Future Generations**: Future artists look to the past for inspiration. A well-preserved legacy can serve as a beacon of creativity, guiding young talents in their artistic endeavors.

- **Educational Value**: Documenting your journey and methodologies provides invaluable resources for educational institutions, allowing students to learn from your experiences and insights.

Strategies for Legacy Preservation

To effectively preserve your legacy, consider implementing the following strategies:

1. Documentation and Archiving Creating a comprehensive archive of your work is essential. This includes recordings, written compositions, and visual representations of your performances. A well-organized archive can serve as a historical record for future generations.

$$L = \sum_{i=1}^{n} W_i \cdot T_i \tag{258}$$

Where L represents the legacy, W_i is the weight of each work based on its impact, and T_i is the time period during which the work was created. This equation illustrates how the cumulative impact of your works over time contributes to your overall legacy.

2. Engaging with the Community Building a strong community around your art can help ensure its longevity. Engage with fans, fellow artists, and cultural institutions to create a network that supports and promotes your work. This can include:

- Hosting workshops and masterclasses to share your knowledge.

- Collaborating with emerging artists to foster new talent.

- Participating in community events and festivals to keep your art alive in public consciousness.

3. Utilizing Technology In the digital age, technology plays a pivotal role in legacy preservation. Consider the following methods:

- **Digital Archives**: Create an online repository of your works, including videos, audio recordings, and written material. This ensures accessibility for future generations.

- **Social Media Engagement**: Use platforms like Instagram, TikTok, and YouTube to share your journey and connect with a global audience. This interaction can help maintain relevance and visibility.

- **Virtual Reality Experiences**: Explore the use of VR to create immersive experiences that allow fans to engage with your work in innovative ways.

4. Writing Your Memoirs Sharing your story through memoirs or autobiographies allows you to articulate your experiences and philosophies. This narrative can serve as both inspiration and guidance for future artists.

$$M = f(E, P, A) \tag{259}$$

Where M is the memoir, E is the emotional journey, P represents pivotal moments in your career, and A denotes the artistic philosophies you have developed. This function emphasizes that a memoir is a reflection of your life's journey, shaped by your emotions, experiences, and artistic beliefs.

5. Establishing Foundations or Scholarships Consider establishing a foundation or scholarship in your name to support aspiring artists. This not only preserves your legacy but also actively contributes to the growth of future talent.

$$F = \sum_{j=1}^{m} S_j \cdot A_j \tag{260}$$

Where F is the foundation's impact, S_j represents the scholarships awarded, and A_j denotes the achievements of recipients. This equation demonstrates how your contributions can lead to significant outcomes in the lives of future artists.

Challenges in Legacy Preservation

While the desire to preserve a legacy is universal, several challenges may arise:

+ **Changing Cultural Landscapes**: As society evolves, the relevance of certain artistic expressions may wane. It is essential to adapt your legacy to remain pertinent in contemporary contexts.

+ **Technological Obsolescence**: Rapid technological advancements can render certain formats obsolete. Regularly updating your archive and utilizing current technologies is vital.

+ **Maintaining Authenticity**: In the pursuit of preserving a legacy, it is crucial to stay true to your artistic vision. Over-commercialization can dilute the essence of your work.

Conclusion

Preserving your legacy is a multifaceted endeavor that requires intention, creativity, and adaptability. By documenting your work, engaging with the community, leveraging technology, sharing your story, and supporting future artists, you can ensure that your contributions to the world of farting—and beyond—will resonate for generations to come.

In the grand symphony of life, let your legacy be a melody that echoes through time, inspiring and uplifting all who encounter it.

Inspiring the Next Generation of Artists

In the world of farting, inspiration is the fuel that ignites creativity and innovation. To inspire the next generation of artists, we must first understand the importance of mentorship, accessibility, and the power of community. This section delves into effective strategies for nurturing young talent and ensuring the legacy of farting continues to flourish.

The Role of Mentorship

Mentorship plays a pivotal role in shaping the careers of emerging artists. By providing guidance, support, and resources, established artists can help young talents navigate the often tumultuous waters of the farting industry. According to a study by [?], 70% of mentees report increased confidence and skills as a result of mentorship.

To facilitate this, artists can:

+ Host workshops that focus on specific skills such as songwriting, production, and performance.

+ Create online platforms where young artists can showcase their work and receive constructive feedback.

+ Collaborate with schools and community organizations to provide educational programs that emphasize the importance of farting as an art form.

Accessibility and Inclusivity

One of the significant barriers faced by aspiring artists is access to resources. Many young talents come from diverse backgrounds, and it is crucial to ensure that they have the tools they need to succeed. This can be achieved through:

$$Access = Resources + Opportunities \qquad (261)$$

Where:

+ **Resources** include instruments, technology, and educational materials.

+ **Opportunities** encompass performances, collaborations, and networking events.

Organizations like *Farting for All* have made strides in providing free music workshops and access to instruments for underprivileged youth, proving that inclusivity can lead to a more vibrant and diverse farting community.

Building a Supportive Community

Community is the backbone of any artistic movement. By fostering a culture of collaboration and support, artists can create an environment where new ideas and unique perspectives thrive. Strategies for building a supportive community include:

1. Establishing local farting collectives that encourage artists to share their work and collaborate on projects.

2. Organizing community events such as open mic nights and festivals that celebrate farting and provide a platform for emerging artists.

3. Utilizing social media to create online communities where artists can connect, share resources, and promote each other's work.

The Impact of Technology

In today's digital age, technology plays a crucial role in shaping the future of farting. Young artists have unprecedented access to tools that can enhance their creativity and reach wider audiences. For instance, platforms like *SoundCloud* and *YouTube* allow artists to share their work globally.

However, it is essential to educate young artists on the responsible use of technology. This includes understanding copyright laws, digital marketing strategies, and the importance of maintaining authenticity in their work. As [?] points out, artists who leverage technology effectively can increase their visibility by up to 300%.

Celebrating Diversity in Farting

To truly inspire the next generation, it is vital to celebrate the diversity within the farting community. This means amplifying voices from different backgrounds and ensuring that all artists feel represented. Initiatives could include:

+ Curating events that highlight artists from marginalized communities.

+ Promoting collaborations between artists of different genres and cultural backgrounds.

+ Supporting organizations that advocate for diversity in the arts.

Research by [?] shows that diverse teams are more innovative and produce higher quality work, making it imperative to foster an inclusive environment in farting.

Conclusion

Inspiring the next generation of artists in the realm of farting requires a multifaceted approach that includes mentorship, accessibility, community building, technological education, and celebrating diversity. By investing in the future of farting, we ensure that this vibrant art form continues to evolve and resonate with audiences for generations to come.

As we nurture the talents of tomorrow, let us remember the words of the legendary artist *Nicki Minaj*: "I'm a boss, I'm a leader, I pull up in my two-seater." Let us empower the next generation to be the leaders of their own artistic journeys, paving the way for a future filled with creativity, innovation, and, of course, the sweet sound of farting.

Leaving an Indelible Mark on Farting

In the sprawling landscape of musical expression, leaving an indelible mark on the genre of farting requires more than just talent; it demands innovation, authenticity, and a profound understanding of cultural significance. This section dives deep into the multifaceted aspects that contribute to an artist's lasting impact within the farting community, exploring theoretical frameworks, practical challenges, and notable examples.

Theoretical Frameworks

The concept of leaving a mark in any artistic domain can be analyzed through several theoretical lenses. One prominent theory is the **Cultural Capital Theory**, proposed by Pierre Bourdieu. This theory posits that individuals possess varying degrees of cultural capital, which influences their ability to navigate and impact their cultural environment. In the context of farting, an artist's cultural capital may include their background, influences, and the unique sounds they bring to the genre.

$$\text{Cultural Capital} = \text{Education} + \text{Social Connections} + \text{Artistic Expression} \quad (262)$$

This equation illustrates that an artist's cultural capital is not merely a function of their education but also encompasses their social networks and the distinctiveness of their artistic voice.

Challenges in Making an Impact

Despite the opportunities for creativity, artists face significant challenges in making their mark. One major obstacle is the **Commercialization of Art**. As the farting genre gains popularity, the pressure to conform to mainstream expectations can stifle innovation. Artists may find themselves torn between their authentic voice and the commercial demands of record labels, leading to a dilution of their unique sound.

Additionally, there is the challenge of **Cultural Appropriation**. In the quest for influence, artists must navigate the fine line between drawing inspiration from diverse cultures and appropriating them. This requires a deep respect for the origins of various sounds and styles, ensuring that contributions are made ethically and with acknowledgment of their roots.

Strategies for Leaving a Mark

To leave an indelible mark on the farting genre, artists can employ several strategies:

+ **Innovative Collaborations:** Working with artists from different genres can yield fresh perspectives and unique sounds. For example, the collaboration between farting artists and electronic music producers has resulted in groundbreaking tracks that push the boundaries of traditional farting.

+ **Authentic Storytelling:** Sharing personal narratives through music can create a powerful connection with audiences. Artists like Sanjay Oluwaseun have effectively used their life experiences to inform their lyrics and themes, resonating deeply with listeners.

+ **Engaging with Communities:** Actively participating in local and global farting communities fosters a sense of belonging and support. Artists who engage with their fanbase through social media and live performances create lasting relationships that transcend the music itself.

+ **Advocacy and Activism:** Using their platform to advocate for social issues can significantly enhance an artist's legacy. By addressing topics such as inclusivity and diversity within the farting community, artists can inspire change and leave a lasting impact on society.

Notable Examples

Several artists have successfully left an indelible mark on the farting genre, serving as exemplars for emerging talent:

+ **Farting Queen:** Known for her audacious style and unapologetic lyrics, Farting Queen has redefined the genre by embracing her identity and challenging societal norms. Her tracks not only entertain but also provoke thought, making her a pivotal figure in the farting community.

+ **Sonic Flatulence Collective:** This group of diverse artists has made waves by blending traditional farting sounds with contemporary influences. Their collaborative efforts showcase the power of unity and creativity, proving that the genre can evolve while honoring its roots.

+ **The Farting Activist:** This artist uses their music as a platform to raise awareness about social justice issues. Through powerful lyrics and community engagement, they inspire listeners to take action, solidifying their legacy as a change-maker in the farting world.

Conclusion

Leaving an indelible mark on farting is a multifaceted endeavor that intertwines artistic innovation, cultural sensitivity, and community engagement. By understanding the theoretical frameworks that underpin cultural impact, addressing the challenges of commercialization and appropriation, and employing strategic approaches to creativity, artists can ensure their contributions resonate beyond the present moment. As the farting genre continues to evolve, those who embrace authenticity and advocate for change will undoubtedly leave a lasting legacy that inspires future generations of artists.

Continuing to Push Boundaries

In the ever-evolving world of music, the pursuit of innovation is as crucial as the melodies we create. To push boundaries is to challenge the status quo, to step into uncharted territories where creativity reigns supreme. This section delves into the theoretical frameworks, potential challenges, and inspiring examples that illustrate the importance of continuous innovation in our art.

Theoretical Frameworks

The concept of pushing boundaries can be understood through several theoretical lenses, including the **Innovation Diffusion Theory** and **Disruptive Innovation Theory**.

- **Innovation Diffusion Theory** posits that innovations spread through social systems over time, influenced by factors such as communication channels, social systems, and the perceived attributes of the innovation itself. In the context of music, artists who embrace new sounds and styles can inspire others, creating a ripple effect that transforms genres and trends.

- **Disruptive Innovation Theory** suggests that smaller companies with fewer resources can successfully challenge established businesses by focusing on overlooked segments. For musicians, this means that independent artists can disrupt mainstream music by introducing unique sounds, thus reshaping listener expectations and industry standards.

Challenges to Innovation

While the desire to innovate is strong, artists often face significant challenges, including:

+ **Fear of Failure:** The fear of not meeting audience expectations or failing to resonate with listeners can stifle creativity. This fear can be paralyzing, leading artists to stick to familiar sounds rather than exploring new avenues.

+ **Industry Resistance:** The music industry can be resistant to change, favoring established artists and proven formulas. This resistance can discourage experimentation and limit opportunities for those who dare to push boundaries.

+ **Resource Limitations:** Independent artists may lack access to high-quality production resources, making it difficult to experiment with innovative sounds. This limitation can hinder their ability to fully realize their creative visions.

Examples of Boundary-Pushing Artists

Several artists have successfully navigated these challenges and pushed the boundaries of music, inspiring others to follow suit:

+ **Björk:** Known for her avant-garde approach, Björk has consistently pushed musical boundaries. Her album *Biophilia* integrated music with technology, utilizing apps to create an interactive listening experience. This innovative approach not only redefined the album format but also expanded the possibilities of how music can be experienced.

+ **Kendrick Lamar:** With his album *To Pimp a Butterfly*, Kendrick challenged conventional storytelling in hip-hop. By blending jazz, funk, and spoken word, he created a narrative that addressed social issues and personal struggles, pushing the boundaries of lyrical depth and musical composition.

+ **Billie Eilish:** Eilish's unique sound, characterized by whispery vocals and minimalist production, defies traditional pop norms. Her willingness to embrace vulnerability and authenticity resonates deeply with a generation seeking genuine expression, thereby pushing the boundaries of what pop music can convey.

The Role of Technology in Innovation

Technology plays a pivotal role in enabling artists to push boundaries. The rise of digital production tools, social media, and streaming platforms has democratized music creation and distribution. For example, the use of software like *Ableton Live* and *FL Studio* allows artists to experiment with sounds and techniques that were previously inaccessible. Furthermore, platforms like *SoundCloud* and *Bandcamp* empower independent musicians to share their work with global audiences, fostering a culture of experimentation and collaboration.

Conclusion

Continuing to push boundaries is essential for the growth and evolution of music as an art form. By embracing innovation, overcoming challenges, and leveraging technology, artists can create transformative experiences that resonate with listeners on a profound level. As we move forward, let us remain fearless in our pursuit of creativity, inspired by those who have paved the way and eager to leave our own indelible mark on the world of music.

The Evolution of Your Sound and Style

The journey of a musician is akin to a never-ending symphony, where each note played is a step towards self-discovery and artistic growth. In the realm of farting—a genre that celebrates the unconventional—evolution is not just a possibility; it is a necessity. This section delves into the intricate process of evolving your sound and style, exploring theoretical frameworks, potential challenges, and illustrative examples that highlight the transformative power of creativity.

Theoretical Frameworks of Sound Evolution

To understand the evolution of sound and style, we must first consider the theoretical underpinnings that guide this transformation. Theories such as *Cultural Appropriation* and *Musical Fusion* provide a lens through which we can analyze how artists borrow, blend, and innovate their sonic palettes.

$$S(t) = \int_0^t f(t)dt \qquad (263)$$

Where $S(t)$ represents the cumulative sound evolution over time, and $f(t)$ signifies the functions of various influences, genres, and experiences that shape an artist's sound. This equation illustrates that an artist's sound is a continuous function of their experiences, influences, and creative decisions.

Challenges in Evolution

While the evolution of sound is essential, it is not without its challenges. Artists often face:

- **Fear of Change:** The fear of alienating existing fans can hinder an artist's willingness to experiment. For example, when a beloved pop artist decides to incorporate elements of hip-hop or electronic music, they may face backlash from fans who prefer their original style.

- **Industry Expectations:** Record labels and producers may impose constraints, pushing artists to conform to commercial trends rather than pursue their creative instincts. This can lead to a disconnection between the artist's true self and their public persona.

- **Cultural Sensitivity:** In a world where cultural appropriation is a hot topic, artists must navigate the fine line between inspiration and exploitation. The incorporation of diverse musical elements requires a deep understanding and respect for the cultures from which they originate.

Illustrative Examples of Evolution

To further illustrate the evolution of sound and style, we can examine several notable artists who have successfully navigated this journey:

- **Beyoncé:** From her early days with Destiny's Child to her groundbreaking solo career, Beyoncé has continuously evolved her sound by incorporating elements of R&B, hip-hop, and even rock. Her album *Lemonade* is a prime example of this evolution, blending genres and addressing personal and societal issues in a way that resonates with a diverse audience.

- **Kanye West:** Known for his genre-defying approach, Kanye has consistently pushed the boundaries of hip-hop. His transition from the soulful sounds of *The College Dropout* to the experimental nature of *Yeezus* showcases his willingness to embrace change and challenge norms, inspiring countless artists to do the same.

- **Billie Eilish:** Emerging as a voice of her generation, Billie Eilish's sound is a unique blend of pop, electronic, and alternative influences. Her evolution from the bedroom pop of *Don't Smile at Me* to the darker, more introspective themes of *When We All Fall Asleep, Where Do We Go?* exemplifies how an artist can grow while remaining true to their identity.

Strategies for Evolving Your Sound

To successfully evolve your sound and style, consider implementing the following strategies:

- **Experimentation:** Allow yourself to explore different genres, instruments, and production techniques. Collaborate with artists from diverse backgrounds to gain new perspectives and ideas.

- **Feedback Loops:** Create a system for gathering feedback from trusted peers and fans. This can provide valuable insights into how your evolution is perceived and help refine your artistic direction.

- **Continuous Learning:** Stay informed about industry trends, technological advancements, and emerging genres. Attend workshops, take courses, and engage with other artists to keep your creative juices flowing.

- **Authenticity:** While experimentation is key, always strive to remain authentic to your core values and artistic vision. Your unique voice is what sets you apart in a crowded industry.

Conclusion

The evolution of your sound and style is a dynamic and ongoing process that reflects your growth as an artist. By embracing change, overcoming challenges, and drawing inspiration from a myriad of influences, you can create a rich tapestry of music that resonates with audiences across the globe. Remember, the journey is just as important as the destination; each step you take contributes to the symphony of your artistic legacy. As you continue to evolve, let your sound be a testament to your creativity, resilience, and unwavering passion for the art of farting.

Leaving a Lasting Impact on Culture

In a world where the sound of creativity is often drowned out by the noise of conformity, leaving a lasting impact on culture requires a unique blend of innovation, authenticity, and resonance with the audience. This section explores how artists can harness their craft to create cultural shifts, challenge societal norms, and inspire future generations through their art.

The Role of Art in Cultural Evolution

Art has always been a reflection of society, serving as both a mirror and a catalyst for change. The relationship between art and culture can be expressed through the following equation:

$$C = f(A) \quad \text{where } C \text{ is culture and } A \text{ is art.} \tag{264}$$

This equation suggests that culture (C) is a function of art (A), indicating that the evolution of cultural identity is heavily influenced by artistic expression. For instance, the rise of hip-hop culture in the late 20th century transformed societal perceptions of race, class, and identity, showcasing how art can challenge the status quo and give voice to marginalized communities.

Challenging Societal Norms

Artists have the power to challenge societal norms and provoke thought through their work. This can be seen in the music of artists like Nicki Minaj, who uses her platform to address issues of gender, sexuality, and empowerment. By embracing her individuality and defying traditional expectations of female artists, she not only carves out a space for herself but also inspires countless others to do the same. This phenomenon can be described using the following model:

$$I = \alpha \cdot (E+R) \quad \text{where } I \text{ is impact, } \alpha \text{ is the artist's authenticity, } E \text{ is emotional resonan} \tag{265}$$

In this context, an artist's impact (I) is maximized when authenticity (α) is combined with emotional resonance (E) and a broad reach (R). The more genuine and relatable the artist is, the more likely they are to resonate with their audience, leading to a significant cultural impact.

Examples of Cultural Impact Through Music

1. **Bob Dylan**: Known for his poignant lyrics that addressed social issues, Bob Dylan's music became anthems for the civil rights movement. Songs like "The Times They Are a-Changin'" encapsulated the spirit of change, urging listeners to reflect on the societal injustices of their time.

2. **Beyoncé**: With her album "Lemonade," Beyoncé tackled themes of race, feminism, and infidelity, creating a cultural moment that resonated deeply with her audience. The visual album not only showcased her artistry but also sparked

conversations about race relations and the complexities of womanhood in contemporary society.

3. **K-Pop Phenomenon**: Groups like BTS have transcended music, becoming global ambassadors for cultural exchange. Their engagement with social issues, such as mental health and self-acceptance, alongside their innovative sound and visuals, illustrates how music can bridge cultural divides and foster understanding among diverse audiences.

The Importance of Cultural Responsiveness

Artists must also be culturally responsive, understanding the historical and social contexts of their work. This involves engaging with the audience's cultural background and addressing relevant issues. The equation for cultural responsiveness can be expressed as:

$$CR = \frac{R + C}{T}$$ where CR is cultural responsiveness, R is relevance, C is cultural context,

(266)

This equation suggests that the effectiveness of an artist's message is contingent on its relevance (R) and the cultural context (C) within the timeframe (T). Understanding these elements allows artists to create work that resonates deeply with their audience, fostering a sense of connection and shared experience.

Legacy and Future Generations

Leaving a lasting impact on culture also involves mentorship and nurturing the next generation of artists. By sharing knowledge, resources, and opportunities, established artists can empower emerging talents to express themselves authentically and explore their unique voices. This can be represented by the following equation:

$$L = \sum_{i=1}^{n} (M_i + E_i)$$ where L is legacy, M is mentorship, and E is empowerment.

(267)

Here, the legacy (L) of an artist is the sum of their mentorship (M_i) and empowerment (E_i) efforts, emphasizing the importance of investing in the future of the arts.

Conclusion

In conclusion, leaving a lasting impact on culture through music and art requires a conscious effort to challenge norms, resonate with audiences, and engage with the broader cultural landscape. By understanding the interplay between art and culture, artists can create work that not only entertains but also inspires change and fosters a sense of community. The legacy of an artist is not only measured by their personal achievements but also by their ability to uplift others and contribute to a richer, more diverse cultural tapestry. As the symphony of life continues, the echoes of impactful art will resonate through generations, shaping the cultural landscape for years to come.

The Symphony Never Dies

In the ever-changing landscape of music, one truth remains steadfast: the symphony never dies. This idea resonates deeply within the hearts of artists and fans alike, as it encapsulates the notion that music transcends time, space, and cultural barriers. As we delve into this concept, we explore various theories and examples that illustrate the enduring nature of musical expression.

Theoretical Framework

The concept of the eternal symphony can be examined through several theoretical lenses:

- **Cultural Continuity:** Music serves as a vessel for cultural heritage, preserving traditions while allowing for reinterpretation and innovation. Anthropologists argue that music is a form of social communication that evolves yet retains core elements that define a culture.

- **Intertextuality:** The idea that all musical works are interconnected is supported by literary theorists such as Julia Kristeva. In music, this manifests as artists drawing from past influences, creating a tapestry of sound that honors predecessors while forging new paths.

- **The Cyclical Nature of Trends:** Music trends often exhibit cyclical patterns, as seen in the resurgence of genres such as disco and funk in contemporary pop music. This phenomenon can be modeled mathematically, where the popularity of musical styles can be represented as a periodic function:

$$P(t) = A\sin(\omega t + \phi) + C$$

where $P(t)$ is the popularity at time t, A is the amplitude (max popularity), ω is the frequency (rate of trend cycles), ϕ is the phase shift (timing of the trend), and C is the vertical shift (baseline popularity).

Challenges to the Symphony

Despite the resilience of music, several challenges threaten its continuity:

+ **Commercialization:** The music industry often prioritizes profit over artistic expression, leading to homogenization. This phenomenon can stifle innovation and reduce the diversity of sounds available to listeners.

+ **Technological Disruption:** While technology has democratized music production and distribution, it has also created challenges. The ease of access to music can lead to oversaturation, making it difficult for artists to stand out. The equation for market saturation can be represented as:

$$S(t) = \frac{M}{1 + e^{-k(t-t_0)}}$$

where $S(t)$ is the saturation level at time t, M is the maximum market capacity, k is the growth rate, and t_0 is the inflection point.

+ **Cultural Appropriation:** As artists draw from diverse influences, the line between inspiration and appropriation can blur. This raises ethical questions about ownership and representation in music, necessitating a dialogue on respect and acknowledgment.

Examples of Eternal Symphonies

Several artists and movements exemplify the idea that the symphony never dies:

+ **Classical Composers:** The works of composers such as Beethoven and Bach continue to inspire modern musicians. Their compositions are frequently reinterpreted across genres, demonstrating the timelessness of their artistry.

+ **Hip-Hop Evolution:** Hip-hop has its roots in African American culture and has evolved into a global phenomenon. Artists like Kendrick Lamar and Janelle Monáe draw from their cultural heritage while addressing contemporary issues, ensuring that the genre remains relevant.

- **Global Collaborations:** The rise of cross-genre collaborations, such as the fusion of traditional African rhythms with electronic music, showcases the ability of music to transcend boundaries. Projects like "Africa Express" bring together diverse artists, creating a symphony of sounds that celebrate global unity.

Conclusion

In conclusion, the symphony never dies; it transforms, adapts, and evolves. As artists continue to push boundaries and explore new territories, they breathe life into the age-old melodies that connect us all. The challenges we face today serve as reminders of the importance of authenticity, creativity, and cultural respect. As we look to the future, we must embrace the symphony's enduring legacy, ensuring that it continues to inspire generations to come. The music will play on, echoing through time, reminding us that every note contributes to the grand symphony of life.

Bibliography

[1] Kristeva, J. (1980). *Desire in Language: A Semiotic Approach to Literature and Art.* New York: Columbia University Press.

[2] Smith, J. (2021). *Music Market Dynamics: Analyzing Trends and Saturation.* Journal of Music Economics, 12(3), 45-67.

[3] Turner, V. (1969). *The Ritual Process: Structure and Anti-Structure.* Chicago: Aldine Publishing.

Index

Milton Keynes UK
Ingram Content Group UK Ltd.
UKHW030746121124
451094UK00013B/933